Television in the Olympics

Television in the Olympics

Miquel de Moragas Spà
Nancy K. Rivenburgh
James F. Larson
(in cooperation with researchers from 25 countries)

John Libbey

LONDON · PARIS · ROME

British Library Cataloguing in Publication Data

Television in the Olympics
Acamedia Research Monograph: 13
I. Title   II. Series
302.2345

ISBN: 0 86196 538 8
ISSN: 0956-9057

Series Editor: Manuel Alvarado

Published by

John Libbey & Company Ltd, 13 Smiths Yard, Summerley Street,
London SW18 4HR, England.
Telephone: +44 (0)181-947 2777: Fax +44 (0)181-947 2664
John Libbey Eurotext Ltd, 127 rue de la République, 92120 Montrouge, France.
John Libbey - C.I.C. s.r.l., via Lazzaro Spallanzani 11, 00161 Rome, Italy

Television in the Olympics International Research Project

Research Directors

Miquel de Moragas Spà
Centre d'Estudis Olímpics i de l'Esport, Universitat Autònoma de Barcelona, Spain

Nancy K. Rivenburgh
School of Communications, University of Washington, Seattle, USA

James F. Larson
Center for Advanced Research and Training in Telecommunications, University of Colorado at Boulder, USA

Central Research Team

At the Centre d'Estudis Olímpics i de l'Esport:
Núria García, Marc Carroggio, Maria Gutiérrez, Muriel Ladrón de Guevara, Gemma Larregola, Nicolás Lorite, Montserrat Llinés, Susanna Ribas, Dolors Aparicio, Carmen Gómez Mont (Universidad Iberoamericana – México) and Sonia Muñoz (Universidad del Valle – Colombia).

At the University of Washington:
Kerry Carnahan

International Research Correspondents

Japan
Nobuko Kosaka
Hiroshi Matsuyama
   Yomiuri Telecasting Corp
Andrew Painter

People's Republic of China
Li Liangrong
   Fudan University
Kong Xiang-an
   Tianjin Institute of Physical Education

Korea
Park Heung Soo
  Yonsei University
Kang Tae-Young
  KBS Broadcast Research Institute

Republic of Singapore
Duncan Holaday
Eugenia Peck
  National University of Singapore

Malaysia
Ramli Mohamed
  Universiti Sains Malaysia

Indonesia
Naswil Idris
  The Indonesian Open Learning University

France
Françoise Papa
  Université Stendhal

Germany
Claus Dieter Rath

United Kingdom
John Izod, Peter Meech, Tim Thornicroft
with Richard Kilborn
  University of Stirling

Greece
Panayote E. Dimitras
  Communication and Political Research Society

Slovenia
Slavko Splichal
with Sandra Basic and Breda Luthar
  University of Ljubljana

United States
Eric Rothenbuhler
  University of Iowa

Canada
Gaëtan Tremblay
with M. St-Laurent
  Université du Québec à Montreal

Colombia
Ramiro Arbeláez Ramos
  Universidad del Valle

México
Carmen Gómez Mont
with Lorena Martín del Campo, Vicente Arancon, Francisco Briseño
and Pablo Herranz
  Universidad Iberoamericana

Brazil
José Marques de Melo
with Nanci Laura Loturco Pittelkow
  Universidad de Sao Paulo

Cuba
Enrique González Manet
  Instituto Cubano de Radio y Televisión

Romania
Peter Gross
with Radu Cosarca and Cristian David
  California State University Chico

Russia
Yassen N. Zassoursky
with Svetlana Kolesnik and Andrei G. Ritcher
  Moscow University

Egypt
Awatef Abd El-Rahman
with Ashraf Abd El Mogeith, Fahima Ahmed Gouda, Hani Mohamed,
Khalid Salah El Din and Mohamed Houssam El Din
  Cairo University

Cameroon
Francis Nguepmenye Wete
  University of Yaounde

Ghana
Kwame Karikari
  University of Ghana

South Africa
Arnold S. de Beer
Elanie Steyn
  University for Christian Higher Education, Potchefstroom
Daan P. van Vuuren
  SABC
Eric Louw
with Nhlanhla Nkosi
  University of Natal

Australia
John Langer
  Victoria University of Technology

Project Translators, Transcriptors and Coders

From Faculty of Translation and Interpretation, Universitat Autònoma de Barcelona:
John Beathie, Guillermo Cariño, Dolors Cinca, Carme Colominas, Marta Corominas, Doris Ensinger, Sean Golden, Yukiko Kimura, Núria Medina, Karen Meltcafe, Zhou Minkang, Deolinda Monteiro, David Owen, María Piñana, Antonia Pujol, Laureano Ramírez, Joelle Rey, Elena Tanqueiro, Maria Isabel Tornero and Javier Vico.

From Centre d'Estudis Olímpics i de l'Esport in Barcelona:
Roc Fages, Belinda Pérez, Carles Tudurí and Daithm MacLochlainn.

From Seattle, Washington:
Youngsoo Yook, Daniel Limawan, Aleks Markovcic, Fenia Mavromichali, Jill Sherensky, Daniella Patrut, Isabelle Vatan, Kate Brown, Susan Brownell, Jiande Chen, Lena Ugarova, Daniella Englisch, Iri Cermak, William Munn, Jennifer Fisch, Kyle Nicholas, Joelle Nole, Pat Radin, Elizabeth Levy, Eric Magnuson, Leonard Rifas, Fenia Mavromichali, Iri Cermak, Alan Coar, Michelle Johnson, Kerry Carnahan and Kevin Kawamoto.

The authors want to recognize the support provided by the following persons and institutions:

The President of International Olympic Committee, Juan Antonio Samaranch
The Olympic Museum Lausanne
European Community Commission
Comisión Interministerial de Ciencia y Tecnología (CICYT), Spain
Comissió Interdepartamental de Recerca i Innovació Tecnològica (CIRIT)
Comissionat per a Actuacions Exteriors, Generalitat de Catalunya, Catalonia
University of Washington Graduate School Fund

Centre d'Estudis Olímpics i de l'Esport, Universitat Autònoma de Barcelona

Much of research for this book was carried out in the Centre d'Estudis Olímpics i de l'Esport at the Universitat Autònoma de Barcelona. The creation of this centre was proposed after a 1987 Seoul meeting on Olympic and Cultural Exchanges in the World System and was set up in 1989 as a Consortium between the Autonomous University of Barcelona, Barcelona City Council, The Spanish Olympic Committee, and the Barcelona Provincial Council. The Center established different cooperation programmes with the Catalan Autonomous Government and with the Spanish Sports Council. In 1995, a general agreement was established with the International Olympic Committee, and consequently the Autonomous University and the International Olympic Committee to establish the International Olympic Chair in Olympism.

The archives of Centre d'Estudis Olímpics i de l'Esport contains the basic materials (videotapes, visual transcription and translation of the ceremonies, reports from international correspondents, original documents, press dossiers and clippings, and so forth) related with this research on Television in the Olympics, as well as books and documentation on other questions related with Barcelona 1992 and Olympic phenomena.

Table of Contents

List of Tables and Figures

Preface

This book highlights the intersection of two phenomena which we consider to be of great interest for the interpretation of cultural forms in modern society. On one hand there exists the phenomenon of television – still rapidly growing on a worldwide scale. On the other hand, there exists the phenomenon of the Olympic Games, celebrating its first centenary in 1996 of their revival by Baron Pierre de Coubertin. The Olympic Games also continue to grow in dimension, complexity and worldwide impact.

Observing the present day Olympic Games is tantamount to having a privileged stage or laboratory at one's disposal for the study of modern day communications in most all its forms. There is the additional methodological advantage of the event being planned for and attended by the largest and most geographically diverse concentration of media organizations in the world.

This book's objective is not to describe all the different aspects that make up modern Olympic communication – from the design of the mascot, to the organization of telecommunications, to intercultural exchange among Olympic actors. Rather, this book is about television – and all that it touches as part of the central role it plays in the organization and diffusion of the present day Olympic Games.

Background

The authors of this book recognize some of the previous research into television and the Olympic Games. In 1984 the International Olympic Committee had already organized its first symposium on the subject and in 1987, preceding the Winter Games of Calgary'88, the University of Calgary organized a symposium with professionals and experts in communications. Issues related to communications have also been addressed in various congresses related to Olympism and culture celebrated in the last few years in Seoul, Quebec and Barcelona.

It was over the course of several of these meetings that the authors discovered their common research interests in communications, Olympics and international comparative analyses. In fact, each of us had already engaged in our own comparative studies of international Olympic broadcasting prior to this project.

Together, however, we have been able to undertake a project of a breadth and dimension without precedent in Olympics research and even rare for its level of international participation in the social sciences more broadly.

The project emanated from the idea that the Olympic Games are a communication phenomenon that is initially produced in a city, but then 'reproduced' in multiple places throughout the world. These reproductions of the Olympics are actually carefully produced 'constructions' of a live event and differ in their presentation and impact as one travels the globe. Our investigation tries to make sense of how these multiple Olympic realities occur by looking at the production conditions in the host city, comparing the resulting broadcast forms of the event, and trying to understand something of the different cultural contexts they are intended for.

Research participants and acknowledgments

In order to accomplish this an international research team was needed which was capable of gathering data in the host city as well as gathering data in a large number of geo-politically representative countries and media environments. We wanted to steer clear of the tendency of some international studies of communication and of Olympism to limit attention to the areas of the richest countries in the world. In no way did we want to confuse the globalization of the Games with their presence in the most developed countries in the world.

A large team of researchers ('study correspondents') was formed (see list of study participants). This team of researchers was chosen based on various criteria including communications interests, relationships with local media, understanding of the Olympics, and so forth. Ultimately, this project covered 25 countries and brought in the talents of close to 120 participating researchers, translators, coders and more. In fact, we were very pleased to find so many individuals so interested in television in the Olympics.

Together with this international team we required a team capable of analysing 'in situ' in Barcelona, recording the process of the Games organization, going behind the scenes during the Games, processing incoming data, and so forth. This team, which we called the 'central team', worked primarily out of the Centre d'Estudis Olímpics i de l'Esport in the Universitat Autònoma de Barcelona. Chapter 1 offers a more detailed discussion of the methods and research process.

Among our acknowledgments we would like to mention first and foremost the President of the International Olympic Committee, Juan Antonio Samaranch, who gave his support to the investigation right from the very beginning.

We would also like to mention the support received from the International Olympic Committee. In particular we wish to acknowledge Fernando Riba for the cooperation of the The Olympic Museum; the General Secretary of the IOC, Françoise Zweifel, who made possible our accreditation in Barcelona; the director of the public communication department Fekrou Kidane who always made himself available for academic activities related to Olympism; as well as José Sotelo and the marketing department, specifically Michael Payne and Mark Dzenick, for the help received.

This research project would also not have been possible without the direct help of the various institutions who appear in the credits of this book of which the administrative and research 'basecamp' provided by the Centre d'Estudis Olímpics i de l'Esport in the Universitat Autònoma de Barcelona was central to the study's success. For this, the authors would like to direct their thanks to the coordinator of this centre, Muriel Ladrón de Guevara. The authors would also like to extend a very special recognition for the technical and research assistance of Dolors Aparicio, librarian of the Centre and Núria García who coordinated the transcription processes for 85 hours of Olympic coverage, along with numerous other research tasks.

Our thanks must be extended to all the researchers, translators and documentalists mentioned in the credits of this publication – the real people responsible for this internationally collaborative work. Our utmost thanks go to those communication and Olympism experts who supported us in different phases of the investigation. We would like to especially mention John MacAloon, from the University of Chicago, Fernand Landry from the University of Laval, Kang Shin Pyo from the University of Inje and Jesús Martín Barbero from the Univesidad del Valle in Cali, Colombia. Their intellectual stimulation has been fundamental to this project.

Certainly, this cooperative effort was not without its difficulties. As we said, an Olympic Games is a very complex event with many different actors and institutions involved from which we sought information. While the specific difficulties have now been forgotten, we encourage all who are involved in the Olympics to give their support to academic research, the ultimate purpose of which is to further our insights into the Olympic ideals of international understanding.

MdeM, NKR, JFL

1   Some Perspectives on Television and the Olympic Games

The latter decades of the 20th century brought great change in the practices, technologies, public uses, and reach of communications media. The world also experienced, beginning in the 1980s, a transformation of its politics, as most Cold War barriers crumbled, only to be replaced in the short term by the outbreak of war and regional conflict based on long-standing political, cultural, religious and economic animosities. There were also major changes in the movement and commercialization of popular culture around the world: music, fashion, telenovelas – and televised sport. The Olympic movement, which by this time had become an important non-governmental actor on the world stage, has both participated in and been changed by each of these areas of transformation. In fact, rather than settling in at the secure old age of 100 years, the modern Olympics has been continuously challenged by these phenomenon – not the least of which has been a highly dynamic protagonist called television.

Scholarly interest in the Olympics and television

The relationship between philosophical or scholarly activities and Olympic sport has a long history. In modern times the relationship between the formal academic community and the Olympics dates from the inception of the modern Olympic movement about a century ago. Indeed, it was no accident that the present International Olympic Committee (IOC) was founded by Baron Pierre de Coubertin in the Sorbonne University of Paris in 1894.

As MacAloon wrote, academics participated in Pierre de Coubertin's 1892 and 1894 Sorbonne conferences. The year following the Athens Olympics of 1896, Coubertin organized what is now considered to be the first Olympic Scientific Congress, in Le Havre, in recognition of the need for more scientific reflection on the developing world of modern sport. 'The scientific preferences of traditional Olympism were shaped to a great extent by the world view of Victorian Europe. Hence, ... when Olympic authorities began to organize "scientific" meetings about sport, they tended to prefer universal humanists,

1

philosophers and artists, on the one side, and psychologists, biologists and medical doctors, on the other side, over sociologists, political economists, comparative linguists and ethnologists.'[1]

In other words for much of the past century sport and Olympic research has been dominated by the concerns of sports physiology and medicine – and more recently biological, biomechanical, technical, individual psychological and philosophy – in contrast to those of anthropology, history, politics, culture, sociology, communications and economics. However, at the 1994 Olympic Congress in Paris there was an acknowledgment that the latter mentioned fields also have much to contribute to the Olympic movement.

Also, Olympics research thus far has resulted from both the independently conceived efforts of individuals and efforts assisted and encouraged by institutions or programmes associated with the Olympics.[2]

The intersection of international communications research and the Olympics

The study of television as an international phenomenon provides an appropriate backdrop to this project. In fact, the primary arenas of international communications research lend themselves directly to looking at the Olympic Games.

The comparison of media systems and the environments which spawn them has long attracted researchers interested in cross cultural definitions of news, levels of press freedom, the media's role as a political and cultural actor, and more. In the study of television in particular, researchers have attempted to connect, for example, attributes of local television content to the specific national environments in which they reside. One approach to this type of analysis has been to compare different international media presentations of the same event or genre of programming – whether superpower summits, United Nations conferences, specific news events, or game shows – in an attempt to reveal more about local cultures and attitudes, as well as to understand how different media presentations might ultimately influence relations among nations.

National self identity and 'ways of seeing'

In much the same way, of course, the Olympic Games as event can be interpreted. As this book will reveal, the production processes for Olympic television result in multiple and different presentations of the Olympics around the world. These can then be analysed and

---

1 MacAloon (1987: 17).

2 Prominent among these institutions are the International Olympic Academy in Olympia, Greece, and the regularly scheduled Olympic Scientific Congresses. A longer list would include the Carl Diem Institute in Cologne, Germany, the Centre d'Estudis Olímpics i de l'Esport at the Autonomous University of Barcelona, the Centre for Olympic Studies at The University of Western Ontario in Canada, the Beijing Institute of Physical Education in China, the Deutsches Olympisches Institut in Berlin, Germany, and the new Olympic Museum in Lausanne, Switzerland. In 1991 the first International Conference on a World Olympic Academic Network was convened in Seoul, Korea, and in 1993 a similar meeting was held in Berlin, Germany.

compared for both similarities and differences offering possible clues as to how different cultural, political and economic contexts affect television presentations. This suggests that one can investigate broadcast presentations of the Olympic Games not only for insights into national and cultural self identity, but also to better understand different ways of seeing global events and issues in the broader schema of international and intercultural relations. The idea of identity influencing 'ways of seeing' is an important theme of this study.

Cultural exchange and community

Prompted by concerns about information imbalance and, as such, skewed perspectives, the late 1970s and 1980s also saw much international communications research related to the flow of media messages around the world, documenting both message direction and quantity. The follow on to this work has been to explore communications flow in terms of cultural exchange (or influence, as the case may be), trying to grasp the international massive flow of entertainment and news messages means in light of intercultural relations, cultural change, and the development of certain types of transnational community.

It is with this last point that an obvious connection with the Olympics can again be made. Not only does the Olympics as a television event reach across virtually all political and cultural borders in the world – however unevenly – but its nature as an event produced and participated in by an unprecedented number of international constituents suggests that it may produce unique and shared meanings that allow diverse 'members' to feel part of an Olympic family or community. While not earth-shattering news, the most widely recognized, introduced and discussed 1992 Olympic participant – across all 28 broadcasts in this study – was Magic Johnson of the US basketball 'Dream Team'. International broadcast commentators came to Barcelona already knowing this athlete. What does this mean? That said, other research documenting the popularity of quality local television programming in the face of international imports and the tendency for news programming to be largely regional also suggests tells us that it is the local dimension of international events that draws – and sustains – the attention and interest of global audiences. This local/global dimension is well suited for investigation in the context of the Olympics as a television event – and clearly emerges as another theme throughout this study.

Television and institutional change

The media have always been looked at for their role in altering societal structures. Whether that means the conduct of politics in a democracy or attitudes toward minority members of society, television in particular has been documented as a participant, catalyst, or at times, obstruction to institutional or societal change. Sports fans have, without doubt, noticed the dramatic evolution in sport formats resulting from the rapidly developing relations among sport, television and commercial enterprise. Sponsorship of athletes and events, competitive bidding for television rights and changes in the rules and timing have produced fundamental changes in sport – including an increase in the popularity of international competition. Television has also adapted to sport. For example, the television industry has developed new camera technology specifically to catch sport images. Television is now an actor in sport. Officials can use television replays to make final judgments.

Sports arenas have become television studios. More broadly, televised sport has even come to mark the seasons in some countries.

The Olympics, as the premier international sports event, is emblematic of many of these changes. Communications-related revenues from sponsorship, the sale of television rights and the licensing of Olympic symbols now constitute the primary capital for the organization of the Olympic Games. There is much to understand here both in terms of grasping the dynamics of these relationships, but also in terms of what impact they have now, or in the future, on the Olympic messages and meaning. As such, a better understanding of the balance – or tension – among various organizations and institutional actors in the Olympics (nations, host city, IOC, sports federations, media, athletes, etc.), each with their own message and motivations, is an important research goal and another overarching theme of this project.

The television industry worldwide

Conversations about the television industry today conjures up words like 'globalization', 'fragmentation', 'personal technology' and 'convergence' – all very real phenomena in the communications industry today. The Olympics Games, with the largest gathering of media in the world in a technologically wired host city, offers a unique window on the worldwide television industry. Not only can trends in technology be confirmed, but the hierarchical character of the industry also emerges. Broadcasters representing extreme resource disparities approach – or grapple – with Olympic television in a variety of ways that are instructive to understanding the impact of such technological and resource diversity more globally. In addition, it becomes quickly apparent in the context of Olympic broadcasting that economic disparities translate into different media presentations – and possibly understandings – of the Olympic Games. The idea of resources as linked to meaning construction will surface repeatedly as a theme in this book

The Olympics as a media-constructed reality

Finally, there has always been a fascination for the ability of television (and other media) to 'construct' reality. There is a fraudulent nature to television. It hides its processes and deficiencies, as best as possible, from the audience. A fundamental goal of its programming – beyond entertainment and information – is to promote its own credibility and prestige.

The Olympic Games is very much a media-constructed reality. There may not be another world event so planned, controlled, produced, yet presented 'live'. Surrounding the spontaneous and very real activities of athletes is a very thick layer of broadcast production personnel and technology swaddling each athletic feat or ceremonial ritual (like a newborn) and presenting it, flawlessly, to world audiences. Much goes on, however, in that layer that relates to our understanding of the reality that just occurred.

All of the above discussion, of course, is relevant in important ways to the Olympic movement itself. The patrons of Olympism need to be wary and kept abreast of the role of communications media as advocate, detractor and interpreter of Olympic values and messages. In that sense, and given the deep involvement of television in the Olympics, it seems imperative for research in this area to grow in breadth of international scope and inquiry if the Olympic movement wishes to preserve itself.

Research on international television and the Olympics

The scholarly activity in this area is already well underway. There have been many attempts, in various disciplines and with different approaches, to grasp the above arenas of study relative to communications media and the Olympics. Just a few examples, in conjunction with the 1984 Los Angeles Olympics, an international team of scholars funded by UNESCO studied media coverage of the Olympics in several countries around the world.[3] The Seoul Olympics gave added impetus to such scholarship. In 1987 a symposium on the Olympics and East-West, North-South Cultural Exchange in the World System, followed by gatherings in 1988 and 1989, convened international scholars to share research separate from and more broadly based than the Olympic Scientific Congress in Seoul. Both the World Academic Conference of the Seoul Olympiad, hosted in Seoul preceding the games and the Seoul Olympiad Anniversary Conference prominently featured themes relating to communication and the media. Around the same time a conference on the Olympic Movement and the Mass Media was convened in Calgary in 1987. Not surprisingly, given the continued growth and maturation of global television and telecommunications, the research interest in Olympic television and the media that gathered momentum in Seoul and Calgary carried over to Barcelona. In April of 1991 a symposium at the Center for Olympic and Sport Studies was held on the Olympics, Media and Intercultural Exchange, bringing scholars and researchers together with many of the key individuals responsible for designing and producing Olympic communication in Barcelona.

The complexity of the Games as research challenge

As a modern cultural phenomenon the Olympic Games must be studied. And, it is clear that television as a central protagonist to the Olympics need be included in such study. But, how to understand it? When approaching the Olympic Games as either process or event one can easily be overwhelmed by its complex character. Even when 'narrowed' to a television perspective, there are still a host of political, technological, cultural, sport and economic actors and relationships to be considered. Further, the involvement of each type of participant in the Olympics is based not necessarily on mutual goals or motivations, but rather on complementary needs.

Because of the diversity of needs and interests which comprise the Olympics it is not possible to approach the Games armed with useful, overarching theory. The phenomenon cannot be readily explained exclusively in terms of theories of Games, interdependence, systems, structure, intercultural relations, social constructions of reality, semiotics, or behavioral dynamics. It therefore becomes necessary to bring a multi-disciplinary perspective to analysis of television in the Olympics. Therefore, rather than the discovery of

---

3   Real (1986).

some new theory of global television, what the reader will find in this book is the application of discrete concepts and analytical approaches in order to explain more manageable aspects of the Olympic television experience. For example, narrative analyses is applied to looking at broadcast commentary of the Games. Concepts related to intercultural perception and identity formation inform the analysis of the presentation of nations. Theories related to the constitution of community offer a framework for analysis for understanding shared Olympic messages in television broadcasts ... and so forth.

This is not an excuse, but rather an acknowledgment that the application of some grand theory relative to television in the Olympics is both naive and dangerous. Quite simply, there are no advantages seen to masking the complexity and truly multi-dimensional character of the Olympics in order to grasp its essence.

Methods

By its nature this study needed to be multi-method and internationally collaborative. Refer to the preface for an overview of the research team structure and a list of all contributors to the project. Ultimately, 130 people worked on this project. The study sample included 25 countries. These countries were selected in order to obtain diversity in terms of geographic region, economic development, cultural orientation, political system and media environment. The final selection of countries included: Japan, China, Korea, Cameroon, Indonesia, Canada (including Quebec), Singapore, Spain (also Catalonia), France, South Africa, United Kingdom, Greece, Slovenia, USA, Australia, Colombia, Mexico, Brazil, Cuba, Romania, Russia, Ghana, Egypt, Malaysia and Germany. They touch all continents, yet fall short in terms of island nations and the Middle East region. Of the participating researchers ('study correspondents') from those countries some worked individually, others in teams. In two of above countries, South Africa and China, there were different sets of correspondents intended to represent different perspectives (Northern and Southern China; Afrikaans, White and Black South Africa).

Each research correspondent was asked to provide the following materials from his or her country related to the Barcelona Olympics: (1) video tape of the broadcasts of the Opening and Closing Ceremonies; (2) video tape of five selected sports events, including the men and women's 400 metre hurdles, men and women's 100 metre sprint and a sport event of high popularity in that country; (3) answers to a questionnaire (discussed below); and, if they so wished (4) any press clippings or other observations they felt relevant to understanding the Olympic experience in that country.

The questionnaire was, in fact, a lengthy report providing information on: the broadcasting system in that country; audience data generally and specific to the Barcelona Olympics (audience levels, composition, viewing behaviors, highest rated sports); Olympic programming features such as scheduling, narrative structures, commentator characteristics; characteristics of the Opening and Closing ceremony broadcasts themselves, including perceptions as to the presentation of Olympic values, national identity, the host city identity, commercial values, politics, and so forth; and a summary of press commentary about Olympic television. Finally, the questionnaire asked about the broader context of the Games in that country. For example, did other events or issues distract from or compete with the Olympic broadcast for attention? Several correspondents provided essays summarizing key themes related to the Olympics in their countries. The above data appear throughout the book in various forms.

Content analysis

Part II of this book represents the results of a comparative content analysis conducted on the video broadcasts of the Opening Ceremony provided by the study correspondents. The broadcasts were also compared to the host broadcaster RTO'92 international signal provided to all broadcasters as a basis for their own productions. The design of the content analysis required that each broadcast be analysed both for visual and verbal features. In order to do this, the ceremony was divided, for analysis purposes, into 245 segments based roughly on meaning 'units' or distinct focal points throughout the ceremony. About 73 of these segments corresponded to the performance and ritual aspects of the Opening Ceremony as planned by the ceremony designers (refer to Appendix D for a list of the primary performance segments for the ceremony). The other 172 segments matched with each national team that marched into the stadium during the parade of athletes. Once these were established, each broadcast was visually transcribed. That is, each shot was viewed, compared to the international signal, and recorded if it was different (e.g. edited) in any way. In that way, the entire structure of each national broadcast, including advertising or interview breaks, were transcribed by location and time. Appendix C offers an abbreviated glimpse at the format in which this was done (although that particular example has been simplified for presentation purposes).

To prepare the verbal commentary for analysis each broadcast was first transcribed by native speakers from that country, then if not in English or Spanish (the working languages for the project) the commentary was translated in full. This part of the data preparation was enormously time consuming and pain staking. Translations were not only subjected to reliability tests, but translators were asked to footnote the translations with explanatory comments as well as code the commentaries for paralinguistic qualities so that during the analysis phase, the authors knew whether broadcast commentators were speaking enthusiastically, sarcastically, with emotion, and so forth. There were close to 30 paralinguistic coding categories.

The content analysis was conducted on two levels. First, a quantitative analysis of each broadcast was conducted using a list of close to 450 distinct categories, representing the primary meaning areas of concern in this study: the presentation of Olympics, nations and the host city, as well as other topics. See Appendix A for a list of content analysis categories. Trained coders were used to assign each distinct meaning association in the broadcast a category. These coded data were checked for reliability and analysed using a statistical data base.

The broadcast visual and verbal transcripts were also analysed in a very different way, using techniques more common to discourse analysis, semiotics and studies of narrative structure. Here is was possible to also look at the interplay between the verbal, visual and sound attributes of the broadcasts. Ultimately, the results from each country broadcast was compared to the others based on structure, as well as by focusing on specific topic or meaning realms (as represented by the chapters in Part II).[4]

The authors, all experienced in international comparative analysis, were well aware of the limitations and pitfalls such cross national analysis holds in terms of linguistic nuance, equivalence issues and more. In that sense, the results as presented in the following chapters are careful not to over-analyse the data by attributing much more than explicit meaning to broadcasts. Here also, the study correspondents and native speaking translators were invaluable for their insights into the broadcasts' meaning and cultural contexts.

Documentation and observation

The other key elements to this analysis were access to both the privileged documentation prepared for the Barcelona Games by the Barcelona organizing committee (COOB'92), the host broadcaster (RTO'92), the International Olympic Committee (IOC) and other organizations involved in its planning and execution, as well as accreditation to go behind the scenes in the Main Press Center, International Broadcast Center and at venue operations – the hubs of all media activity – during the Games themselves. This type of access allowed for fairly systematic observation by the central research team of different facets of broadcast production. Interviews were also conducted with different broadcasters. Every attempt was made to interview each of the broadcasters whose Olympic presentations were content analysed for this study in order to have a sense of the individual broadcaster circumstances that led to each final broadcast. Interviews were also conducted well before and after the Games with others involved in broadcast and ceremony planning and production. These data sources allowed for the detailed investigation of economic, organizational and technological infrastructures and processes presented in Part I of this book. Without question, one of the benefits of studying an event such as the Olympic Games is the ability to pre-plan literally years in advance for its occurrence.

Ultimately, the greatest methodological challenges of this project simply had to do with the logistics and intercultural obstacles related with conducting such a large international project – everything from research correspondents coming down with malaria, to others caught in dangerous political turmoil, to the geographic distance between the primary authors (each on a different continent during this project). All can contribute to slowdowns or miscommunication about important project related processes. In that sense, this project offered a tremendous – yet very rewarding – learning experience for those interested in this type of work. At the same time, the authors feel confident that the integrity of the research design and methods, in face of such above noted obstacles common to international communications research, were preserved throughout.

---

4   The astute reader will notice that in different chapters, the broadcast sample occasionally varies in size from 25 to 28. Depending what was being looked at, visual or verbal attributes, a few broadcasts were not able to be used because of some characteristic (as with Colombia's Canal A incomplete broadcast due to electricity rationing) or some particular obstacle for that part of the study.

Overview of chapters

Besides this introductory and some concluding thoughts in the final chapter, the book is divided into three Parts, each corresponding to a different broad dimension of this research undertaking.

Producing the Olympics

Part I, 'Economic, Organizational and Technological Infrastructure for Olympic Television', has four overriding objectives. The first is to investigate the central role of communications- related phenomena, particularly television, in the structure and organization of the Olympic Games. The Olympics has clearly evolved in conjunction with changes in the communications environment. Chapter 2 outlines the major sources of funding for the Games and looks at the evolution of the economic dynamics of the Olympics. Emphasis is placed on the role of television rights and sponsorship revenues in the organization of the Games. Chapter 3 first continues the look at Olympic infrastructures by presenting a picture of the host broadcaster in Olympic television and the media community which descends on the host city. This imported 'culture' of broadcast production is both a distinct and dynamic part of the Olympic experience, literally surrounding every sport and ceremonial activity with cameras, cables, computers and hundreds of broadcast personnel. To understand it, even visualize it, is highly relevant because it is a part of the Olympics not seen on the television screen. The other section of Chapter 3 looks at the Olympics as a site of converging technologies and showroom for the major actors in the global communications industry.

It is within Chapter 3 that the second objective of this part of the book starts to take shape: using the Olympics as a window through which to make observations about characteristics and trends in the international television and communications industry.

A third objective of Part I of this book is to provide a context for understanding the production processes for the international broadcasts analysed in Part II. It is necessary to understand how they are constructed in order to see how and why they influence meaning. Chapter 4 details the production process, specifically focusing on ways in which international broadcasters customize or personalize the broadcasts for home viewers, using the host broadcaster-provided 'raw' (i.e. visual and natural sound only) international signal as a basis. The second section of Chapter 4 begins the cross national comparative analysis by looking at the various programming strategies used for Olympic television in each country. How much programming? When is it offered? And so forth. The results presented here also contain inferences for how, and with what level of interest, various cultures choose to attend to this global television event.

One final objective of Part I of this book is to show how meticulously planned and produced, in fact, this 'live' event really is. It sheds light on television and the process of meaning construction taken up in Part II by showing how a single Olympic event, such as the Opening Ceremony, becomes multiple presentations in as many countries with different structures, narrative flows, visual and verbal imagery, and thus, meaning.

Television and construction of meaning

Part II tackles this issue of multiple presentations directly, by meticulously comparing 28 broadcasts of the Barcelona 1992 Opening Ceremony. The Olympics as a television event is very much a constructed reality – virtually all is controlled except the moments of athletic endeavor. But this Olympic 'reality' results from much more than a set of production processes. Instead it is the convergence of various broadcaster conditions in the host city combined with the influence of cultural (political, economic, social, etc.) contexts at home. In that sense, analysis of these broadcasts offers perspectives on both those contributing phenomena.

As a frame of reference, Chapter 5 describes what was intended for the Opening Ceremony and the processes of planning a three hour spectacle which: adheres to Olympic ritual and regulation; presents the host culture (in this case a fascinating dynamic between Catalonia and Spain); and allows for the presentation and admiration of the athletes who are the supposed soul of the Olympic Games. The next part of the chapter begins the direct comparison of broadcasts in terms of structural differences. Chapter 6 continues this overall comparison of Opening Ceremony broadcasts by looking at different narrative approaches, orientations to the Olympics, and commentator style and roles.

Chapters 7, 8 and 9 each focus on a different sphere of meaning. Chapter 7 is concerned with how broadcasters present and define elements of Olympism to home audiences. An overall objective in this chapter is to ascertain whether this international movement does in fact create any sense of community or connection among its participants. The search for this is done by looking for common meanings expressed across broadcasts for Olympic symbols and rituals, as well as the attention to shared elements of community (such as collective memory, past Olympic heroes, etc.)

Chapter 8 focuses on an analysis of the athletes' parade. How do broadcasters choose to present others? This chapter becomes a good example of how various cultural contexts affect broadcast presentations. It demonstrates how cultural aspects such as religion, politics, language, or even dress influence broadcast presentations. In this sense, Chapter 8 is very much about television and national or cultural self identity.

The hosting of global events is a well known image management strategy. In the case of the Olympics, millions of dollars are invested to prepare for the Games. In addition there is a high level of self consciousness and concern about just what kind of image of the host will travel around the world. As is described in Chapter 5, much thought and planning went into the design of the Barcelona Opening Ceremony as a stage to present Catalonia as a distinct, yet complementary host, with Spain. This 'dual' host relationship is a fascinating story unique to the 1992 Games. Chapter 9 explores how well the host image strategy worked. It compares broadcaster presentations of the host city and cultures in terms of attention, understanding, depth and interest and finds intriguing variations.

The final chapter of this section, Chapter 10, offers some useful quantitative data on the presence of advertising in Olympic television. The increase of commercialism surrounding the Games is an area of increasing concern and discourse among many Olympic observers. This chapter explores both the explicit and implicit presence and mix of commercial messages with Olympic messages in television programming.

The viewing experience

Finally, the study – through a reliance on the study correspondents, press accounts and other data – begins to make sense of Olympic audiences. First of all, nearly every broadcaster in this study claimed the Opening Ceremony was being simultaneously watched by 3.5 billion people. This figure, for academics at least, certainly begs the question. So Chapter 11, although cognisant of the difficulty of this enterprise, attempts to grasp the size and shape of this 'global' audience. How large can it really be? More important, what are the key factors which influence viewership of the Olympic programming? And finally, how do people view the Games? For this part of chapter on audience composition and viewing behaviors, the study relies on some systematic, but mostly anecdotal inputs of study correspondents and their experiences during the Games.

Chapter 12 keeps at this local perspective by choosing a few countries from the study sample for a closer look at their experience with the 1992 Olympics. Chosen were countries from Africa, Latin America, as well as Russia, China and Slovenia, partly because of difference in culture and media environments, but perhaps more important in the decision to focus on them was what was going on in those countries in 1992. These local perspectives serve as an important reminder than local circumstances can greatly colour the experience of a global event like the Olympic Games.

PART I
Economic, Organizational and Technological Infrastructures for Olympic Television

Introduction

In communications there is a widespread recognition of the interaction among economics, organizational and corporate practices and technological change on both national and global scales. Yet it is far from clear exactly what the dynamics of these relationships are as change occurs. For example, increasingly rapid technological change affects the economics, organizations and production practices of the media. Yet in reciprocal fashion, economics certainly constrain technological and organizational possibilities. In this part of the book, the Olympics provide a window on all these phenomena as the modern Games have been characterized by a rapid and linked evolution in these infrastructures which both support and influence the essence of the event. From the growth in television rights income and commercial sponsorship to increased worldwide exposure and live broadcasting of the Games, television has been fundamentally involved in the evolution of the modern Olympics. In this sense, this part of the analysis both confirms and adds to what we know about television's role as a change agent in so many aspects of national and international society – whether politics, sport , or cultural understanding.

This part of the book is also intended to set the stage for the multi-dimensional comparative analysis of international television broadcasts which takes place in Part II. Constructing the Games for television requires literally thousands of professional personnel living in a thick and amazingly complex blanket of cameras, cables, monitors and computer electronics which surround and interact with the Olympic athletic events and ceremonies. In order to compare and better understand the meanings which ultimately emerge from Olympic telecasts – as a window to cross cultural understanding of the modern Olympics – one must first appreciate the dimensions of human interaction and production processes that go into broadcasting an Olympic Games worldwide.

2   The Economics of the Olympics: television and sponsorship

An analysis of the financing of the modern Olympic Games demands a primary distinction between three main concepts of expenditure:

- Expenditures necessary for the organization of the Games that are not reusable as services once the Games are over (e.g. human resources and services costs).

- Expenditures necessary for the organization which are later reusable as services in the host city (e.g. improvements in sports facilities).

- Finally, expenditures on infrastructure (e.g. highways, telecommunications), which are useful for the celebration of the Games and constitute a long term investment in the organizing city and country.

The total cost of organizing the Barcelona Games was reported by COOB'92 at 1,635 million US dollars. The primary organizing committee costs (listed here in descending percentage of expenditure for COOB'92) fell into the areas of: installations and preparations of facilities (23.5 per cent), services to the Olympic Family (19 per cent), telecommunications and electronics (12.7 per cent), support structure (11.7 per cent), radio and television services (9.3 per cent), competitions and events (7.2 per cent), commercial management (5.5 per cent), ceremonies and cultural acts (4.6 per cent), image (4.1 per cent) and security (2.4 per cent).[1]

---

1   Brunet (1993: 37). Services to the Olympic Family include such items as transport, medical care, accreditation and protocol services, language services, and accommodation outside the Olympic village. Commercial management involves primarily tickets and commercial operations.

This chapter draws upon the research of Marc Carroggio. The section on the IOC and the negotiation of television rights benefits from the contributions of Susanna Ribas. The section on NBC and the Pay-Per-View experiments benefits from the contributions of Kerry Carnahan. The authors gratefully acknowledge the collaboration and contributions of these people.

To offset these expenditures, Table 2.1 shows the principle categories of income for an Olympic organizing committee and in particular for Barcelona'92. As can be seen, the Barcelona Olympics, with revenues at 1,638 million dollars, netted a small profit of about 3 million dollars (368 million pesetas). More important to note is that a significant portion of COOB'92 income, at 58.2 per cent, was derived from communications-related enterprises – television rights, sponsorship, licensing of symbols – underscoring the fundamental role these areas play in the organization of the modern Olympic Games.

Of course, the economics involved in being an Olympic Games host are much broader than this. It should be noted that the organizing committee activities constitute only part of the economic impact of hosting an Olympic Games. As an example, the COOB'92 budget comprised only about 17 per cent of overall Olympic related costs. The 1992 Games saw direct costs (public works investments) in Barcelona and environs estimated at 8,012 million dollars for highway construction, housing, telecommunications, hotel and sports facilities and general environmental improvements. Taken together, this urban transformation improved transportation, communications, conference and other facilities in and around Barcelona with obvious long term economic and social impacts. It is interesting to note that of these expenditures only 9.1 per cent was devoted to the improvement of sports facilities. This reflects not so much a lack of effort in this area, but the enormous overall investment made in a range of structural and communications related improvements in and around Barcelona in preparation for the Olympic Games.

Finally, added to the above noted organizing committee and public works expenditures totaling 9.4 billion dollars, economists estimated the induced economic impact of the 1992 Games to be approximately 16.6 billion dollars, bringing the total economic impact of the Barcelona Games to close to 26 billion dollars.[2]

Television rights in the Olympic Games

Table 2.1 also offers a comparative analyses of the organizing committee's budgets from the last eight summer Olympic Games. It should be acknowledged that a comparison of these budgets is complicated by differences that exist between the management systems of each new host organizer and by the continued evolution of commercialization strategies (e.g. changing definitions of income categories). In reviewing Table 2.1 one should also bear in mind the various forms of investing public resources to finance the Games. These resources, which reached their highest percentage of the budget in Moscow'80, are also important in all the Games prior to Los Angeles'84. In the case of the Seoul Games, apart from the contributions of state resources, other items such as promotional donations that were not strictly commercial in character became very important. An example was the donation of approximately 52,400 won by Korean residents in Japan. Also, public contributions made to offset the deficits of the Games in Munich (approximately 686

---

2   The COOB'92 expenditures of 1635 million dollars plus public works investments at 8012 million dollars actually totals 9.6 billion dollars. However, as detailed in Brunet (1993), various adjustments bring the final figure down to approximately 9.4 billion dollars in total direct and indirect costs and investments related to the Olympic Games.

Table 2.1. Summer Olympic Games organizing committee revenues (1964–1992)

Main budget categories	Tokyo 1964 mill. Yen	%	Mexico 1968 mill. US$	%	Munich 1972 mill. Mark	%	Montreal 1976 mill. US$	%	Moscow 1980 mill. Rble.	%	Los Angeles 1984 mill. US$	%	Seoul 1988 mill. Won	%	Barcelona 1992 mill. Pstas.	%
Sponsorship and licenses	855	8.6	4.3	5.6	181.0	14.1	9	1.5	207.1	27.8	126.7	16.5	74,516	8.2	59,686	30.5
Sponsorship	805	8.1							7.8	1.0	111.6	14.5	70,833	7.8	58,152	2.9
Licenses	50	0.5							199.3	26.8	15.1	1.9	3,683	0.4	1,534	0.8
Television rights	600	6.0	7.4	9.6	47.4	3.7	32	5.2	61.1	8.2	286.7	37.3	224,694	24.7	54,164	27.7
Ticket sales	1,871	18.9					27	4.4	20.2	2.7	139.9	18.2	27,494	3.0	9,454	4.8
Accommodation	327	3.3					2	0.3			20.5	2.7	13,863	1.5	8,866	4.5
Services	41	0.4			10.3	0.1	1	0.1			10.1	1.3	26,493	2.9	14,981	7.6
Subscriptions, collections	5,115	51.6	56.9	74.0	922.0	71.6	526	87.0	451.7	60.6	66.3	8.6	367,194	40.4	46,349	23.7
Lotteries	1,030	10.4			250	19.5	235	38.8	368	49.5			118,804	13.0	9,952	5.0
Commemorative coins & stamps	963	9.7			639	49.5	115	19.0	71	9.5	35.9	4.7	138,167	15.2		
*Public & private donations	3,122	31.5	56.9	74.0	33	2.6	176	29.2	12	1.6	30.4	3.9	110,223	12.2		
Sale of assets	285	2.8							3.1	0.4			131,411	14.4	2,094	1.0
Other	831	8.4	8.2	10.7	122.6	9.5	9	1.5	1.6	0.2	118.0	15.3	44,175	4.8		
TOTAL (local currency)	9,901	100	76.8	100	1,286	100	606	100	744.8	100	768.2	100	909,840	100	195,594	100
TOTAL (million US$)	27.5		76.8		352.3		606		*		768.2		1,272.5		1,638.1	

Source: Carroggio, Marc (1995).
Notes: The conversion rate of the local currency into dollars has been established as the following: 1 US dollar = 360 yen, 3.65 deutschmarks, 715 won, 119.4 pesetas.
The data offered in this table are derived from a standard interpretation of the data offered by the respective organizing committees in their Official Reports.
*No accurate conversion rate was available for the rouble.

million marks), Montreal (990 million dollars) and Moscow are not included in the revenue figures.

Despite these qualifications, Table 2.1 clearly shows the change in balance of revenue sources for the Olympic Games from Tokyo'64 to Barcelona'92, with a nearly consistent increase in the portion of revenues coming from sponsorship and television rights.

The evolution of revenue from television rights

In the 1960s and 1970s television rights constituted a minimal proportion of budgets. Los Angeles'84 represented a radical turning point with 37.3 per cent of revenue coming from television rights. The later decrease to 24.7 per cent in Seoul'88 could be interpreted as showing the importance of public and private participation and the lottery in the budget for those Games. Overall, however, the continuous increase in television rights income from 1.17 million dollars in Rome'60 to 635.6 million dollars for Barcelona'92 has been tied to both the increase in worldwide audience figures and the volume of Olympic programming. According to the IOC, the cumulative global audience of the Barcelona'92 Games was 16.6 million people in 193 countries, and the number of programming hours offered by Radio Televisión Olímpica (RTO'92) to international broadcasters amounted to 2,800 hours (an increase of 89 per cent over Seoul'88).[3]

As a result, one can see that revenue from sponsorship and television rights have taken over the leadership that revenue from ticket sales once held. While revenue from ticket sales represented 18.8 per cent of total revenue in Tokyo'64, this has decreased to 3 per cent and 4.8 per cent respectively in Seoul'88 and Barcelona'92. The Games organized in the United States are an exception to this general decrease in revenue from ticket sales (18.2 per cent in Los Angeles'84 and 16.5 per cent forecast for Atlanta'96), probably as a consequence of the non-intervention of the public sector in the organization of the Games along with the high sports interest and purchasing power of the domestic market. In short, television's financial role, in Olympism and in sport in general, tends to quickly eclipse the logic of ticket sales and public resource subsidies. More generally, this growing tie between television broadcasters and the Olympic Games has major economic and social implications for the international Olympic movement.

Table 2.2 summarizes the evolution of television rights fees paid by geographic zone. These figures include all income from television rights which are then allocated by the IOC to the organizing committee, international sports federations and national Olympic committees as described later in this chapter. (That explains the discrepancy between the television rights figures shown in Table 2.1 and Table 2.2. Table 2.2 shows *total* rights income. Table 2.1 represents the organizing committee (OCOG) allocations only.) The geographic distribution and sums of the economic contributions from television describe not just the increasing role of television rights income in the Olympic Games, but the relative influence of broadcasters on a worldwide scale with US broadcasting companies greatly influencing the financing the broadcasting operations of the Olympic Games.

---

3   IOC (1994a).

Table 2.2. Television rights income by geographic zone: summer games 1960 to 1992

Zone	Broadcaster Union or Pool	Rome 1960 US$'000	Tokyo 1964 US$'000	Mex. City 1968 US$'000	Munich 1972 US$'000	Montreal 1976 US$'000	Moscow 1980 US$'000	L.A. 1984 US$'000	Seoul 1988 US$'000	Barcelona 1992 US$'000	Atlanta 1996 US$'000[5]
North America USA	ABC				6,500 TS 6,000	12,500 TS 12,500		225,000			
	NBC		1,500	4,500			22,333 TS 50,000		300,000	401,000[1]	456,000[5]
	CBS	395									
Canada	CBC			250	257	300	1,044	3,000	3,600		20,750
	CTV									16,500	5,450
Latin America	OTI			2,500	300	300 TS 300	1,060	2,150	2,920	3,550	
Europe	EBU	668		1,000	1,745	2,275 TS 2,275	4,703 TS 950	19,800	28,000	66,000 TS 24,000	250,000 TS 5,000
	OIRT	66			300	1,000 TS 1,000	1,500	2,500	3,000	4,000 TS 500[2]	
Arab States	ASBU					75 TS 75	300	350	420	500	3,750
Africa	URTNA					25 TS 25	64	110	170	200	
South Africa	SABC Africa Pool[9]					1,050 TS 1,050				6,000[3]	6,750 250
Asia	ABU						150			2,200	5,000
	BOTP[4]									1,100	
	BOKP[4]									7,500	[8]
	NHK[4]	48		1,000	1,000			18,000	52,000		
	BOJP[4]									62,500	99,500
	ANB						4,500				
Oceania Australia New Zealand	Ch. 7						1,360	10,600	7,000	33,750	30,000
	TVNZ Pool			500						5,900	8,000
Others	Caribbean	0.6	78		990	31 TS 31	20	6,793	10,613	860[6]	[8] 190
Total[7]		1,178	1,578	9,750	17,092	34,862	87,984	288,343	407,133	635,560	5

Sources: Brunet (1995); Atlanta Committee for the Olympic Games (1995); COOB'92 (1993b: 391); IOC documents
Notes: 1. In addition to the rights fee, NBC paid a further 10 million dollars in free advertising space for COOB'92 and $5 million for the IOC.
2. A few months after the contract was signed, OIRT dissolved and the rights were subrogated to the EBU for the Games.
3. To assist South Africa's re-entry into the Games after so many years, 2 million dollars were set aside for the South African Olympic Committee.
4. These acronyms stand for 'Barcelona Olympic Taiwan Pool', 'Barcelona Olympic Korea Pool' and 'Barcelona Olympic Japan Pool' each made up of several broadcasters from those respective countries.
5. Data on Atlanta'96 is provisional and correspond exclusively to the proposed budgets of ACOG'96 and rights negotiations concluded by November 1995.
6. As an example, for Barcelona'92 other rights fees were negotiated with broadcasters from the Philippines, Caribbean, Puerto Rico and Australian radio.
7. The television rights figures shown on Table 2.1 represent the portion of the above total rights income figures allocated to each organizing committee.
8. All negotiations for rights with had not yet concluded at press time, so no figures were available.
9. For Atlanta '92 there is an Africa 'pool' arrangement totalling $7 million of which $6.75 million represents the rights fee paid by SABC, the South African broadcaster, and the remaining $250,000 was paid by an agent for resale to various African broadcasters.
TS = Technical services.

However, changes in the European television system with the appearance of private television channels and the break-up of monopolies, has led to a constant and exponential increase in the rights fees paid by the European Broadcasting Union (EBU) for the Olympic Games and for sports spectacles in general. The Atlanta'96 organizing committee (ACOG) managed to sell the broadcast rights for Europe to the EBU for 250 million dollars, an increase of 233 per cent in respect to Barcelona'92 (where the EBU paid 90 million dollars, including technical services).

Despite these increases, revenue from television rights in Barcelona'92 (27.7 per cent) and as projected for Atlanta'96 (35.1 per cent of revenues) do appear to reflect a general stabilization of this source of revenue.[4] In that sense, these 1990s figures offer no clear indication of direction. It is yet to be seen what will result from the increased revenues coming from corporate sponsorship, as well as from the advent of the multimedia or information highway era, in which the number of channels will increase in such a way as to likely alter the structure of distribution of the Games programming. It is also highly unlikely that audiences and programming quantities can continue to grow in the same way they have since the 1960s.

The IOC and the negotiation of television rights

The International Olympic Committee is the sole owner of the Olympic Games and holds all the rights to them, especially those relating to their organization, symbols and transmission. Revenue that comes about as a consequence of IOC ownership is redistributed among the IOC, the organizing committees of the Olympic Games (OCOGs) and the national Olympic committees (NOCs) according to various formulas that have been developed throughout the years.

Television cameras were first present at the Olympic Games in Berlin in 1936. However, it was not until London in 1948 that the organizers received the first economic contributions as recompense for television's presence. The organizing committee in London charged the BBC 1,500 pounds sterling to broadcast the event.

The experience of the Cortina d'Ampezzo winter Olympic Games and the summer Games in Melbourne, both in 1956, saw the first difficulties emerge in the negotiations between television stations and the host organizers. In part, this was because television broadcasters wanted the same status enjoyed by radio broadcasters who were allowed to freely broadcast the Games as news, not entertainment. This issue led the IOC to include the question of television rights in the 'Olympic Charter'. Thus, in 1958 a new article was passed, number 49, which established that 'the rights shall be sold by the Organizing Committee, with the approval of the International Olympic Committee' and the revenues from this sale would be 'distributed in accordance with its instructions'.[5]

In those days the host city paid 100,000 Swiss francs to the IOC when it was chosen to

---

4   Atlanta Committee for the Olympic Games (1995).

5   Ribas (1993).

host the Games. For that reason, and because the fees paid had been relatively low thus far, the IOC chose not to keep any revenue from the sale of television rights. That situation was soon to change when in the 1960 Games, with the presence of the US network CBS, the first significant sums came to an organizing committee from television rights; CBS paid $50,000 for the winter Games in Squaw Valley and $394,000 for the summer Games in Rome. Four years later the Tokyo Games saw the first use of communication satellites, more broadcast coverage, and another significant increase in television rights fees paid.

As a result, in 1966, Session 65 of the IOC established a new distribution formula for television revenue. These new criteria dictated that the first million dollars go entirely to the IOC, who would take a third for itself and would distribute the rest, in equal thirds, between the national Olympic committees and international sports federations. Of the second million dollars the first third would go to the organizing committee, then the rest would be divided up again into thirds and distributed equally among the IOC, the national Olympic committees and the international sports federations. For the third million, two thirds (and any remaining millions) would go to the organizing committee and a third to the IOC.

In 1971 the IOC added a paragraph to article 21 of the 'Olympic Charter' further consolidating its control of the use of this increasingly important revenue source; in this paragraph it was established that revenue from television rights belonged exclusively to the IOC, and the IOC should decide on the form of distribution among the international federations (IF), the national Olympic committees (NOC) and the organizing committee (OCOG). Despite these controls the organizing committee of the Munich Games in 1972 managed to sign a double contract with the US network ABC from which it received 7.5 million dollars from television rights and another 6 million from 'technical services'.[6] In this way the rules established by the IOC only affected one part of the contract and allowed the organizing committee to keep 6 million dollars for themselves. Looking back at Table 2.2 one can see that the inclusion of 'technical services' as parts of rights agreements continues today with, for example, the EBU committing 5 million dollars in 'technical services' under its agreement with the Atlanta Committee for the Olympic Games (ACOG'96).

The Los Angeles Games in 1984 brought about a radical change in Olympic budgets and the way in which resources were managed. Television rights and sponsors became the two pillars on which the Olympic Games were organized, with a surplus left over. However, the economic success in Los Angeles'84 impelled the IOC to, once again, introduce new and stricter controls both for the sale of television rights and the management of sponsorship programmes (discussed below), the application of which began in Seoul and continues along the same basic lines for Atlanta'96.

The Seoul Olympic Organizing Committee (SLOOC) experienced some difficulties in the negotiation of television rights for the 1988 Olympic Games as its expectations for large rights revenues clashed with broadcaster unwillingness to let the fees go too high. The

---

6   *Ibid.*

Seoul organizers had optimistically expected along the lines of 500 to 600 million dollars based on the past rate of increase in rights fees paid, but NBC (US), for example, countered with its concerns about the large time difference (which placed most key events well outside of US prime time), possible boycotts by socialist nations, and internal and external terrorist threats.[7] They settled on 300 million, still a one third increase over what ABC paid for the Los Angeles Games.

For the Seoul Games, the IOC negotiated jointly with the organizing committee and, as such, was an equal and interested party in the contract. This arrangement caused some difficulties when differences of opinion arose. Therefore, in Barcelona'92 the IOC negotiated 'in consultation' with the organizing committee. While both were still involved parties in the contract with each broadcaster, the IOC reserved the final judgment should conflicts arise.

Difficulties with rights negotiations don't always relate just to money. In Barcelona, COOB'92 negotiators ran into problems bargaining with the Arab countries due to both the timing of the Gulf War and the fact that those countries could not broadcast women's events, complicating the assessment of rights fees. Also, several months after rights negotiations were concluded with the Eastern European broadcast union of OIRT. That entity dissolved, and the rights were subrogated to the EBU. In effect, the two entities merged operations for broadcasting the Games.[8]

The distribution of rights fees in Barcelona

In the Barcelona Olympic Games revenue from the sale of television rights to the entire world (635.5 million dollars) was distributed by the IOC in the following manner: 73 per cent was set aside for COOB'92 (of which 20 per cent went for host broadcasting operations), while the IOC received the remaining 27 per cent.[9] The money that went to the IOC was divided up into three equal parts: one third for IOC operations, another third to international sports federations (IFs) whose sports figured in the programme for the Olympic Games, and the final third went to the national Olympic committees (NOCs).

The amount set aside for the NOCs was distributed through the Olympic Solidarity programme to assist national Olympic committees with the greatest economic needs. This programme includes grants for athletes and trainers, as well as the purchase of sports equipment. Besides grants, Olympic Solidarity offers financial help to the NOCs for their actual participation in the Games, covering the travel costs, accommodation in the Olympic village and equipment costs for a certain number of athletes and officials.

For the Atlanta Games it is estimated that 60 per cent would be set aside for the ACOG'96, with the remaining 40 per cent divided in equal shares among the IOC (13.3 per cent), the international federations (13.3 per cent) and Olympic Solidarity (13.3 per cent).

---

7   Larson and Park (1993: 74–81).

8   COOB'92 (1993b: 393).

9   IOC (1992a).

Rights negotiation criteria

Historically, the IOC has been guided by two basic criteria for the sale of television rights. First, the IOC seeks to obtain the maximum possible dissemination of the Games to world audiences. For example, during the negotiations for the European rights for Barcelona'92 some private channels offered proposals superior (in terms of money) to that of the European Broadcasting Union (EBU). Despite this, the IOC decided to sell the rights to the lower bidding EBU (made up of the main European public channels) because of the broadcast union's ability to reach more people across Europe.

Second, the IOC seeks exclusivity. Thus, in Barcelona'92, NBC (USA), CTV (Canada), HSV (Australia), TVE (Spain), RAI (Italy) and others all received exclusive rights to broadcast the Olympics in their home country. That said, the IOC did allow certain channels and broadcast unions to negotiate a resale of the rights they acquired, allowing the original buyer to recuperate part of the investment made and, at the same time, assure a wider diffusion of the Games.

This was the case, among many others, of the deals struck between NBC and Televisa in Mexico and between NBC and the pay-per-view system discussed below. Televisión Española (TVE) and Televisió de Catalunya (TV3) negotiated to create a new channel, Canal Olímpic, for the transmission of the Games in Catalan in Catalonia. Agreements were also forged between TF1 and Canal Plus in France, the two Russian television stations (Ostankino 1 and Russian State Television Channel 2). In a similar way, broadcasters in both Korea and Japan formed temporary 'pools' for gaining broadcast rights. In these latter cases, however, once the rights were obtained, the broadcasters were largely competitive – although some division of sports and broadcast scheduling did take place.

The US experiment with Pay-Per-View

As television rights fees have climbed, these types of cooperative arrangements have become more prevalent as broadcasters seek ways to mitigate costs related to covering the Olympic Games. In 1992, NBC of the United States experimented with a new strategy to enhance Olympic broadcast revenues: the use of Pay-Per-View (PPV) cable service in addition to its traditional broadcast.[10] This effort, dubbed the 'TripleCast', was a joint venture between NBC and Cablevision, a large US cable operator. The TripleCast, which offered three channels of continuous, 24-hour coverage of the entire Olympic Games, was the largest and most complex sporting event ever to be offered via PPV television. The PPV service allowed a viewer to order a variety of programming packages based on 1,000 hours of Olympic competition. At the time, it was also seen by many as an experiment that would make or break this new service. The PPV venture on the part of NBC was never intended to make a profit, but rather to show the ability of this new option to defray the

---

10 Pay-per-view service allows a viewer to order a specific cable television program and pay only for what is ordered. This service is made possible via a converter/decoder box placed in a subscriber's household by the cable company, who sends out scrambled versions of the programmes. For a one-time only fee, subscribers receive an unscrambled version of the selected broadcast.

rising costs associated with gaining exclusive rights to broadcasting premier sports events.[11]

The TripleCast, by nearly all accounts, was a failure. While the actual programming itself got rave reviews and customers showed high levels of satisfaction, the number of subscribers barely topped 250,000 instead of the projected (and needed) 2.5 million. This failure to attract subscribers caused NBC and Cablevision together to lose nearly $150 million.

As for an explanation, some observers pointed to the complexity of the TripleCast setup in terms of the logistics of working with local cable company channels and promotional confusion over the hodgepodge of packages available. All can't be blamed on these factors. In fact, general awareness of the service was extremely high. In the end, NBC seemed to have discovered that there are simply limits to the number of Olympics fans who have the time and desire to pay money to view the Games beyond what's offered 'free' on network coverage.

Rising costs and broadcast segmentation

The PPV experiment is only one example of how the evolution of television rights in the Olympics has moved from a story of a few big broadcasters to a host of different participation strategies where Olympic programming is becoming segmented, fragmented, shared, resold and more specialized (as with the use of sports channels). In part this reflects changes in the television industry worldwide, but it also reflects the need to share or minimize costs for television rights of this 2-week mega-event.

The overall trend of rising costs for broadcasting the Games does present a challenge for many broadcasters – large and small. As noted earlier, many world broadcasters rely on broadcast unions or other 'pool' strategies to afford to obtain rights to broadcast the Games. Here still, rising costs are passed along to member broadcasters, putting particular pressure on small-sized broadcasters. For example, EBU member broadcaster fees for the television rights for the Barcelona Games were based on a 'basic units system' formula (which considers number of households served and other factors) whereby, for example, the BBC paid the EBU on basis of its 66 basic units versus a lesser contribution was made by Icelandic National Broadcasting (RUV) based on its three basic units. Even so, once in Barcelona the costs for on site broadcast services such as commentator positions, IBC space and editing suites (explained in Chapter 4) did not differentiate broadcasters by size or resources (with some exceptions). The combination of rising broadcast union member fees plus on site costs made RUV an example of a borderline 'participant' in Olympic broadcasting. The public broadcaster services 75,000 households in Iceland and could barely send 3 people to Barcelona, let alone afford studio facilities and other services once

---

11 For discussions of NBC's experiment with pay-per-view, see 'Recent Growing Pains Can't Stop PAY-PER-VIEW Gains', *Advertising Age* 63:34 24 August, 1992, p. S1 and 'NBC Girds For Olympic PAY-PER-VIEW: Oh, The Agony Of The Feat', *Advertising Age* 6 April 1992, p. S14.

there.[12] Other broadcasters, notably from the African continent, cannot afford to send personnel at all and simply receive parts of the international signal or a 'borrowed' signal (as in the case of some African broadcasters using French broadcasts).

Even the $401 million that NBC in the United States could afford to paid for the Olympics broadcast rights to Barcelona was far more than the company expected to recoup from advertising sales during its broadcasts. While NBC's PPV experiment actually increased the total hours of Olympic viewing, the idea of paying to view the Olympics is an uncomfortable one – philosophically – for many Olympics observers who worry that revenue-generating schemes like PPV will simply exacerbate social divisions between 'haves' and 'have nots' and, if expanded, would prevent viewers from seeing their favourite athletes or sports, effectively undermining IOC goals of maximum distribution.

In this sense, these linked phenomenon of rights sharing and programming segmentation as new financing strategies presents a challenge for the Olympic movement. First, while technology easily allows decentralized coverage of the Games (that is, a broadcaster receives the television signal in their home country and adds commentary after the fact), the financial inability to be present in the host city also has important qualitative consequences for the ability of those broadcasters to customize and convey the Olympic 'experience' to home audiences. Can a commentator outside the host city really communicate the spirit and excitement found inside an Olympic venue? Can a French TF1 commentator inspire national pride in a viewer from Cameroon?

Second, if the strategy becomes one of sharing, segmenting or in some way 'breaking' up of the Olympic telecast into different sizes and shapes to meet the financial capabilities and constraints of international broadcasters one must also ask how this is beneficial to the goals of the Olympic movement as a whole. Whether they watch or not, does an audience with access to only a handful of Olympic events at limited hours 'experience' the Games in the same way as those audiences confronted with a full two-week, 200 hour programming schedule of Olympic ceremonies and events?

Sponsorship and the Olympics

Sensitive to an over reliance on television rights income, the IOC has made a conscious effort to expand the revenue base for the Olympic Games. Barcelona'92 represented the first Olympic Games where revenue from sponsorship and licensing outstripped broadcast rights fees. Referring back to Table 2.1, Los Angeles'84 revenue from sponsorship and licenses represented 16.4 per cent (126.7 million dollars) of the budget, down to 8.2 per cent (104.3 million dollars) for Seoul'88, then dramatically rising to 30.5 per cent of total revenue (or 499.9 million dollars) for Barcelona'92. This figure should increase for Atlanta'96. These data confirm the increasing importance of sponsorship in the financing of the Olympic Games. Sponsorship as a revenue source, however, directly links to television in the Olympics as the increase in sponsorship dollars is due, in large part, to

---

12 Interview with Ingolfur Hannesson, Head of Sports, Icelandic National Broadcasting Service Radio and Television, Barcelona, 9 August 1992.

the increasing popularity and reach of television around the globe. Because of the nature of the Olympic Games as 'more' than just a sporting event, sponsorship and advertising exposure is highly desirable for companies interested in reaching as wide a profile of the public as possible.

The growth in sponsorship dollars also correlates with a growing sophistication on the part of the IOC and Olympic organizers in designing attractive sponsor packages selling Olympics 'prestige'. Various surveys commissioned by the marketing division of the IOC confirm that it is largely the perceived prestige of Olympism (modernity, world leadership, excellence, etc.) that makes Olympic sponsorship desirable for inclusion in corporate advertising strategies. Perhaps more important, however, is the IOC-sponsored research showing that the Olympics is considered by the majority of consumers in major global markets to 'the most important' sports event and one that promotes 'international cooperation and brotherhood'.[13]

The evolution of Olympic sponsorship

Although the Greek patron Averoff offered to finance the 1896 Athens Games, the first real sponsorship experience in the Olympic Games took place in Rome in 1960 when several companies contributed material resources free of charge. For example: the Gillette company contributed 10,000 boxes with shaving equipment for the participants; Olivetti provided 1,000 typewriters; Omega offered the stopwatches; Zanussi provided the 60 refrigerators needed for the Olympic Village; Fiat put 34 cars at the disposal of the organizers; Coca-Cola gave a present of 200,000 bottles; Banca Nacionale del Lavoro acted as the Games' official bank and paid for the expenses of the various publications and services; and the popular motorcycle company Lambretta offered transportation to journalists and photographers.[14]

Thus started a trend that was to be expanded on in Tokyo'64 when nearly 100 companies answered the organizers call and provided a wide array of goods free of charge for the celebration of the Games. For example, Daishowa contributed 9,200 rolls of toilet paper, Sanyo gave a present of hair-dryers for the swimmers as well as 14 washing machines for the Olympic Village.[15] IBM attended the Games for the first time, contributing its computer technology and providing an electronic calculation system which then had to be supplemented with other contributions – a printing machine and refrigerator to prevent the heavy computer from overheating. In Tokyo'64 goods were also contributed by sponsors whose brands were in direct competition. For example, Olivetti, Brother, and Kusuda – three rival companies – provided typewriters for the press centre. Both Coca-Cola and Pepsi-Cola contributed soft drinks free of charge.

---

13 For example, surveys carried out by International Sport, Culture and Leisure Marketing (ISL), an international agency commissioned by the IOC to run the international Olympic sponsorship programmes. See: ISL (1985).

14 Rome Olympic Organizing Committee (1960).

15 Tokyo Olympic Organizing Committee (1964).

In Mexico'68, the budget contained 8,752,000 dollars direct profit from royalties. Adidas and Puma, who were by then in strong competition, fought to provide the participating athletes with their sports shoes, paying them large sums of money in the process. The need to regulate sponsorship became apparent.

The strategy of exclusivity

The number of sponsors did not stop growing. In Montreal 168 sponsors took part, but this figure grew to 200 in Moscow and to 381 in Lake Placid in 1980. This rapid proliferation of commercial brands linking themselves with the Olympics both alarmed and provoked Games organizers to consider a new strategy: exclusivity in terms of number of sponsors and their commercial sector.

The organizers of the Los Angeles Games (LAOOC) limited the number of sponsors to 35 and, for the first time, clearly established the model of exclusivity which became a central part of future Olympic sponsorship programmes. According to this model, a list of 35 commercial sectors was devised; only one company could associate itself as a sponsor of the Games in each category. The results were positive for the LAOOC: instead of the 10 million dollars that the organizers of the Winter Games in Lake Placid had made, they achieved a revenue of close to 180 million dollars.

So, it was in Los Angeles'84 that the potential 'value' of the Olympic Games as a vehicle for commercial sponsorship became clear. After the financial and political setbacks of the 1972, 1976 and 1980 Games, this new 'business' approach was judged by the majority of observers as a great success and, in fact necessary, for the Games to survive.[16] After the financial deficits of Montreal'76 and Moscow'80 Games the IOC was having difficulty finding cities willing to host the Games. Today, cities and countries go to great lengths to become nominated as Olympic host.

The exclusive rights model has brought about something very important in modern commercial competition: the establishment of the reputation of certain brands, as opposed to their most direct rivals, based on an association with the positive values of sport and Olympism. This strategy is followed by large companies such as Coca-Cola in relation to Pepsi Cola, VISA in relation to American Express, Kodak in relation to Fuji, and so forth. (Something very similar has taken place in the case of television, with the competitive bidding for television rights in some countries largely a pursuit not for profits, but for prestige.)

This situation also has its downsides. For example, the desirability of associating one's product with the Olympics has given birth to 'ambush marketing', a (sometimes question-able) practice of companies who try to neutralize the image benefits that exclusive sponsorship provides for their competitors by 'ambushing' the event through other means besides sponsorship. For example, American Express attempts to frustrate the advantage of official sponsor VISA by not only contracting directly with broadcasters to advertise

---

16 The consortium of business leaders led by Peter Ueberroth made a profit of US$230million, which was unusual in the organization of the Olympic Games up until then. See Ueberroth (1985).

during the Games, but using Olympic themes in its advertisements in an effort to dilute the benefits of the official sponsor's exclusive association with Olympics symbols.

To try to protect its sponsors' goal of exclusivity from television broadcasters willing to look askance at ambush marketing techniques in order to sell advertising space, the IOC introduced a policy as part of the sale of the television rights that obliges broadcasters to guarantee Olympic sponsors some kind of preference for acquiring advertising time during the broadcast of Olympic events.[17] These preferences are also applicable to the sponsors of the national Olympic committees.

Typology of Olympic sponsors

The present regulations group sponsors into three main categories: World Olympic Sponsors, Sponsors of the Olympic Games Organizing Committee (in 1992, the sponsors of COOB'92) and Sponsors of the national Olympic committees (NOC). Within the latter two categories there are also some sub-types of sponsorship.

World Olympic Sponsors (TOP)

This group of sponsors are in a programme known by the initials TOP (The Olympic Program). This is a small group of exclusive sponsors generally associated with both a winter and summer Games. TOP was first applied in 1988 for both the Seoul and Calgary Games in 1988 (TOP–1 had 9 companies) and then again for the Barcelona and Albertville Games in 1992 (TOP–2 with 12 companies). The interests of TOP sponsors was highly influential in the decision by the IOC to begin holding summer and winter Games in different years, starting with Lillehammer (1994) and Atlanta (1996). Rather, than an intensive and expensive burst of Olympic activity in a single year, the new two-year spacing of the Olympic calendar offers more incentive to sponsors to participate as they can exploit their association with the Olympics on a more continuous basis.

TOP has enormously simplified the path to be followed by companies that want to link themselves to Olympism on a worldwide scale. Before 1988, a company that wanted to be a global sponsor had to negotiate with each one of the national Olympic committees. Today a single contract is negotiated through a management agent of the IOC (for 1988 and 1992 it was a firm called International Sport Leisure Marketing) who in turn negotiates the respective contracts with all the NOCs to allow sponsors the use of the five rings, the emblems and mottos of the various NOCs and the OGOC, all in the same package.[18]

This combination of global and national Olympic rights is particularly attractive for large companies who make an effort to transmit a global concept of marketing (e.g. Coca-Cola, 'Global Sponsor of the Barcelona'92 Olympic Games') while, at the same time, encouraging its national subsidiaries or distributors to remain close to their clients with promotions on a national level (e.g. Coca-Cola, 'Sponsor of the Spanish Olympic team'). Also, sponsors maintain global exclusivity in their respective product category (e.g. soft drinks);

---

17 IOC (1992b: 28).

18 For more detailed information on this subject, see Hitchen (1992: 173–174).

when one of these categories is occupied, no other company can acquire the rights for a similar product. Table 2.3 shows the company and sector profile of the first three TOP sponsor programmes.

Table 2.3. TOP Sponsors 1988–96

TOP–1 1988	TOP–2 1992	TOP–3 1996	Commercial sector
Coca-Cola	Coca-Cola	Coca-Cola	soft drinks
Kodak	Kodak	Kodak	photography
Sports Illustrated/Time	Sports Illustrated/Time	Time, Inc.	publications
VISA	VISA	VISA	credit cards
	Bausch & Lomb	Bausch & Lomb	optical, dental
		Xerox	photocopies
Brother	Brother		typewriters
Philips	Philips		audio and television
3M	3M		magnetic tapes
Federal Express	United States Postal Service (USPS)	United Parcel Service	couriers
Matsushita Electric (Panasonic)	Matsushita Electric (Panasonic)	Matsushita Electric (Panasonic)	video
	Ricoh		fax
	Mars		food
		IBM	data processing
		John Hancock	insurance

Sources: IOC (1993); Atlanta Committee for the Olympic Games (1995).

TOP sponsors are able to exclusively contract advertising spaces on numerous television channels and acquire special hospitality services during the Games. In Barcelona'92, for example, TOP sponsors enjoyed the use of luxury boats moored in Barcelona port for their public relations operations.

Revenue derived from TOP has increased since its beginnings in 1988. The present trend of the programme is to hold the number of companies in the programme down and to increase the entry cost, presently about 40 million dollars per sponsor, following the 'less is more' strategy encouraged by the organizers of the Los Angeles Games

Sponsors of the Organizing Committee of the Olympic Games (OCOG)

Each organizing committee's sponsorship programme (COOB'92's programme, for

29

example) is designed not to compete with TOP, in that once a product category is filled it is excluded from the worldwide programme (or vice versa).

The sponsors of OCOG programmes are able to use the symbol and mascot of the host (whose design might include Olympic symbols such as the rings, but they cannot use Olympic symbols alone). Although the OCOG programme is not a worldwide one, it can take on an international character when those companies also make agreements with other NOCs.

Further, the organizing committees of the Games can establish bilateral agreements both on a national and an international level with each of the national Olympic committees as long as they respect the general conditions of TOP. For example, COOB'92 had separate contracts with the Spanish Olympic Committee for the commercialization of the Games in Spain, as well as with the national Olympic committees in the large economic world powers such as the United States, Canada, Japan and Germany. In Atlanta, the organizing committee (ACOG) entered into a joint venture with the United States Olympic Committee (USOC) to create the Centennial Olympic Games Partners programme, providing exclusive joint marketing and sponsorship rights to the 1996 Games and the US Olympic Team. About eight companies are named Centennial Olympic Games Partners.[19]

OCOG sponsorship categories. Olympic sponsorship deals are made for both financial contributions and the contribution of goods and services. Once the only sponsorship formula in the modern Olympics, sponsorships that include in-kind supply of materials and services have once again become very important in the Games. In Barcelona'92, for example, COOB'92 had the following types sponsorship relationships:

- *Joint partners* were companies that took part in vital areas of the organization of the Games and made a minimum contribution of 2,500 million pesetas. These companies also provided computing technology, cars, banking services, insurance, telecommunication equipment and services, photocopies, uniforms and electronics.

- *Official sponsors* were companies that wanted to associate their image with the Games and that contributed a minimum of 600 million pesetas. These included companies ranging in products from ice cream to sun glasses to sports equipment.

- *Official suppliers* were companies that contributed professional technical products or goods or services for the organization with the minimum value of their contribution being 150 million pesetas. This materials sponsorship area is particularly important for television in the Olympics which is an technically complex and expensive undertaking. To this end, official suppliers contributed software, power, cables, screens, signal links, and more.

- *Suppliers of official sports material* provided COOB'92 with an amazing array

---

19 Atlanta Committee for the Olympic Games (1995).

of sports material, including basketball hoops, track surfaces, volleyballs, clay pigeons, sports nets, scales and weighing systems, swimming pool chemicals, boxing gloves and saddles.

- *Licensees* were those who obtained the license to use the symbols of the Games (host venue symbol and mascot) in the commercial exploitation of certain products (t-shirts, hats, towels, stickers, dolls, pajamas, perfume, etc.). For the Barcelona'92, 63 companies produced nearly 450 different products, not counting differences in size and colour.[20]

Sponsors of the National Olympic Committees (NOCs)

The main aim of sponsorship programmes for the national Olympic committees is to finance the national sportsmen and sportswomen who will represent their countries at the Olympic Games. The sponsors of these programmes can use one or various emblems of the national Olympic committee as their main compensation. The case of the United States is especially important. Their national Olympic committee (USOC) enjoys great prestige as a consequence of its economic support of athletes participating in the Games.

In Spain a specific plan, known as *Programa ADO'92* (Asociación de Deportes Olímpicos) was developed and a similar programme launched for Atlanta'96. It received a total of 2,400 million pesetas a year for five years, mainly from Spanish companies. Each company could contribute a variable amount of money, with a minimum amount set at 40 million pesetas, to sponsor a specific team (athletics, soccer, gymnastics, etc.) or the entire Spanish delegation. Thus for example, during the five years leading up to the Games, Coca-Cola sponsored the Spanish athletics team contributing 1,500 million pesetas and the Spanish tobacco company, Tabacalera, sponsored the sailing team, contributing 1,200 million pesetas. The programme also included discounts on television advertising, the use of the phrase 'the official sponsor of ...' and emblem of the Spanish Olympic Committee and ADO'92, and the inclusion of the sponsoring company's logo in ADO'92's advertising campaigns.

Television and sponsors

Television plays an important role in the success of Olympic sponsorship. The need to be present in Olympic telecasts is undeniable if a company's sponsorship is to be successful. As will be discussed at more length in Chapter 10, the analysis of all the advertising spots aired during the broadcasting of the Barcelona'92 opening ceremony across 28 international television broadcasts revealed that 46 per cent of all advertisements belonged to sponsoring companies. TOP sponsors such as Coca-Cola and Kodak are notable for their presence in broadcasts from nearly all geographic zones. As noted earlier, however, television broadcasters also allow non-sponsoring broadcasters to advertise using non-regulated Olympic themes and references raising some issues of concern.

20 See COOB'92 (1991b) and COOB'92 (1991c).

Protecting Olympic symbols

A challenge inherent in linking the Games' financial health to sponsorship programmes is to the need to maintain the integrity of Olympic symbols and the positive presence of the Olympic movement. After the experience of Los Angeles'84 it was felt that the Olympic movement had not benefited proportionally from the revenue derived from the use of its symbols by companies so the IOC, once again, reviewed its regulations concerning the privileges and limits of sponsorship.

Following are some of the key rules, contained in the 1992 version of the 'Olympic Charter' pertaining to commercial presence in the Games:[21]

- Rule 2, point 9: '[The IOC] opposes any political or commercial abuse of sport and athletes.'

- Rule 61 does not allow any form of publicity in and above the stadia and other competition areas which are considered as part of the Olympic sites. It also states that 'The IOC Executive Board alone has competence to determine the principles and conditions under which any form of publicity may be authorized.'

- Rule 17 states that, 'All rights to the Olympic symbol, the Olympic flag, the Olympic motto and the Olympic anthem belong exclusively to the IOC.' And, part of the bye-law to this rule states that 'The use of the Olympic symbol, flag, motto and anthem for any advertising, commercial or profit-making purposes whatsoever is strictly reserved for the IOC.' Other points contained in the bye-law detail the specific issues referring to the use of these elements for advertising purposes.

Two points remain clear having read the above rules: the complete prohibition of advertising in the competitions and the Olympic stadium and the IOC's position as the only valid interlocutor in negotiating the use of the Olympic signs and symbols, its exclusive property, for advertising purposes. Recently, the IOC revised another relevant bye-law (revision in italic).

- Paragraph 11.4 of the Bye-laws to Rules 12–17 states that, 'the use of an Olympic emblem must contribute to the development of the Olympic Movement and must not detract from its dignity; *any association whatsoever between an Olympic emblem and products and services if such association is incompatible with the fundamental principles of the Olympic Charter or the role of the IOC as set out therein.*

While it is unknown by the authors whether the IOC or an OCOG has refused a company as Olympic sponsor based on having an 'undesirable' image for the Olympics, in Malaysia, for example, there was a controversy over the sponsorship of the local Olympic television broadcast by a cigarette company. Besides public complaints, this was also disturbing to

---

21 IOC (1992c). See Chapter I, rules 11 to 18, and Chapter III, rules 61 and 63, and their respective bye-laws.

the local Ministry of Health who been engaged, for several years, in an active anti-smoking campaign. The cigarette company in question, Dunhill, was not an official Olympic sponsor.[22]

How well the above rules are observed by companies, broadcasters and Olympic organizers is addressed, to some degree, in Chapter 10 on advertising and commercial messages in the Games where some absolute and 'gray area' violations were found to be present in the international broadcasts of the Barcelona Olympics. Chapter 10 also raises this topic in a more philosophical sense as a fundamental tension in the Olympic movement in terms of Olympic meaning.

While the commercial impact on the Olympic Games has increased dramatically, it is important to remember that, from a technical point of view, sponsorship of the Olympics still differs significantly from sponsorship of other sports events in that only the regulated association of Olympic symbols with the image of the brand, advertising and packaging of the firms providing sponsorship is accepted. This eliminates the huge advertising opportunities provided by the inside of competition venues and by putting multiple logos on athletes' clothes and equipment – all advertising formats developed with television in mind.

Whatever the current concerns, the profitability of using television rights and sponsorship financing for the Games organizers has been clearly demonstrated in their bottom lines since Los Angeles' 84. On the other hand, the commercial benefit for companies (including broadcasters) is a bit more ambiguous. It seems to depend upon a complex commercial strategy in which the presence of a brand in sports events is linked not just to a single Olympic Games, but rather to a long term strategy of advertising and public relations. In this sense, the case of Kodak, present in the Games since Athens in 1896, or Coca-Cola, present since Melbourne in 1956, are the kinds of companies that have both given and reaped from their long term interdependent relationship with television, sports, the Olympic movement.

Still, one must question whether these kinds of long term corporate associations are healthy as an image strategy for the Olympic movement. Does the repeated linkage of a few high profile corporate images with the Olympic symbols result in the Olympics becoming inseparable from those corporations in audience minds?

One thing that is clear is the need for further coordination of the conduct of sponsors and broadcasters so that both benefit, rather than lose, as a result their positions of exclusivity. While the IOC goes to great length to protect Olympic symbols and prestige, a closer look at the regulation of advertising amount, types and timing – all in light of a changing television environment – seems imminent for future telecasts of Olympic events.

---

22 Mohamed (1992).

3 The Olympics as a Showcase: Media organizations and information technologies

As with all major organizations and activities in the late twentieth century, the Olympic movement requires a sophisticated infrastructure in order to function effectively. It is necessary not only for the worldwide telecast of the Olympic Games, but also for preparation, planning and the continuous operation of those organizations that constitute the modern Olympics.

Modern technology has contributed to the Olympic Games in various areas: telecommunications networks for the transmission of picture, data and sound signals; information management for the organization of the Games; information dissemination to the mass media and other Olympic constituents; the security of the installations and people; measurement methods and results data for athletic events; and the tools that mass media need to produce programming.

This chapter's focus on media organizations and communication technologies is not intended in a technologically deterministic spirit. Rather, it is the manner in which media organizations adapt, shape, use and are influenced by these technologies that is a most interesting and important part of the story of television in the Olympics. Quite simply, the human and 'meaning' aspects of the modern Olympics cannot be adequately understood without attention to the set of technologies and accompanying organizational framework that help construct each Olympic Games.

The media organization for the Olympics

As indicated in Chapter 2, the International Olympic Committee (IOC) heads the Olympic movement which comprises the international sports federations (IF), national Olympic committees (NOC) and the organizing committees of the Olympic Games (OCOG). The

The section on high definition television draws upon contributions from Gemma Larregola, and the section on radio draws upon contributions from Maria Gutiérrez. The authors gratefully acknowledge their cooperation.

35

main tasks of the OCOG are to: organize the competitions; stage the opening and closing ceremonies; provide the infrastructure at sports or other related venues; supply the necessary technical services, facilities and personnel to run the operation; design and implement security arrangements; promote the Games; and obtain financing. The enormity of this job requires the full six years of preparation time. While each of these OCOG tasks are books in themselves, the focus here is to give a sense of the enormity of just one: the technical services, facilities and personnel needed to stage Olympic broadcast operations.

Radio and television organization: the host broadcaster

Up until the 1988 Olympics the broadcaster covering the Games for the host country was generally contracted by the IOC to provide international broadcasters with coverage (e.g. ABC for Los Angeles' 84). Over time, however, this arrangement proved inadequate. First, as the Games grew in number of sports competitions, so did the broadcasting requirements in terms of the personnel and equipment necessary to cover it all. It became increasingly difficult for a single broadcaster to produce a national, as well as an international, signal that could satisfy the needs of diverse world broadcasters. Second, because serving their own national clientele was the priority for the host country broadcaster, this led to problems of bias in attention to certain sports and athletes in the signal. It was clear that a new strategy was needed for organizing the broadcasting of the Olympics.

Beginning with the Seoul Olympics, each OCOG has had its own radio and television organization (RTO). For Seoul, the organizing committee (SLOOC) contracted with the largest public broadcaster Korean Broadcasting System (KBS) to act as RTO for the 1988 Games. KBS, needing even more resources than it had available to devote to the enormous task of acting as host broadcaster, in turn signed an agreement with the second largest broadcaster in Korea, MBC, to jointly form the Seoul Olympics Radio and Television Organization (SORTO).

In Barcelona' 92 the host broadcaster, RTO'92, was fully under the auspices of the organizing committee (COOB'92). The rationale for this was efficiency, shared responsibility, neutrality of the signal, and economies of scale. By the time of the Games, RTO'92 had 3337 people of many nationalities working to produce the international signal, although the organization relied primarily on agreements for cooperation from Spanish television (TVE), the Corporación Catalana de Radio y Televisión (CCRTV), and the European Broadcast Union for personnel and technical assistance in meeting its goals as host broadcaster.[1]

RTO'92 acted as 'host' broadcaster in several ways. It set up the broadcast facilities and attended to the needs of the world broadcasters who descended upon the Olympic city, providing them with a range of support services during the Games. However, the primary role of RTO'92, as with all host broadcasters, was the production of the 'international signal' used by all broadcasters covering the Games. The international signal is an

---

1   RTO'92 (1992: 198).

aggregate of all camera and sound signals from all sports venues, as well as non-competition sites and activities such as press conferences. RTO'92 also produced daily 'summaries' for use in sports and news programmes around the world.

The international signal is a visual and sound only television signal which does not favour any national, political, or cultural viewpoint. That said, it is also produced by an elite cadre of sports broadcast professionals – many of whom are familiar faces in the technical operations at World Cups and other international sports events around the world – and as such, are driven by the standards and trends of their professional genre. Chapter 4 describes, in more detail, the character and creation of the international television signal.

The official responsibility of RTO'92 as host broadcaster ended with the delivery of the international signal to the International Broadcast Center (IBC) where rights-holding world broadcasters simultaneously edit the signal, add commentary, graphics, or other preferences before sending a television signal home live or on delay. Chapter 4 describes in more detail the options for 'customizing' the international signal. Part II of this book investigates and compares these different broadcast versions of the Olympics Games as received in 26 countries around the world.

Rights-holding broadcasters

As described in Chapter 2, the broadcast rights to the Olympic Games in a certain territory are awarded to broadcasters by the IOC in consultation with the organizing committee. Rights-holding broadcasters include independent organizations, like NBC of the USA or CTV of Canada, broadcast unions such as the European or Asian broadcast unions (EBU and ABU), or temporary 'pools' of national broadcasters who join resources in order to obtain the rights to broadcast the Olympics. For example, for the Barcelona Olympics six normally competing Japanese broadcasters came together to create the Japan pool, BOJP. Broadcasters from Korea and Taiwan each formed pools as well. Once in Barcelona as rights holding broadcasters, each pool varied on how much its members shared resources and final product. Some made internal agreements as to which sports and times each pool member would broadcast. These agreements didn't always hold, especially for broadcasters from competitive national markets. In Japan, viewers ultimately received six different broadcast versions of the Olympics. In Korea, there were many audience complaints about duplicate coverage by competing broadcasters of the Korea pool.[2]

Prior to the actual Games representatives of these world broadcasters met with RTO'92 representatives to discuss the production and distribution of Olympic television. It is during this time leading up to the Games that broadcasters work with an RTO on issues such as arrangements for unilateral (their own) 'extra' cameras to be placed at certain venues; the scheduling of events; space, power and lighting needs in the international broadcast centre, and so forth.

National Olympic committees and international sport federations also play a role in the

---

2   Park and Kang (1992).

television coverage of the Games during this time in that they intervene on behalf of their teams and athletes when broadcasters make requests that affect sports event schedules and procedures. An example here would be when (as happened for Seoul'88) influential broadcasters request that finals be scheduled to enhance their own audience strategies by coinciding with local prime time. Depending the host city location, this event timing is not always optimal for athlete performance.[3] In another example, Atlanta'96 broadcasters wanted some changes made in the colour and face mask design of fencing outfits to work better for viewing the sport on television. The resolution of these requests require negotiations with the IF that governs each sport.

The media in Barcelona

No event in the modern world is capable of generating such an effective information and organizational system as found by international media upon arrival in an Olympic city. Upon arriving in Barcelona, the accredited media found three Olympic villages prepared for their accommodation, facilities at 38 official sports installations, and an enormous, centrally located Main Press Center (MPC) and adjoining International Broadcasting Center (IBC) with everything, including restaurants, that they could need. It was a self-contained media 'world' only necessary to leave for sleep (on a bed at least) since every sport event could be viewed from the premises.

Main Press Center (MPC)

The media facilities occupied the most extensive closed spaces available in the city of Barcelona: the Montjuïc fairground areas. The Main Press Center took up 51,158 square metres. This was an increase on the order of 248 per cent in respect to Los Angeles'84 and of 64 per cent in respect to Seoul'88. Like the athletes' Olympic village, this huge expanse was also highly secured, allowing only the entrance of accredited personnel and authorized guests.

The MPC was in operation 24 hours a day. Its heart was a main hall with room for journalists to work simultaneously surrounded by several walls of giant modular television screens, capable of displaying a single large image or multiple images from different Olympic venues or city locales. Different levels and areas of the MPC housed: 125 offices and production areas available for rent to the media; a telecommunications centre; a video library containing the televised production of the Games; television monitors connected to all the sport installations; computers and information kiosks for instantaneous sports results, news and other information; various size press rooms for interviews offering simultaneous translation services (one of them with a capacity for 1,200 people) and for the over 650 press conferences that would be held during the Games; different news services such as telephone lines prepared for the transmission of photos, and more. The combined effect of walking into the MPC was to enter a highly visual, interactive and electronic experience of the Olympics.

---

3   Larson and Park (1993: 76).

The International Broadcast Centre (IBC)

Adjacent to the Main Press Center in Barcelona was the International Broadcast Center or IBC, the nucleus of radio and television operations. At more than 45,000 square metres the IBC housed RTO'92 and rights-holding world broadcasters. As noted above, the IBC receives the audio and video signals coming from the different competition installations which are immediately distributed among the broadcasters occupying it. The IBC is a conglomeration of television and radio studios, editing and post-production rooms, commentary ('off-tube') booths,[4] office services, new technology showrooms, telecommunications equipment rooms, meeting rooms and other facilities to service close to 8,000 radio and television personnel.[5] Unlike the more open, 'grand hall' atmosphere of the MPC, the IBC, because the extensive production facility requirements was more a series of closed off, soundproof and climate controlled spaces housing different specialized equipment and broadcaster offices and studios.

The largest on-site Olympic 'community'

Media personnel easily outnumbered athletes at the Barcelona Olympic Games. In fact, the media represented the largest single temporary 'community' to converge at the Olympics. Table 3.1 shows the tremendous growth in media attention given to the Olympic Games since 1960. In a sense this growth is paradoxical given the increased efficiencies in the ability to transmit information around the world (eliminating the need to 'be there' in order to get information). But the growing numbers of media organizations and personnel at the Olympics reflect several factors: the continued development of the media industry worldwide; the increased technical complexity (and thus personnel needed) to broadcast the Games; the desire of broadcasters to customize the output for their distinct audience needs and, of course, the allure for any professional of being where the action is.

Geographically, media personnel in Barcelona were distributed as follows: 16.6 per cent from Spain; 41 per cent from the rest of Europe; 26 per cent America (this study lacks differential data on North and South America); 11 per cent Asia; 2.6 per cent Africa and 2.8 per cent Oceania.[6]

In total, there were 147 radio and television stations – 56 radio broadcasters and 91 television broadcasters – accredited for the coverage of the Barcelona Olympic Games. Of these 118 had the use of their own studios and offices in the IBC where they prepared

---

4   Off-tube commentary booths are small rooms equipped with a microphone and a colour monitor on which the journalist can receive the international signal of the event and add commentary to it. For broadcasters with limited personnel or financial resources to able to afford commentary positions at the actual competition venues, the use of off-tube booths in the IBC provided a relatively economical alternative -- although without the excitement of 'being there'.

5   At the sports venue themselves there are facilities for unilateral camera positions, commentator positions, ENG camera positions, observer seats, as well as 'mixed' zones for completing athlete interviews. There was also a television studio in the athletes' Olympic Village.

6   Barcelona Press Service (1992).

and carried out their broadcasts. The remaining 29 stations worked only through broadcast organizations or unions to which they were members. For example, there were seven international broadcasting organizations covering the Barcelona'92 Games: the Asian Pacific Broadcasting Union (ABU), the Arab States Broadcasting Union (ASBU), the Caribbean Broadcasting Union (CBU), the European Broadcasting Union (EBU), the Organisation Internationale de Radio et Télévision (OIRT), the Organización de Televisiones Iberoamericanas (OTI) and the Union Radio Télévision National d'Afrique (URTNA). See Appendix B for a summary of accredited broadcasters in Barcelona.

Table 3.1. Accredited media representatives at the summer Olympic Games

Rome'60	Total number of representatives		1,442
	Print press	1,146	
	Audiovisual media	296	
Tokyo'64	Total number of representatives		3,984
	Print press	1,507	
	Audiovisual media	2,477	
Munich'72	Total number of representatives		8,000
	Print press	3,300	
	Audiovisual media	4,700	
Los Angeles'84	Total number of representatives		8,200
	Print press	4,000	
	Audiovisual media	4,200	
Seoul'88	Total number of representatives		15,740
	Print press	5,380	
	Audiovisual media	10,360	
Barcleona'92	Total number of representatives		12,831
	Print press	4,880	
	Audiovisual media	7,951	

Sources: OCOG Official Reports.
Note: Print press figures include photographers. Estimates of non-accredited media put these figures higher. For example, Barcelona'92 total media personnel estimates would be close to 19,000.

An overview of television broadcasters

Of the rights holding broadcasters, NBC of the United States contracted for the most space in the IBC and invested the most technical and human resources for the coverage of the Olympic event. It had almost 7,000 square metres at its disposal. This amounted to more than 15 per cent of the total available space in the IBC. NBC's four television studios, eleven recording rooms, 77 cameras, 286 video recorders (VTRs), 957 monitors, 2 satellites and 18 kilometres of cable and the collaboration of 1,300 professionals made it possible for the broadcaster to carry out a very unique and personalized broadcast of the Olympic Games from Barcelona. NBC was the source of both envy and scorn among broadcast personnel in the IBC. It was the only broadcaster to bring a separate security set up to prevent entry into its area, creating an aura of 'secrecy' around its operations. Being, by far, the largest rights holding broadcaster in terms of dollars, NBC expected a certain return on its investment in terms of priority camera and commentator positions, last minute technical requests and other services in the IBC, making its presence felt by all.[7]

The presence of Televisión Española (TVE) was the second most notable due to both the size of the space booked in the IBC and the personnel and infrastructure used for the coverage of the Barcelona Games. TVE had almost 1,500 square metres at its disposal in the IBC: 600 square metres were used as offices (dispatches for editing, production, realization, logistics, operations, administration, etc.) and, in the remaining 870 square metres it built its own technical area with two complete television studios, recording, editing, post-production and signal emission rooms, a video library, characterization and sound-effects. There were also 500 professionals selected by TVE to carry out its Olympic programming.

After TVE the most significant deployment of resources by European television stations was carried out by the German broadcasters ARD and ZDF, who sent 350 professionals to Barcelona to cover the Olympic event. In the IBC both broadcasters had the use of a large television studio with four cameras in which there were two quite different sets: one for interviews, in which the decoration and the furniture created a scene resembling the Olympic symbol, and another smaller one for the presentation of news and for transition anchor commentary between events. Although both the Spanish and German broadcasters had significant unilateral (customized) signal capability, they were also members of the EBU, using that signal as the base for their broadcasts. This was also the case with French broadcasters.

The Japanese television station Nippon Hoso Kyokai (NHK) built two studios inspired by Gaudí architecture in its reserved space in the IBC, from where it offered its Olympic programming for both the station's conventional channel and its specialized news channel.[8] Nearly 100 professionals were dedicated to carrying out these programmes; this figure does not include the team NHK sent to Barcelona for the production of high definition broadcasts (discussed later in this chapter). There was less of a presence of the rest of the other five television stations in the Barcelona Olympic Japan Pool (BOJP) although this does not mean that they were of little importance. Thus, for example, Tokyo

---

7   Kim Sung Soo, coordinating producer for the Korean Broadcasting System, revealed something of the general attitude toward NBC by other broadcasters. Mr. Kim told a story about the women's marathon in Barcelona where NBC had a vehicle to film the leaders in the final 500 metres of the race up Montjuïc to the Olympic stadium. By mistake, however, COOB'92 security personnel would not let the NBC vehicle go up the hill, thus missing the last sprint before entrance into the stadium. According to Mr. Kim, despite the serious error on the part of the security people, other broadcasters were 'secretly pleased' with the story, feeling that it 'served NBC right'. (Interview, 4 August 1992, Barcelona).

8   Antonio Gaudí was a famous turn-of-the-century designer and architect whose modernist inspired buildings and other creations are distinctive landmarks in and around Barcelona, including the famous Sagrada Familia and Park Güell.

Broadcasting (TBS) had the use of a television studio from which it produced its programmes with the aid of 70 professionals. Fuji TV (CX), Asahi National Broadcasting (ANB) and Nippon Television Network Corp (NTV) each had one studio and 65, 44 and 45 professionals respectively, while the smallest of the Tokyo stations, Television Tokyo (TX) sent 8 people to Barcelona.

For Latin America, there were 20 member organizations of the Organización de Televisiones Iberoamericanas (OTI). OTI also offered a daily hour and a half summary to affiliated countries. In Barcelona there were broadcasters from Chile, Colombia and Venezuela, Brazil and Mexico with the latter two bringing, by far, the most personnel.

Canada's CTV sent 135 people to Barcelona to cover the Olympic event; Network 7 from Australia sent 154 people. By contrast, the entire group of East European countries that made up the Organisation Internationale de Radio et Télévision (OIRT) sent 200 people to Barcelona and took up very modest spaces in the IBC.

Africa and southeast Asia were the world zones that had the least presence in Barcelona and, consequently, the least chance to directly intervene in the televised production of the Olympic event.

The 28 broadcasters analysed for this study demonstrate the range of physical 'presence' international broadcasters have at an Olympic Games – ranging from the no investment, no presence and a 'borrowed' broadcast of Ghana TV to hundreds of millions dollars invested, 1000 plus people and a technology-driven custom broadcast produced by NBC of the USA. As might be imagined, the Olympic 'experience' is entirely different for viewers in these two countries in terms of broadcast content.

Radio in Barcelona '92

The first radio broadcast of the Olympic Games took place in Amsterdam in 1928, but only reached a Dutch national audience. After that time, radio's increased prominence as an Olympic medium coincided with its wide proliferation around the world. And even today, with the strong audience preference for seeing the athletes' performance on the television screen, radio still fills an important role in the coverage of sports events, by reaching those corners of the globe still unattainable by television and supplementing television in other areas.

While international radio broadcasters constituted a significant showing of media personnel at the Barcelona Games, their physical presence in the IBC tends to be that of a second class citizen (with the exception of large broadcasters such as the BBC, RAI and Radio Nacional de España, the public radio station of Spain who locate themselves among the big television broadcasting organizations).

Accredited radio stations had access to the same services of the MPC and IBC as television broadcasters. The majority of radio broadcasters, however, were set up far from the nerve centre of the IBC (along with the least resource endowed television broadcast organizations). In general, this area lacked an approach road, computer terminals, vending machines and other amenities common to the main thoroughfares of the IBC. Radio stations as important as Radio France, ARD-Radio, Cadena SER (the most important private broadcaster in the Spanish state) and Catalunya Ràdio (Catalonia's public broadcaster) shared this space with the more modest radio stations of the developing world. This hierarchical system inside the IBC directly correlates to the amount of financial investment made by radio broadcasters relative to television rights holders.

As with the television broadcasters, differences in economic investment also affected the working conditions of radio broadcasters. For example, a larger investment by the radio station resulted not only in a larger number of square metres in the IBC and possibly the construction of a radio studio, but better commentator and reporting positions at the sports installations. Nearly all radio broadcasters use the RTO'92 international sound transmission (that is part of the international television signal) as a background to the journalist's narration.

While radio broadcasters experience some disadvantages in facilities compared to television, a distinct advantage for radio broadcasters was the ability to rent and use mobile telephony at the Games, a technology that allowed them great mobility in the sports installations and, therefore, a distinct coverage of the Olympic events in the sense of multiplying the points of interest of the event and speed of reporting. There were many broadcasters (ARD-Radio, Cadena SER, Radio France, among others) who combined the narration coming from the commentator position and their IBC studios, international sound (RTO) and the mobile telephone to result in the highest of quality radio broadcasts. Those broadcasters with fewer financial resources did much of their reporting from the IBC watching television monitors or by using hired mobile telephony. In several cases, as with South African and Russian radio and television broadcasters, the two media types shared commentators and other personnel. In addition, many radio stations belonged to the same broadcast unions mentioned above and thus used those facilities. For example, OTI (Organización Internacional de Televisiones Iberoamericanas) offered its installations to accredited radio journalists whose radio stations did not have the use of unilateral space in the IBC: such as the Colombian stations Radio Cadena Nacional Colombia, Radio Caracol, Radio Datos y Mensajes and the Brazilian stations Radio Italiala and Radio Gaucha. Other stations, such as Radio Record (Mexico) and Radio Bandeirantes (Brazil), who had unilateral space, used the OTI organization to represent their interests in matters concerning the logistics of media in Barcelona'92.

Press and photography in Barcelona

Despite the central role and popularity of radio and television in disseminating the Games, the presence of the printed press at the Games has continued to grow. In Barcelona there were 4880 accredited print media professionals, 1,800 of whom were inside the stadium for the live coverage of the opening ceremony. While television may boast large audience figures, such high press interest is significant for the Olympic Games and movement in general as print coverage tends to be drawn out over longer periods of time, offering more reporting about the preparations, circumstances, issues and actors involved in the Games – in effect keeping the topic alive between Games.

In contrast to times gone by, print journalists had the use of sophisticated information systems in Barcelona. These included the installation of the new 'electronic journalist desks' equipped with a television monitor for 16 Olympic channels, a connection to the results channels, and telephone and computer connections. In other words, print journalists did not have to be at the sports competitions in order to adequately cover them. Television and electronic information thus provided the raw material for a large portion of Olympics reports that would eventually show up in print.

In the Rome'60 Games there were only 6 accredited photographers for each venue. The first accreditations then were granted to the large worldwide agencies (AP, UPI, TASS, Reuters, Agence France Presse) which continue to receive privileged treatment by the IOC and the organizing committees today. After Montreal'76, in which 600 requests were received from photographers, various steps to regulate photography began to be established. In Barcelona, photographer pool systems were in active use to limit the numbers at various venues.

Internal dynamics in the IBC

It is a credit to the planning and know how of literally thousands of people that the Olympics Games were able to be broadcast simultaneously to 193 countries around the world in 1992. In this sense, the work inside the MPC and IBC represented the Olympic value of international cooperation at its best: members of this large community linked by a sense of professional collegiality and their common knowledge of broadcast technology and/or sports journalism. Many of these professionals from the largest media broadcast organizations see each other at different international sports events. Others are broadcast free lancers, not typically attached to any one particular organization, but bringing their talents in broadcast operations to one event after another around the world. While the operations are busy and media personnel largely tend to their own jobs, there is a good amount of sharing and observing that goes on among broadcast organizations.

As an example, the South African athletes were not the only ones to be 32 years out of an Olympic Games. The South African broadcaster, SABC, also felt a bit 'out of it' in terms of the Olympic broadcasting culture at Barcelona. The broadcaster was also ill-prepared because of the late IOC approval of entry of the South African team into the Barcelona Games. According to SABC personnel, however, the broadcasters of the UK (BBC), Canada (CTV), New Zealand (NZTV) were enormously helpful and supportive of SABC's efforts, sharing commentators and unilateral camera feeds to augment the SABC broadcast.[9]

The Head of Sports for Icelandic National Broadcasting Service, Ingólfur Hannesson, also

---

9 Interview with Trevor Quirk, sports commentator for SABC. 3 August 1992, Barcelona.

commented on the positive aspect of 'collegiality' associated with world broadcasters coming together in the IBC. He said that the Scandinavian broadcasters readily, and informally, shared programming such as interviews. Being a relatively small broadcaster (three people in Barcelona and a member of the EBU), Hannesson also mentioned that there was much to learn walking the halls of the IBC from the technical operations of the largest broadcasters, several of which are described above.

This enormous feat of putting out an Olympic broadcast to the world, of course, is not without certain trials and tribulations. Also imagine putting 8,000 broadcast personnel, speaking an array of languages in the same building, under enormous deadline stress for 17 days, 24 hours a day (because of world time differences). In this sense, life at the IBC could also get stressful. It is a world of 'production', largely out of touch with the outside world of the Olympics events or Barcelona as a city. Not much was seen of the Olympics by most broadcast personnel except for a television monitor, VTR cubicle space, signal switch, or lens of a camera. It was not unusual to find IBC broadcast personnel who had no idea which athletes from what countries had won medals or not.

The primary complaints by broadcasters which arose during the broadcast operations in Barcelona (and tend to be the same for other Olympics as well) generally revolved around three issues: (1) access and transportation logistics; (2) add on costs; and (3) the quality and content of the international signal.

Particularly during the first week of the Games issues related to getting media personnel to and from – as well as inside – venues are paramount. Despite the best laid transportation and accreditation plans there are always problems and complaints related to travel and access to and favourable positioning inside of the sports venues. Daily meetings of broadcast representatives in the IBC dealt with an array of such concerns about missed or lost buses, accredited media being denied facility access, cameras blocking commentator visibility, last minute schedule changes, and so forth.

Another, more general area of complaint related to on site costs. Once broadcasters pay for rights, all is not free. There was much pay-as-you-go activity in the IBC (for the use of editing rooms, to obtain commentator positions, etc.) This added up quickly for some broadcasters. And, although RTO'92 allowed some variable pricing for the most financially strapped outfits, it still was a problem when a broadcaster wanted to send someone to cover a sport, but could not pay for the commentator position in time (or at all) to do it. Small, under financed broadcasters are at a distinct disadvantage for covering the Games in the 'real' sense of being at the venue while the competition is going on or the ceremonies unfolding. They are often restricted to commentating 'off tube' from the IBC and using the signal which is fed to them there by RTO'92 or their broadcast union. Others still as noted in Chapter 2, like Ghana TV, must remain at home because of a lack of resources to send a broadcast team to Barcelona at all.

Another area of tension with broadcasters arose from the constitution of the international feed. Every broadcaster represents a distinct sporting culture. While there are sports popular to most, some broadcasters wish to broadcast more of particular sports. For example, badminton is an important sport to Southeast Asian broadcasters, table tennis to Korean and Chinese broadcasters, and so forth. Because of the enormity of sports happening concurrently during the Games RTO'92 professionals are often faced with difficult decisions as to what goes on the international signal. Further, broadcast unions also 'produce' a version of that feed to distribute to their member organizations, acting as another gatekeeping step. Thus, for example, on a typical day in the IBC, the broadcast team leader for SBC Singapore could be seen lodging 'yet another' complaint to the Asian Broadcasting Union (ABU) questioning why the end of a badminton match was cut off to switch to the start of a basketball game.[10] To a lesser degree, there were also complaints related to the technical quality of the international signal. Particularly during the first days of the competition, international broadcasters made known to RTO'92 their preferences in terms of attributes of the international signal – from camera positions to use of graphics. However, as might be expected, not everyone can be pleased as some broadcasters might prefer, for example more graphics, others less. Some want more frequent display of scores, others less, and so forth.

The Olympics as technology showcase

In essence, the temporary home of all broadcast personnel coming to Barcelona is inside a thick layer of technology which surrounds the Olympic events – a complex web of electronics which comes between the sweat of the athlete and world wide audiences. Yet for television viewers, other than glimpsing some cameras and timing equipment on screen, this vast technological infrastructure is largely transparent.

The technological challenge of being a host city

A city can no longer just be a friendly place with suitable geographic features to host an Olympic Games. A candidate city's 'technology profile' – especially in the information technology sector – has become one of the most vital conditions in the nomination of a city as an Olympic host. In fact, organizing the Games puts the entire technological capacity of a host country to the test.

When Barcelona was chosen as the host city of the XXV Olympiad, the city still lacked the optimal technological conditions necessary to host the Games. However, just as in Seoul a few years beforehand,[11] the Games provided the impetus for technology development across the country. To meet the challenge in a way that would serve the long term, planning for the Olympics became a central focus of an 8-year information and telecommunications development initiative that would ultimately benefit all of Spain.[12]

Even before its official nomination as Olympic host city, Barcelona had initiated the

---

10 Interview with Hah Tee Goh, team leader for SBC Singapore television. 3 August 1992, Barcelona.

11 Larson and Park (1993).

12 For more information about Barcelona's technology strategies see Pastor and López (1995).

BIT'92 (Barcelona Informática y Telecomunicaciones) programme.[13] The first objective of this programme was to identify and prioritize the fields in which to focus research and development efforts and financial resources in preparation for the Games. The key areas identified were: signal development (picture, sound, texts, data, security control); Olympic installations (competition areas, Olympic village); hardware (computer networks, terminals, printers); systems to group users (athletes, journalists, police, spectators, VIPs); and systems to manage categories of information (transport, medical services, accreditation, accommodation, results). Identifying these critical areas then helped define the nature of the communications network (wide band, optical fiber, security circuits, etc.) and infrastructure (communication towers, satellite link stations, etc.). Before proceeding, the cost and design of the programme was weighed against the interests of local businesses and reviewed in light of European Community rules.

The information services budget for the media in Barcelona'92, including the MPC, was 1,189.8 million pesetas with income by way of rent and contributions from the TOP–2 programme worth 410.9 million pesetas. The Press Village had a budget of 2,709 million pesetas of which it was able to recuperate 1,868 million by way of rent and service payments.[14]

Information services in Barcelona'92

The Main Press Center for the Rome Games in 1960 had a large main hall filled with 1,400 Olivetti typewriters and a fleet of 50 motorcycles for press to get to the sports venues. In the Tokyo Games in 1964 was the first IBM experiment in the computerized treatment of results. In Munich'72 Siemens added to its version of a computerized results programme a data base with historical information for use by journalists reporting the Games. In Los Angeles'84 ATT used an electronic messaging system which allowed access, by means of a personal key word code, to community terminals supplying information on results, athletes and competitions.

As described, media personnel entering the MPC and IBC at Barcelona experienced the latest in information technology available for end use. The initiative started by the BIT'92 programme had allowed the creation of a system through which a wide variety of voice, video and data information flowed. It would be difficult to overstate the number of levels and layers of processed information or the density of the communications network. Hence the following treatment is not intended to be exhaustive. Instead it deals with some of the major information services carried by Olympic communications networks which benefited media operations. As an indication, Table 3.2 simply lists the quantities of information equipment used in the organization of the Games.

COOB'92's information programme was developed in two main blocks: internal systems and organizational systems. Internal systems corresponded to administrative and business

---

13 Dirreción General de Electrónica e Informática (1986). The first draft of the BIT project was dated March 1985.

14 Data base 'Barcelona'92', Alcatel Project, 20 September 1991, No. 202557.

management needs (accounting, expenses, personnel, inventory, etc.) by means of the Sistema Informátic de Gestión Empresarial (SIGE).[15]

As for organization systems, the primary programmes for the organization of the Games included the security management programme and the Sistema Gestió Operativa (SIGO) management programme. The SIGO programme, for the exclusive use of the organization personnel, managed multiple organization measures: accreditation, accommodation, health, transport, tickets, press reservations, etc. In addition, and critical to media operations, were four programmes related to providing information for the mass media: the SIR (results information programme) and three others discussed in more detail below.

Table 3.2. Information equipment used in the organization of the Barcelona Games

Technology	Quantity
Private telephones	10,000
Public telephones	1,000
Standard telephones	2,000
Fax terminals	617
Ibermic lines	225
TMA terminals	407
Press terminals	3,900
Radio-trunking terminals	2,110
Portable transceivers	3,800
Pagers	3,340
Televisions	10,000
Videos	1,200
Heads	53
Displays	31
Photocopiers	700
Giant screens	3
Sound at venues	65
Conference rooms	47
Accreditation lines	38
Access control bar-code readers	550
Hand-held metal detectors	1,850
Metal detector archways	387
CCTV cameras	470
Portable terminals for the press	4,000
PS/2-AMIC Terminals	1,510
PS/2-SIGO Terminals	300
PS/2-CIS Terminals	1,050
PS/2-SIR Terminals	950
DOCUMENT terminals	605
Office automation computers	715

Source: COOB'92 (1993b: 118)

---

15 For a description of all information systems see COOB'92 (1993b, Volume III).

AMIC: Multiple Access to Information and Communication

The main programme in respect to information for the 'Olympic Family' (organizers, guests, athletes, officials, media) was AMIC (Acceso Múltiple a la Información y a la Comunicación or Multiple Access to Information and Communication).[16] The acronym also means 'friend' in Catalan, the national language of the Olympic host. The system provided, by means of easily accessible and uncomplicated computers, sports information such as timetables, start lists, results, statistics, athlete profiles, records and other subjects. It was also the source of a variety of general services data on such subjects as the cultural Olympiad, the torch or the Olympic movement and useful information on transport timetables, weather forecasts, medical services and lost property. All this information generated by 157 news writers and 77 translators was provided in the four official languages (English, French, Spanish and Catalan), and was accessible to accredited people in the more than 500 places. In addition, AMIC's electronic mailing system allowed the sending of messages between the members of the Olympic family.

From 11 July to 12 August 1992(the Games started 25 July) the AMIC system was consulted by users a total of 8,067,972 times as is shown in Table 3.3. During the Games themselves the system was consulted an average of 450,000 times a day. This included a total 1,200,000 electronic messages among the Olympic family. For the first time in Olympic history the AMIC system allowed the large centres of computer activity at the Game – the MPC and IBC, the Olympic village, the hotels where the delegations were accommodated, the operations centres and sports installations – to be interconnected with a high capacity network.

Table 3.3. Summary of user consultations of the AMIC

	% of users*
By Language	
English	49.9
Spanish	26.8
Catalan	18.1
French	5.2
By subject and service	
Results, medal table, calendar	28.1
Other consultations	24.2
News	19.6
Electronic Mail	14.8
Biographies	13.3

Source: COOB'92 (1993b: 136).   *Total number of users = 8,067,972

16 The AMIC programme replaced a videotext system called 'Proyecto Alcatel' which began to provide a service in October 1990 and was in operation during the organization period of the Games. Alcatel was a joint project of COOB'92 and the Alcatel company, with the involvement of Toshiba. Under the project, notebook computers were distributed free of charge to 3,600 users, almost all of whom were journalists from around the world. The computers were especially made up of software allowing users to access a database of information on the Barcelona'92 programmes and projects. The Alcatel project went off line at the start of the Games, when AMIC started up.

EPH: Electronic Pigeonholes

The Electronic Pigeonholes (EPH) was an electronic system for consulting and printing results, start lists, summaries and other statistics. Users were able to ask for diverse information on the day's competitions and obtain this data printed on paper, by means of a touch-sensitive screen. Developed by Rank Xerox, there were 600 terminals available in the main mass media installations, in the MPC, in the IBC and in other Olympic installations.[17]

CIS: Commentary Information System

A third system, CIS (Commentary Information System), allowed the radio and television commentators in charge of the different sports broadcasts to have rapid access to a broad selection of information on the athletes by means of a touch-sensitive screen: start lists, results, summaries, statistics, records and biographies. At the beginning of each sports session, the monitor showed the start lists and the competitions planned for that day. Competition results appeared on the screen as they came about (without having to be requested) to allow for instantaneous event coverage. For the opening ceremony CIS included special background information to assist commentators in relation to political, sporting, cultural and historic aspects of the ceremony. It also indicated to commentators, through a red, yellow and green light system when the best times were for the commentator to talk and not 'disrupt' the viewing experience of the ceremonies. Needless to say, broadcasters did not necessarily adhere to those instructions.

Photographic services

The Barcelona MPC made available an instant photograph developing service, run by Kodak, the official sponsor, with a capacity for developing 1,410 rolls of film an hour. According to various sources the number of photographs generated by the Games could be counted in millions. On 9 August, two days before the end of the Barcelona Games, COOB'92 sources were giving the figure of 130,000 developed rolls of film, which could have been equivalent to more than 3 million photographs. There were only 650 accredited photographers for the opening ceremony who, according to COOB'92, managed to take up to 685,000 photographs.

These photographs found their ways into newspapers, books, magazines, and more. From the point of view of cultural analysis it is surprising to note how, from this multitude of photographs, not more than a few dozen finally stood out as representative of the key images of the Barcelona Olympics. Also, there was a surprising degree of similarity between the photographs chosen for publication, even by professionals and media from different backgrounds.

---

17 In the authors' experience, the delay time from viewing the live finish of a race to the results posting on an EPH terminal in the MPC could be as fast as 2–8 seconds. Not all media personnel, however, were comfortable with these new technologies. Minutes of daily broadcaster meetings in the IBC revealed that RTO'92 officials had to constantly encourage some broadcasters – who complained about the lag time in getting printed start lists and results (which RTO'92 also provided) – to simply access the computer terminals which they apparently resisted.

Central information operations

All the above (and more) information systems with their respective programmes were coordinated in a single centre (CIOT- Centro de Información y Operaciones de Tecnología or Technology Information and Operations Centre) which, due to its strategic role, was declared a maximum security centre and given the purposefully misleading name of Center for Auxiliary Services. Nearly 300 people worked day and night shifts in the CIOT, controlling all the possible incidents (repairs) that could take place in any one of the 60 different operations units in relation to any one of the nearly 20 information (AMIC, SIR, SIGO, EPH, etc.) or telecommunications projects used (CATV, telephony system, lost persons, closed group radiotelephony or walkie-talkies, electronic security, etc.). Altogether 5,500 people were mobilized by COOB'92 for the entire set of technological operations.

The actors (or partners) of the information technologies programme

Once the nomination had been secured, and based on the parameters of the BIT'92 initiative, COOB'92 devised a 'Technology Plan' to direct the awarding of hardware and software projects. They turned to a large number of specialized firms, taking into consideration the guarantee and efficiency of the services contracted and whether the companies were official sponsors of the Games. Organizers also attempted to support local and regional companies (Catalans, Spaniards, Europeans) or multinational companies established in the area. This chapter provides names for many of these technology suppliers because it presents an interesting picture of the players in global communications technology.

Among the many technology suppliers for the Barcelona Olympics, the contributions from IBM and Telefónica were particularly large and significant. IBM continued their historic presence in the organization of the Olympic Games as a joint partner of COOB'92 and played a decisive role in the most basic aspects of the computing system in Barcelona'92. As a joint partner IBM contributed central systems, local systems, basic software, local networks and so on, worth close to 5,000 million pesetas. IBM also played a decisive role in important projects for the mass media such as the information system for radio and television commentators (CIS) and the information system for the Olympic family (AMIC) discussed above.

IBM was the main supplier for the Olympic Calculation Center, the real brains behind the organization of the Games, contributing two ES/9000 computers, one in use and the other one as back-up, with a capacity of 120 to 150 gigabytes on disk. These computers, connected to a network with some 3,600 PS/2 terminals, were able to execute 120 million instructions a second. IBM provided the CIS programme with IBM PS/2 computers with a touch-sensitive screen (IBM 8516).[18]

Telefónica's role also deserves special mention. This company has a monopoly in the telecommunications field in Spain and, as is happening with other telecommunications

---

18 *PC Week* (1992).

companies in Europe, it plays a fundamental role in the technological and industrial development programmes in its country. Telefónica was involved in the Barcelona'92 project from the very beginning of the candidature, in the planning of the services needed for the Games as well as in the adaptation of its regional growth under these new circumstances.

From 1988 onwards Telefónica invested nearly 350,000 million pesetas in Barcelona, 92,000 of which can be considered investment directly linked to the Olympic Games while other investment was considered as 'advances' in medium term plans to facilitate the organization of the Olympics. Telefónica's main areas of concern were the renovation of the telecommunications network, the installation of new mobile links, improvements in microwave links, the introduction of optical fiber in Barcelona, the construction and initiation of a satellite communications centre, a teleport and a new digital telephony centre in the Olympic Village, as well as the construction of two big new communications towers.[19]

Other big companies also supplied equipment in this sector: Retevisión provided the television hertzian network; Alcatel provided a telematic information programme for journalists ('Proyecto Alcatel') as well as installing the optical fiber necessary for the construction of the network; Teletra España provided the microwave network, the radio link-up systems and the codification of the television signal; Panasonic provided the radio and television installations; Sintel the central node and coaxial cable equipment for narrowcasting; Philips supplied digital technology for Telefónica's telecommunications network, television sets, the sound system and the communications instruments and mobile telephony; Sony provided the giant 115 m^2 'Jumbotrónic' screens. Pesa Electrónica, official supplier of broadcast equipment for RTO, provided the installation and back-up for the radio and video production systems, etc.

The Spanish company EDS was put in charge of the results information programme (SIR) and represented an investment of 1,000 million pesetas in R&D and 600,000 man-hours in preparation.[20] Other companies, such as Càlcul i Gestió, ERITEL and the British firm Sema Grup T&G (UK), made, respectively, various contributions of software for managing the results, business management, information for the Olympic family (AMIC), operations management, etc. Table 3.4 offers an overview of technology services suppliers in Barcelona.

Telecommunications networks for modern Olympics

In keeping with the general advances in telecommunications, the organizations and media coverage of the contemporary Olympics require the construction and use of a large number of communications networks, along with the provision of various services throughout those networks including built in security and back up systems. These networks range

---

19 Telefónica (1992).

20 *PC Week* (1992).

from the global to the local and are increasingly interconnected and integrated, forming a large 'network of networks'.

The telecommunications network available in Barcelona'92 was 'still' not, at least in a strict technological sense, an Integrated Network (digital) of Information Services. However, it was a 'network of networks' made up of different technologies (radio links, optical fiber cable, coaxial cable, satellites) and run in an integrated manner for the different information services, among them services specifically for the mass media. In the next chapter on producing the Olympic telecasts, Figure 4.1 diagrams the telecommunication set up for Barcelona'92.

Table 3.4. Technology service suppliers in Barcelona'92

Project	Service	Company
Internal telephones	Network	Telefónica
	PBXs	Ericsson
	Cabling	Sintel
Public networks		Telefónica
Transmission network	Ibermic	Telefónica
Terminals	Telephone	Telefónica
	Fax	Ricoh
	Video conference	Telefónica
	Radio communications	Philips/Indelec
	Portable transceivers	Motorola
Radio network		Telefónica
Wavelength control		Dirección General Telecom
CATV	Head ends	Jerold/Televes
	Cabling	Sintel
	Receivers	Philips
	Videos	Panasonic
	Transmission equipment	Alcatel
Scoreboards, Timing Instruments	Alphanumeric	Seiko
	Sport	Baybor/Olimpex
Giant screens	Vidiwall	Philips
	Jumbotron	Sony
Public Address		Philips
Sport CCTV		Panasonic
Accreditations	Photography	Kodak
Personal access control		IECISA
Materials access control	Metal detectors	Kryptos/Garret

	X-ray	Siemens
Security CCTV		ECV
Intruder detection system		AISA
Project tracking methodology		SCYT (CCS)
Computing systems	Central, local, basic systems	IBM
	Technical design & support	IBM
	Simulation	IBM/UIM
	Monitoring and control software	IBM/BIDISA, SELESTA
Management software (SIGE)		Càlcul i gestió
Results software (SIR)		EDS
Commentator software (CIS)		IBM
Results distribution system		Xerox
AMIC software		Eritel
Operations software (SIGO)		UTE (Sema Group, T&G)
Photocopying		Xerox
Archiving and documentation		Xerox
Space management and CAD		Disel
Facilities management		Sema Group
Local support for users		Centrisa
Office automation		Apple
Office automation		Compuservice
Olympic Games promotion		Alcatel
Olympic database		CIDC

Source: COOB'92 (1993b: 108).

One characteristic of modern telecommunications networks that belies their powerful role and influence is that, like computer software, they are largely invisible to the public. One ordinarily does not see fiber optic cables which girdle the globe underground or undersea, nor does one see microwaves travel through the air or the increasingly powerful satellites that circle the earth in geostationary orbit. However, the construction of network infrastructure for the Barcelona Olympics left two highly visible landmarks on the sky line of the city. One is the Telecommunications Tower on Collserola hill ('Collserola tower'), the other one is the 'Calatrava tower', named in reference to the architect who designed it, situated right beside the Olympic Stadium on Montjuïc hill.

The Collserola tower is the tallest structure in Spain, standing 288 metres high, including the 20 metre long upper antenna. During the Olympic Games it was a key pivot of the telecommunications system, serving as a base station for mobile services, a link for television broadcasting and providing data links for other telecommunications systems. The tower is directly linked by optical fiber to Barcelona's metropolitan digital ring (connecting the four main Olympics areas) and during the Olympics was linked by that means and also microwave backup channels to the IBC and virtually all other Olympic facilities. The Calatrava tower served a similar range of technical functions. Because of its location in the Montjuïc Olympic Area, it became one of the most recognized symbols of the Barcelona Olympic Games. The tower is 119 metres high and was a mainstay of transmissions from this area.

Along with construction of these towers, Barcelona undertook the modernization and digitalization of its telephone system, construction of a new telephony station in the Olympic village, a satellite communications centre and a teleport.[21]

It is not possible to go into detail in this book on the technical nature and the telephony services available in Barcelona during the 1992 Games. It is enough to give the following examples: in certain moments the network had to handle 30,000 telephone calls in an hour; it had to handle the 70,000 calls made each day just from the media centres. Journalists had Modular Press Card Telephones, which operated with telephone credit cards. These telephones were capable of data, telefax and telephoto transmission and were located in press centres at all the Olympic venues.

For the public or 'Olympic family', Barcelona increased the number of public telephones by more than 42 per cent, installing 1,750 new devices over and above the 4,000 normal public phones. Of these 594 were placed in the press centres, 602 in public kiosks, 481 in different Olympic sites and 65 more in public telephones centres.[22]

It would be impossible to catalogue the many ways in which mobile communications support can influence the organization and media coverage of the Olympics, but one small example may suffice. During the open and closing ceremonies in Barcelona, an author of this book was given a cellular telephone and from his position in the crowd he was continually interviewed by Catalunya Radio (National Catalan radio station) and commentated on the development and content of the ceremonies.

The transmission of television signals (CATV project) used a optical fiber network of approximately 150 kms. length, completed with nearly 250 kms. of coaxial cable, with a capacity to carry many simultaneous television signals, to some 11,000 terminals distributed throughout the various Olympic facilities.[23]

Within the Olympic facilities themselves, a variety of communication networks and systems were installed to support broadcasters and other media representatives. For example, at the IBC, CATV permitted the viewing of up 72 signals or channels. This cable system provided international broadcasters with access to sports coverage from the major

21 The Barcelona Teleport, installed in Castellbisbal, required nearly 3,500 million pesetas investment, and the Granada satellite communications center (Barcelona), with a capacity for broadcasting up to 43 simultaneous television signals, required an investment of nearly 5,000 million pesetas, and through which 90 per cent of the international signals of the Games were passed.

22 Telefónica (1992: 6).

23 Each television panel was able to receive six local channels in the installation itself, three commercial channels, one statistical information screen and 16 Olympic channels with pictures of what was going on in other installations.

Olympic venues, along with RTO'92 summaries, briefings at the Main Press Center, coverage from the Olympic Village, views from beauty cameras around Barcelona and such commercial cable channels as CNN, Sky News and MTV.

Many broadcasters also set up their own local area networks (LANs) to support the planning and production of their Olympic telecast. Such local area networks would allow a broadcaster like NBC to link its computers at the IBC with other Olympic venues in and around Barcelona, and also with its studios in New York City or other locations. Such networks handle many applications, including the organization and retrieval of videotaped material, databases on the history of athletes and the Olympics, management of work schedules and personnel information, and TelePrompTer links similar to those in a modern, electronic newsroom.

The INTELSAT global satellite system served as the backbone for worldwide dissemination of the television signal while the EUTELSAT system served the same purpose for the European region. The international distribution of television signal was carried out in Spain by means of a ground network of national and international links provided by Telefónica and Retevisión.[24] The links carried television programmes from the IBC through the satellites communications centres in Barcelona (Penedés) for permanent links, and Guadalajara and Buitrago (Madrid) for occasional link-ups to satellites for global coverage, and countries bordering Spain which linked through terrestrial circuits permitting the transport of signals to other European countries and the Mediterranean area.[25]

Development of new broadcasting technologies

Every Olympics serves as a marketing showcase for some of the latest in communications technologies and Barcelona was no exception. The panoply of new or 'state of the art' technologies introduced for media coverage probably exceeded that for any prior Olympics. There were two main characteristics to the innovations seen in Barcelona: *digitalization* (production, treatment, diffusion and storage) of the video signal, and *new techniques for capturing pictures* which converted television cameras into eyes that were able to capture the event from limited positions or positions that were inaccessible for the human eye. Both technologies allow for increasing spectacular television coverage of sport.

The adoption by the host broadcaster of a ½" digital standard (Panasonic) for production of Olympic television and the large scale application of digital technology enabled a significant improvement in video picture quality. It also meant that the 2,800 hours of recorded international signal contained in the audiovisual archive for Barcelona'92 would be easily and rapidly accessible in its various segments and would not deteriorate over time or copy generations thanks to digital VTRs.

Research and development led to cameras and camera systems with a greater number of

---

24 For the first ten minutes connection a rate of 1,150 dollars was charged in the case of INTELSAT and 1,440 dollars in the case of EUTELSAT. Retevisión and Telefónica (1990).

25 RTO'92 (1992b: 6).

options and flexibility for shot types. For example, devices called snorkels were introduced for coverage of certain swimming and canoeing competitions. They consisted of a submarine periscope that allowed coverage of underwater images without submerging the camera. By allowing vision above and below the surface of the water, the snorkels allowed television shots of a body half submerged, as in synchronized swimming and water polo.

For coverage of other swimming events, underwater cameras were mounted on tracks on the bottom of the pool, allowing them to follow the progress of a swimmer from an underwater vantage point. Similarly, a track-mounted camera in the main Olympic stadium allowed the television camera to move along with runners from an overhead point of view.

The host broadcaster in Barcelona also expanded the use of the Wescam, a system in which the television camera is placed inside a stabilizing bubble in order to eliminate any sudden movements. Wescam zoom lens systems were used from helicopters and ships to enhance coverage of the sailing and rowing competitions (mini-cams on the boats themselves were also used). Self stabilizing lens were also used for cameras in electric cars.

High definition television (HDTV)

The experiment with high definition television systems in Barcelona also deserves mention. During 1992, both Barcelona and the Olympic Winter games in Albertville were used as a large-scale field test to launch the European HDTV standard (Vision 1250). RTO'92, Retevisión, Pesa Electrónica S.A. and TVE collaborated to provide 12 hours of live and recorded programming daily produced in HDTV during the Barcelona Games. This project received direct support from the European Union which provided a total of 13,853,079 ECUs for this promotion.[26] For satellite broadcasting large European companies (Thomson, France; Philips, Holland; Nokia, Finland; Seleco, Italy) joined television stations who were members of the European Broadcasting Union (EBU) to collaborate in the Vision 1250 project.[27] NHK, continuing the experiences of Seoul'88, broadcast ten hours a day to Japan using their own HDTV standard. They also provided a viewing room so that visitors to the IBC could experience for themselves the quality of HDTV.

Technology convergence and future Olympic television

The information age heralds an era of multi-media, interactive, mobile and personalized communications. One scenario centres on Personal Communication Services as delivered through Personal Communication Networks. It suggests that there will be a network of networks in which the conventional cellular networks will be linked to office buildings, neighbourhood and sidewalk or subway networks, all of which will be in turn connected to a central Advanced Digital Network which will coordinate such a network of networks. The primary personal communications services will be one phone number for each person

---

26 CCE (1992).

27 Larregola (1993).

in the network and that number could eventually follow an individual anywhere in the world.

Such a vision would obviously materialize first in the advanced industrialized nations, those furthest along the path to becoming information societies. This, of course, raises some serious questions about universal access to Olympic messages – visual, audio and verbal. These new services will cost a great deal, and what does that mean for the already problematic lack of development in many of the poorer nations of the world?

However, given the strong trend toward informatization of the Olympic host city and the global network with which it is connected to convey Olympic television, it is quite plausible, even probable, that the delivery of Olympic messages will become much more personalized, mobile and interactive in the future. If a host city and Olympic venue-wide network of mobile communications services are available, together with lightweight, portable and easy to use personal communication devices, it requires no great leap of the imagination to think of how they might be used. During the Seoul Olympics, Samsung provided each spectator at the opening ceremony with a miniature FM-radio receiver through which it was possible to receive a commentary describing the ceremony in eight different languages. In Barcelona, hundreds of broadcasters at the opening ceremony were equipped with touch-screen CIS monitors alongside television monitors carrying the international television coverage of the games. In a future era of personal digital assistance and multi-media, both spectators in the stands and viewers at home are likely to have an expanded range of information options available during their viewing of the Olympics. Properly designed, such technologies might offer depth of explanation and information support to the opening ceremony, along with a wealth of information on sports, teams, athletes, the host city and so forth. In short, they could open up a much wider network for the sort of information services that are now expanding, but still relatively limited, within the Olympic family. Through connections to the global network, such services could be extended around the world.

There are several parallels between telecommunications policy, as conventionally conceived, and the television and communications policy issues facing the Olympic movement. Traditionally, telecommunications services in most countries around the world were provided by government PTTs (Post, Telephone and Telecommunications) organizations. They functioned as monopoly suppliers (the regulator is also the supplier) of such services, based partly on the argument that telecommunications formed a natural monopoly in which economies of scale allowed a single supplier to offer services at lower cost than if there were competing services. Another of the traditional underpinnings of telecommunications policy has been the ideal and goal of a worldwide system which has experienced a wave of new technologies and services and has been accompanied by moves toward market liberalization or deregulation and privatization.

Although Olympic television is not a monopoly in exactly the same sense as government PTTs, the IOC relies on the host broadcaster and Games organizing committee to provide an international television signal. Furthermore, the policy has called for broadcast rights to be limited to one broadcast organization or union per country. As in telecoms generally, developments in media technology have already put pressure on the IOC to open up television coverage to competitive organizations, a trend that is likely to continue.

The goals of Olympic universalism imply for television and the media something very similar to the goal of universal access to telecommunications services. Indeed, given the centrality of television to the Olympic experience for most people in the world, the IOC cannot claim to have achieved its goals until everyone in the world has access to approximately the same range of Olympic media programming. Today this goal is still a long way from realization, as is that of the International Telecommunications Union (ITU) for universal access to basic telecommunications services.

4 Producing and Scheduling the Olympic Telecast

While the economic, technological and organizational infrastructures reviewed in the prior chapters set the context for Olympic broadcasting, it is during the production phase of the Olympic telecast that the Olympic Games begin to transform into the multiple international presentations of the event which become the basis for the comparative analysis of Opening Ceremony broadcasts presented in Part II of this book. The first section of this chapter describes the process of producing the Olympic telecast and more specifically the Opening Ceremony, both by RTO'92 and international broadcasters. This discussion picks up where the prior chapter left off and continues to underscore the complexity of staging a live international television production. However, this chapter is also intended to provide a better understanding of why international Olympic telecasts are different in both structure and content for television viewers around the world.

In addition to content and structure, international television broadcasts of the Olympics also vary in terms of the amount and scheduling of programming from country to country. The second section of this chapter begins this book's comparative analysis of 27 Olympic broadcasters by analysing the differences in programming strategies engaged in by each.

Producing the Olympic telecast

The sporting events of the Barcelona Olympic Games took place in 41 venues, located in four different areas of Barcelona – Montjuïc, Diagonal, Vall d'Hebron and Parc del Mar – as well as in 15 other cities which served as Olympic sub-sites. Of these sports venues, the two main installations in Montjuïc, the Olympic stadium (ceremonies and athletics) and the Palau Sant Jordi (gymnastics, volleyball, handball), contained permanent production control rooms and a large number of fixed and mobile cameras. Television production

This chapter draws heavily upon the research of Montserrat Llinés whose collaboration the authors gratefully acknowledge. The section on sound in the Opening Ceremony benefits from the contributions of Maria Gutiérrez with technical advice from Joan López. The authors gratefully acknowledge their cooperation.

in the remainder of the competition installations was carried out using mobile production units (45 in total) and 25 ENG teams.

In the Olympic stadium the host broadcaster RTO'92 had five control rooms which received images from 46 cameras inside the stadium: four of these control rooms were dedicated to the complete coverage of four different competitions occurring simultaneously in the stadium (as would be common for athletics events), while the fifth control room was used to integrate the production of the first four, creating the definitive signal from this installation. In the Palau Sant Jordi RTO'92 used a similar system with an internal installation which included 34 cameras, 29 VTRs and 4 control rooms (3 production and one integrated). This allowed a better and more complete coverage of one of the Games' most popular sports: artistic gymnastics.

It should be noted that these RTO'92 camera quantities do not include additional camera positions purchased and placed at venues by individual rights holding broadcasters (discussed below). For example at the Barcelona Opening Ceremony, in addition to the 46 RTO'92 cameras in the Olympic stadium there were 53 'unilateral' camera positions; that is, there were 53 cameras for the exclusive use of broadcasters such as the BBC (UK), NBC (USA), TVE (Spain) and others. The RTO'92 cameras are devoted solely to the production of the international television signal. The unilateral cameras are used by individual broadcasters to enhance the international signal with additional camera shots and perspectives.

Production of the international television signal

As introduced in Chapter 3, the prime responsibility of the host broadcaster is to produce the international signal for distribution to rights holding broadcasters situated in the IBC. It is important to understand that what all world television audiences ultimately see is essentially an enhanced version of the international signal for, at a minimum, all international broadcasters must add verbal commentary to this visual and natural sound only signal and many broadcasters, as will be discussed, customize the signal even more by editing it, adding images, graphics and so forth to create distinct unilateral broadcasts. No broadcaster uses only unilateral camera images to the exclusion of the international signal.

The 'Olympic Charter' demands that the international television signal is neutral and avoids any distinctive treatment of athletes or countries – except, of course, special attention to moments of sports drama, whether victory or defeat. Given the number of sports events and national athletes competing simultaneously during an Olympic Games it is a difficult challenge to achieve total impartiality. In addition, the international signal must be of high technical quality in order to meet standards of all international broadcasters.

The international signal provided by RTO'92 to international broadcasters was a colour video signal of 625 PAL lines, free of commentary and possessing surround sound. It included action replays and slow motion replays, as well as other optional information such as the graphics with the start lists, the athletes' names and numbers, the flags and abbreviations of the participating countries, results and records, all of which were in Latin characters. All the stations made use of the graphic information system with the sole exception of the US broadcaster NBC which substituted its own graphics for use in its broadcast. RTO'92 also inserted a selection of videos into the international feed for broadcaster use. These included two daily sports summaries and short videos on the Olympic venues, sub-site towns around Barcelona, Olympic medals, introductory animation with music and other options. Consistent with the format, these selections were visuals and natural background sound (or music) only, awaiting a voice over commentary by each broadcaster.

Table 4.1. RTO'92 Olympic sport coverage

Live coverage only	Live and delayed coverage
Opening and Closing Ceremonies	*Preliminaries delayed; finals live:*
Athletics (5 feeds)	Fencing
Gymnastics (4 feeds)	Table Tennis
Volleyball (4 feeds)	Shooting
Swimming	Roller Hockey
Diving	
Synchronized Swimming	*Preliminaries delayed; semis and finals live:*
Modern Pentathlon	Taekwondo (2 feeds)
Waterpolo	Yachting
Volleyball	
Rhythmic Gymnastics	*Preliminaries delayed; quarters to finals live:*
Weightlifting	Badminton
Football	Archery
Jumping and Dressage (Equestrian)	
Modern Pentathlon	*Certain events live; others delayed:*
Cycling Track	Canoeing – Flat Water
Tennis	Equestrian 3-day event
Baseball	Rowing
Basketball	
Boxing	*All delayed:*
Hockey	Basque Pelota (exhibition sport)
Handball	
Shooting	
Canoeing	
Marathon	
Walks – 10, 20, 50 km	
Cycling	
Wrestling (3 feeds)	
Judo (2 feeds)	

Source: RTO'92.

In addition, for the Barcelona Games the international signal was, for the first time in the history of televised Olympics, almost 100 per cent live. In fact, as shown in Table 4.1, RTO'92 offered live broadcasting of all competition sports, which amounted to about 2,500 hours of live coverage of the Barcelona Olympic Games (out of 2800 hours total

RTO'92 coverage). In many cases, the entire competition – from preliminary rounds to finals – were live, while in others only the final rounds were broadcast live. Even of the exhibition sports, only Basque pelota was broadcast completely in a recorded form. Also shown in Table 4.1 are those sports requiring more than one feed because of multiple events happening simultaneously inside the same venue location – as with gymnastics, athletics or wrestling.

Sports venue production strategies

In order to achieve premium quality sports coverage, several strategies were used by RTO'92. First, the television professionals at each sports venue relied on a 'spotter', a specialized adviser fully versed in the nuances of that particular sport, who was at the director's side to forecast decisive moments of the event and suggest what the possible reactions of the athletes were going to be.

Another strategy employed by RTO'92 was to take advantage of its cooperative agreement with the EBU and multinational organizational makeup in such a way as to assign technicians, directors, or production teams experienced in television coverage of particular sports to those sports. Thus, for example, television coverage of canoeing and archery was produced by professionals of the French station FR3; yachting and shooting were in the hands of the German stations ARD and ZDF; fencing used a crew from RAI of Italy; handball used NRK of Norway; table tennis had a Swedish SVT crew; and tennis and equestrian events employed BBC production crews. Although most RTO'92 personnel came from Spanish and other European broadcasters, baseball, for example, was covered by combination of professionals of Cuban Television ICRT and NBC (USA). NBC also assisted with boxing.

In order to have the signal coming from the 41 venues be absolutely complete, exhibit the same professional quality, and look compatible when the international signal switched from one venue to the next, RTO'92 put together a production style book for each sport. Everything was thought of in this book, from the position of the athletes in the starting grid to the presentation of the medals.

Finally, as discussed in Chapter 3, the latest in remote picture capture and sound technology was installed to meet the challenges of particular sports venues – from periscope cameras and underwater microphones for swimming, to self stabilizing lens for yachting, to track mounted moving cameras for swimming and track events, and other innovations.

Signal relay: from the venues to the IBC, IBC to the world

As shown in Figure 4.1, a fibre optic ring built in anticipation of the Olympics, with backup terrestrial links, formed the heart of the Barcelona signal relay system, connecting the four main Barcelona venues to the International Broadcast Center (IBC). The signals coming from the exterior sub-sites were sent to the IBC via the Collserola Telecommunications Tower. Outside races and yachting used mobile communications with, for example, helicopter relay.

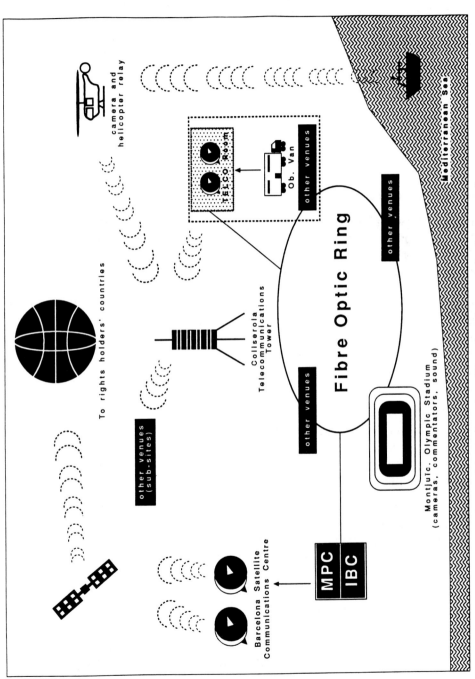

Figure 4.1. The Barcelona Olympics telecommunications network

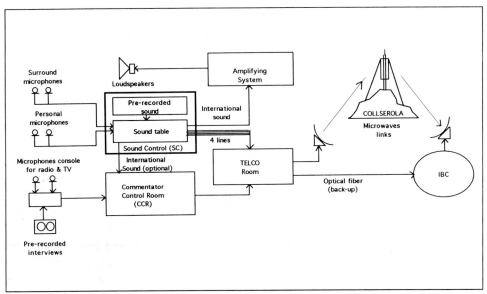

Figure 4.2. Sound signal relay system from sport venue to IBC. [Source: Joan López]

The specific route of the sound signals from venues to the IBC is demonstrated in Figure 4.2. In the sound control (SC) centre both direct sound from each venue and pre-recorded sound signals (except those of the commentators) were received and sent to the TELCO Room production centre, where the sounds were mixed with the visual images and sent on to the IBC, as well as back to the commentator control room (CCR). The sound (mostly verbal commentary) received from the radio and television commentators' positions also goes through the CCR, where its quality was controlled and it is then optionally mixed with the international sound. This combination was then sent back to TELCO Room, where, together with the images, it passed on to the IBC distributed to rights holding television and radio broadcasters.

Upon arrival in the IBC, the international signal was delivered, recorded and filed in the IBC documentation centre. The systemization in the filing of this information allowed RTO'92 to make all the televised material available to radio and television broadcasters who might want to incorporate highlights from earlier events into their broadcasts. As required by the IOC, the documentation centre also made a daily summary of each day's events which it distributed without charge with the aim of guaranteeing a minimum broadcast of the Olympic event to the world. It should be mentioned that these types of archival systems are increasingly being instituted as part of Olympic host broadcasting and contribute in important ways to the development of Olympic visual archives for historical, media, research and other uses over time.

Producing the ceremonies

Any observant Olympics fan can link the trend toward visual spectacle in the Olympic Ceremonies to the increased desire of Games organizers to appeal to television audiences.

Since the Los Angeles Games of 1984 the Olympic ceremonies have been clearly adapted to the preferences of television. One of the preferences of modern day television is to assert control over the event by knowing its timing, players, sphere and order of play so that the technological needs of capturing and maximizing the event are sure to be met. At the same time, broadcasters and organizers alike want to produce a 'live' spectacle. For it is the fundamental, dramatic element of 'liveness' that in part draws the tens of thousands in the stadium or millions of television viewers around the world to watch the Olympic Games.

Constructing and controlling a 'live' event

To reconcile the desire for control with the need for live appeal, the most significant adaptive changes in the ceremonies for television have actually occurred behind the scenes, focusing on enhancing technical quality and intervention in order to minimize the margin for error in a live broadcast. This requires meticulous planning and control by organizers and broadcasters in producing the Olympic Games and ceremonies. The Opening and Closing ceremonies are still live events, but events more or less safely bundled in visual and sound enhancements. (This does not mean, however, that those involved are not without knots in their stomach as the events unfold!)

In this sense, the televised production of the Opening and Closing Ceremonies and the sports events are very different – not in technical quality, but it other important respects. While much is planned to guarantee consistency and quality coverage of the sports events, sports venue coverage is ultimately reactive to the competition itself. For RTO'92 it was also guided by the philosophy of impartiality in message. In the case of the ceremonies, however, the international signal was intended from the outset to be used to promote certain meanings which reflected those political and cultural features that the organizers wanted emphasized (see both Chapters 6 and 8 for discussions of intended meaning of the ceremonies). Prior to the event, a story-board was made out for the televised coverage of the ceremonies. This guide outlined, step-by-step, the actions that were to take place in the stadium, indicating which was the most appropriate camera shot for each instance. Ceremony designers worked with RTO'92 to take advantage of the story-telling abilities of television cameras to create moods and focus attention on different iconic features of the ceremony.

For the Opening Ceremony the production team chose to use only four of the five control rooms available at the Olympic stadium. One of them was used for the coverage of the athletes' parade and the choreography and movements of the actors on the stadium floor, using the signal from 16 cameras (half of which were mobile). A second control room received the images of 7 cameras aimed at recording the reactions of the dignitaries' box and the public, as well as on the speeches podium. Ten cameras, coordinated from a third control room, covered all the actions that took place on the stage at one end of the stadium. And a fourth control room, under the command of the director of television production of the ceremony, was responsible for the synthesis of the programme with the aid of panoramic shots from cameras located in unusual positions ('beauty cameras'), such as a helicopter or a crane. The Closing Ceremony, in contrast to the Opening Ceremony, only had the use of 29 cameras for the production of the international signal produced by RTO'92.

The construction of the Opening Ceremony sound track

Without a doubt, one of the most unrecognized and interesting aspects of the production of Opening Ceremony was the degree of control and manipulation of sound. Unbeknownst to most television viewers – as well as to most spectators in the stadium – was the fact that virtually all sound for the Opening Ceremony was pre-recorded months in advance. This strategy was not exclusive to music and song, but to every aspect of the ceremony – from the roar of airplanes crossing the sky, to opera singers, to the applause of the spectators. That said, this is not an unusual strategy for television broadcasting in general although it was a big decision for ceremony planners given that millions of people were expecting to watch a 'live' ceremony in all its facets. While forfeiting some opportunities for spontaneity in the event on the part of spectators and musical performers, it was felt that the advantages to this approach outweighed the 'risks'. Ultimately convincing the ceremony planners to pre-record the sound were the following points:

- Pre-recorded sound simplifies the installation and infrastructure of the sound system.

- Pre-recorded sound allows for near perfect synchronization of the technical aspects of the spectacle, offering the ability to link sound, lights, camera movement and other enhancements.

- Pre-recorded sound assures optimal quality for television, allowing for stereophonic sound (stadium spectators only hear monophonic sound), as well as mixed in enhancements.

- Pre-recorded sound allows a better 'experience' or sense of proximity to the event for television viewers. For both television and stadium spectators pre-recorded sound also can direct attention to specific events happening in a very large stadium in a way that live sound can not.

- Unforeseen weather conditions, such as the rain or the wind, do not affect the pre-recording but can affect live music leading to irreparable distortions in a live broadcast.

- Unforeseen noises, such friction between the microphone and the actors' clothes, movements of the announcers in respect to the microphone or various feedback effects, can be avoided.

- The use of pre-recorded sound is more comfortable for the performers in the stadium, especially for the opera singers some of who, in fact, preferred that their music be pre-recorded.

Most important, of course, is that pre-recorded sound allowed ceremony producers to have more control over a live spectacle of three hours duration. The decision to use pre-recorded sound also demonstrated the priority consideration given to the ceremony as a television spectacle, as many of the above factors relate specifically to concerns over the production quality for global audiences, rather than for stadium spectators. Also, there were a limited number of microphones strategically situated in the stadium to pick up sound elements, which came about spontaneously during the event, in the form of applause, booing, cheering, etc. This relatively minor element of sound information was picked up and added to the pre-recorded sound for the making of the final mix.

Nearly 50 sound technicians were in charge of guaranteeing the correct sound production in the Opening Ceremony. All the signals from the ceremony were received by sound control (SC), where they were combined using sound mixing tables (as shown in figure 4.2). In fact, two mixes were made using different power sources, lines and relay routes to ensure the availability of back-up sound at all times in case of problems.

The athletes' parade. The most 'live' portion of the ceremony was the athletes' parade in the sense of having some flexibility in case of the very real possibility of last minute changes in the delegations marching in (especially because they march in alphabetical order). During pilot sound tests of the parade segment numerous human errors resulted in the wrong music being played for entering countries due to changes in participating teams, the appearance of new countries, the confusion of names and flags, etc. In order to avoid these errors a very novel reproduction method was chosen: CD-I (Compact Disc-Interactive). This system permitted the reproduction of different recorded music on CD with the aid of a screen that, interacting with the computer, ensured that the music was matched to the entering country team by asking certain verification questions.

As such, the sound for the athletes' parade was largely pre-recorded, but also flexible and interactive. A television camera in front of the athletes' entrance linked to an internal television monitor. When a delegation came entered the stadium and appeared on the monitor the presenters announced the delegation's name (for example, 'Afghanistan'). Simultaneously the RTO'92 technicians showed the image and the corresponding title. Those in charge of sound in the ceremony indicated 'Afghanistan' in response to the CD system prompt so the pre-recorded music, composed for the occasion to fit a team's size and maintain the athletes' pace (essential for television programme timing) as they passed the stands, was heard at the same time in the stadium and on the small screen. As a final note here, the applause (a combination of live and recorded applause mixed at the sound table) that was heard by television viewers did not strictly coincide with the images (e.g. entering team) that could be seen on the screen.

The production of unilateral signals

Every broadcaster, except those using High Definition Television (HDTV), used the images and live sound (international signal) offered by RTO'92 as the basis of their coverage of the Barcelona Olympic Games. This was just as much the case in the Opening and Closing ceremonies as with sporting competitions. As mentioned previously, this base material was then customized by broadcasters. In all cases, commentary was added. But, in addition, the signal could be edited – reduced in length, have its order changed, have images and sounds coming from different sports installations mixed, and so forth. Some broadcasters, with the means available, chose to also enhance the signal by adding images from their own (unilateral) cameras placed at sports venues and from studios and inserting custom graphics or live or pre-recorded features or interviews. The amount of modification or enhancements to the international signal tended to directly correlate with the amount of personnel and financial resources available to a broadcaster.

Thus, for example, the US broadcaster NBC was able to offer its viewers a clearly different and consequently personal version of the Opening and Closing Ceremonies by using a large amount of different images provided by its own cameras situated inside and outside the stadium as well as the international signal offered by RTO'92. This gave a different rhythm and logic to the spectacle that developed in the stadium by making a particular montage of all the audiovisual material that was at its disposition. Appendix C demonstrates how, during one segment of the Opening Ceremony, NBC presented a somewhat different view of the event. Chapter 5 investigates just how much the different broadcasters in this study altered the structure of the Opening Ceremony.

Unilateral camera locations for popular national sports

To enhance the signal with different camera perspectives certain broadcasters paid for the privilege of placing their own (unilateral) cameras at different venues. NBC (USA) had the most unilateral cameras. It had unilateral camera positions for its cameras in the Olympic stadium and the Palau Sant Jordi and in 30 of the 43 competition installations. In fact, NBC was able to personalize all the sports except fencing, the pentathlon, tennis, Basque pelota 30m., yachting, Basque pelota 36m., roller hockey, cycling 15 km. and the football matches played in sports installations outside Barcelona.

The Spanish television station TVE situated its own cameras in 10 competition installations, the Olympic stadium, Palau Sant Jordi, as well as in the venues where the following events were held: swimming, waterpolo, diving, rhythmic gymnastics, tennis, basketball, handball and football. The BBC (UK) had unilateral cameras in the Olympic stadium and also in the installations where the swimming, tennis, hockey and rowing events took place. ARD (Germany) was able to cover the following with its own cameras: the Olympic stadium, wrestling, cycling, tennis, table tennis, equestrian events and basketball.

The Japanese pool (BOJP) had camera positions in the Olympic stadium and also in the swimming installations and around the marathon circuit. The Mexican station Televisa had cameras in the Olympic stadium and where the football was held. The Australian station Channel 7 and the French stations A2 and Canal Plus were also present in the Olympic stadium and Piscines Bernat Picornell where the swimming events took place. The Canadian station CTV, RMC Monte Carlo and TF1 France had cameras in the Olympic stadium, while DRT Denmark had its own cameras in the Port where the yachting events took place. (Table 5.2 in the next chapter lists which of the broadcasters in this study had unilateral cameras available to them.)

As noted above, the Olympic stadium was the venue with the largest number of unilateral cameras. The main use of these cameras by broadcasters during the Opening and Closing Ceremonies was to increase the number of shots of the athletes from that country. They were also used to try to bring their athletes closer to the audience by means of close up shots. During the athletic competitions the unilateral cameras were used primary for 'stand ups' before and after the events in a manner common to sports broadcasting. These 'stand ups' were takes in which the journalist presented or evaluated the development of the events in front of the camera with the competition track as a background, carried out some brief interviews, or fixed the viewer's attention on the performance of that country's athletes.

Another venue with a large number of unilateral cameras was the Palau Sant Jordi, where the gymnastic, volleyball and handball events where held and which had 26 unilateral camera positions during the handball competition. The Piscines Bernat Picornell, where the swimming events where held, had 24 unilateral camera positions to cover the synchronized swimming events.

A few broadcasters, such as SABC of South Africa, did not have its own extra cameras at the Games, but through a series of cooperative relationships were able to use some of the unilateral camera images of other broadcasters such as the BBC (UK), CTV (Canada), TVNZ (New Zealand) and Australia's Channel Seven.

Adding customized commentary to the signal

As noted, all broadcasters needed to add commentary to the international signal, whether the signal was customized visually or not. Chapter 6 discusses the different strategies broadcasters used to select and position their commentators. Generally, broadcast commentators worked in a complementary manner moving back and forth between positions in the sports installations and television studios or commentary cabins (off tube) in the IBC. In the case of the pan-European Eurosport channel, different language commentator teams were used for the coverage of the Opening Ceremony and certain events (English, German, Dutch and French).

Every competition venue had commentary positions from which accredited broadcast journalists and commentators could follow the live development of the events, while at the same time view the international signal or their broadcaster's unilateral signal on a colour television monitor so they could comment specifically on what television audiences were viewing. There were 159 commentary positions in the Olympic stadium, 96 in the Piscines Bernat Picornell (swimming), 86 in the Palau Sant Jordi (gymnastics) and 66 in the Palau d'Esports de Badalona (basketball). In the majority of venues the commentators also had a CIS (Commentary Information System) terminal at their disposal. As described in more detail in chapter 3, this system included information on, among other things, starting line-ups, results, summaries, statistics, records and biographies.

Broadcasters without commentary positions in the competition installations (usually because of financial constraints), but which were present in the IBC as accredited media, rented 'off tube' commentary cabins. These were small rooms equipped with a microphone and a colour monitor on which the commentator could receive the international signal of the event to be commentated on.

It is through the structural, visual and verbal customization of the international signal that broadcasters can significantly influence the narrative structure, 'feel' and meaning of the Olympics for home audiences. Part II of this book investigates how the variety of broadcast constructions of the Olympic ceremonies resulted in different interpretations of Olympics values, other nations, the host city and sport in general.

Olympic programming schedules and strategies

Olympic programming hours and schedule by region

While the absolute number of hours dedicated to the coverage of the Olympics by broadcasters varied, most attempted to maximize their financial investment to obtain rights by dedicating a large part of their broadcasting hours to the Olympic programming. Some even extended their regular broadcast hours. That said, broadcasters varied in the way they placed Olympic programming in their daily schedule in terms programming strategy. Using the sample of 27 broadcasters analysed in this study, this section gives an overview of the programming amounts by geographic region and then looks at some of the different programming strategies and their outcomes.

Olympic programming in Europe

This study included nine European countries. Of those countries belonging to the European Union (Germany, Spain, France, Great Britain, Greece), the average number of hours dedicated to programming on the Games exceeded 250 hours. It is also significant that at least three national stations (Canal Plus in France and TVE 2 and Canal Olímpic in Spain) and a European satellite TV station (Eurosport) were converted, for a while, into dedicated Olympic channels and offered uninterrupted coverage of the Games. Table 4.2 offers some examples of European programming quantities.

Table 4.2. Examples of Olympic programming in Europe

Country	TV Broadcaster	Broadcasting hours
France	A2, FR3, TF1	260
	Canal Plus	300+
Germany	ARD, ZDF	360
Great Britain	BBC1, BBC2	240
Slovenia	2nd Channel	150
Romania	RTV	150
Greece	ERT 1, 2, 3	240
Spain	La 2 (TVE)	400
Catalonia	Canal Olímpic	400
Russia	RTO/RTR	100

Source: Correspondent reports.

In Germany, the public channels ARD and ZDF broadcast a total of 360 hours from Barcelona alternating in daily shifts from 9 am to 12:30 am so as not to compete head to head. In Spain, the second channel of Spanish state television (TVE 2) and the second channel of Catalan television (Canal 33) which was converted into Canal Olímpic, each programmed 400 hours of the Games, uninterrupted, for 24 hours a day.

French viewers could enjoy more than 100 hours a week of the Olympic Games thanks to the complementary strategy of the two public channels (A2/FR3) which programmed from 9 am to 10:30 pm almost uninterrupted. Subscribers to Canal Plus were able to watch 22 hours a day of Olympic programming.

The BBC (UK) broadcast coverage of the Games on its first channel, BBC1, practically every day, from 8 am to 11:30 pm; BBC2 only included some events in its usual programming to complement the breaks on BBC1. The three Greek channels also opted for a similar complementary broadcasting of the Games, programming a total of 240 hours.

These hours do not necessarily represent upper limits on programming available to some audiences. For example, the pan-European Eurosport channel and other satellite services offered Olympic programming which could be received via cable or satellite dish in many European countries.

Among the countries of Eastern Europe, the number of programmed hours was less, between 100 and 150 hours in total, but the amount of resources spent on the coverage of the Games was also less.

Influential to European broadcaster attention to the Games, of course, was its location in Barcelona, offering not just a host setting of regional interest, but a host setting in the same – or nearly the same – time zone for optimum live programming opportunities.

Olympic programming in the Americas

Table 4.3 shows some examples of programming quantities from the Americas. NBC's (USA) Olympic programming added up to a total of 160 hours, most of which was in the form of delayed broadcasts due to the 9-hour time difference with Barcelona. Most of the programming was concentrated in the evening prime time period from 7:30 pm to 11:30 pm and from 0:30 am to 1:30 am, although the Games were also broadcast from 7 am to 9:30 am and from 12 pm to 5:30 pm on weekends.

Parallel to its regular broadcast, NBC also tested out a pay-per-view TripleCast operation by means of its subsidiary Cablevision (discussed in chapter 2). Three channels (blue, red and white), divided according to sports and sections, broadcast 12 hours live, without advertising breaks, and another 12 hours of repeated coverage. This amounted to a total of 520 hours of live coverage and more than 1,000 Olympic broadcast hours total.

73

Table 4.3. Examples of Olympic programming in America

Country	TV Broadcaster	Broadcasting hours
USA	Cablevision TripleCast	520
	NBC	160
Canada/French language	TVA	181
Cuba	Tele Rebelde	123
Colombia	Canal A	28
	Deportes 44	300
Mexico	Televisa	238
	Canal 13	292
	Multivision	17
	Cablevision	331
Brazil	TV Globo	88
	Bandeirantes	201
	SBT	78
	TV Manchete	86

Source: Correspondent reports.

The French language Canadian station TVA broadcast the Barcelona Games, almost without interruption, from 9 am to 6 pm. At night, between 7 pm and 10 pm, it dedicated three hours a day to coverage of the most noteworthy events of the day for its viewers along with reports and interviews. CTV of Canada, not shown here, also broadcast the Games for nearly the same number of hours.

In Mexico, a large number of hours were also dedicated to the programming of the Games. Televisa broadcast live from Barcelona on its second channel from 2 am to 4 pm daily. Channels 4 and 5 offered summaries between 9 pm and 11:30 pm. Canal 13 covered the Games for 318 hours; it only stopped broadcasting Olympic programming from 7 am to 9 am, from 7 pm to 9 pm and from 11 pm to 0:30 am. In addition, Mexican viewers had access to much of the NBC TripleCast cable programming, increasing available pro-gramming by nearly half.

Deportes 44, the Colombian subscription television broadcasters' sports channel, broad-cast the Barcelona Olympic Games virtually without interruption.

The Cuban station Tele-Rebelde offered most of its Olympic programming in delayed form, due to the time difference of 6 hours with Barcelona: of the 117 hours broadcast 99 were recorded. On the other hand, the Brazilian stations opted for live programming despite the time handicap with a total 453 of programming.

Olympic programming in Asia, Southeast Asia and Australia

Table 4.4 offers some programming examples from Asian, Southeast Asia and Australia. CCTV (China) programmed 272 hours of coverage: 40 hours more than for the Seoul Games and 40 hours more than for the Asian Games of 1990. The CCTV Olympic broadcast broke the record for the longest broadcast in China. From 6:25 am on 7 August 1992 until 10 pm on the 10th of the same month it broadcast 90 hours of uninterrupted coverage of the Games, while a usual programming day spanned only 10 or 12 hours. It also broke the national record for a live broadcast: of the 126 hours that it dedicated to the sports broadcasts, 49 were live from Barcelona. Korean broadcasters also extended their typical broadcast hours to accommodate the Olympics.

Table 4.4. Examples of Olympic programming in Asia and Australia

Country	TV Broadcaster	Broadcasting hours
China	CCTV	242
Korea	KBS	215
	MBC	172
	SBC	159
Indonesia	TVRI	100+
Japan	NHK	177
	NTV	30
	TBS	32
	CX	28
	ANB	27
Malaysia	RTM1	197
	RTM2	86
	TV3	233
Singapore	SBC 12	240
Australia	Channel 7	300+

Source: Correspondent data.

In Japan, although 6 channels broadcast the Games, NHK offered the most complete and notable coverage. It dedicated 22 of the 24 hours of programming of its news channel to broadcasting the latest on the Games and to carrying out broadcasts of the various competitions; 11 hours of its general channel's programming was dedicated to the broadcasting of reports on Barcelona, Catalonia and Spain and also sports rebroadcasts; and, finally, 8 hours a day was devoted to HDTV Olympic programming.

The Australian station Channel 7 was converted into a Olympic channel during the Olympic Games, with a single pause in sports programming between 6 pm and 7:30 pm, in order to broadcast local news, a current affairs show and a soap opera.

Olympic programming in Africa

Finally, as shown in Table 4.5 the African countries, which spent a lot less resources and experienced technical problems concerning the broadcasting by means of the French satellite station Canale France International (CFI), were the ones which dedicated the least time and, consequently, the least attention, to the Barcelona Olympic Games. This table represents, of course, only a limited sample of the African continent.

Table 4.5. Examples of Olympic programming in Africa

Country	TV Broadcasting	Broadcasting hours
South Africa	SABC	104
Ghana	GBC	75
Egypt	ERTU 1, 2, 3	92
Cameroon	CRTV	52

Source: Correspondent reports.

Program types and strategies

In general, all of these broadcasters offered their viewers a variety of programmes within their Olympic programming. They combined the broadcasting of the sports competitions with Olympic summary shows and 'magazine' style interview or discussion shows – although for all broadcasters the main programming was, of course, sports. However, broadcasters did present more of certain sports according to the national interests. For example, Ghana Broadcasting Corporation Television (GBC-TV) dedicated most of the little time it was able to programming of the Olympic Games to the soccer competition. In fact, the Ministry of Information which supervises the GBC, largely underwrote the costs of the soccer matches because the GBC could not afford the bill and it was felt that it was necessary to telecast the Ghanaian matches in particular to avoid public outrage resulting in unknown political or social consequences.[1]

The use of live or delay broadcasts was clearly influenced by the time difference that existed between the time the competitions were taking place in Barcelona and the time of their broadcast in various countries. In this sense, Europe was the continent which benefited the most due to the few time differences between the countries. The Americas benefited – particularly for early morning (before work) programming and weekends, since the time difference led to an earlier broadcasting time in the countries of that zone than in Barcelona and the finals and many of the most relevant events could be shown live in the morning hours.

Olympic programming models

Reviewing the Olympics scheduling of about 30 broadcasters, the following programming models for the Games emerge. These models can also be related to in terms of the levels and types of competitive broadcast structures within different countries.

Broadcasters that were able to dedicate all their programming to the Olympic Games without altering their regular programming strategy: This strategy was only the case with monothematic broadcasters (e.g. Canal Plus in France or dedicated sports channels like Eurosport) and television companies that had more than one channel so that one channel

---

1 Karikari (1992).

could be converted to Olympic programming (e.g. TVE 1 and 2 in Spain, or the Catalan channel Canal Olímpic).

Broadcasters that dedicated a large part of their programming to the Olympic Games without being able to offer their audience adequate alternatives: In states with national television monopolies (the case of Cuba and China) or which have a small number of television channels (the case of Rumania and Egypt), the presence of Olympic broadcasts in the programming schedule drastically reduced what was available to audiences on the television, to the consequent detriment of viewers who were not interested in sports. Some Rumanian viewers called the broadcaster RTV to complain about being under an 'Olympic dictatorship' because, as the only national channel, Olympics programming severely limited programming options.[2]

This reflects the limited competitive broadcast environment within these countries. For example, while there were 469 regional or local television stations across China, Chinese Central Television CCTV is the only national broadcasters in China and uses two channels. Channel 1 only broadcast within certain time bands (30 minutes in the morning, 30 minutes in the evening, 30 minutes at night, each day). Channel 2 dedicated practically all its programming to Olympic events (48 hours of Olympic news in total, 126 hours of live broadcasting and 105 hours of recorded broadcasting, a total of 279 hours, twice the amount of 1984).

Broadcasters that dedicated a large part of their programming to the Olympic Games while keeping on certain areas of their usual programming, preferably the most popular and informative ones. This is the case of numerous broadcasters and countries, according to different formulas. It often relates to a competitive broadcast environment where broadcasters are reluctant to forego the most popular regular programming so as not to lose certain audiences and advertisers. This is the case, for example, of the French (A2, FR3), US (NBC), British (BBC) and Mexican broadcasters (Televisa) stations A2 and FR3. These broadcasters tried to keep on their most popular programmes during the Olympic Games. Thus, the BBC broadcast its most important soap operas: *EastEnders* and *Eldorado*. NBC kept on its daily time allotment of soap opera programming in the schedule, as the profile of those particular viewers and advertisers (important customers often with long term contracts) are not well matched to Olympic programming. The Australian station Channel 7 only interrupted its Olympic programming in order to offer its audience a news bulletin, a local current affairs show called *Real Life* and the soap opera *Home and Away* (which apparently provided a striking contrast with the internationalist perspective which tends to govern the Olympics). In these countries, viewers did not suffer from a lack of programming options due to the multiple channel environments in which they live.

Broadcasters within the same country offering complementary programming strategies. This programming model has two sub-groups: those that succeeded and those that failed. Broadcasters from several countries – such as Germany and Greece – successfully

---

2   Gross (1992).

employed a strategy of alternating programming days, times or sports for broadcasting the Games. This general strategy was also attempted in Korea and Russia, but shortly after the start of the Games these 'complementary' programming agreements largely fell apart due to competition. The two Russian channels, Ostankino 1 and RTR, together acquired the Olympic broadcasting rights and agreed to alternate the broadcasting between them, dividing up the two ceremonies and agreeing to day on, day off alternate broadcasting of the most popular sports. However, Ostankino 1 broke the pact. RTR denounced this and from that moment on the two channels broadcast simultaneous Olympic programming. This broadcaster conflict was such that it also made news in the print media and led to problems and complaints by that part of the audience which did not want to see the Olympic Games. Some people compared the situation to what took place in Brezhnev's era, when every station used to broadcast the same programming.[3]

A similar situation happened in Korea where the three members of the Korean 'pool' ignored sharing arrangements and began to compete head on, often showing the same programming at the same time. This situation prompted many viewer complaints and was also the subject of press criticism.[4]

There was also some middle ground in this circumstance where rights were shared by competitive broadcasters. In some countries, there was some duplicate Olympic coverage, but occurring at different times during the day. For example, three Brazilian broadcasters all offered coverage of the Opening Ceremony, but some at different times. Or, Olympic programming quantities were distributed so unevenly in the rights agreement as to not conflict. In Japan, there were six television networks that finally broadcast the Games in Japan. NHK, the Japanese public network that had four channels at its disposal had acquired 80 per cent of the rights. The remaining 20 per cent was distributed among a group of private television stations amounting to little or no head on competition.

Olympic radio programming

Olympic television programming, of course, does not amount to the only coverage of the Games available in any country. Both print press and radio offer alternative Games coverage. In some countries, such as Indonesia, both radio and television played an extremely important and pervasive role in Olympic coverage.[5] While this analysis does not have coverage quantities for those media, radio strategies, in many ways, mimicked the television programming models, employing both exclusive Olympic coverage (e.g. sports radio formats) and mixed programming coverage (inserting special shows, news reports, interviews, etc.).

Those members of the Olympic Family who gathered in Barcelona, also constituted a media audience of sorts. To serve those needs, a Spanish radio station, Radio 4, belonging

3   Zassoursky *et al.* (1992).

4   Park and Kang (1992).

5   Idris (1992).

to the state public radio network, was converted during the celebration of the Games into Olympic radio. The broadcasts began 15 days before the Games and ended coinciding with the Closing Ceremony. A total of 98 people, worked exclusively for Radio Olympic. Its objective was to offer general programming (music, features) and special interest news (results, competition schedules) to the Olympic family (sports delegations, etc.). The station broadcast in the four official languages of the Barcelona Games (Spanish, Catalan, French, English) throughout the day, but also offered news bulletins in other languages, such as Russian, Basque, Japanese and Arabic between 11 and 12 pm at night.

The process of Olympic meaning production

The Olympic broadcast, received in any country, starts as a technologically and logistically complex production surrounding 41 different sports venues pulsating with cheering crowds, split second action and multiple focal points. At a series of stages, decisions are made – based on a variety of factors from professional norms to financial resources – as to what moves forward through the broadcast production process to 'become' the Olympic Games for television viewers. RTO'92 was concerned with issues such as professional quality, neutrality, breadth and sound mixes to produce an international signal. Technicians and producers from different broadcast companies further revise the technical imagery and select which sports and athletes will be broadcast based on standards within their own broadcast specialty, available technical resources, and under the stresses of time. Commentators for those broadcasters select what information, emotion and imagery they wish to evoke based also on professional norms and levels of preparedness, as well as on perceptions of their audience and – of course – by reacting to what they see. Broadcast owners and managers choose the amount and timing of programming that will be shown to home audiences based on financial resources, time zones and various attributes of the broadcast environment. Based on all of those processes, viewers will choose whether or not to watch. But even viewing environments differ in the number of options available. Each step irrevocably alters each event of the Olympic Games in some way before reaching television viewers.

The purpose of this chapter was to begin to see how and why the Olympic television 'experience' is different for viewers around the world, as well as offer important background knowledge for the chapters in Part II which explore, in more depth, how broadcast similarities and differences might link more broadly to the construction of meaning and, as such, to an understanding of the modern Olympics.

PART II
Communicating Culture, Olympism and Politics in the Opening Ceremony: a Comparative Analysis

Introduction

It is hoped that the chapters in Part I demonstrated the meticulous planning and control by organizers and broadcasters in producing the Olympic Games and ceremonies. The Opening and Closing ceremonies are still live events, but in television terms they are also highly produced. As described in Chapter 4, part of the production process involves broadcaster modifications to the host broadcaster international signal. In this way, a single Olympic Ceremony quickly becomes many different ceremonies as a result of structural, verbal and visual modifications by international broadcasters. Structurally, broadcasters have the ability to add or subtract programming elements within and around the ceremony. Then, all broadcasters must add verbal narration to the event because the international signal is visuals, music and natural sound only. Finally, broadcasters may superimpose additional visual elements, such as graphics, or insert images produced by their own cameras.

Part II investigates the outcome of these customization processes in the sense of how they contribute to varying interpretations of the event for home audiences. This part of the book starts off by describing the design process of the Opening Ceremony and the ways in which the ceremony planners attempted to direct what meanings would be associated with the Barcelona Opening Ceremony. Then begins a detailed comparative content analysis of 28 Opening Ceremony broadcasts from all parts of the world. In successive chapters, broadcaster interpretations of the Opening Ceremony are compared in terms of broadcast structure, verbal and visual narratives, attention to the values of Olympic community, the presentation of other nations, and the understanding of the host culture. In the final chapter, the broadcasts are analysed for the presence and character of commercial messages.

Taken together, these areas of analysis offer a sense of how the Olympics might be understood to viewers around the world and, in a broader view, of how television constructs various realities of events, peoples and ideas located beyond daily reach. What is revealed, however, is not only the many ways in which international perspectives diverge, but also the ways in which television in conjunction with Olympic planners may contribute to the cultivation of globally shared meaning.

5   The Planning and Structure
of the Ceremonies

It was the longest commercial 'spot' in my career. There are those who say the longest in history, too. And perhaps the most complex, from the first briefing in 1989 until D-Day 25 July 1992. From the product analysis to the determination of creative techniques. From the gestation of ideas to the production of the image. From forging the strategy to choosing the performers'.[1]

Lluís Bassat, President, Ovideo Bassat Sport, creators and producers for the Barcelona '92 ceremonies

An advertising spot? Others have characterized the Olympic ceremonies as the ultimate global ritual, a media spectacle, an entertaining show, a prelude to a sports event, and more. MacAloon is most likely correct in stating that the Olympics is all of the above – at once spectacle, ritual, festival and game.[2]

The origins of the Barcelona ceremony

In 1989 the Barcelona Olympic Organizing Committee (COOB'92) distributed a summary of recommendations on the content and promotional objectives of the ceremonies to the companies interested in producing the Opening and Closing Ceremonies for the 1992 Barcelona Olympic Games. These recommendations were accompanied by a dossier containing the 'Olympic Charter', video documentation of the 1984 Los Angeles and 1988 Seoul ceremonies, various technical data, and research based on the Seoul ceremony.[3] According to these recommendations the ceremonies needed to meet the following objectives:[4]

- Be conceived as a spectacle for television and, at the same time, as a spectacle for the spectators who would see it 'in situ' in the stadium.

---

1   Bassat, Lluís, (1992).

2   MacAloon (1991).

3   Moragas Spà (1989).

4   Subsequent chapters offer more detail on the success or not of these objectives.

83

- Respect the norms established in the 'Olympic Charter', although it is possible to adapt the representation of the rites to new televising methods.

- Begin the spectacle in the streets of the city, with the aim of increasing participation. (This proposal had to be abandoned in the end due to the demands of the security forces.)

- Display the city and the host country, that is to say, 'Barcelona, Catalonia and Spain, acting as a background to a feeling of solidarity with the whole world'. As regards Barcelona, it was suggested to capture the following ideas: a Mediterranean, Spanish, European city, capital of Catalonia, open to the world, 2000 years of history, a city of contrasts, modernity and universality, and the balance between modernity and tradition.

- Investigate and study in depth the use of folklore, introducing innovations which would underscore its universal values and make it more vivid for television and stadium spectators.

- Draw attention to the values of the Olympic movement (peace, harmony, integration, etc.).

- Design the ceremonies in accordance and coherence with the aesthetic style of the design of the previously approved symbols, especially the logo and mascot.

The struggle to win responsibility for the creation and production of the Barcelona ceremonies became a high stakes competition among a variety of advertising and production houses. Finally COOB'92, faced with good ideas in several different proposals, backed by exemplary qualifications, suggested the merging of three candidates and the forming of a new company. This move merged three types of companies: Ovideo TV, a company from the visual production sector; Bassat, a prestigious advertising agency from Barcelona associated with the multinational Ogilvy and Mather; and Sport Sponsoring, a leader in press production and sports information. This new company became Ovideo Bassat Sport.

Ovideo Bassat Sport was organized and operated in a way similar to how the great cinematographic producers work. There were directors in three main areas: art, production and management, as well as people in charge of specialty areas of music, sound, stage, dressing rooms, transport, and so forth. Ovideo Bassat Sport comprised 150 people who, in turn, coordinated the participation of a total of 20,573 people involved in the ceremonies, including athletes, volunteers, artists, actors, technicians, and others.[5]

Political and cultural guidance for the ceremonies remained under the control and consensus of COOB'92, that is to say, representatives of the Spanish and Catalan governments, the Barcelona City Council and the Spanish Olympic Committee. (See Chapter 9 for an understanding of the Barcelona / Catalonia / Spain relationships.)

---

5   COOB'92 (1992d: 63).

In a press conference the day before the Barcelona Opening Ceremony, Ovideo Bassat Sport president Lluís Bassat characterized the 2½ year preparations for the ceremony as a very difficult creative and logistic struggle challenged not only by the need to present a variety of image agendas (IOC, Spain, Catalonia, Europe, etc.) in a way that had global appeal, but by the sheer numbers of bodies that would be in the Olympic stadium at the same time – spectators, media, athletes, volunteers, dignitaries, performers – all with a part to play and only a relatively few actually paid to be there doing a professional job.[6] The large number of rehearsals that the preparation of the Olympic ceremony required gives an idea of its complexity. Besides the three general public rehearsals of the Opening Ceremony, there were also numerous partial rehearsals. Some performance segments, such as the 'Mediterranean' segment, required 45 partial rehearsal sessions.

The budget earmarked for the Opening Ceremony consisted of 2,800 million pesetas (approximately 119 pesetas = 1 US$ in 1992) of which 200 million came from outside sources. The costs of the most important sections, according to various newspaper sources, were structure (650 million pesetas.), music (150 million pesetas.), artists and designers (260 million pesetas) and lighting (180 million pesetas). This budget was considered modest given the size and duration of both ceremonies (over five hours) compared to the cost of the production of commercial spots for the advertising campaign of a high profile Olympic sponsor.

The strategy: a visual, musical experience

There is little question that the ceremonies were conceived from the outset as major televised and musical super productions. The basic strategy according to Bassat and ceremony director Manuel Huerga was 'to create a spectacle more than a ceremony' while respecting the 'Olympic Charter'.[7] The organizing concept was to frame the entrance of the athletes (the athletes' parade) as the central performance segment of the ceremony. The 'Barcelona' thread that was to tie all the performance parts together was art and, most important, music. As Huerga stated:

> The most important thing to remember was that an Olympic ceremony in Barcelona cannot evidently be the same as an Olympic ceremony in Los Angeles or Seoul – to give the most recent examples – for several reasons: Los Angeles is in Hollywood and, therefore, has an experience in the entertainment world we cannot compete with ... Seoul has a wealth of folklore which is totally unlike ours, and it also has a feeling of anonymity in spectacles which we do not have either. We consider that the difference between Catalonia and ... Seoul and Los Angeles, is

6   One example of the literally thousands of potential problems that needed to be addressed was a concern about the 10,000 or so athletes not walking fast enough during the Parade segment. The solution was to train the leaders (those carrying the country name placard) to march quickly and to use fast-paced music as an accompaniment. Also, there were several segments of the ceremony which involved stadium spectator participation, holding up masks and waving light sticks. Despite receiving very simple instructions before the ceremony began, people waved the lights at the wrong time.

7   Manuel Huerga and Lluís Bassat, Press Conference, 24 July 1995, Barcelona, Spain.

perhaps the individuality and large number of artists per square metre existing in this country.[8]

To this end, stars from the world of music and show business, famous for their presence in the world media, were contacted. Josep Carreras, the Catalan opera singer, was put in charge of musical direction and, not without controversy, invited other major 'divos' from the world of the 'bel canto' to participate. Famous representatives from the world of modern popular music also took part: Ryuichi Sakamoto, Mikis Theodorakis, Angelo Badalamenti, Carles Santos, Sir Andrew Lloyd Weber, and more. There were also representatives from the world of Catalan and Spanish folklore and music such as Cristina Hoyos and the cellist Lluís Claret, and design such as Peret and fashion designer Antonio Miró, and more. A long list of specialists, such as artistic director and costume designer Peter Minshall and choreographer Judy Chabola also took part, along with those listed above, under the direction of experts in the field of television and cinema productions.

Perhaps realizing the challenge of appealing to global audiences, the Ovideo Bassat Sport planners also said that they intended a musical and visual experience that would not require commentary to grasp its basic meaning. In this sense, the technology of television was also employed as a narrator to the event. And for their part, the host broadcaster RTO'92 professionals involved with the Opening Ceremony took this artistic challenge to heart. As Joan Serra, director of planning for RTO'92, put it: 'Do you want an experience or a documentary? ... We intended an experience'.[9] To this end, ceremony planners worked with RTO'92 to create certain 'moods' (e.g. solemnity during rituals, joy during dance), identify protagonists (Magic Johnson, IOC President Samaranch, King Juan Carlos, cultural 'story' characters) and add drama to performances by using camera and sound techniques.[10]

One of the most outstanding novelties in the production of the Barcelona ceremony was the participation of independent theatrical groups. The performances of the theatrical companies 'El Tricicle', 'La Fura dels Baus' and 'Els Comediants' introduced the independent style of theatrical creation into the ceremonies, a style which was significantly different from that of the traditional uniformed gymnastic teams found in so many prior Olympic ceremonies. (It is quite possible that the avoidance of this particular format was motivated by the bad memory that many Spaniards have in respect to the union representations of Franco's regime, which included similar folk gymnastic demonstrations.) In

---

8   Huerga and Sol (1992: 202).

9   Serra, Joan (1993).

10 Interview with José Ramón Díez, Deputy Director of Production for RTO'92, 24 July 1992. Mr. Díez said that, for the most, part the planners let the television production specialists do their job as they know best. The greatest challenge, he said, was to present coherently to television audiences performance segments that had numerous focal points. The night performance required the heavy use of lights – another significant challenge for camera technicians. Also, some of the opera celebrities presented difficulties by insisting on certain camera angles, in order to highlight their 'best' profiles, that were not optimal placement in television terms.

addition, the use of pantomimed humor by these theatrical groups in the Closing Ceremony was an Olympic ceremony first.[11]

Guiding ceremony interpretations

While the planners did not want to rely on broadcaster commentary – something they can't control – to narrate the ceremony, every effort was made to guide media interpretations of the ceremonies. This effort achieved varying success in terms of accuracy and depth of interpretation as this and subsequent chapters will reveal. COOB'92's extensive media relations programme included publications, on-line computer information services, press releases, organized visits and tours, newsletter, press dossiers, events, press briefings and press conferences, audiovisual scripts, and more. At one point or another, all of these contact points were used to provide background and interpretive information about the Olympic ceremonies.

The most important interpretive tool, however, were the specialized media guides provided for on-site coverage of the Opening Ceremony and later on for the Closing Ceremony.[12] These guides consisted of a synthesized document (85 pages in the case of the Opening Ceremony) that contained four basic levels and types of information: a description of the structure and exact timetable of the ceremony; a synopsis of each performance segment; a detailed 'script' that commentators could paraphrase or use verbatim to narrate each ceremony part (except the full athletes' parade); and finally, background information about actors, symbols and other attributes of the ceremony (actors' nationality and background, number of dancers for different segments, size of Olympic flag, the meaning of Olympic symbols, historical data, etc.). These documents, eagerly awaited for by all media anxious to prepare their stories and commentary, were not distributed until the night before each ceremony.

The barriers of surprise

The organizers attempted to keep the content of the ceremonies a strict secret during the preparation period. The reasons for this secretiveness were in part to protect from and limit local journalistic controversy about the contents and part a belief that the 'surprise' effect adds to the spectacular nature of the ceremonies. Neither effort is fully effective as journalists readily speculate about aspects of the Opening Ceremony. And, as for the element of surprise as enhancing somehow the experience of the event, this latter reasoning works directly against the objectives set forth by the organizers by limiting the time and thus ability for international commentators to interpret and assess the contents of the most crucial cultural and political aspects of the ceremonies. This barrier is particularly acute for broadcasters not native to one of the Olympic languages that the ceremony guides are published in (English, French and the host language – in this case, Spanish and Catalan).

---

11 The Catalan group 'El Tricicle' performed a parody of a marathon, pantomiming humorous antics by runners and spectators alike.

12 COOB (1992a).

In fact, the Indonesia TVRI commentator repeatedly complained to home audiences about organizers keeping things 'secret' and the difficulty of obtaining names and information.

Despite the late access to the ceremony guides by media personnel, there is clear evidence of its use by international television commentators. These 'scripts' do play some role in encouraging shared descriptions and interpretations of ceremony segments for global audiences. However, how broadcasters choose to use them varies greatly – with language and preparation time emerging as factors in its use. By comparing broadcast commentary scripts with the media guide 'scripts' this study analysed the use the ceremony guides during both performance and ritual segments of the ceremony. The results show broadcasters falling in five basic categories of use, progressing in order of reliance on the media guide:

- The Tele-Rebelde commentator from Cuba stood alone in using the Spanish version of the media guide verbatim for most performance and Olympic ritual segments. There was little elaboration beyond the media script. (Ironically, the study correspondent from Cuba, Enrique Gonzalez Manet, reported that the commentary was 'not helpful' in understanding the cultural segments of the ceremony.)[13]

- Canada's TVA and Mexico's Canal 13 also often used the media script verbatim, but limited its use mostly to cultural performance segments.

- Several broadcasters, such as ARD (Germany), BBC (UK), NBC (USA), 2nd Channel (Egypt), had obviously read through and studied the script to understand the cultural performances, but then paraphrased its contents staying essentially true to each segment's story line and then elaborated freely beyond the bounds of the media guide.

- Other broadcasters, such as Channel 7 (Australia), CTV (Canada), NHK (Japan), TF1 (France) and SBC12 (Singapore) used the guide much more superficially, reading script sub-heads ('Hercules in victorious in the first Olympic Games') or pulling out key words or phrases ('The sun, the force of life' or 'Hercules, hero of heroes') when appropriate to describe what was happening on the field. There is much less effort given to narration of performance and often long silences without any explanation at all.

- The commentators of CCTV (China), TVRI (Indonesia), Canal A (Colombia), Romanian TV and Ostankino 1 (Russia) mostly ignored the media guide except for the occasional performer or segment name. They were clearly not comfortable using the provided scripts as written in non-native languages and had not taken (or had) the time to translate the guide in any way that would be useful to enhance their commentary.

The organizing committee not only attempted to steer interpretative commentary by

---

13 Gonzalez (1992).

providing narrative scripts, but also the timing of when comments were made. Broadcast commentators sat next to a mechanism installed by RTO'92 consisting of a three colour light signal (red, green and yellow), similar to traffic lights, which indicated to the commentators the opportunity to make verbal comments or remain silent so as to best capture the live sound atmosphere of the spectacle. Just as commentators varied considerably in their reliance on the ceremony guide, not all commentators followed these timing recommendations.

For their part, some broadcasters made use of special consultants to interpret the ceremonies – although this was the exception (Chapter 6 profiles the international commentators). Others used the public rehearsals, several days before the start of the Games, to prepare their commentaries. Others still (e.g. Japan's NHK, USA's NBC) spent well over a year preparing background data for use in both the ceremony and subsequent sports commentary.

The experience of Barcelona shows that, in whatever case, the quality of interpretation does not depend upon maintaining the secret of the ceremony, but rather the amount of preparation of the commentators and language accessibility of explanatory materials. While broadcasters ranged dramatically in their levels of advance preparation due to both resources and experience, the availability of information adapted to timing, stylistic needs and language preferences of broadcasters clearly influence the interpretive quality of the ceremony commentaries.

The structure of Olympic ceremony

No planners for the Olympic ceremonies start with a completely empty stage. The Olympic system of symbols is expressed through a series of pre-determined rituals: the transference of the Olympic flame from Olympia, Greece to the host city, the Opening and Closing Ceremonies, the prescribed steps for awarding of medals, and so forth. MacAloon quotes a 1910 statement by Baron Pierre de Coubertin to the effect that without such rituals the Games would cease to be 'Olympic', and would become merely large multi-sport world championships.

Looking closer at the ceremony rituals as outlined in the 'Olympic Charter' and following the models applied in Seoul'88 and Barcelona'92, one can divide the Opening Ceremony into the following parts: opening cultural performances; Olympic rituals, including the athletes' parade; and the final culmination of the spectacle.[14] See Appendix D for a chronological listing of the ceremony segments at Barcelona.

Considering this ceremony breakdown, there has been a significant expansion in duration and scale of the cultural performances and the athletes' parade over time, shifting the balance of audience attention away from the Olympic rituals embedded within the programme. In addition, the ceremonies have shifted from a tone of overall solemnity to

---

14 Technically, the athletes' parade is an Olympic ritual, but for the purposes of analysis this study routinely distinguishes between the parade and other ceremony rituals such as the entrance and lighting of the Olympic flame.

being more cheerful, particularly in regards to the athletes' parade.[15] In all parts of the ceremony, there has been an obvious trend toward more visual grandeur linked with the desire to appeal to television audiences.

The ceremony parts

Opening cultural performance

The first part of the Opening Ceremony plays the dual role of welcoming world audiences to a familiar event, the Olympic Games, and presenting a new host city and its culture. In Barcelona'92 the opening cultural performance took approximately 52 minutes and was made up of five acts: an initial act of welcoming, with evocative images of the city of Barcelona; a second act consisting of the arrival of the King and Queen of Spain and the symbolic representation of the Catalan, Spanish and Barcelona flags; third and fourth acts representing Catalan folklore and the folklore of different regions of Spain, especially Andalusian folklore (flamenco); and, finally, a great spectacle reminiscent of the mythological epics in which the protagonists were Hercules, the human spirit, Olympic history, the Mediterranean and its culture.

Olympic rituals

The athletes' parade. In accordance with the rules of protocol established in the 'Olympic Charter' (rule 69, edition 23 July 1992) the Opening Ceremony is made up of five major ritual acts, starting with the athletes' parade. The parade of the athletes and the Olympic delegations constitute a fundamental part of the Opening Ceremony not only in terms of time, but symbolic implications. As MacAloon says:

> In the Opening Ceremony each nation is presented in the same way, at least from a formal point of view, each one being equally visible, equally worthy and equally 'Olympic'.[16]

This important sentiment and quality to the athletes' parade, equal visibility, also creates the greatest challenge for ceremony planners. In part because of the difficulties the size of the parade represents for the television spectacle (long, slow moving) and the limits 10,000 or more athletes put on the effective use of the stadium for cultural performances, it is a recurrent issue among Olympic hosts, broadcasters and NOCs as to whether all Olympics athletes should be allowed to march in the parade. To date, the wish of the NOCs for total participation has been respected, although the result in Barcelona was a parade one hour and 20 minutes in duration and an easy target, as addressed in Chapter 8, for advertising breaks and other types of broadcaster departures. In accordance with the rules, the respective countries are required to parade in alphabetical order, with only two exceptions: Greece heads the parade and the host country brings it to a close.

While the 'Olympic Charter' specifies the format for the parade, teams as well as

---

15 This start of this trend is traced back to the Munich Games. See Alkemeyer and Richartz, (1993).

16 MacAloon (1991).

individual athletes use their entrance to express themselves or culture through dress and demeanour, often violating rule 69 bye-laws that forbid such activities as the waving of national flags and the carrying of signs or cameras. The rule also requests that athletes salute the Head of State and IOC president as they march by – although in each Olympiad fewer teams seem to respect this act of protocol. In addition, the athletes' new demands for national or regional identification have become a significant challenge for the Olympic rituals as the forbidden presence of armbands, flags, as well as formal requests by athletes for special ethnic or national recognition increases. In the Barcelona Games, for example, the Unified team from the ex-Soviet Union paraded under a single Olympic flag, although some athletes within the group displayed their nation's flags. As with other international structures, such as the United Nations, conceived with a nation-state system in mind the Olympic movement is sure to face increasing pressures of this kind reflecting a changing world political structure.

Television cameras on the field also encourage some athletes to fall out of step with the formal requirements of parade marching to wave to friends and family at home. Here we see television directly intervene with the ritual process by identifying and highlighting those athletes who break protocol in some way. Different national broadcasters also instruct their unilateral camera personnel to seek out team personalities – sometimes for impromptu interviews.

Institutional speeches and protocol. The athletes' parade is followed by the official speeches allowed for by the 'Olympic Charter': the president of the organizing committee's speech, the president of the International Olympic Committee's speech and the host country's Head of State speech. The order and the selection of these speakers is also established in the 'Olympic Charter' (Rule 69 and its bye-laws). The Head of State's speech is really a declaration of opening. All speeches are especially brief (and limited in the bye-laws). The official opening was about 2 minutes in Seoul'88 and about 3 minutes (the maximum allowed) in Barcelona'92. As mentioned above, with the growth in duration of cultural performance and parade, these exceptionally short prescribed rites seem to recede in prominence, swallowed up in surrounding spectacle. Further, despite their brevity not all broadcasters choose to translate the speeches (if in a non-native language). Instead some paraphrase or simply announce who is speaking and leave it at that. And, as Brownell points out, when broadcasters do translate the speeches they don't always do so correctly. Referring to the Chinese CCTV broadcast, she said:

> The translations of the speeches were ... sparse, and in some cases inaccurate. At one point Juan Antonio Samaranch said movingly in English, 'The greatest festival of our contemporary times, the Olympic Games, is about to begin.' The Chinese translation was something like, 'This is the greatest festival day of our nation'. Thus, Samaranch's appeal ... to the notion of a global festival was transformed in to a comment on its significance to Spain – and since Samaranch is himself Spanish, this could be perceived as parochial nationalism.[17]

17 Brownell (1993).

The enthronement of symbols. The institutional speeches give a role not only to the Olympic authorities, but to the political authorities of the host city and country. Once these are over, the essence of the Olympic ritual begins with the introduction of the symbols, the Olympic flag, the torch and the administration of oaths to the judges and participants.

In the staging of these rituals there is a growing tendency towards spectacle which uses theatrical techniques (music, light, stages, movement, surprise, etc.) to achieve maximum emotion and solemnity. The lighting of the Olympic cauldron with a flaming arrow in Barcelona'92 was a spectacular display of imagination very representative of this tendency. Interestingly, the first idea was to use a laser beam but it was thought that using the traditional form of archer would, in fact, be more spectacular.[18]

New ritual acts in Barcelona. Different modern Olympic Opening Ceremonies have been known to introduce rituals not originally prescribed in the 'Olympic Charter', such as the introduction of the torch relay in the Berlin 1936 Games. Some of these 'new' ritual acts are then repeated in successive Olympic ceremonies and, as such, become tradition without being incorporated into the 'Olympic Charter' as ceremony protocol. Barcelona organizers also attempted to add new, as well as alter traditional ritual acts. They added a segment consisting of the parading of an Olympic flag in representation of the previous 24 host cities of the summer Olympics (along with the flag of peace – Picassos dove – to represent the Games that were not held in 1916, 1940 and 1944 due to war). They also added a dramatic unfurling of a 'giant' Olympic flag over the top of all the athletes gathered in the centre of the stadium (see Chapter 7 for broadcaster interpretations of this new rite). An alteration occurred after the oaths, when for the first time the host's national anthem (in this case the Spanish one) was not played as Rule 69 bye-law 1.14 suggests.

Celebration and final culmination of the spectacle

Once the official rituals are complete, a final celebratory segment begins. In Seoul this was given the title 'cultural manifestations' and in Barcelona'92 'Music and Europe'. As discussed in Chapter 9, this part was dedicated to promoting the image of Europe in the ceremony, first through the linkage of Catalan folklore (the human towers) to symbols of the European Community (there were 12 towers and blue and yellow lights to mimic the EC flag), but also through the representations of opera and the singing of the 'Ode to Joy'. In a somewhat unusual twist for an Olympic ceremony, the EC contributed financially to COOB'92 to have this distinct presence both in the ceremonies and Barcelona city during the Olympic Games.[19] The EC also provided broadcasters with a supplemental 'script' in

---

18 Bassat, Lluís (1992). Press Conference, 24 July 1995, Barcelona, Spain.

19 Commission of the European Communities (1992: 4). This document, distributed during the Barcelona Games, outlined the general strategy taken by the Commission to promote the idea of European unity during both the 1992 Albertville and Barcelona Games. In 1991, the European Parliament approved 15.5 ECUs in funding for the Commission's Olympic Programme, allocating 4 million ECUs to the Albertville organizing committee (COJO), 6 million ECUs to COOB'92, 1 million ECUs to the 1992 Paralympic Games; and 4.5 million ECUs toward an accompanying information and communications campaign. Included in the Commission's cooperative activities with the organizing committee was to have a 'visual presence' in the Olympic Opening Ceremonies.

an effort to encourage commentary about the European Community. This succeeded only marginally with several broadcasters mentioning the EC at the appropriate moment, but ignoring the suggested script, as well as most background facts and figures.

The Closing Ceremony

In comparison with the Opening Ceremony, the Closing Ceremony takes place in a more 'informal' way allowed by less stringent 'Olympic Charter' rules than those which govern the Opening Ceremony. The athletes enter the stadium in a disorganized way, without necessarily grouping themselves into national formations. This substitutes the connotations of 'national' order for that of disorder and spontaneity with the intended symbolism of new friendships having been formed.

The Closing Ceremony is also distinguished by its timetable. While the Opening Ceremony took place during the evening in Barcelona, it began – as seems tradition – in full daylight (in Seoul on 17 September from 10:30 to 13:30, in Barcelona on 25 July from 19:00 to 22:15). The Closing Ceremony traditionally takes place at night (in Seoul on 2 October from 19:00 to 20:25 and in Barcelona on 9 August from 21:30 to 23:30).

The most representative rituals of the Closing Ceremony are the extinguishing of the Olympic flame, the parade with the Olympic flag and the transfer or handing over of the flag to the representatives of the next host city, with the consequent exhibition of the new symbols (logo and mascot), thus communicating the message of the continuity of the Olympic movement. In Seoul this continuity was expressed by the simultaneous raising into the air large representations of the old and new mascots, 'Hodori' and 'Cobi', until they disappeared into the darkness of the night.[20] In Barcelona the logo of Atlanta'96 was unfolded and its mascot 'Whatizit'[21] was presented, along with the first representative performance of North American music and dance.

Comparing broadcast structures

Considering the efforts made by the IOC to regulate the presentation of Olympic symbols and rituals, as well as the extraordinary planning effort that goes into the minute-by-minute execution of the ceremonies, it begs the question of what broadcasters 'do' to the essential structure of the ceremony – if anything – before it reaches television audiences. How respectful are broadcasters to the integrity of the event as planned?

All broadcasters in this study claimed to show the 'complete' Opening Ceremony to their audiences (rather than highlights). While none of the broadcasters in this sample changed the chronological ordering of the ceremony segments as outlined above, 17 of 26 broadcasts analysed for structural alterations did change the ceremony structure by: (1)

---

20 SLOOC (1988). See also MacAloon and Kang (1991).

21 The Atlanta'96 mascot 'Whatizit' underwent a name change to 'Izzy' after its introduction in the Barcelona Closing Ceremony in part because of the confusion non-English speaking broadcasters and audiences had understanding the embedded humour in the spelling and intended meaning of the name.

departing for advertisements, news breaks, interviews or studio visits; (2) eliminating parts of the ceremony through technical means allowed by broadcasting on delay; (3) lengthening the programme by adding introductory or concluding segments; and/or (4) making visual alterations (e.g. the use of unilateral camera and custom graphics). In this sense, 'complete' broadcasts, that is to say, broadcasts showing the Opening Ceremony exactly as intended by its planners are rare. All broadcasters added their own commentary.

Table 5.1. Comparative Opening Ceremony broadcast structures (distribution of parts as a percentage of broadcast*)

Nation (broadcaster)	Cultural display % of broadcast	Olympic rituals % of broadcast	Parade of athletes % of broadcast	News, features % of broadcast	Com- mercial % of broadcast
RTO'92 international signal	39.0	19.0	42.0	0.0	0.0
United Kingdom (BBC)	38.0	19.0	42.0	1.0	0.0
Indonesia (TVRI)	39.0	17.0	42.0	2.0	0.0
Russia (Ostankino 1)	39.0	19.0	38.0	0.0	4.0
France (TF1)	39.0	19.0	37.0	0.3	4.7
Greece (ET1)	39.0	19.0	36.0	0.0	6.0
Catalonia (Canal Olímpic)	38.0	19.0	37.0	0.4	5.6
Singapore (SBC 12)	38.0	19.0	37.0	0.0	6.0
Eurosport	37.0	18.0	38.0	0.0	7.0
Spain (TVE2)	36.0	19.0	37.0	2.0	6.0
South Africa (SABC)	35.0	18.0	37.0	0.0	10.0
Malaysia (TV3)	35.0	17.0	37.0	0.0	11.0
Canada (TVA)	34.0	16.0	34.0	0.0	16.0
Australia (Channel 7)	32.0	14.4	36.0	0.6	17.0
Canada (CTV)	30.0	15.0	29.0	5.0	21.0
Korea (MBC)	41.0	25.0	23.0	0.0	11.0
USA (NBC)	29.0	7.0	26.0	10.0	28.0

*N = 11,382 seconds (3 hour 10 minute official ceremony)
Notes: The first line, RTO'92, represents the baseline measurement or the official ceremony. Only broadcasters which altered the structure of the ceremony are included in this table. They appear, from top to bottom, in increasing order of total amount of structural alterations to the ceremony in terms of time with the BBC (UK) making the fewest and NBC (USA) the most changes to the official RTO'92 version. Missing from this figure is Colombia's RCN which altered the structure with commercial breaks, but was an incomplete broadcast because of electricity shortages in that country. Also missing is the distribution for Cameroon CRTV which would be the same as that for France's TF1 (Cameroon received the French broadcast). However, instead of going to a commercial break as in France, CRTV audiences went to a home studio in Cameroon. Egypt's 2nd Channel is also not shown above although the broadcaster misses the first 1 minute 35 seconds of the ceremony due to a commercial break, then stays with the full ceremony.

Table 5.1 summarizes and compares broadcasters that changed the structure of the ceremony before transmitting it to home audiences. The baseline structure – or official ceremony – is represented by the top row of the table showing the RTO'92 international signal and its percentage distribution of the ceremony spent on the athletes' parade, other Olympic rituals and cultural performances (42 per cent, 19 per cent, 39 per cent respectively to equal 100 per cent). The broadcast structures of international broadcasters who altered this balance in some way descend from that in order of degree of deviation from the official ceremony, ending with the USA's NBC broadcast which revised the broadcast structure most substantially from the RTO'92 version. Note, in particular, the large among of time NBC spent on non-ceremony aspects within the time frame of the ceremony. Broadcasters that did not deviate from the RTO signal are not included in this table.

Departures from the Ceremony

The biggest structural difference across broadcasts resulted from various interruptions or breaks, mainly for advertisements. A majority (60 per cent) of the broadcasters analysed interrupted the Opening Ceremony to show advertisements. The broadcasters in this study which did not interrupt the ceremony with advertisement breaks were: BBC (UK), ARD (Germany), CCTV (China), Tele-Rebelde (Cuba), CRTV (Cameroon), TV Globo (Brazil), Canal 13 (Mexico), NHK (Japan), 2nd channel (Slovenia), Romania TV and TVRI (Indonesia). Although some of those broadcasters, such as Canal 13, used superimposed advertising in its broadcast. Some of these broadcasters (e.g. ARD of Germany) are commercial broadcasters yet did not choose to interrupt the Olympic ceremonies, despite the commercial attractiveness of a large national audience. Table 5.2 summarizes the number and time of advertising and others breaks international broadcasters inserted into their respective broadcasts.

There are also differences between how, and for how long, broadcasters interrupted the ceremonies for advertising breaks. Some stations showed most of their advertising at the beginning or at the end of the ceremony, such as in the case of TF1 in France or TVE in Spain.[22] Some did not exceed 5 minutes of advertising within the bounds of the ceremony, as was the case of 2nd channel in Egypt, while others exceeded 15 minutes: MBC (Korea), CTV and TVA (Canada), Canal A (Colombia), TV3 (Malaysia), and SABC (South Africa). A more limited group of broadcasters, which could be called supercommercial, exceeded 30 minutes of advertising (Channel 7, Australia) and 40 minutes (CTV, Canada). NBC led the ranking at just over 62 minutes of commercial breaks, eliminating 38 per cent of the official ceremony through departures for ads and newsbreak.[23]

Whether and how broadcasters depart from the ceremony are influenced by competitive

---

22 Table 5.2 only represents commercials shown 'inside' the official ceremony. It does not reflect commerical time right before and after the ceremony.

23 The number and time of breaks listed for NBC represents the broadcast of one affiliate (Seattle KING 5) station. Each NBC affiliate might vary somewhat in the number of local advertising and news breaks inserted in the ceremony. Therefore, these figures might be considered typical. All US broadcasts were delayed.

pressures and structure, advertising regulations, perceptions of the 'sacredness' of the Opening Ceremony, broadcast concerns about audiences switching channels, broadcaster resources available to produce and insert interviews and studio visits, as well as technical problems, as with the Colombian Canal A broadcast starting late due to electricity shortages and the Ghanaian version of the ceremony hopelessly scrambled because of a glitch concerning television standards conversion. In general, one sees wealthier, commercial broadcasters more willing and able to change the ceremony structure.

Table 5.2. Broadcaster departures from the ceremony

Nation (broadcaster)	Ads (time)*	Ads (number of breaks)	News and others (time)	News and others (number)	Number breaks (total)	Time breaks (total)
Australia (Channel 7)	33' 45"	12	0' 54"	6	18	34' 39"
Brazil (TV Globo)	0	0	0	0	0	0
Cameroon (CRTV)	0	0	11' 37"	2	2	11' 37"
Canada (CTV)	40' 35"	15	8' 17"	8	23	48' 52"
Canada (TVA)	30' 55"	22	0	0	22	20' 55"
Colombia (Canal A)	21' 20"	19	0' 33"	1	20	21' 53"
Cuba (Tele-Rebelde)	0	0	0	0	0	0
China (CCTV)	0	0	0	0	0	0
Egypt (2nd Ch.)	1' 35"	1	0	0	1	1' 35"
France (TF1)	8' 58"	3	0' 25"	5	8	9' 23"
Germany (ARD)	0	0	0	0	0	0
Greece (ET1)	10' 24"	4	0	0	4	10' 24"
Indonesia (TVRI)	0	0	3' 38"	2	2	3' 38"
Japan (NHK)	0	0	0	0	0	0
Korea (MBC)	14' 12"	3	0	0	3	15' 12"
Malaysia (TV3)	20' 25"	5	0	0	5	20' 25"
Mexico (Canal 13)	0	0	0	0	0	0
Romania (RTV)	0	0	0	0	0	0
Russia (Ostankino 1)	6' 35"	19	0	0	19	6' 35"
Singapore (SBC 12)	11' 55"	10	0	0	10	11' 55"
Slovenia (2nd Ch.)	0	0	0	0	0	0
South Africa (SABC)	19' 0"	19	0	0	19	19' 0"
Spain (Canal Olímpic)	10' 25"	5	0' 47"	1	6	11' 12"
Spain (TVE–2)	10' 55"	5	2' 46"	7	12	13' 41"
United Kingdom (BBC)	0	0	2' 12"	1	1	2' 12"
Eurosport	12' 15"	8	0	0	8	12' 15"
United States (NBC)	62' 32"	22	10' 15"	4	26	1: 12' 45"

*This does not include superimposed advertising.

Delayed and re-broadcasts

Time zones are certainly a factor in Olympic ceremony programming, with some commercial broadcasters even attempting to influence the 'start' times of Olympic events during rights negotiations to coincide with prime time viewing in that broadcast nation.[24] Table 5.3 shows, among other broadcast attributes, which broadcasts in this study aired on delay in their respective countries. Among these there are examples of delayed, first time broadcasts (Canada's CTV, USA's NBC, Cuba's Tele-Rebelde) and daytime re-broadcasts of the original live broadcast first shown in the middle of the night (Australia's Channel 7, Korea's MBC, Singapore's SBC 12). The five delayed broadcasts in this sample still used original, 'live' commentary. In Russia, however, when the Games were re-broadcast several days later (not the version in this sample) a new, 'improved' ceremony commentary was added responding to local criticisms that the original commentary was shallow and inadequate.[25] Broadcasting on delay provides unlimited opportunities for altering the structure of the ceremony. Our sample included the following distinct approaches to this:

- Australia's Channel 7 first broadcast the Opening Ceremony live in the middle of the night without interruptions. The network then re-broadcast the ceremony later the same day. The re-broadcast included commercial breaks, but did not alter the structure of the ceremony in any other way.

- Korea's MBC is an example of a re-broadcast that significantly edited the ceremony, eliminating a full hour of cultural performance and the Athletes' Parade. MBC did not eliminate any part of the Olympic rituals. Although a live version aired in the middle of the night, the highest ratings, by far, are associated with the re-broadcast. These viewers missed much of the official ceremony, including 116 of the teams that marched into the stadium.

- NBC of the USA is probably the most unusual case. The first US broadcast was at 8 pm Eastern Standard Time, six hours after the end of the live ceremony. NBC did not mention this delay to audiences, but instead matched its own start time for the broadcast to the 8 pm start time in Barcelona, so the 'live' NBC commentary, for example comments about the evening sky in Barcelona, fit nicely with the US broadcast time. Anyone with a basic knowledge of time zones would know that the broadcast was not truly live.

For its delayed broadcast, NBC took the liberty of manipulating the structure of the ceremony, shortening some parts, lengthening others, as well as inserting commercial breaks, studio visits and interviews. Entire sections of cultural performance were removed. However, NBC was careful to edit back into the broadcast important moments that would have otherwise been lost due to commercial breaks if the broadcast was truly live. The

---

24 For a discussion of how this worked in the Seoul 1988 Olympics, see Larson and Park (1993: 54, 76–77).

25 Zassoursky *et al.* (1992).

interesting point here is the lack of any acknowledgment on the part of NBC to audiences of the event as both delayed and edited. It broadcast just as if it was live.

Supplementary programming

Several broadcasters added programming to the front and back of the official ceremony, both to set the mood and debrief the event. This was more common with live broadcasts that coincided with popular viewing times (rather than the middle of the night broadcasts). Table 5.3 also lists those broadcasts which included supplementary programming.

Table 5.3. Broadcast schedule and production attributes

Nation (broadcaster)	Timetable	Own introduction	Own conclusion	Live or delayed	Own cameras
Australia (Channel 7)	Prime time	Yes	No	Delayed[1]	Yes
Brazil (TV Globo)	Afternoon	Yes	No	Live	Yes
Cameroon (CRTV)	Afternoon	Yes	No	Live	No
Canada (CTV)	Prime time	Yes	Yes	Delayed[2]	Yes
Canada (TVA)	Morning	No	Yes	Live	Yes
Colombia (Canal A)	Prime time	Yes	No	Live	No
Cuba (Tele-Rebelde)	Prime time	Yes	Yes	Delayed[2]	No
China (CCTV)	Early morning	Yes	No	Live	No
Egypt (2nd Ch.)	Prime time	No	No	Live	No
France (TF1)	Prime time	No	No	Live	Yes
Germany (ARD)	Prime time	Yes	No	Live	Yes
Greece (ET1)	Prime time	No	No	Live	No
Indonesia (TVRI)	Early morning	No	No	Live	No
Japan (NHK)	Early morning	No	No	Live	Yes
Korea (MBC)	Morning	No	No	Delayed[1]	No
Malaysia (TV3)	Early morning	No	No	Live	Yes
Mexico (Canal 13)	Afternoon	Yes	Yes	Live	Yes
Romania (RTV)	Prime time	No	No	Live	No
Russia (Ostankino 1)	Prime time	No	No	Live	No
Singapore (SBC 12)	Early morning	Yes	No	Live	No
Slovenia (2nd Ch.)	Prime time	No	No	Live	No
South Africa (SABC)	Afternoon	Yes	Yes	Live	No
Spain (Canal Olímpic)	Prime time	Yes	Yes	Live	No
Spain (TVE–2)	Prime time	Yes	No	Live	Yes
United Kingdom (BBC)	Prime time	Yes	No	Live	Yes
Eurosport	Prime time	Yes	No	Live	No
United States (NBC)	Prime time	No	No	Delayed[2]	Yes

[1]There was a live middle of the night broadcast of the Barcelona Opening Ceremony in this country. However, this study analysed a delayed version re-broadcast during normal viewing hours;
[2]This was first showing of the Barcelona Opening Ceremony in this country.

The importance of this add-on programming relates to the narratives and explanations put forth – before and after the event – and how they might influence audience interpretations of the ceremony. In Cuba, for example, the delayed ceremony broadcast was preceded by 'Hoy Mismo', a regular interview programme that was used on that day as an introduction to the ceremony. During the programme, however, at least 7 minutes of the Opening Ceremony was highlighted and previewed, along with comments, clearly framing the upcoming experience for viewers.

Visual alterations

Unilateral cameras. A large number of television stations broadcast the ceremony using only the visual images provided by the cameras of RTO'92 as host broadcaster. In these cases there are no differences in television shots, selection of images, and so forth of the ceremony itself. The only differences would be if the broadcaster inserted breaks or commercials in the ceremony. This is the case in more than half (16) of the broadcasts (the broadcasts of Cameroon, Catalonia, Colombia, Cuba, China, Egypt, Ghana, Greece, Indonesia, Korea, Romania, Russia, Slovenia, Singapore, South Africa and Eurosport). These broadcasters did not have their own cameras in the stadium. (The broadcasters from Cameroon and Ghana were not present in Barcelona.)

Because of the high costs of negotiating for and installing one's own cameras in the Opening Ceremony stadium only the most developed countries tend to use unilateral cameras to 'personalize' their coverage. Table 5.3 shows that this is the case for 12 of the broadcasters in this study: United States (NBC), and to a lesser extent in terms of numbers of cameras, of Germany (ARD), Australia (Channel 7), Canada (CTV and TVA), Spain (TVE), France (TF1), UK (BBC), Japan (NHK), Malaysia (RTM), Mexico (Canal 13) and Brazil (TV Globo). Specifics on unilateral camera locations chosen by these broadcasters, as well as the production of unilateral signals was discussed in Chapter 4. Also noted was the fact that some broadcasters, such as SABC of South Africa, 'borrowed' some unilateral images to use in its broadcast thanks to informal arrangements made directly with other broadcasters during the Games.

Generally, broadcasters employed their own cameras in the Opening Ceremony to show extra visuals of one's own team. For example, Australia's Channel 7 added 29 extra shots of the Australian team. Germany's ARD and USA's NBC added 16 or more extra shots of its own team. The rest of the broadcasters with unilateral cameras added from 1 to 8 shots of their own national team to their broadcast. Spain's TVE–2 and Japan's NHK inserted shots of their national dignitaries sitting in the stadium tribunal. Other broadcasters, such as the UK's BBC and Canada's CTV, did the above, but also used their cameras to offer a greater assortment of camera angles and types of shots to their broadcasts beyond that provided by RTO'92. Still, these broadcasters altered an average of only 3 1/2 minutes of the international signal by inserting unilateral camera shots. Table 5.4 lists the unilateral shot time by broadcaster (i.e. the amount of time broadcasters used their own cameras and did not rely on the international signal). NBC (USA), however, used its unilateral cameras to such a degree (and combined with editing manipulations to the international signal) that it was, in fact, impossible to calculate accurately exact unilateral usage except to confirm that it was the most, by far, of any broadcaster in this sample and included extra shots of the US team (and other teams' star athletes) along with a greater variety close-ups and images of their commentators themselves. For an example of unilateral camera use refer to Appendix C which shows the ways in which NBC chose to alter the entrance of the King of Spain from the host broadcaster version.

Table 5.4. Unilateral manipulations to the international signal

Nation (broadcaster)	Time unilateral shots	Time superimposed advertising	Time unilateral graphics
Australia (Channel 7)	6' 21"	0	2' 28"
Brazil (TV Globo)	1' 41"	0	0
Cameroon (CRTV)	0	0	0' 09"
Canada (CTV)	6' 28"	0	6' 04"
Canada (TVA)	2' 52"	0	1' 27"
Colombia (Canal A)	0	5' 01"	1' 02"
Cuba (Tele-Rebelde)	0	0	0
China (CCTV)	0	0	2' 30"
Egypt (2nd Ch.)	0	0	0
France (TF1)	0' 32"	0	1' 12"
Germany (ARD)	5' 17"	0	0' 07"
Greece (ET1)	0	47' 25"	0' 12"
Indonesia (TVRI)	0	0	3' 58"
Japan (NHK)	1' 45"	0	0' 03"
Korea (MBC)	0' 53"	0	34' 11"
Malaysia (TV3)	1' 43"	0	1' 07"
Mexico (Canal 13)	0' 54"	3' 50"	0
Romania (RTV)	0	0	0
Russia (Ostankino 1)	0	0	0
Singapore (SBC 12)	0	0	1' 37"
Slovenia (2nd Ch.)	0	0	0
South Africa (SABC)	2' 35"	1' 14"	3' 30"
Spain (Canal Olímpic)	0	0	0
Spain (TVE–2)	2' 19"	0	0
United Kingdom (BBC)	12' 40"	0	0' 45"
Eurosport	0	0	0' 24"
United States (NBC)	*	1' 38"	0' 31"

*It is impossible to accurately calculate the frequent unilateral camera use by NBC.

Table 5.5. Summary of broadcaster unilateral alterations to and departures from the official Barcelona Opening Ceremony

Nation (broadcaster)	Total time of unilateral alterations to and departures from ceremony	As % of the official ceremony N = 11382 sec (3 hr, 10 min)
Australia (Channel 7)	43' 28"	22.6
Brazil (TV Globo)	1' 41"	1.1
Cameroon (CRTV)	11' 46"	6.3
Canada (CTV)	61' 24"	32.1
Canada (TVA)	22' 15"	11.6
Colombia (Canal A)	27' 56"	14.7
Cuba (Tele-Rebelde)	0	0
China (CCTV)	2' 30"	1.6
Egypt (2nd Ch.)	1' 35"	1.1
France (TF1)	11' 07"	5.8
Germany (ARD)	5' 24"	2.6
Greece (ET1)	58' 01"	30.5
Indonesia (TVRI)	7' 36"	4.2
Japan (NHK)	1' 48"	1.1
Korea (MBC)	50' 16"	26.3
Malaysia (TV3)	23' 15"	12.1
Mexico (Canal 13)	4' 44"	2.6
Romania (RTV)	0	0
Russia (Ostankino 1)	6' 35"	3.7
Singapore (SBC 12)	13' 32"	7.4
Slovenia (2nd Ch.)	0	0
South Africa (SABC)	26' 19"	13.7
Spain (Canal Olímpic)	11' 12"	5.8
Spain (TVE–2)	16' 00"	8.4
United Kingdom (BBC)	15' 37"	8.4
Eurosport	12' 39"	6.8
United States (NBC)	*	over 50

*See text for discussion of NBC.

Graphics, super-imposed images. Another form of visual alteration is the use of partial and full screen graphics, and super-imposed images onto some existing scene. Some broadcasters superimposed advertisements over the images of the ceremony, raising serious questions regarding the blurring of the boundaries between the commercial and the Olympic (addressed in Chapter 10) . This is the case of Canal A (Colombia), Canal 13 (Mexico), SABC (South Africa), and above all ET1 (Greece) which had advertisements superimposed in the corner of the screen for nearly 48 minutes, which represents approximately 25 per cent of the total ceremony time. It was also common for commercial broadcasters to add their own logos to the screen during transitions to commercials or periodically throughout the broadcast as an identifier. Many created specialized logos which intermingled the network logo with Olympic logos. Other broadcasters, such as MBC (Korea) added significant amounts of Korean language graphics to the athletes' parade showing country statistics. Table 5.4 also lists the amount of time broadcasters added their own superimposed graphics (both advertising and information) to the international signal.

Table 5.5 summarizes totals *all* structural alterations to and departures from the official Olympic ceremony made by broadcasters in this study, including departures (for ads, news, interview, etc.), unilateral camera use, graphic and superimposed advertising additions. Across all broadcasters (excluding NBC) an average of 8.8 per cent of the official ceremony is altered, in some way, before reaching home audiences. The range, however, is from 0 per cent to well over 50 per cent (again, NBC is a unique case where the percentage figure is well over the majority of the broadcast, but not possible to calculate as an exact figure). Only in Cuba, Romania and Slovenia did audiences see the ceremony exactly as it was intended by the Barcelona planners – that is, in terms of the visual experience. (The verbal commentary is unique to all countries.)

While one event happens in the Olympic stadium, television broadcasters are well within their capabilities and rights to alter the broadcast in any way they choose. While audiences might assume they are seeing the 'real' thing, this is far from the truth. Broadcasters range significantly on the amount of changes they make to the structure and flow of the Olympic ceremony. The question becomes how much is too much? As will be further addressed in Chapter 7, Olympic rituals were left, for the most part, untouched by broadcasters. Chapter 8, however, reveals the significant number of entering national teams that are unseen by the world because of commercial and other breaks. Chapter 10 will explore further the initial question raised here as to the implications of commercial breaks and super imposed graphics inserted 'inside' the ceremony. Each of these areas need to be considered distinctly, for each have a different set of implications for the integrity of the Olympic movement or national pride.

6   Opening Ceremony
       Narratives

Since the 1936 Olympics when world radio broadcasts described a dramatic lighting of the Olympic flame at Berlin, electronic media and Olympic planners have joined together in a story telling venture of global proportions.[1] Although international radio broadcasts of the Olympics still exist and are an important means of experiencing the Olympics for some audiences, the Games are now a story primarily told through a partnership with television.

The Olympic ceremonies contain several levels of story. There is the meta-story of the modern Olympic era with its founder, heroes, villains, victories, locales and memorable events. In fact, the Barcelona planners attempted to condense this story into a ceremony segment where Olympic flags representing all of the modern Olympiads ran across the stadium floor amid the latest generation of Olympic athletes. Like familiar tales which find expression in different cultures there is a common story line to these successive Olympiads derived from storytellers who have collectively characterized them over time. The extent of the Olympics as a shared story is apparent when commentators from Indonesia and Slovenia alike are able to refer to 'the Munich tragedy', 'Moscow boycotts', or 'Carl Lewis' without further elaboration for their audiences. Chapter 7 expands on the idea of the Olympics as a shared community.

There is also the story of the Olympic Games at hand. As with all narrative structures, this more specific level of story has an implied author, the host city Barcelona (the real author being the international collaborative planning efforts described in prior chapters), protagonists on stage as well as behind the scenes, the television commentator as narrator, national television audiences (and co-commentators) as narratee and implied 'reader'. It is at this level, when the narration is directed toward a perceived national viewer, that the ceremony presentations notably diverge in their character as commentators reflect varying broadcast norms and cultural contexts more deeply rooted than the professional uniformity found at an Olympic international broadcast centre.

The most localized story level, of course, surrounds the nuances of national teams and

---

1   For a discussion of the Berlin Games, see Alkemeyer and Richartz (1993).

athletes. Although some of these nation-specific narratives are shared, as when commentators told of the difficulties of the Bosnian team getting to Barcelona or of the antics of the USA's basketball Dream Team, many are unique to the sports dialogue within a nation.[2]

Chapter 5 began the comparative analysis of international broadcasters by looking at different structural presentations of the Opening Ceremony. These are differences created by the technical manipulation of the international broadcast signal – inserting advertisements, adding graphic or unilateral shots, editing segments – and do not address the role of television commentators as the primary narrators and interpreters for the event. This chapter compares approaches to narrating across international broadcasters. These approaches, as defined, do not so much dictate what is said in terms of content as they reflect certain verbal styles and roles of the commentators *vis-à-vis* the audience. It is suggested that these approaches likely influence how audiences will characterize and understand the Opening Ceremony. And, while some of the variety in narrative approaches reflect only the personality of individual commentators other differences link to local culture and broadcast environments in ways which are instructive for understanding how international television broadcasters present global events.

Narrative approach: history, party or show

This analysis revealed three distinct approaches to the presentation of the Opening Ceremony: as historical event, celebration and entertainment 'show'. Just as commentators move among narrative levels described above, most broadcasts offered a combination of narrative approaches, shifting in tone and style for distinct ceremony segments. That said, broadcast commentators did display preferences for certain approaches with the most significant stylistic difference emerging between broadcasters from the more developed countries with competitive, multi-channel broadcasts systems (the United States, Canada, Japan, etc.) and broadcasters from countries with a more centralized system of television (China, Cuba) or belonging to systems with limited channel competition and commercialization on television (Egypt, Romania, Slovenia). While it is obvious that the analysis of these commentaries are not directly representative of a nation or culture (i.e. 'the Koreans do this', etc.), this study does take the position that the broadcast commentators are 'chosen' and therefore accepted by their respective national cultures as capable (not deviant) event mediators. This sentiment was reflected by some of the study correspondents as well as in this description of the Australian Channel 7 commentator and former athlete Lisa Forrest's transition from the world of swimming to Olympic commentating:

> It might also be noted that her physical appearance might be a factor in facilitating this move. Events like the Olympics tend to call out in television terms certain stereotypical 'national characteristics' ... National broadcasters may assume, consciously or unconsciously, that audiences want some kind of recognition and

---

2   Some broadcasters, such the USA's NBC and Japan's NHK, spend both time and resources traveling the globe ahead of the Games to collect these nation-specific athlete stories for later presentation during the Games as human interest anecdotes.

confirmation of a 'national type' in the face of the remarkable plurality which is the Olympics. Forrest, whatever her abilities as a broadcaster or athlete, also happens to fit a certain kind of female character which in media terms typifies a 'national' archetypal Australian female – light coloured hair (blonde, but not too blonde), an open 'toothy' smile, a certain enthusiasm and optimism combined with a pragmatic approach and a 'down-to-earth' straightforward manner.[3]

The ceremony as a historic event

Some broadcasters interpreted the ceremonies as if dealing with a unique historic event taking place in that moment, although forming part of a historic chain. According to this interpretation the ceremony serves as a renewal of the Olympic myth. This orientation is characterized by a focus on the importance of Olympic ritual and repetition and a more mythic level of character, portraying nations as interacting in a sacred arena. The event has gravity and each ritual holds great symbolic import. Sport is a symbol for transcendent, universal values. This characterization of the ceremony is also the most 'Olympic' in the sense that it assists in the reproduction of the cycle of the Olympiad.

There is great unanimity across broadcasters in considering the Olympic ceremonies as historic events. Several broadcasters directly label the Opening Ceremony as 'historic' and refer, with reverence, to an 'Olympic family' (e.g. ERTU2, Egypt and 2nd Channel, Slovenia as a new member of that family). However, thematically not all broadcasters are interested in the same historical aspects. For example, ET1 (Greece) and MBC (Korea), put major emphasis on mythological aspects and historical cycles while some of the western broadcasters (and particularly the Spanish) seemed to be more interested in their own nation's participation in history (the opening day is a special day in the memory of each country). Still others placed the 1992 Games in its broader historical context of a post Cold-War era, in effect setting the groundwork for a collective definition of the Barcelona Olympiad.

> 'These young athletes marching into a new era ... a dramatically altered new world' (CTV, Canada, Opening Ceremony)

> '[The] first Olympics that hasn't been disturbed by political intrigues and disagreements' (Ostankino 1, Russia, Opening Ceremony)

> The 'first boycott-free Games' and the 'first Cold-War-free Games' (SBC 12, Singapore, Opening Ceremony)

NBC of the United States put major emphasis on the importance of the day for world history and international relations:

> When we left Seoul following the Closing Ceremony of the 1988 games, we could not possibly have imagined how very different a set of circumstances would greet us here in Barcelona. Geopolitically, the world is in its most fluid state since the

---

3   Langer (1992).

end of World War II. In some cases, it's as if pieces of a jigsaw puzzle have been tossed into the air, and some have yet to land. Elsewhere, while borders are made clear, new and old conflicts and political divisions rage. As always, the Olympics are touched directly and indirectly by these realities, and over the next sixteen days we will, as we believe pertinent, talk about these situations and their effects on the athletes here. (NBC, USA, Opening Ceremony)

As did the BBC of Britain:

... in the spell of four years between Olympic Games the world changes, but surely, in recent history, never on the scale that's altered the face of so many nations since 1988 ... Who could imagine in Seoul in '88 the dominant Soviet Union would no longer exist in '92, Estonia, Latvia and Lithuania march as independent nations and the remaining 12 republics march in a group behind their national flags, the Unified Team. South Africa is back with a promised end of apartheid. Germany is now united. After the Gulf War, Kuwait and Iraq march in the same parade. Serbia, Montenegro and Macedonia from the crumbling remains of Yugoslavia compete as individuals. Slovenia, Croatia take part in their own right and athletes from Bosnia have escaped for a few days from the horror of Sarajevo ... The Olympic marchers tonight reflect the very different world in which we live. (BBC, UK, Opening Ceremony)

The commentator as observer

When commentators engage in these forms of historical interpretation they suggest that an exceptional and unforgettable event is taking place. 'Being there' is a privilege which they communicate to their spectators. In this approach, the commentator plays a role of the humble *observer* of history, awed and lucky to be present, intervening only when necessary to introduce or underscore the significance of events unfolding (and as such leaves much to silence).

While several broadcasters, like those quoted above, include historic 'moments', the more solemn and formal styles of the CCTV Chinese and MBC Korean broadcasts fit this historic approach throughout most of their broadcasts. These broadcast narratives incorporate more poetic forms of scripted sounding speech delivered without any hint of humor or triviality.

190 birds spread their wings(...). Oh torch, taking peace to humanity, crown with your light the winners of this sacred contest. (CCTV, China, Opening Ceremony)

A festival for all mankind ... to establish world harmony and peace and to present a new lantern for the future of mankind (MBC, Korea, Opening Ceremony)

Other broadcasters, such as from Russia (Ostankino 1), Great Britain (BBC), Egypt (ERTU2), Germany (ARD) and Greece (ET1) offer a sense of an historic approach not so much through a formality or poetry of tone, but through a willingness to convey a sense of personal awe, thereby connoting respect for the Olympics as a tradition. For this approach, the source of emotion is the transcendent nature of the Olympic movement symbolized by events in stadium.

> Keep the tissues hand, because I promise you it is going to be a very emotional hour to three hours. (SABC, South Africa, Opening Ceremony)

> Now you see an athlete in the arena of this stadium who will carry the Olympic torch around the circle. And the lights of the amateur photographers are breaking out – thousands of people want to record this moment for themselves for the rest of their lives ... Here they are, the Olympic Games. The celebration that unites all of humanity has finally begun. (Ostankino 1, Russia, Opening Ceremony)

The ceremony as a celebration

Another narrative approach is the presentation of the ceremony as a celebration or festival. Less transcendent, this approach to the Opening Ceremony pays significant attention to its cultural aspects. Here, the source of emotion comes from the energy of people coming together in celebration in the stadium. The ceremony is an event to be relished, a festival of humanity, a party of youth. The ceremony is not described as just any festival, but rather as an exceptional one of maximum spectacle and colour, which cannot be equaled. It is a peak experience: an explosion of culture, theatre and joy. This orientation characterizes music and dance as the common language. Music and art are central to the event, and the commentary in regards to this is both exuberant and superlative.

The commentator as participant

The commentator, in this approach, is more of a *participant* in the celebration attempting to share with audiences the feelings of happiness and excitement in the stadium. And, through their enthusiastic tone the commentators encourage television audiences to join in these feelings. Many of the Latin-based broadcasts (except that of Cuba) are excellent overall examples of this orientation frequently using words like 'fiesta', 'joy', 'celebration', and clearly relishing the music and dance performances.

> [A] fiesta filled with culture, mythology, human warmth and happiness. Emotional fiesta. (Canal 13, Mexico, Opening Ceremony)

> Let me confess to you, you who accompany TV Globo in this opening parade, that this is one of the greatest emotions we have felt in all of our lives (TV Globo, Brazil, Opening Ceremony)

This approach characterizes much of the broadcasts of Mexico (Canal 13), Spain (TVE–2), Colombia (RCN) and Brazil (TV Globo). However, other broadcasters joined in the celebratory mood during certain performance moments.

> Five Olympic rings have been formed by the dancers and the heart which they draw in the stadium reflect their excitement for having gathered here all the people of the world (ET1, Greece, Opening Ceremony)

> [A] Mediterranean explosion of joy ... festivity of all the sports world (Romanian TV, Opening Ceremony)

> There's such an air of enjoyment and freedom in the Olympic stadium tonight. There's an incredibly happy and gay atmosphere ... Young people from every corner of the earth enjoying themselves and really it's everyone's dream, I suppose, to compete in the Olympics. (BBC, UK, Opening Ceremony)

The ceremony as entertainment

Other broadcasters paid less attention to the cultural and ritual structures behind the ceremonies. Rather than a transcendent or peak experience, the ceremony is an entertaining introduction to the 'real' excitement: the sports competition. Yet, this orientation takes full advantage of such a spectacular start. This third narrative approach, which contained the least amount of references to mythology and emotion, relied on the event's 'liveness' for interest. The commentators reacted to activities in the stadium, employing the improvisational manner of professional sportcasters calling a game rather than adhering to a rehearsed script. In these cases the commentators tended to describe the images that the television audiences could see for themselves on their screens. Accordingly, there is a lack of silence in this narrative form. In some cases the commentators even prevented the viewers from enjoying the spectacle and instead offered themselves as part of the entertainment:

> E: And the climax will be a youngster, eleven years or younger, who will 'shimmy' up the building pyramid [actually a 'human tower' made of several levels of people standing on each others shoulders], and when he finally gets to the top, with a nervous wave, that will signal the end of the construction.

> C: Well, Dick, pretty much what we used to do when the 'whiffle' ball got stuck on the roof, right?

> E: (laughter) Here's the youngster who will have the honor. And your mother was worried when you climbed that big tree in the backyard!

> C: Memo to Nicole, Emily and Ted Enberg, and Keith and Taylor Costas [the commentators' children]: 'don't even think about it!' (laughter) (NBC, United States, Opening Ceremony)

Commentators engaging in this approach were also concerned with the quality of the event and commented on the skill or ability of the organizer to produce the show or spectacle. For example, the French TF1 commentators made at least six references to the Opening Ceremony as a spectacle, noting it as an organizational, cultural and technological success – also one 'made for television'. Others offered similar assessments.

> [An] absolutely unforgettable show ... magnificent show ... one of the most colourful (TVA, Canada, Opening Ceremony)

Tonight is for celebration, pageantry, and maybe even a sense of wonder (NBC, USA, Opening Ceremony)

Now the fun's over ... it [the ceremony] had grace, it had colour, it had excitement, it had class' ... [a] spectacular spectacle (CTV, Canada, Opening Ceremony)

[A] super event ... world class (NHK, Japan, Opening Ceremony)

The commentator as insider

This entertainment-oriented approach is greatly influenced by narrative techniques common to competitive broadcast environments where broadcasters survive by maintaining both anticipation in audiences, as well as their own credibility as the 'best' broadcaster (e.g. the broadcasts of NBC, USA; TF1, France; Eurosport; CTV, Canada; and on occasion Channel 7, Australia). To do this, commentators tended to present the ceremony as a spectacle full of surprises for the audience. The commentator role here is one of informed experts or *insiders* commenting on the development of the ceremonies. They are impressed, but not over-awed or surprised themselves by what they see (because of their implied position of omniscience). In fact the commentators made it known they were privy to the surprises ('Stay tuned. You're really going to like what's coming up next') and, at times, revealed the secrets by telling their viewers what was about to take place. This technique attempts to enhance the credibility of the commentator and suggests an essential role for television as narrator and interpreter – without which, the implication is, viewers would not understand what was going on.

Interestingly, in these broadcasts the commentators also intervene more often visually. There are shots of the commentators at their stadium seats inserted periodically throughout the ceremony broadcasts particularly in the case of CTV (Canada) and NBC (USA). This serves both as a reminder to audiences of the commentators privileged position, as well as to suggest that they are an integral part of the ceremony experience.

The verbal style of the entertainment approach is similar to the most popular television forms common to highly developed and competitive media cultures. The commentary represents a mix of talk show, sports broadcasts and variety show mixed together in a more or less improvised manner. These broadcasts are also characterized by good amounts of insignificant and carefree dialog between two or more commentators who joke, explain anecdotes and improvise word games. Referring to the 'human towers' segment, the French commentators sarcastically discuss its viability as a future Olympic sport:

We're seeing the essence of Catalonia ... The one who's going down headfirst! There's an Olympic sport for next time – see who can build the highest tower. Catalonia will contribute to the genius of the Olympics.' (TF1, France, Opening Ceremony, segment from 'Els castellers')

Triviality: entertaining by distorting

The desire for some of these commentators to be entertainers themselves, however, gives rise to a narrative style which can distort the basic cultural and ritual meanings of the ceremony: triviality. Trivial, in this sense, is not the same as informal or casual. The informality of the commentators is not always 'triviality'. In Latin America, for example, a festive and carefree tone is frequently employed to speed up the festival, expressing in this manner the deepest cultural values of the ceremonies by means of a festive form of interpreting the events

Triviality, on the other hand, refers to the consideration, or rather the lack of consideration some commentators seemed to express for certain cultural acts or countries. While the remarks may be intended as humorous, or entertaining, ('Well, I didn't know Hercules rode a bicycle!' BBC, UK, Opening Ceremony, commenting on the giant mechanical Hercules entering the stadium on wheels) some certainly come at the expense of others. The following sentences only serve as representative examples of this triviality (also see Chapter 8 for additional examples):

> MP: Seeing the Mongolians has also been a spectacle [referring to their traditional dress – or lack of dress], they are ...
> OV: They look fresh, huh!
> MP: Very fresh, yet in Seoul they did it the same way. I think it [the dress] is useful year after year.
> (TVE, Spain, Opening Ceremony)

> C: 'The French are traditionally strong, and will be again this year, in fencing, which is appropriate for the nation of Alexander Dumas, the creator of 'The Three Musketeers', and we're told that the French, while they may not win the most medals, will, as always, live well. They brought their own wine to Barcelona.'
> (NBC, USA, Opening Ceremony)

> EB: Attention because now the team from Zambia, which is second to last before the delegation which will close this parade, the delegation from Spain. The Zambians ... precede the Zimbabweans.
> LI.C: Zimbabwe, an hors d'oeuvre [to the Spanish delegation].
> (Canal Olímpic, Catalonia, Opening Ceremony)

The tone of triviality in this last example then became an emotional account when referring to their own national delegation.

> It's a reduced delegation [Zimbabwe]. And now will come the largest ovation [referring to the entrance of Spain]. (Canal Olímpic, Catalonia, Opening Ceremony)

Not all broadcasters who interpreted the ceremony largely as entertainment portrayed commentators act as clever 'insiders' or used this narrative technique. The broadcasts of Japan (NHK), Romania (RTV), Slovenia (2nd Channel), and at times Russia (Ostankino 1) treated the ceremony as an entertainment spectacle preceding a major sports event and included plenty of improvising and spontaneous remarks, yet without the humor or sarcasm of the examples above. The presentations were relaxed and casual, but not colloquial or trivial. That said, this more straightforward narrative style easily shifted to enthusiastic or admiring references when certain referents (countries or situations) arose that allowed comments which, in one way or another, were inappropriate in another political era. This can explain the interest of Romania in the US athletes or the Russian admiration for the aesthetics (spontaneity, creativity, freedom of expression) that were shown in the representations of Barcelona 92:

> And you know, it's very interesting to watch what's happening in Barcelona, how the settlers of Barcelona are waiting for the Games! The balconies of all the houses are decorated with all kinds of flags and here one can be jealous of the Spanish inventiveness. ..The whole city is coloured, it is all gleaming, glowing, everybody smiles friendly. The delegation of Venezuela appeared ... Look what a thrilling view! Now you could get an idea, though still incomplete, of the events; how beautiful it is, how wonderful. (Ostankino TV, Russia, Opening Ceremony)

In general, the various narrative approaches to the ceremonies show the existence of different televised commentary models around the world with the primary difference being the attitude taken toward the use of colloquialisms or the informality of the commentaries. While the majority of western television broadcasters used a mixed narrative model, the primary interpretative style was that of the 'televised show' with a supposedly knowledgeable, often well known host presenting him or herself as integral to experiencing the ceremony. Thus, for example, NBC adopted an extremely colloquial tone for references to North American athletes. They adopted a style more in line with news bulletins than with sports programmes for the commentaries on the athletes' parade. They also adopted a mix between a historical report and the chronicle of events for describing the culture and political identity of the host city (Barcelona). The formality of some non-western commentators could also be interpreted as the result of a prudent attitude or even of one of political fear. This prudence is not only stylistic but also thematic, opting to ignore conflictive aspects in the meaning of the ceremony.

How much talk?

Beyond levels of formality and the use of humor, the next most dramatic difference across broadcasters is simply how much is said. The length of the commentaries during the ceremonies, measured in time and in the amount of comments made, varies considerably and has implications for audience experience of the ceremony. Table 6.1 shows the general distribution of commentary by line count for commentaries translated into a common language. Of course, this table should be reviewed understanding the limitations of this type of analysis using translated text. Still, it does demonstrate that the amount of narration that occurred in an 3-hour, 10-minute ceremony varies considerably across broadcasters in this study.

The differences displayed above relate generally to preferences for narrative approach, with the more 'historic' characterizations (e.g. China's CCTV, Korea's MBC) of the ceremony the least verbose and the more 'entertainment' orientation engaging in significantly more talk.

Table 6.1. Amount of commentary by broadcaster

Approximate number of commentary lines in English (at an average 12 words per line)	Broadcaster – Nation
250–500	CCTV – China MBC – Korea ERTU2 – Egypt
500–750	2nd Channel – Slovenia Tele-Rebelde – Cuba RTV – Romania TVRI – Indonesia SABC – South Africa
750–1000	Ostankino 1 – Russia ET1 – Greece ARD – Germany TF1 – France CTV and TVA – Canada Channel 7 – Australia TVE – Spain
1000–1250	BBC – UK SBC12 – Singapore
1250–1500	NHK – Japan
1500–1750	NBC – USA Canal 13 – Mexico Canal Olímpic – Catalonia

Narrative depth and focus

Even in the most verbose broadcasts, few television commentators made analyses inspired by cultural anthropology that brought to light any deeper structure and meaning of the cultural aspects of the event. Instead, excessive description became a way of camouflaging an inability to interpret the cultural structures behind the event.

> At this moment we're seeing these people who represent the Sun and are located in the centre of the stadium. In other parts we also see people who in this case represent ... plants or herbs that currently are also entering the stadium(...). In another part we see what eventually will be the Mediterranean Sea, logically the sea which will be the origin of civilization and culture. (Canal Olímpic, Catalonia, Opening Ceremony)

Richness of description, poverty of interpretation

In other cases the narrative poverty or the lack of interpretative ideas was camouflaged by a litany of facts, such as, for example, the day, month and year in which Spanish princess

Cristina was born, the age of the composer Carles Santos, the length of the Olympic torch in centimetres, etc. This abundance of detail, selected from the media script sidebars, is surprising until one understands that its rhetorical function was to maintain active commentary, to keep it alive, even during scenes in which the commentators did not know what to tell their audiences.

As noted in Chapter 5 with its discussion about the use of the ceremony media script, broadcasters vary in their efforts to interpret for audiences the cultural and ritual meanings embedded in the ceremony. While a very few read verbatim from the script (which offers broadcasters a summary of intended meaning), many commentators chose to merely highlight actions, read key words from the script, or briefly paraphrase the 'story' of a performance segment.

Cultural distance and understanding

There was, however, an interesting example of cultural divergence in the interpretation of the most abstract cultural segment of the ceremony: the 'Mediterranean Sea, Olympic Sea' performance produced by the avant garde Barcelona theatrical group La Fura del Baus. The segment begins with a mythical, giant mechanical Hercules participating in the first Olympic Games. Then the Olympic spirit, symbolized by a boat, travels metaphorically through time and space from the first Games of ancient Greece, crossing the Mediterranean Sea (the stadium floor covered with performers elaborately costumed in blue), to the Barcelona Games of 1992. On its way, the ship and its crew confront a variety of fantastical monsters representing the evils that have plagued humankind and threatened the existence of the Olympic Games over the centuries: illness, war, hunger, etc. In this end, good triumphs and Hercules' renewed spirit arrives in Barcelona 1992 to pay homage to the achievements of modern civilization and stage a new Olympic Games. Key symbolic elements in this performance segment are water (the Mediterranean Sea), the sun and Greek mythology related to Hercules as son of Zeus, hero and Olympic victor.

Few broadcasters attempt to interpret this extraordinary performance much beyond the level of detail demonstrated in the above paraphrase of the segment story. From what they do choose to say, however, emerges evidence of varying cultural orientations (possibly East/West) or rather the effects of increasing cultural distance from the source of the myth. For example, western broadcasters (e.g. ARD Germany and TF1 France) were able to base their comments on a basic familiarity with Greek mythology. The focus in these commentaries is on Hercules as hero, powerful victor and 'a species of superman in ancient Greece' (ARD, Germany, Opening Ceremony). In the interpretations of the broadcasts such as Indonesia (TVRI), Korea (MBC) and China (CCTV) Hercules is not a competitor, but rather a discover, spreading knowledge and civilization with him in his travels. He's also an unfamiliar character, as evidenced in this tidbit by the Indonesian TVRI commentator: 'if we're not mistaken, the name Hercules is popular'.

In another example, the European and Egyptian (ERTU2) broadcasters uniformly focus on the sea as the central 'element' to the story. The Greek commentators (ET1), in particular, are pleased with the central role of the Mediterranean sea and discuss its importance repeatedly. The broadcasts of Japan (NHK), Korea (MBC) and Indonesia (TVRI), by contrast, focus on the sun as the central element, highlighting its power as a source of life and energy. For example, the official name of the segment was 'The Mediterranean Sea, Olympic Sea'. The Indonesian TVRI commentator introduced it instead as 'The Sun Story'.

In fact, the Indonesian broadcast offers a good example of cultural distance leading to a completely different framing of the segment story. The commentator misses the universality of the story intended by its creators and describes the performance as an enactment of a familiar Spanish sports legend which, ultimately, explains the existence of mixed races in Catalonia (because it shows how people traveled there from other lands). There is no mention of the intended Olympic allegory at all. For example, the Indonesian commentator starts off by saying:

> This is an ancient story widely known and enjoyed by the Spanish especially by those that like sports. Because this ancient story has been recited from generation to generation ... so ... to inspire ambition to ... be better in the world of sports (TVRI, Indonesia, Opening Ceremony)

Later on during the performance, when the 'monsters' of humankind (hunger, war, disease) are confronting the ship, the commentator, described it as a literal, rather than metaphorical, attack by robbers and pirate and reminded audiences that he was holding the definitive source (the media guide):

> This is a fight which truly happened described in a book given to [me] (TVRI, Indonesia, Opening Ceremony)

By contrast, the German ARD commentator underscored the story as nothing more than creative imagination:

> This is not in any encyclopedia. This is a modern Olympic story. Now we must dream a bit. (ARD, Germany, Opening Ceremony).

For all broadcasters in this study, however, the response to the spectacular staging of Mediterranean segment was extremely enthusiastic, albeit mostly confused. When the segment came to a close the British BBC commentators had the following, probably revealing, exchange:

> D.L.:Have you understood all the symbolism?

> G.L.:Well, I think we have to expect something a little bit different from the country that brought us Gaudi, Dali and Miro ... eh ... I thought it was certainly different, wasn't it?

> D.L.Definitely different ... and ... visually exciting
> (BBC, United Kingdom, After the 'Mediterranean Segment' of the Opening Ceremony)

If the broadcasters had difficulty interpreting this segment, then their viewers were likely frustrated with their narrative. This was expressed by some print journalists who clearly came away less enthusiastic and even more confused as to the segment's meaning. For example, a few journalists in Malaysia interpreted the performance as depicting the Moorish invasion of Spain and responded harshly in the press after the ceremony. The choice of this story for an Olympic Opening Ceremony, they claimed, was an insult to Muslims around the world. One editorial said that the performance:

> ... violated the principle of friendly spirit which is a fundamental tenet of the Olympics. And it is stretching our imagination to expect the Muslim community all over the world to accept this [insult] within the spirit of sports because the [performance] tried to sustain western prejudice on whatever is perceived as Islam ... Spain and its people do not have the right to use the world stage to sabotage the fledgling good relations among Muslim and non-Muslim communities ... Certainly not at a sports festival which aims at uniting mankind.[4]

Using a somewhat different approach to his vent his confusion about the symbolic aspects of the ceremony, a South African television critic offered this sarcastic summary:

> The grand opening of the Olympic Games left me puzzled and confused, totally unable to decode the message of the drama. Basically there were all these leaves. They danced. Then some seaweed joined them and a dead bird. They danced as well. With a crash of cymbals, no doubt to indicated the passing of time, five fork-lift trucks wrapped in aluminum cooking foil drove into the arena, through the leaves and seaweed.
>
> More music and a puff of smoke turned the trucks into a ship. The crew dressed in leather knickers, climbed up and down things. Some blew on conches, others carried around a bleeding lady. Then there was a giant sea urchin and octopus (David Basckin, August 2, 1992, *Sunday Tribune*)

Who are the storytellers?

A primary factor to consider in any analysis of the quality and kinds of interpretations made of the Opening Ceremony is the backgrounds and professional training of the narrators. In the Opening Ceremony commentaries of Barcelona'92 one can find the following categories of broadcast commentators:

- Famous television presenters, not specialized in sports

- Celebrity or well known sports announcers and reporters, often with previous Olympic participation or known for a broad range of work in the sports world

- Sports announcers and reporters without 'celebrity' or well known status

- Former athletes invited to comment on the ceremony

---

4 An excerpt of a 29 July 1992 editorial from *Utusan Malaysia* in Mohamed (1992).

- Intellectuals invited to comment on cultural and political aspects of the ceremony

As introduced in Chapter 5 and demonstrated above in the brief description of the Mediterranean Sea segment, the structure of the ceremonies is made up of different episodes and aspects which are inherently difficult for just one, and one type of, commentator to cover. Despite this reality, all broadcasters except for two in this study used sports commentators to narrate the Opening Ceremony. This choice is representative of how most broadcasters approach Olympics television. Also, with the exception of MBC (Korea) and CCTV (China), each with only one ceremony announcer, the international broadcasters used commentator teams of 2 to 5 persons, in a set up similar to sports event narration.

For several broadcasts, such as NBC (USA), RTV (Romania) and CCTV (China), the primary commentators were long time, highly regarded sports 'personalities' in those countries. By contrast, the Russian Ostankino 1 broadcast was criticized in the Russian press for not using top quality television commentators, but instead lesser known sports reporters. (Because of this Ostankino 1 re-broadcast the ceremony a few weeks later, on August 29th, less the athletes' parade, using a more 'qualified' cultural commentator.) Only in the Opening Ceremony broadcasts of Japan (NHK) and Brazil (TV Globo) were the commentators from other than the world of sports. NHK hired all purpose, celebrity television 'talento' primarily for ratings purposes. TV Globo also used reporters not specialized in sport.

It is fair to conclude, across all broadcasts who used them, that sports announcers have difficulty adequately explaining the more political aspects of the ceremonies (the athletes' parade), as well as the cultural representations (local folklore). To deal with this shortcoming, several broadcasters supplemented their sports commentary team with some 'knowledgeable interpreters' as with TF1's (France) use of writer Jean La Couture or Canal 13's (Mexico) use of newsman Javier Solorzano to comment on the political and cultural aspects related to Spain of the Opening Ceremony. Others changed commentators for different ceremony parts. Thus, for example, Egyptian (ERTU2) television changed the commentator of the first part of the Opening Ceremony for a new one at the beginning of the athletes' parade. Canal Olímpic of Catalonia used the same formula, substituting two general commentators (a man and a woman) for sports specialists. This choice can explain why this broadcast's commentaries during the parade of the nations consisted more of a sport dialogue full of trivial anecdotes than an appreciation of the geopolitical reality of 172 nations coming together in the stadium.

Another strategy was to have different commentators to represent different audience sectors. This was for the primary purpose of addressing multi-lingual audiences. For example, the SABC South African broadcast included three commentators representing the different language groups of English, Afrikaans and Xhosa. Similarly, two Cameroonian (CRTV) studio commentators switched between English and French.

Despite such attempts to offer more well rounded commentary, it was to be expected that most of the sports commentators used for the Opening Ceremony were more comfortable narrating with a sports 'style' that mostly consisted of a descriptive, fact-based, play-by-play type narrative of the events happening in the stadium, rather than engaging in more a mythical, anthropological journey into the meaning of cultural symbols. In surveying more generally across the international broadcasts, it was the Russian sports commentators who were most 'comfortable' with the meeting of sport and art which takes place in Olympic Opening and Closing Ceremonies. After a particularly abstract and theatrical segment of the Closing Ceremony ('The Fire of Celebration') meant to evoke sorcery, passion, imagination, energy, interaction and the origin of life bundled up into an abstract display of stars, planets, monsters and disorder through fire and dance the Russian commentator, clearly thrilled with the performance, said:

> Arts in the highest meaning of the word are present here, at the Closure. But they are directly linked with sports. In this synthesis of arts and sport lies the future of the Olympic Games. (Ostankino 1, Russia, Closing Ceremony).

By contrast, the Australian Channel 7 commentator made a brief and uncomfortable mention about the fusion of sport and art, but could find no other words with which to follow up. The Eurosport commentator had reached his limit. As the athletes spilled out onto the field after this performance (as was planned at that point in the Closing Ceremony), he chose to interpret this as a spontaneous event in revolt of too much symbolic 'art':

> Frankly, Simon, I think the athletes have got fed up. I personally think – it's a personal view – that it's all been a little bit staid and heavy and symbolic as we've been saying, and they've had enough, and they just want to be part of the show now ... It think it's all a wee bit solemn and pompous, and now the party's starting ... (Eurosport, UK, Closing Ceremony)

At moments such as these, the commentator role is not that of a participant, insider, or even observer of the event, but rather he or she serves as a sort of barrier to understanding by refusing attempts at narration altogether – and even, in a very few cases as above, disparaged those artistic elements of the ceremony. In fact, press commentaries from several of the countries in this study – Greece, Malaysia, Britain, Australia, Germany, Egypt, and others – readily suggested that some broadcast commentators acted as an hindrance to understanding and criticized the overall quality of the ceremony commentaries. Looked at another way, however, it should not come as a surprise that there would be limits to the interpretations of performance art in an event narrated largely by commentators hired for their sports expertise.

A comment about visual narratives

The aim of this section is not to deal with the visual narrativity or the television language in all its aspects, but rather to comment briefly on visual narratives in Olympic sports television. Not all Olympic programmes are 'sports programmes', but nevertheless, the production conditions of sports television are present in every aspect of Olympic programming, including the transmission of the ceremonies – which take place in a sports stadium. Clearly, the spectacular nature of the transmission of the ceremonies benefits from the state-of-the-art technology developed for sport (refer to Chapter 3 for a discussion of technology in the Games).

Spectators inside the stadium readily experience cameras interacting with ceremony actors and activities in the stadium. But to the viewing audience, these intercessions are largely transparent. Instead, television guides audience eyes beyond their natural capacity by employing a dazzling array of camera position and movement. Television virtually extends the human senses.

The mobility of the television view

One of the finest examples of the adaptations of camera technology to sports narrative has been in capturing the reality of movement. Sport is basically movement (jumping, running, throwing, rhythm, etc.). Television has also become addicted to movement so when objects do not move, move a little bit or move very slowly, then television becomes mobile, employing the many narrative resources at its disposal: close up, zoom in, or the distancing of images, zoom out, pans, the linking up of shots, etc.

In order to do this, producers have the most modern techniques at their disposal: from the most sophisticated optical lenses, to various forms of camera mobility, from light ENG cameras to helicopters and the most precise underwater cameras. Each one of these technological possibilities becomes a form of language, of narrative resources, in the hands of producers.

Thus, for example, the closing in on the image using the zoom in has major implications for the person viewing the event. The solemnity required for the swearing in of the athletes or the awarding of the medals calls for long, ponderous shots and the fade-out of images. Segments of the festive spectacle demand, in contrast, maximum variety, mobility of images and the short duration of shots. One study correspondent described this phenomenon well in terms of the 'Fires of Celebration' segment of the Closing Ceremony mentioned above:

> During the 'devil's reign' segment, the camera alternated between long shots and shots which seemed to be right in the middle of the action. The long shots showed the stadium from a distance – the camera sitting somewhere over and above the action. This might have been a point of view typical of any spectator in the stadium itself ... When this shot appeared on screen, the intensity of the moment – its drama and energy – simply dissipated; the segment became no more than several clusters of people in costume moving around an oval shaped field in time to music. The middle of the action shots, however, hummed with vibrancy, and were made to do so – the shots changed quickly, the camera jiggled and tilted, the angle of vision swerved from side to side. Here we were, right in the midst of the devil's power, participants close to the action.[5]

---

5   Langer (1992).

Visuals as narrative guide

Olympic television uses all the conventional modes of camera use – close ups, extreme close ups, medium, full, long, overhead, zooms, etc. Each play a semiotic role in the Olympic narrative. Thus, for example, 'close-ups' that frame a detail, the part of a whole: the face of the human body, a part of a musical instrument, some dancing feet are suitable for expressing of passionate messages such as dramatism and effort, as well as any detail that comes about during the development of the spectacle.

Close-ups, familiar to sports transmissions for athletes' expectations before a race begins, the image of happiness as the athlete wins the race, the sadness of defeat, effort in the race, the emotion in the awarding of the medals are also of great importance in the dramatization of the ceremony and in the consecration of the Olympic rituals (flags, flame, torch, etc.).

Extreme close-ups not only dramatize, but bring the television viewer into the event. Thus, for example, before Carl Lewis' last attempt in the long jump, RTO'92 offered, for 35 seconds, an extreme close-up of the famous American athlete's face on which his emotions, concentration and effort could be seen. The television viewer could not feel closer, not only to the event, but to the athlete's feelings.

Shots dedicated to capturing the presence of political authorities and dignitaries in the dignitaries' box are treated differently, in a less intimate manner. The extreme close-up is not used for this task. In its place is a range of medium shots which allow identification while at the same time keeping the distance demanded by protocol. In Barcelona'92, for example, the image of the King of Spain (Juan Carlos I) was interpreted on nearly every television station around the world as a popular and accessible image, far from formal, but all the same this image appeared in only a very few occasions in extreme close-up. Generally, his image was captured in a close to middle shot which, at least, left the tie and first button of his jacket visible. The camera closed in on the monarch's face when it attempted to capture his emotions and it drew away when it attempted to show his authority. The same rhetorical function could be discovered in the analysis of the images offered by RTO'92 of the president of the International Olympic Committee, Juan Antonio Samaranch, during his opening speech.

However, looking at Appendix C, which compares the RTO'92 international signal to the NBC (USA) unilateral version, one can see an example of how NBC constructed a slightly different narrative spin to the segment, one that made the King even more of the central, heroic and accessible protagonist, through the alteration of the visual narration that included more shots of the King and a smiling, rather than overly serious Monarch.

The extreme close-up is only used when an attempt is made to show a feeling reflected by an important person. For example, when the RTO'92 producer discovered Princess Elena (daughter of the King and Queen of Spain) crying during the parade of the Spanish delegation, he broke with protocol and closed in on her face with an extreme close-up. The producer was unable to find in the available images another more direct manner of transmitting emotion and identification with the event to the television viewers.

119

The medium shots also capture of the idea of unity or team spirit by focusing on parts of the scene or small groups of people. This is the case, for example, of the images in which a group of opera singers appeared in the ceremony, or of the players of a team lined up, or of athletes on the starting line on the athletics track. The medium close up is the most used shot in the athletes' parade during the Opening Ceremony. The television viewer's attention is directed towards the group of the best sports people in a delegation. The camera will draw forward into a close up or extreme close up when the 'big stars' are parading (Magic Johnson or Carl Lewis)

The full or long shot takes in large areas of the installations. It is used, for example, to show more than a quarter of the crowd in the major parts of the spectacle in the stadium, or of various delegations in the athletes' parade. For the ceremony this dramatizes its size and impressive coming together of so many people in cooperation. The best version of this, however, is the overhead. This involves an aerial shot which allows images to be captured of not only the stadium, including the stands and the playing field, but also the entire Olympic area, in the case of Barcelona, the whole of Montjuïc hill.

Thanks to these shots, producers enable television viewers to see and contextualize, from these heights, the images of the geographic site where the events are taking place, besides making out up to the smallest details in the extreme close-up. Thanks to these resources, the television viewer 'arrives' flying high above the site of the events and penetrates them right to the very limits of human perception.

These narrative forms can only be finally interpreted in their 'audio-visual' setting. The sound accompanies, and is adapted to, the differences in shots. The technical section of Chapter 4 reveals how the experience of the close-up forces the producers to establish a sound programme which works with the visual narrative.

The transformation of images

The rhetorical possibilities of television language are not limited to the mobility and selection of shots. There are also other forms of manipulation or transformation of the image and of the combination of the shots.

From among all the new resources of the electronic image, television sports language has exploited three of them to their utmost: the replay, slow motion and the multiplicity and mobility of the cameras within the sports arena.

These resources help to resolve one of the big problems of the 'perception' of sport: the ephemeral, rapid, even elusive nature of its culminating moments. The goal in soccer is a paradigmatic example of the contrast between the fleetingness of the event and its social importance. It is known that a goal can cause an entire nation to celebrate if it comes about in the last minute of an important match. Then the cameras are there to repeat it , or 'eternalize' it, to slow it down, to multiply the points of view in this magic and fleeting moment. In fact, soccer goals have ceased to be fleeting moments and are now visual objects which can be digitized. Television viewers can see the goal from a great variety of positions (sideview, frontal view, counterpoint), they can see it at different speeds and, finally, they can even add it to their library.

The example of the soccer goal could be applied to many other sports. In fact, each sport has its own conditions for television, and this is precisely what could make a determined sport see its popularity increase or decrease. The popularity of sports (their audience) depends on their ability to adapt to the new conditions of the television spectacle.

An interesting example of the beneficial influence of television in the popularity of a sport is the case of diving. Spectators of this sport have to keep their 'eyes well open' when the diver begins to dive. In hardly a few seconds the diver will have disappeared into the water in the swimming pool. On television, on the other hand, different shots and camera takes manage to achieve the maximum spectacle. Television allows us to see the diver preparing the dive, followed by the jump into the air and, without interruption, his movements within the swimming pool, making the view of the dive longer. Immediately afterwards we are able to see these images repeated, or new shots of the dive, from a side position, from top to bottom or vice versa, with the image slowed down or even frozen in the most improbable positions of the dive

The same process takes place in the transmission of an athletics race such as the 100 metres in which it is possible to see the athletes from both sides of the track, from a camera positioned above their heads, from a shot in which all the athletes can be seen together, or a shot in which an individual athlete's effort can be observed, in various repetitions and in slow motion.

Each one of the possibilities of the electronic image has other applications in other important aspects of modern sport, especially in the evaluation of the judges' decisions. The replay allows attention to be fixed on a punishable detail (offside) or a decision on who was really first over the line in a close race. The former photo finish has been replaced by a permanent capacity of slowing down, or even freezing, the images produced by new digital video equipment.

The replay has also arrived in the transmission of the rituals of the Olympic ceremonies. Thus, for example, RTO'92 used this technique to repeat the images of the archer firing the arrow to light the cauldron in the Barcelona Games.

The same thing took place in the Opening Ceremony of Lillehammer'94, this time to repeat the images of a ski jumper with the Olympic torch in his hand, before passing it on to the last relay participant.

New forms of seeing reality and sport

All these techniques shape new ways of seeing reality and, to be more specific, new ways of seeing sport. The spectators, accustomed to seeing sport by means of the many possibilities offered by television, and used to being television viewers, could find the live offering of the sport in the stadium to be insufficient.

The ultimate reason that will stimulate people to go to the stadium in person will not be an interest in 'seeing' the competition but rather the need to participate in the event, the shouts, the warmth of the people, the sandwiches, the company, going to and coming back from the stadium, etc. These reasons will be the real stimuli that will lead to people giving up their privileged position as television viewers in order to become spectators.

Even so, it will become more frequent to see spectators depending on the audiovisual media to follow the spectacle in the stadium. This is already taking place with the use of radios as a complement for information on what is been observed. In Seoul'88 portable television sets were provided as an experiment to follow the events. In the athletic events in the Montjuïc stadium spectators were often to be seen turning their heads around to watch the replays of the events on the stadium's giant screens. Seating was priced not just according to the direct vision of the events but also according to the possibilities of seeing these giant screens. However, the spectators were not the only people to make use of the images on the stadium's giant screen: the athletes themselves looked for the verification of the results or an explanation of a defeat immediately after taking part in an event. The screen contained the reason for their joy or their disappointment.

It is therefore not surprising that in the future spectators will demand, in a more and more insistent manner, the presence of these images in the stadium. Spectators will not want to give up being 'television viewers'. In the same way as the television viewers, thanks to sound and image techniques, they have begun to feel the most privileged of the 'spectators'.

The modern Olympic ceremonies are therefore the result of the coming together of various factors all linked to narrative outcomes. There is the structural 'setting' or flow of the event related to camera editing, advertising breaks and amount and timing of commentary. There is also the ceremonies' script designed to influence narrative choices made by broadcasters. Finally, there are the commentators' multiple communicative and cultural filters, conditioned by their level of preparation and their respective political, cultural and historical contexts which come to bear on their presentation of ceremony narration.

7   Television and Olympic Community

I s there really an Olympic family? This chapter attempts to identify the nature and bounds of shared Olympic meanings as evidenced in the international broadcasts of the Olympic Opening Ceremony. This is approached by conceptualizing what is required to sustain a community. Common definitions suggest that a community – whether of individuals, cultures, or nations – exhibits the following characteristics:

- shared meanings for central symbols and rituals;

- commonly expressed values which guide behaviour within the bounds of the community;

- a collective memory that includes a common repertoire of personages, institutions and events;

- discourse that links to shared myths and beliefs.[1]

As Smith notes, 'human beings retain a multiplicity of allegiances in the contemporary world', suggesting that communities may share members, but each community can be distinguished by variables such as time, size, range, focus and level which, in turn, define the source and character of its key symbols, rituals, history, institutions, and so forth.[2] MacAloon suggests that as the presentative aspects of a 'transnational, Olympic, "human community"' the symbols of Olympism can easily co-exist with national symbols within the context of the Games because of their seemingly 'non-ideological', but in fact broadly humanist ideology. Referring specifically to performance rituals unique to the Olympic Games (such as the awarding of medals or the raising of the Olympic flag), he says that: 'symbols of the Olympic community are positioned hierarchically over and above the symbols of the nation-states, but without contravening them'.[3] In this way, these two

---

1   See, for example, Smith (1992: 21) or Schlesinger, Philip (1991:300).

2   *Ibid.* Smith (1992).

3   MacAloon (1984).

distinct types of communities are theoretically able to share the same physical and psychological space for members common to both during the Olympic ceremonies.

The 'Olympic Charter' provides the foundation and encouragement for the development of an Olympic community through its articulation of the goals of the Olympic movement. By carefully regulating the use and occurrence of Olympic symbols and rituals the IOC guarantees their repetition over time, as well as attempts to hold their meaning constant. Both the IOC and Olympic host have a vested interest in maintaining the integrity and value of Olympic symbols, such as the five interlocking rings, both as condensational symbols evoking a broader Olympic movement, as well as to sustain their appeal for corporate sponsors so critical to the financing of the Games.

However, as with all aspects of the Olympic ceremonials and events, once these symbolic images transmit to the international broadcast centre (IBC) any control by the International Olympic Committee (IOC) or host city organizers over how they are presented is lost. Therefore, Olympic broadcasters necessarily play a primary role (for better or worse) as oral and visual historians and interpreters of Olympism for each new generation of Olympic viewers. In that sense, this analysis doesn't just assume audience understanding of modern Olympism as defined by the IOC, but instead looks for explicit efforts by broadcasters to bring attention to and explain the Olympics beyond simple identification of its symbols and rituals. It looks at the role of television in the 'socialization' process for an Olympic community.

This is not an easy task for television. Anecdotes abound as to the ability of the Games atmosphere to inspire its participants; athletes, organizers, volunteers and visitors may reaffirm their belief in the existence of a transnational Olympic family based on the overwhelming sensation of 'being there'.[4] Media audiences, of course, miss the same kind of full sensory involvement. So, in order to play a significant role in the development of an Olympic community, television needs not only to legitimize the institutional structure which perpetuates it (IOC, NOCs, International Sports Federations, etc.) and pass along a sense of shared heritage (of symbols, myths, heroes), but also must allow audiences to experience the Olympic ceremonials as more than a spectacle. It must offer audiences some sense of participating in a community ritual. This is a tall order for a small box.[5]

The architecture of Olympic community

Attention to Olympism

In order to explore the role of broadcasters as patrons of an Olympic community, 'Olympic' commentary topics were distinguished from those related more directly to

---

4   In particular, refer to MacAloon's (*ibid.*) discussions about the festival aspects of the Olympic Games.

5   As MacAloon suggests, spectacle involves both choice and a separation of performer and spectator. These are requisite for television entertainment, but do nothing for the maintainance of community. Ritual, however, implies behaviours which are participatory and obligatory, and as such, encourages an emotional commitment to its purpose (*ibid.*).

nations (see Chapter 8) or the host city (see Chapter 9) and included discussion or mention in the broadcasts of: (1) Olympic and sport values; (2) Olympic symbols and rituals; (3) past Olympic feats, facts, or locations; (4) Olympic-related emotions or feelings; (5) Olympic personalities (non-sport) and institutions; and (6) discourse about general Olympic topics (e.g. professionalism, commercialism, politics in the Games). Refer to Appendix A for a full list of topic categories.

Figure 7.1 ranks 24 broadcasts by the percentage of the ceremony commentary spent on Olympics topics. These data are most useful in a comparative sense because the official structure of the Opening Ceremony (as described in Chapter 5) tends to guide the balance of commentary (e.g. the length of the athletes' parade encourages a disproportionate amount of discussion about nations).[6] While the total volume of commentary varies significantly across broadcasts, this percentage figure offers some measure of the relative importance placed on topics identified above as fundamental to the existence of an Olympic community. Results range from a high of 30 per cent of the broadcast commentary devoted to Olympic topics for Indonesia's TVRI to a low of 4 per cent of the commentary for the Cuban broadcast. Figure 7.2 shows the same data but by absolute frequency of comments. Commentator attention to Olympics topics ranged from 25 distinct comments in the Cuban broadcast up to 187 for Canal Olìmpic of Spain. These measures should not be construed to say that the Indonesian broadcaster, for example, is the most devoted disciple of Olympism. In the particular case of TVRI, the commentators were clearly impressed with the logistic feat of hosting the Games, and as such, spent much time discussing different venues, costs and unique features of the Games environment. That said, this type of commentary does pass along 'community' knowledge, but its specific value in terms of encouraging Olympism as a shared experience is certainly unknown.

Olympic values: a very few, broadly expressed

The first section of the 'Olympic Charter' outlines the 'fundamental principles' of Olympism as defined by the IOC as leader of the Olympic movement.[7] These principles represent the clearest official articulation of the values and goals of modern Olympism. Drawing directly from the IOC text these include the humanistic values of friendship, international solidarity, peace, equality and the preservation of human dignity, as well as values related more to sport: equal participation, excellence, joy in effort, friendly competition, fair play and the balanced development of body, will and mind through the blending of sport with culture and education.[8]

The most prominent Olympic value found across the international broadcasters in this

---

6   Olympic rituals comprised 19% (or 36 minutes, 10 seconds) of time in the official ceremony. Refer back to Figure 6.1 for a structural (time spent) overview of the ceremony parts. Related is Table 8.1 which shows the amount of commentary spent on Olympic-related topics as compared to other topics by each broadcaster.

7   International Olympic Committee (1992: 10-11).

8   *Ibid.*

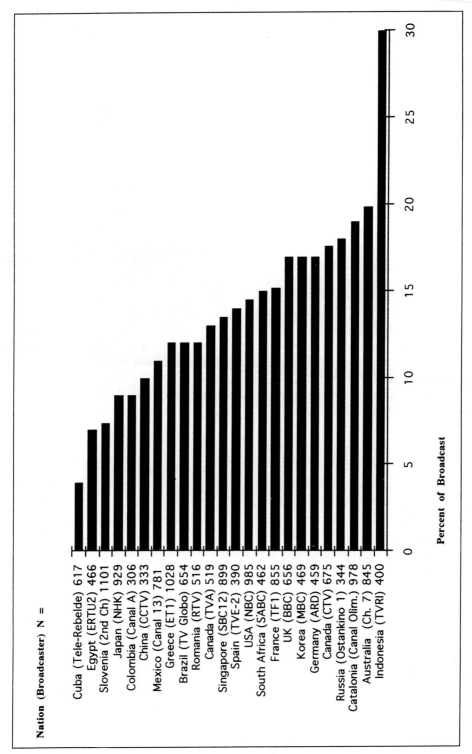

Nation (Broadcaster) N =

Cuba (Tele-Rebelde) 617
Egypt (ERTU2) 466
Slovenia (2nd Ch) 1101
Japan (NHK) 929
Colombia (Canal A) 306
China (CCTV) 333
Mexico (Canal 13) 781
Greece (ET1) 1028
Brazil (TV Globo) 654
Romania (RTV) 516
Canada (TVA) 519
Singapore (SBC12) 899
Spain (TVE-2) 390
USA (NBC) 985
South Africa (SABC) 462
France (TF1) 855
UK (BBC) 656
Korea (MBC) 469
Germany (ARD) 459
Canada (CTV) 675
Russia (Ostankino 1) 344
Catalonia (Canal Olim.) 978
Australia (Ch. 7) 845
Indonesia (TVRI) 400

Percent of Broadcast

Figure 7.1. Olympics-related topics as a percentage of broadcast commentary

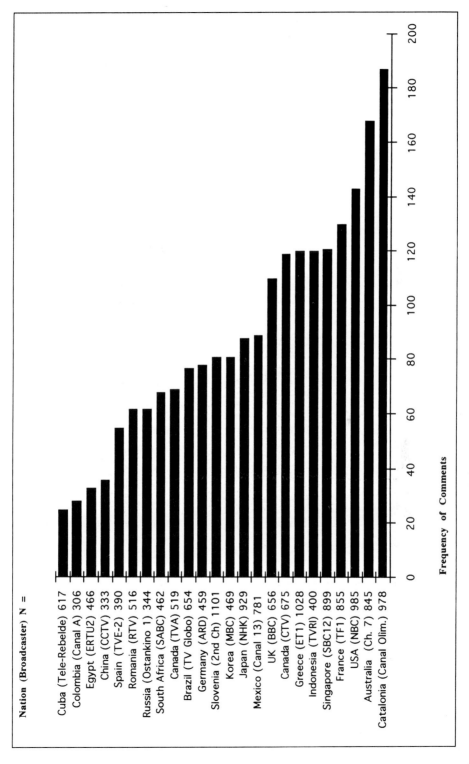

Figure 7.2. Olympics-related topics frequency by broadcaster

Frequency of Comments

Nation (Broadcaster) N =

Cuba (Tele-Rebelde) 617
Colombia (Canal A) 306
Egypt (ERTU2) 466
China (CCTV) 333
Spain (TVE-2) 390
Romania (RTV) 516
Russia (Ostankino 1) 344
South Africa (SABC) 462
Canada (TVA) 519
Brazil (TV Globo) 654
Germany (ARD) 459
Slovenia (2nd Ch) 1101
Korea (MBC) 469
Japan (NHK) 929
Mexico (Canal 13) 781
UK (BBC) 656
Canada (CTV) 675
Greece (ET1) 1028
Indonesia (TVRI) 400
Singapore (SBC12) 899
France (TF1) 855
USA (NBC) 985
Australia (Ch. 7) 845
Catalonia (Canal Olim.) 978

study, however, is not explicitly referenced in the fundamental principles of the 'Olympic Charter'. Rather, it is simply the act of showing up. Every international broadcaster identified participation as a value central to the Olympic movement. Besides virtual unanimity across broadcasters on its importance, 'participation' was also the most frequently cited value overall. Further, it is clear that the meaning of participation related much more directly to nations than to the hard-fought efforts made by individual athletes to compete in the Games.

Table 7.1. Most frequently mentioned Olympic values

Nation (broadcaster)	Most frequently mentioned value	Second most frequently mentioned value
Australia (Channel 7)	peace	participation
Brazil (TV Globo)	peace	friendship
Canada (CTV)	peace	participation
Canada (TVA)	participation	no other value reference
China (CCTV)	friendship, peace	meeting place
Colombia (Canal A)	participation	peace
Cuba (Tele-Rebelde)	participation	peace
Egypt (ERTU2)	participation	youth
France (TF1)	participation	meeting place
Germany (ARD)	participation	friendship/peace (tie)
Greece (ET1)	participation	friendship
Indonesia (TVRI)	participation	peace
Japan (NHK)	friendship	no other value reference
Korea (MBC)	peace	international cooperation
Mexico (CANAL 13)	peace	friendship
Romania (RTV)	peace	international cooperation
Russia (Ostankino 1)	participation	one mention all others
South Africa (SABC)	peace	friendship
Singapore (SBC 12)	participation	excellence
Slovenia (2nd Channel)	participation	peace
Catalonia (Canal Olìmpic)	participation	culture and education
Spain (TVE–2)	participation	peace
United Kingdom (BBC)	participation	friendship
USA (NBC)	friendship	meeting place

The mention of participation was closely followed by 'peace' and 'friendship'. Table 7.1, which shows the two most frequently mentioned Olympic values for each broadcaster, reveals the monopoly this triad of ideals – participation, peace and friendship – has on broadcaster interpretation of the Games. Next in both breadth (mention across all broadcasters) and frequency was a set of closely aligned sentiments: 'international cooperation' and the Olympics as a 'meeting place' for athletes from around the world. For example, commentators labeled the Olympics variously as the 'celebration that unites all humanity' (Ostankino 1, Russia, Opening Ceremony), 'the friendship Games' (Channel 7, Australia, Opening Ceremony); a 'global family festival' (MBC, Korea, Opening Ceremony) or 'a celebration of unity' (CTV, Canada, Opening Ceremony).

Table 7.1 displays a broad consensus that the Olympic Games are perceived as an important meeting of nations and people meant to promote the values of peace, international cooperation and friendship. In terms of overall frequency, 12 of the broadcasts reference Olympic values in a range of 10–20 times during the Opening Ceremony. However, considering that this represents only 1 per cent to 3 per cent of those broadcasters' total verbal commentaries, it does not speak well to the role of television broadcasters as attentive teachers of the philosophies or values of Olympism. The commentators of TVA of Canada, for example, never mention any Olympic or sport values directly except for a single reference to the number of nations participating in the Barcelona Games. It should be acknowledged, however, that simply the visual impact of the international athletes in the stadium may evoke sentiments in an audience related to equality, internationalism, youth and other ideals – as anyone who has experienced emotional shivers or tears watching an Opening Ceremony would attest.

It should also be said that while values of peace, participation and cooperation may certainly be more or less 'etic' or universal in their meaning across these broadcasting nations, other ideas associated with Olympism – equality, moral principle, human dignity – most likely translate or express themselves quite differently in various cultures. For example, according to Zassoursky, 'ism' words such as internationalism or Olympism, don't sit well with many Russians tired of 'isms' in their lives. Thus, these terms are avoided by commentators.[9] Louw suggested that South African commentary about internationalism implied more of a sense of 'relief [by South Africa] at being once again part of the international community'.[10] To Slovenian audiences, participation meant recognition and legitimacy for this new political entity by an international community – and as such became a central focus of the ceremony narrative. According to Splichal, 'This is ... the main reason that all other values and issues which normally pertain to such sports events were not present and discussed, at least not in the Opening Ceremony'.[11]

Only a relatively few broadcasters, such as Russia's Ostankino 1 and Korea's MBC, even attempt to cover the breadth of fundamental principles of the Olympics as outlined in the 'Olympic Charter'. Here is one impressive attempt at summarizing Olympic values by the Korean broadcaster:

---

9   Zassoursky *et al.* (1992).

10 Louw (1992).

11 Splichal *et al.* (1992).

[The Olympics,] a festival for all mankind, regardless their difference of race, custom and culture. For the sake of establishing a world peace and a beautiful global village, they together will become good neighbours, friends and families ... Sports, which is inseparable from human history, is a challenge and a testing ground for the human ability to run faster, to jump farther and high, as the slogan of 'in a healthy body lives a sound spirit' implies (MBC, Opening Ceremony)

Other broadcasters, like China's CCTV, bundle more nationally relevant concepts with Olympism to put a slightly different spin on the Olympic movement: 'the Olympic Games symbolizes peace, friendship, progress and civilization' (CCTV, Opening Ceremony). This and subsequent Chinese commentary presents the Olympic Games as an emblem of progress.[12]

To participate is grand ... to win is divine

Sport values did not express themselves with nearly the same breadth as the more universal ideals of peace and participation. There were some shared mentions of friendly competition, fair play and sport as a common or universal language.[13] About half of the broadcasts mention at least one of those three ideas. The broadcasts from Russia, Brazil, France and Cuba suggested Olympic sport as the exaltation of youth. Commentators from France, Romania, Korea, South Africa and the USA brought up the idea of joy as derived from athletic effort. The Olympic motto – *Citius, Altius, Fortius* – was noted in some form by several commentators. The Egyptian (ERTU2) and Canadian (TVA) broadcasts stood alone without any reference to sport values as outlined in the 'Olympic Charter'.

Instead, the most common sports value association had to do with competition, team rivalries and – of little surprise – winning. As Holaday and Peck wrote about the broadcast of SBC 12 of Singapore, 'Winning was what the Olympics was made to appear all about'.[14] This was expressed, across all broadcasters in this study, through the consistent reporting of medal counts, past gold medalists and potential medal contenders. Langer noted the prevalence of commentary phrases such as, 'winning gold', 'take home gold', 'looking for more this year' and 'here to win' in the Australian Channel 7 commentary.[15] Rather than being unique to western, competitive and capitalist nations this is a shared phenomenon spanning the cultural globe of broadcasters. It is also encouraged by the vast amounts of information about records, medals and competitions made available to broadcasters by Games organizers for use during the ceremony broadcast.

---

12 Brownell (1993) notes that slogans such as 'Peace, Friendship, Progress' are commonly evoked in the Chinese sportsworld.

13 Sport values, even more so than the aforementioned values are subject to varied cultural expression. See, for example, Brownell's chapter on varying interpretations of 'Face' and 'Fair Play' in Brownell (1995).

14 Holaday and Peck (1992). It was common to receive comments about broadcaster focus on winning from the study correspondents.

15 Langer (1992).

Table 7.2. Attention to Olympic symbols, rituals, institutions, personages (frequency of mention)

Nation (broadcaster)	Reference to Olympic symbols and rituals	Reference to Olympic institutions, personages	Total references
China (CCTV)	4	4	8
Cuba (Tele-Rebelde)	4	4	8
Egypt (ERTU2)	8	1	9
Australia (Channel 7)	7	10	17
Brazil (TV Globo)	6	11	17
Romania (RTV)	10	7	17
United Kingdom (BBC)	13	8	21
South Africa (SABC)	13	10	23
Colombia (Canal A)	14	10	24
Russia (Ostankino 1)	17	8	25
Canada (TVA)	10	16	26
Spain (TVE–2)	18	9	27
Japan (NHK)	21	7	28
Germany (ARD)	6	23	29
Mexico (Canal 13)	13	16	29
Korea (MBC)	15	18	33
Slovenia (2nd Channel)	18	17	35
Canada (CTV)	25	14	39
Singapore (SBC 12)	21	19	40
France (TF1)	31	17	48
Greece (ET1)	25	31	56
Catalonia (Canal Olìmpic)	36	24	60
United States (NBC)	37	24	60
Indonesia (TVRI)	43	4	67

Olympic symbols as commentator prompts

For broadcasters, Olympic symbols in the stadium function much like cue cards where commentators are prompted, then only read what's on the card. In other words, the timing of mention of Olympic rings, flag, music, or torch correlate directly to their visual presence on the television screen. However, there is little to no explanation of the meaning or history of the symbols.[16] Table 7.2 summarizes the frequency of mentions of Olympic symbols

---

16 There were some curious interpretations of the five-ring Olympic logo, as when Canal Olímpic of Spain said that the rings represented the five senses (rather than the continents). Most broadcasts did not offer any explanation.

and rituals (flag, torch, oaths, speeches, etc.), then personalities and institutions (IOC, President Samaranch, NOCs, etc.) by broadcaster. These are rank ordered by total attention to these symbols of Olympic community. Again, this should not be interpreted to mean that the US broadcaster, for example, represents one of the most devoted Olympic nations. Instead, this table may reveal how much 'guidance' or narration of the ceremony elements broadcasters felt necessary to provide to their viewers. This might relate as much to local broadcasting and cultural norms as to interest in promoting Olympic symbolism. Still, it does represent relative levels of awareness on the part of broadcasters of the Olympic symbols as having a meaningful presence in the Opening Ceremony – enough so to be identified when they appear 'on stage'.

These data also do not get at *how* the symbols are presented. Olympic symbols were consistently introduced with a sense of import and dramatic flair in commentator tone at key moments of a ritual act, as exemplified in the following passage on Romanian television emotionally delivered when the torch entered the stadium:

> The Olympic torch, the symbol of eternal Olympic energy, the symbol or life and the purity of the Olympic Ideal.
> (Romanian TV, Opening Ceremony)

The importance of this kind of reverent tone could be argued to surpass any relative frequency counts as the commentators demonstrate their own emotional association with an imagined Olympic community and, as such, encourage viewers to become involved in the steps of a ceremonial sequence.

Not surprisingly, the primary institutional references across all commentaries were to the IOC and its president Juan Antonio Samaranch. References to Samaranch were clearly prompted by the 20 camera shots of him sitting in the tribunal which appeared as part of the international signal. References to Baron Pierre de Coubertin as founder of the modern Games came up fewer times – and most often as part of the text of Samaranch's speech, not by broadcaster initiative.

Olympic rituals

The 'Olympic Charter' specifies exactly when and how all the ritual acts within the ceremony will take place. These regulations for organizing committees remain virtually unchanged since the 1936 Berlin Games. Yet, broadcasters are not bound by the same requirements as the host organizer which explains why 10 broadcasts missed some parts of the Olympic rituals for commercial or other breaks.[17] Canada's TVA fully eliminates an official ritual; it skips the oaths (taken by representatives of the athletes and sports judges) due to a commercial break. NBC (USA) shaves time off of every ritual act, except the entrance of the torch, in order to depart for commercial breaks, bringing NBC's overall

---

17 The broadcasts of Australia, Canada (TVA and CTV), Eurosport, Indonesia, Malaysia, Colombia, USA, South Africa, and Catalonia (Canal Olìmpic) all miss parts of Olympic rituals. In the case of Catalonia, however, the time missed is only 40 seconds. A more complete discussion of these types of structural changes made by broadcasters was found in Chapter 5.

attention to Olympic rituals down from the official 19 per cent of the ceremony to only 7 per cent of its broadcast. Significantly, no broadcast misses the two ritual highlights of the ceremony: the entrance of the torch or the raising of the Olympic flag.

Even so, the ability of broadcasters to reposition the prominence of Olympic rituals, both verbally and visually, raises important questions about the lack of control the IOC holds over these 'sacred' moments beyond the reach of the live stadium act. Further, the juxtaposition of these moments of high solemnity with commercial messages raises questions about the impact of commercial blurring on the meaning of these acts.

Commentator roles

Easily the most dramatic moment of the Barcelona Opening Ceremony (and typically of any Opening Ceremony) is the entrance of the torch and lighting of the Olympic flame. Broadcast commentaries present this as the climax of the ceremony. Viewers are cued in from the start of this segment, through excited commentary tone, that this is a most important moment of the ceremony. Important to the idea of a Olympic community is the shared understanding of the basic steps of this ritual act (the torch enters, circles stadium, then the cauldron is lit) by all who narrate, and hopefully view, it. However, it is a surprise as to who will carry the torch in and around the stadium and *can* be a surprise for viewers just how the cauldron will be set aflame.

As with all the ceremony parts, the broadcast media are in a privileged role in narrating this ritual. In the case of Barcelona, the torch bearers' identities were a surprise until moments before their entrance, but all media were privy to the fact that an archer would light the Olympic cauldron with an arrow. Interestingly, this segment is an example of how broadcasters tend to position themselves either as 'observers', 'participants', or 'insiders' (see discussion in Chapter 6) during the ceremony as a whole. The observer role is reactive, letting visual images take the lead in narration. Other broadcasters, because of the desire to appear authoritative, competitive pressures to heighten anticipation, or simply an inability to keep a secret preferred to exploit this privileged knowledge, as insiders, by telling audiences about the archer before the segment unfolded. In fact, Eurosport commentators 'spoiled the drama of the moment' by letting viewers know far in advance how the Olympic flame would be lit.[18] Still other commentators attempted to enter the ritual as surrogate participants on behalf of audience by trying to convey the emotional aspects of the moment ('I can't really express how excited I am for being here in the Montjuïc Olympic Stadium ... and even more now as you are going to see why' – ET1, Greece, Opening Ceremony).

It is also during the torch entrance where television commentary seemed most lacking in its attempt to link television audiences to some shared meaning for the ritual. While it's tempting to say that 'words can't describe' such dramatic moments, few commentaries fall to silence. In fact, they range significantly in their comments during this ritual segment. Possibly because of the familiarity of the ritual steps, most broadcasters choose to ignore

---

18 Izod *et al.* (1992).

the media script provided to them and simply describe what is happening on screen. As a sample of the diversity of the commentary for Greek commentators the moment was national:[19]

> Ladies and gentlemen, take your seats ... you are going to watch the Olympic flag entering the stadium. This is the hour of Greece and of the ideals this country stands for. (...) We will stop talking now so that you can hear her sing. But we are so proud for being Greeks. If you could only see what's going on inside the Montjuïc Olympic Stadium. If you could only see. The festivities are an ode to Hellenism, to our ideals, the ideals of our country, Greece. (ET1, Greece, Opening Ceremony)

For US commentators it was one more chance to talk about the US basketball 'Dream Team'. About the same time Greek audiences heard the aforementioned quote, US audiences learned the identity of the torch bearers, then heard:

> E: This has been a highly kept secret. Menéndez, a surprise selection for the first half of the trip, and even the archer who will light the flame with his arrow, not announced until just minutes ago [note insider role]. The lights, blue and yellow, signifying the EC. Blue flag with the twelve golden stars.[20] And now, Menéndez to Epi, the basketball hero, and a dream trip for him. The 'Larry Bird' of Spanish basketball.
>
> C: Look at Magic [Johnson of the US 'Dream Team' basketba ll team]. 'Hey Epi', he calls out to him. 'Maybe we'll see you down the road, on the court.' (NBC, USA, Opening Ceremony)

However, Korean audiences heard the torch described as:

> ... a symbol of liberty, equality and peace. Praying for a happiness and a welfare of mankind, the torch will burn forever in order to save people from darkness and to deliver them to the bright future. (MBC, Korea, Opening Ceremony)

Egyptian audiences received a detailed explanation of the torch as a symbol of the ancient Greek Games, a description of its travels from Greece to Spain, and the meaning of the torch in the modern Games. Then, falling silent, Egyptians commentators allowed the

---

19 The ET1 Greek broadcast is somewhat unique in its focus on the ancient Greek Olympics and corresponding sense of ownership and pride embedded in the commentary concerning the modern Olympics.

20 This comment brings up a particularly interesting circumstance. What occured at this moment in the ceremony was the accidental insertion of images of the European Community within an Olympic ritual. The blue and yellow EC light sticks, in seat kits for all stadium spectators, were planned as part of the ceremony script to be lit by spectators later during the cultural component of the ceremony. Instead, participants reached for their light sticks the first time the lights went out in the stadium – during the entrance of the torch. So, rather than the torch being the only light in the stadium as planned by ceremony designers, it was surrounded by thousands of lights in what turned out to be a magical moment as spectators actually joined in the ritual. Some broadcasters, like NBC (USA), allowed the EC its premature appearance by mentioning the European Community as represented by the lights. Others merely commented on the lights without explanation.

viewers to be surprised at the novelty of the archer lighting the torch, later confirming its uniqueness as an Opening Ceremony feat.

The creation of global meaning

As noted, it may be the perceived familiarity of the torch ritual (and the fact that it highlights specific athletes, drawing the attention of more individualistic oriented broadcasters) which allows broadcasters to narrate the segment in a more impromptu, and thus varied, fashion without reliance on any host-provided scripts. By contrast, it was a new and never before seen Olympic ritual, the unfurling of a giant Olympic flag over top of all the athletes gathered in the centre of the stadium, that inspired the most universally shared interpretation of any Opening Ceremony part and seemed to evoke a shared essence of Olympic community. The symbolism of the flag easily conjured up common interpretations of unity and friendship across all international broadcasters. For example:

> What a beautiful idea. United under one flag (TF1, France, Opening Ceremony)

> This has a very profound meaning that they are united under the Olympics, under the spirit of the Olympics (TVRI, Indonesia, Opening Ceremony)

> The Olympic flag is wrapping the heads of athletes. They are promising each other to march together for the future. (MBC, Korea, Opening Ceremony)

> Look, isn't that symbolic: the whole Olympic Family is covered under the huge Olympic flag ... We could say that all the Olympians and perhaps all the people who are devoted to Olympism, are gathered under the same roof. (Ostankino 1, Russia, Opening Ceremony)

> Let this unfolding of the Olympic flag be a symbol of the Olympics, peace, friendship, love. (2nd Channel, Slovenia, Opening Ceremony)

> The flag is the symbol of friendship between countries and of peace ... A flag which embraces and covers all the athletes and binds them in the spirit of the Games. (SABC, South Africa, Opening Ceremony)

> As it's unfurled, it's passed over the heads of the athletes and they're invited to make it come alive in their hands. Those famous interlaced rings of blue, yellow, green and red on a white background representing the union of the five continents, the joining together of people from all over the world. This giant Olympic flag has bound the Olympic family together as never before. (BBC, United Kingdom, Opening Ceremony)

Olympic history

Discussing the elements of community, Anthony Smith once said that a memory-less society creates no community.[21] The Olympic Games themselves constitute a specialized history that includes stories of its origins in ancient Greece, long forgotten lists of winners

---

21 Smith (1992).

and statistics, as well as oft-repeated modern Olympics stories about world record performances, come-from-behind victories, violent tragedy, boycotts, and more. Table 7.3 summarizes the frequency of references made by commentators about past Olympic athletes, teams, records, events, performances and participation.[22]

Broadcasters did demonstrate the existence of a significant, shared Olympic memory through references to common historical events (e.g. the Munich tragedy), Olympic eras (e.g. Cold War boycotts) and athlete scandals and triumphs (e.g. Ben Johnson, Jesse Owens). Nearly every broadcaster placed the Games origins in Greece. It is in the amount of attention to Olympic history that broadcasters diverge with those who represent nations with long Olympic participation histories and/or a fascination with Olympic sport trivia, tending to rank higher on attention to Olympic history (e.g. Australia, USA, Canada, United Kingdom, Japan), as well recalling Olympic stories particular to the broadcast nation. For example, for the Korean broadcaster virtually all 'historical' references related to the 1988 Seoul Games.

Table 7.3. References to Olympic history

Nation (broadcaster)	Total	Nation (broadcaster)	Total
Australia (Channel 7)	264	Japan (NHK)	139
Brazil (TV Globo)	47	Korea (MBC)	62
Canada (CTV)	107	Mexico (Canal 13)	27
Canada (TVA)	107	Romania (RTV)	49
China (CCTV)	10	Russia (Ostankino 1)	61
Colombia (Canal A)	27	South Africa (SABC)	54
Cuba (Tele-Rebelde)	19	Singapore (SBC 12)	191
Egypt (ERTU2)	24	Slovenia (2nd Channel)	218
France (TF1)	71	Catalonia (Canal Olìmpic)	92
Germany (ARD)	42	Spain (TVE–2)	31
Greece (ET1)	29	United Kingdom (BBC)	127
Indonesia (TVRI)	47	United States (NBC)	132

Olympic discourse

Olympic discourse is defined as debate or discussion which links to normative beliefs about the Olympic movement. Most commonly, Olympic discourse relates to commentary about trends or behaviors (of athletes, nations, hosts, officials, etc.) which exemplify or violate such beliefs. For example, beliefs regarding fairness in sports behavior or non-commercial intervention might spur commentator mention of drug use in the Olympics or the role of commercial sponsorship in financing of the Games. One long-running example of Olympic discourse would be the debate over the retention of amateurism in the Games.

---

22 It should be noted that, in addition to the giant flag segment just mentioned, the Barcelona host organizers introduced a new ritual segment whereby flags representing each of the prior Olympiads entered the stadium (flags with Picasso's dove of peace ran in place on the war years without a Games). This segment prompted, by its nature, commentary about past Olympics which might not have occurred otherwise.

Another common area of discourse would be the evaluation of the host city in its ability to stage the Games. This type of dialogue reveals a sense of shared 'community' standards against which to evaluate each host (related to security, transportation, quality of sports venues, etc.)

All in all, there is very little negative discourse to be found in any of the broadcasts of the Opening Ceremony. The most common type of discourse overall was the positive assessment of Barcelona's efforts to host the Games. Beyond this, the primary areas of discourse among broadcast commentators related to money and conflict.

Money as discourse

Brought up by just over half of the broadcasts, commercial and financial-related issues provided a natural area of discourse given current trends of financing the Games through commercial sponsorship programmes and broadcast rights (see Chapter 2). With most commercial broadcasters inextricably linked with this trend it is not surprising to find that the discussion of increased commercial presence in the Games seemed mostly reflective of a general interest in the economics, planning and financing of the Games rather than blatant disapproval of such trends.

Some commentators, such as TVRI from Indonesia and Romanian TV, did report the seemingly high costs of tickets, structures, hotels and taxis, associated with the Barcelona Games. Also, there was an undercurrent of cynicism displayed by a few broadcasters concerning the relationships among the Olympics, athlete performance and money. For example, German ARD, British BBC and Greek ET1 commentators suggested that the increasing size of the Games might be forcing undesirable levels of commercialization into and around the Olympic movement.

> YT: We have to say that the Olympic Games ... are not for romantics. This hosting country is now profiting from the huge investments made by the sponsors and from television. The truth, however, is that 90 per cent of this money goes back to the Olympic committees.

> YS: And we should consider the fact ... that the Olympic Games are growing bigger by the years. Naturally therefore, the money to cover the Olympic expenses have to come from somewhere. And it is better being done this way than having the citizens of the hosting country pay them in the form of taxes (ET1, Greece, Opening Ceremony)

A little more bluntly, as was characteristic of this broadcast, the Eurosport commentator offered the following pronouncement upon the entrance of professional tennis player Stephen Edberg as flagbearer for Sweden: 'I think that symbolizes the change in the Games – a millionaire carrying the flag.' Over a third of the broadcasters mentioned professionalism in the Games. Or perhaps more biting is this comment by the Brazilian commentator:

> Now the motto of the Games might be that the important thing is to participate, to take part rather than to win. But the truth is that people know that victory goes

to the richest countries, to those that invest the most ... (TV Globo, Brazil, Opening Ceremony)

These sentiments shared across several broadcasters do reveal an underlying Olympic discourse that says despite the purity of purpose, the influence of money continues to make its mark on the Olympic Games.[23]

Olympic truce

In ancient Greece, Olympic participants were asked to lay down all weapons for the duration of the Games in an Olympic Truce. For Barcelona 1992, this was no exception. The IOC, with participating countries as signatories, formally asked the peoples of the world (notably in Bosnia-Herzegovina at that time) to stop all fighting during the period of the Barcelona Games – to little other than symbolic effect. In probably an Olympic first, the head of COOB'92 and mayor of Barcelona, Pasqual Maragall, incorporated into his speech a plea by the United Nations for a truce in the former Yugoslavia. In response and perhaps to underscore the pursuit of peace as an important Olympic value, at least half of the broadcasters made mention of the sadness of conflict raging in other parts of the world during the Olympic Games, exemplified by the comment of the Greek ET1 commentator when 1500 doves were released in the stadium. He said, '... they represent peace; peace which we all need'. This act provoked a nearly identical comment on the part of the Slovenian (2nd Channel) commentator. He said: 'Peace and friendship through the world is symbolized with 1500 doves released from the stadium. In the old Greece, during the Olympic Games all the wars came to a stop. Unfortunately, today's reality does not follow the old Greek habit.'

Breaking the rules

There was virtually no discourse critical of the 'system' of Olympism and Games structures beyond concern for costs and size. The structures and institutions associated with the Games were clearly supported, and thus legitimized, in the television presentations. Instead, what little negative commentary there was to be found during the Opening Ceremony was reserved for individual athlete behavior that seemed to deviate from some Olympic norm (representing the breaking of community rules). Members of the US 'Dream Team' (although strangely exalted by most broadcasters) were also criticized for not staying in the athlete's Olympic village, as is traditional 'community' behavior, as well as Olympic regulation. The use of drugs by athletes, some examples of judging bias, and the general use of the Games for political goals, *except* for ethnic or national identification, were also criticized behaviours.[24]

---

23 These relationships were not mentioned by all broadcasters. Wete (1992) of Cameroon reported that because of the lack of commercials and free coverage of the Games provided Cameroon, the Olympics is perceived quite differently in his country from other international sports events in this regard.

24 An excellent example of this type of 'breaking the rules' discourse was during the 1988 Seoul Games when numerous broadcasters offered negative comments about the antics of the US and some other nations' athletes marching around the track who dropped out of formation to snap pictures, wave signs, and so forth. Such behaviour were, at the time, considered deviant for an Olympic marchpast.

Other relevant discourse, such as security issues, gender balance in the Games, or IOC regulations concerning new sports received only cursory mention by a few broadcasters. It is interesting to note that the three East Asian broadcasts in this study – CCTV of China, NHK of Japan and MBC of Korea – mentioned not one controversial theme or topic throughout the Opening Ceremony.

A community bound by sports

If there is some form of Olympic family which meets every four years under the broad, wishful banners of peace and friendship, it is a family bound by a shared interest and understanding of sport. General sports banter accounts for from 4 per cent (Greece, ET1) to 34 per cent (Slovenia, 2nd Channel) of overall commentary discourse during the Opening Ceremony and, while broadcasters display preferences for different sports, there is a large degree of shared sports data passed on by Olympic broadcasters which ultimately contributes to a sense of collective memory and common experience. Table 7.4 shows both the absolute frequency, as well as percentage for each broadcast, of pure attention to sports statistics, stories, trivia and forecasts in each broadcast (these figures overlap with those for Olympic history by also including past Olympic sports names and facts). As noted above, the information systems compiled and made available to commentators by successive Olympic organizers creates and perpetuates a mainstay of sports dialogue. Also, the primary backgrounds of the commentators as sports broadcasters easily influences this aspect.

Table 7.4. Attention to sports statistics and stories

Nation (broadcaster)	% of broadcast (total number of comments)	Nation (broadcaster)	% of broadcast (total number of comments)
Australia (Channel 7)	29% (244)	Japan (NHK)	19.5% (182)
Brazil (TV Globo)	10% (60)	Korea (MBC)	10% (48)
Canada (CTV)	15% (103)	Mexico (Canal 13)	14% (108)
Canada (TVA)	22% (114)	Romania (RTV)	11% (57)
China (CCTV)	15% (49)	Russia (Ostankino 1)	10% (34)
Colombia (Canal A)	12% (36)	South Africa (SABC)	22% (102)
Cuba (Tele-Rebelde)	5% (33)	Singapore (SBC 12)	15% (137)
Egypt (ERTU2)	7% (34)	Slovenia (2nd Channel)	34% (372)
France (TF1)	9% (79)	Catalonia (Canal Olìmpic)	13% (130)
Germany (ARD)	30% (138)	Spain (TVE-2)	12% (49)
Greece (ET1)	4% (45)	United Kingdom (BBC)	16% (103)
Indonesia (TVRI)	12% (48)	United States (NBC)	18% (174)

Unity in abstraction

Gusfield would argue that, with or without television, the Olympic Games themselves create the conditions necessary for a viable Olympic community to exist.

Admission to contest each other is itself an admission of a level of equality and community which might otherwise be absent. In the sense that the old custom of dueling made it taboo for an aristocrat to duel a commoner, the entry into the conflict of common games is itself a form of peace and amity. What it symbolizes is the willingness to abide by common rules and thus the communal membership of each with each. Hence the very staging of the Olympics becomes an admission of community; the contrast with nationalism.[25]

Whether television plays a role in the perpetuation, or better yet the strengthening, of this Olympic community is another question entirely. Without a doubt there is the perception and presentation of the Olympics as something bigger than the event at hand. Examples of this could be found in commentary about 'trends' in the Olympic movement, or as the Russian commentator noted, the Olympics embodies ideals that 'remain unchanged' in a constantly changing world (Ostankino 1, Russia, Opening Ceremony). A handful of broadcasts noted that the Olympic movement seemed to be gaining in importance in this post-Cold War era as in this comment by the BBC (UK) commentator:

There's an incredibly happy and gay atmosphere in the stadium. One really does feel this Olympic movement is not only growing but it really in important (BBC, UK, Opening Ceremony)

Or this comment on the Greek ET1 broadcast:

The Olympic movement has greatly suffered over the years but managed to carry on. At a time when ideologies start to crumble, the Olympic movement grows stronger every day. It has brought everyone here (ET1, Greece, Opening Ceremony).

One could argue that these kinds of comments imply a perceived substance or 'meaning' to the Olympics that clearly transcends the Games as event. The Greek ET1 commentator even used television as an indicator of importance by adding to the above remark, 'It has been estimated that 3.5 million people will watch these broadcasts. I think this says it all.'

The identification of commonly held values, while not unique to the Olympics in their nature (peace, friendship, participation), are explicitly linked with Olympism by virtually all broadcasters revealing a shared definition of the transcendent purpose of this movement. That said, values more unique to Olympic sport (for example the linking of sport with culture and education) are virtually non-existent in international television commentary. Less desirable perhaps in terms of the fundamental principles, but demonstrated here as a commonly held belief, is the importance of acquiring medals and being home to athletic heroes.

Responding to Smith's challenge that communities need memories, the abundance of historical information available on line for use by media easily bolsters a sense of collective history by encouraging commentators to recite a plethora of Olympic sport fact

---

25 Gusfield (1987).

and figures – which, by and large, they do. Television commentators also offer remarkably common evaluations of significant Olympic events and eras (boycotts as negative, terrorist acts as tragedy, come-from-behind victories as heroic story) despite the nationality of the perpetrators or victors.

Olympic discourse on the part of television commentators, while limited and mostly positive in the context of the Opening Ceremony, does seem to reveal a similar view of institutional trends and protocol, as well as demonstrate a shared sense of 'expected' behaviors on the part of individual and organizational members of an Olympic community. Most important, perhaps, is that criticisms are reserved for isolated, individual behaviour and not the Olympic system or structure itself.

It is in the aspect of teacher or guide where television loses its grip on the essence of Olympic community – and thus may lose in audiences a sense of membership in an Olympic family beyond their own national team. The symbols and rituals are readily acknowledged by all broadcasters, but commentators diverge significantly on their willingness – or perhaps ability – to imbue them with meaning and ask audiences to participate in the Opening Ceremony as a reaffirming ritual, rather than an entertaining spectacle. Some scholars warn of the dangers of Olympic meanings becoming too 'open' through changing ritual behaviors (e.g. athletes' increasingly informal behaviors during the athletes' parade) and the increased 'show' like quality of the ceremony. Because television participates in and even provides incentive for these trends there is a very real danger of television trivializing Olympism.

That said, it might just be this lack of 'guidance' in the tenets of Olympism that allows such diverse cultural audiences to safely experience some imagined bond without having to resist the prescriptions of yet another ideology. Maybe it is the openness of meaning, the abstraction of the purpose which transcends the sports competition, that allows spectators and participants alike to find comfort in the idea of an Olympic community.

8   The Presentation of Nations

While some point to television's capability to bring the world into our homes as fundamental to our increased awareness of others,[1] in practice television is not a forum conducive to intercultural learning and understanding. The mass media, whose products are primarily created and used by members of a dominant national group, are predisposed to observe and construct realities about the world through a distinctly national lens. This is quite understandable given that most media structures develop within the norms, rules and needs of a particular political and economic ideology. In this way, the linkage between communication systems and notions of national identity is inevitable. As Anderson suggests nations are imagined communities. With relatively few exceptions, the majority of a nation's people never come face to face with each other and so need to establish a meaningful repertoire of shared symbols and knowledge in order to join together in an abstraction called a nation.[2] Media play an important role in the mass reproduction of these standardized representations which reinforce national identity. This is done by drawing on the most potent cultural values, beliefs, myths, history and sentiments of its constituency and embedding them into daily media fare.

However, as Melucci points out, identity is not only a system of representations, but of relations.[3] In this sense, national identity is also constituted through the ability to identify and characterize collective 'others' in the international arena. Here the mass media also play a fundamental role. Research on national images show that media presentations repeatedly select, position and evaluate others relative to the home nation by dimensions of salience, hierarchy and similarity. For example, television news attention tends to be skewed toward elite nations or those which hold some particular economic, political, or geographic salience for the broadcasting nation. Once selected for attention, nations are not simply described to audiences, but positioned in cooperative, oppositional, or stratified postures *vis-à-vis* the home nation through the use of language and visual techniques. Related to this is the consistent finding that media portrayals of nations tend to be more

A version of this chapter first appeared in *Journal of International Communication* **2**, 1, 1995.

1   See, for example, Russett and Starr (1992: 442).

2   Anderson, (1991: 6).

3   Melucci (1982: 62-68).

favourably valenced toward those 'most like us' in terms of political ideology, economic philosophy, value systems, language and so forth.

These findings reflect fundamentals of intergroup and intercultural relations. However, the formats of media also influence portrayals of nations. The visual quality of television means that presentations must respond, to some degree, to the pictures available. Television broadcasters – given pressures of time, budget, journalistic routines, or need to entertain – tend to select visual images and produce stories which are accessible to themselves as well as recognizable to home audiences. This often translates into a reliance on vague labels (e.g. Marxist, developing, rebel), visual and verbal stereotypes, repetitive story frames, and official viewpoints which cast international events in terms that are simplistic and even misleading by virtue of missing context. Simply put, the incentives don't exist – in either a government-supported or private broadcasting system – to present nations in a way that increases audience understanding for an alternative view of the world.

This is the general profile of broadcasters who came to the Barcelona Olympic Games in 1992 to cover an event intended to promote international understanding and exchange through sport. The Olympic Opening Ceremony, in particular, showcases rituals and icons (Olympic rings, flag, lighting of the flame, etc.) meant to symbolize peace, friendship and international community. Despite this, the structure and design of the Opening Ceremony also promotes a nationalistic perspective – from the use of national flags, colours, costumes, host anthems and performances, invited Heads of State, to the centrepiece segment: the athletes' parade. In fact, some observers see nothing less than a stylized introduction to a metaphoric war between nation-states.[4]

Whether one agrees with the war analogy or not, at the very least, participation in the Olympics is seen as a presentation of national membership, ability and identity in a global arena as expressed through athletic teams. The burden of this perspective becomes more acute for some national athletes than others during the sports competition, but it is unmistakable listening to broadcast commentaries during the athletes' parade. For example, when the Chinese team marched into the stadium in Barcelona, the Chinese CCTV commentator said that its athletes, 'compete in good faith and get good results in the representation of the will and spirit of the Chinese people and for the glory of the country'. In fact, international commentators commonly note the (always great) amount of applause given their respective teams upon entrance as if to say, 'See, the world respects our nation'. For some nations, the Opening Ceremony is their only distinct appearance in the broadcast version of the Games if they have few athletes or are not contenders in any event, underscoring the importance of the Parade as a source of national pride and identity.[5]

The relationship of mass media to national identity within the Olympic context gives rise to a series of questions which guided this part of the study. How much attention is given to the presentation of nations in the Opening Ceremony broadcasts around the world? How

4   See, for example, Eriksen (1993: 111).

5   For the Closing Ceremony athletes enter the stadium intermixed.

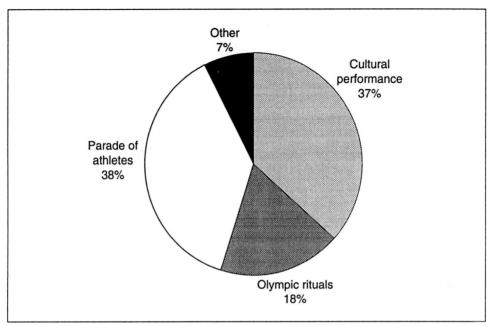

Fig. 8.1. Broadcaster attention to Olympic ceremony parts (average % across 26 broadcasts)

do national broadcasters choose to describe others? By what criteria do broadcasters choose to judge or evaluate others in a broader world context? By looking at broadcaster images of others, what can be said about the role of television in expressions of national self identity?

To better understand the presentation of nations during the Barcelona Olympic Opening Ceremony the content analysis for this part of the study utilized a coding guide of which approximately 75 categories specifically referred to aspects of nations (see Appendix A), as well as textual analysis of commentary correlated with visual images and sound elements. Coding categories related to nations were organized under the following headings (1) Olympic history; (2) sport or team attributes 1992; (3) feelings or sentiments of nation or team; (4) natural geography; (5) political or geopolitical; (6) economic or development; (7) social or cultural; and (8) national trait or character.

Attention to nations in the Opening Ceremony broadcasts

To set the context within which to compare the presentation of nations it's important to understand that attention to nations (beyond the host nation) make up a large portion of the Opening Ceremony broadcast. While the full ceremony was analysed for this study, most of the visual and verbal attention to nations occurs during the athletes' parade segment. In Barcelona 172 teams entered the stadium during the Parade which constituted 1 hour and 20 minutes, or 42 per cent, of a 3-hour, 10-minute official ceremony.

The format of the Parade is repetitive with only the flag, clothes and faces changing as each team enters the stadium. RTO'92, responsible for the international signal (visuals and natural sound only) used by all broadcasters, occasionally inserted shots of spectators waving flags or an approving head of state in the tribunal box. For commercial broadcasters who conceptualize audiences as having short attention spans, the Parade becomes victim to commercial breaks, interviews, graphic creations and other visual diversions as discussed in Chapters 4 and 5. Such departures bring the average time spent on the Parade segment, across all broadcasts, to 38 per cent as shown in Fig. 8.1. The other primary parts of the ceremony are the Olympic rituals at 18 per cent of the ceremony (entrance of the Olympic torch, raising of the Olympic flag, official speeches, oaths), host cultural performances at 37 per cent (song, dance, music, etc.), and other at 7 per cent (commercials, interviews, or news breaks).

Table 8.1. Commentary topic distribution

	$N =$	Nation topics %	Olympic topics %	Host city topics %	Performance topics %
Australia (Ch. 7)	845	71.6	19.9	5.1	3.4
Brazil (TV Globo)	654	78.0	12.0	7.0	3.0
Canada (TVA)	519	71.0	13.2	11.2	4.6
Canada (CTV)	675	65.8	17.6	12.0	4.6
China (CCTV)	333	80.0	10.0	5.0	5.0
Colombia (Canal A)	306	53.0	28.0	13.0	6.0
Cuba (Tele-Rebelde)	617	88.0	4.0	4.0	4.0
Egypt (ERTU2)	466	82.0	7.0	5.0	6.0
France (TF1)	855	58.3	15.2	18.7	7.8
Germany (ARD)	459	68.0	17.0	9.0	6.0
Greece (ET1)	1028	58.0	12.0	25.0	5.0
Indonesia (TVRI)	400	41.0	30.0	20.0	9.0
Japan (NHK)	929	80.0	9.0	5.0	6.0
Korea (MBC)	469	71.0	17.3	6.8	4.9
Mexico (Canal 13)	781	72.0	11.4	10.7	5.9
Romania (RTV)	516	66.0	12.0	12.0	10.0
Russia (Ostankino 1)	344	58.0	18.0	16.0	8.0
Singapore (SBC12)	899	68.0	13.5	13.0	5.5
Slovenia (2nd Channel)	1101	83.5	7.4	4.7	4.4
S. Africa (SABC)	462	71.0	14.7	10.6	3.7
Spain (TVE–2)	390	72.0	14.0	7.0	7.0
Catalonia (C. Olímpic)	978	58.4	19.1	14.1	8.4
UK (BBC)	656	75.5	17.0	4.8	2.7
USA (NBC)	985	61.7	14.5	19.9	3.9

Notes: The broadcast of Cameroon TV is not included in this table. Cameroon TV used the French TF1 broadcast, returning to its home studio during TF1 commercial breaks. Colombia's relatively low N is because of limits on electricity in that country which caused the broadcast to begin after the start of the ceremony.

Table 8.1 represents the amount of verbal comments about nations relative to commentary about the cultural performances, Barcelona and Spain, or Olympic topics (rituals, values, heritage) throughout the Opening Ceremony. It compares substantive commentary – distinct facts, explanations, feelings and other specific image associations – and displays them as a relative percentage for each broadcaster, demonstrating an overall emphasis on commentary about nations.

As indicated in the variety of N totals in Table 8.1, this study shows that broadcasters vary significantly in the sheer quantity of comments (beyond a nation's name) they make about entering national teams. The quantity ranges are demonstrated in Table 8.2. This table simply totals the number of statements (not sentence counts, but distinct ideas or facts put forth) made by each broadcaster about other nations. The disparities result from several influences ranging from cultural orientations toward language use, to national broadcast norms, to familiarity with Olympic languages, to the number of commercial and other breaks which serve to shorten time spent on the ceremony. For example, Korea's MBC showed the ceremony on a significant time delay and, as such, edited out over half of the Parade segment.

Table 8.2. Amount of commentary about nations

Number of statements	Broadcaster (Nation)
0–99	CCTV (China) TVRI (Indonesia) Ostankino 1 (Russia)
100–199	RTV (Romania) TVE–2 (Spain)
200–299	TVA (Canada) ERTU2 (Egypt) ARD (Germany) MBC (Korea) SABC (South Africa)
300–399	TV Globo (Brazil) CTV (Canada) Tele-Rebelde (Cuba) TF1 (France) Canal 13 (Mexico) BBC (United Kingdom) Canal Olímpic (Catalonia)
400–499	Channel 7 (Australia) ET1 (Greece) SBC 12 (Singapore) NBC (United States)
500–599	NHK (Japan)
910	2nd Channel (Slovenia)

Broadcaster descriptions of 'others'

The athletes' parade is the one part of the Opening Ceremony where broadcasters are not 'surprised'. They know exactly what will happen and in what order. Therefore, advance preparation of commentary about the entering teams by broadcasters is indeed possible – limited only by broadcaster resources. In addition, COOB'92's commentary information system for broadcasters provided team and some country data literally at the touch of a finger on special monitors as the event unfolded. Despite this, some quick math concerning the number of teams in Barcelona and the length of the athletes' parade reveals that the average broadcast time allotted per nation is less than 30 seconds. So, there is no illusion that commentators can offer audiences more than a few tidbits about each team. Perhaps because of this time pressure, it is instructive to analyse what commentators chose to highlight about each national team.

In terms of focus, the broadcasts differ on whether they are introducing athletic teams or nations. The content analysis revealed that 60 per cent of the broadcasters tended to frame their comments more in terms of the *team* and its members (e.g. the Chinese divers are almost certain to win a gold medal); 25 per cent of the broadcasters focused on the entering *nation* (e.g. China is the most populous nation on earth); and 15 per cent presented a *balanced focus*, alternating between or combining both approaches (e.g. China, the most populous nation on earth, enters with its largest team ever.) These differences are not readily explained. The broadcasters that focused most on nation versus team were CTV (Canada), ERTU2 (Egypt), ET1 (Greece), MBC (Korea) and Canal 13 (Mexico).

Next, the study analysed the frequency of subject categories specifically related to nations. Given the extreme time constraints surrounding each team's appearance, it is not instructive to look at the breadth of information presented about each national team as is common to national image analysis.[6] All would be 'narrow'. However, narrow breadth did exist *across* nation introductions. Table 8.3 shows the relative topic distribution about nations for each broadcast nation, revealing that descriptions about nations tended to fall into six primary subject areas. Within these groupings, of course, broadcasters varied considerably in the specific references made. For example, NBC (USA), CTV (Canada) and TF1 (France) broadcasts presented a much greater variety of nation or team data than the broadcasts of MBC (Korea), Tele-Rebelde (Cuba), or 2nd Channel (Slovenia) which provided highly patterned and repetitive delivery of information, giving the same type of data (e.g. medal rank, capital city, team size) about each team that entered – as in the case of the Cuban commentator who provided the gender balance (e.g. 5 women, 15 men) for 139 teams he introduced.

NBC of the USA, in particular, showed its need to keep audiences entertained at all times. Given only a brief moment as the teams marched by NBC commentators chose to offer everything from sport statistics to such 'vital' information as: 'Barbados comes from the Portuguese word for 'beard' after the bearded fig trees on the island' or 'The Sultan of Brunei owns the Beverly Hills Hotel'.

---

6   Rivenburgh (1992).

Table 8.3. Descriptive breadth: relative subject distribution during athletes' parade

Nation (broadcaster)	N = 100%	Sport/ team %	Olympic history %	Political %	Sentiments feelings %	Natural geography %	Economic %	Social/ cultural %	Other %
Australia (Ch. 7)	446	30.0	29.5	32.7	2.0	0.2	3.1	0.5	2.0
Brazil (TV Globo)	324	60.0	8.3	24.0	5.0	0.9	1.5	0.0	0.3
Canada (TVA)	237	34.2	32.0	29.0	2.0	0.8	0.8	0.4	0.8
Canada (CTV)	309	25.8	19.0	44.0	3.2	2.9	4.2	0.9	0.0
China (CCTV)	94	61.0	8.5	24.0	4.2	2.3	0.0	0.0	0.0
Colombia (Canal A)	90	59.0	13.0	20.0	4.0	0.0	0.0	0.0	4.0
Cuba (Tele-Rebelde)	371	86.0	4.5	8.0	1.0	0.5	0.0	0.0	0.0
Egypt (ERTU2)	216	37.9	8.3	43.0	8.3	0.4	0.4	1.3	0.4
France (TF1)	312	49.0	9.4	22.0	4.9	4.5	0.0	10.2	0.0
Germany (ARD)	226	65.6	13.7	13.7	5.3	1.3	0.0	0.4	0.0
Greece (ET1)	465	28.7	2.3	64.0	1.3	0.6	2.1	1.0	0.0
Indonesia (TVRI)	75	52.0	37.6	5.8	1.1	0.0	0.0	0.0	3.5
Japan (NHK)	558	45.0	15.9	32.6	1.0	3.0	1.0	0.8	0.7
Korea (MBC)	281	18.0	19.0	60.0	0.7	0.3	1.0	0.7	0.3
Mexico (Canal 13)	378	46.0	6.0	32.2	7.1	0.2	4.0	4.0	0.5
Romania (RTV)	196	57.6	22.4	18.5	0.0	0.5	0.5	0.0	0.5
Russia (Ostankino 1)	98	50.0	25.5	23.5	1.0	0.0	0.0	0.0	0.0
Singapore (SBC12)	435	35.8	30.8	25.5	4.1	2.5	0.9	0.4	0.0
Slovenia (2nd Channel)	910	45.8	40.4	10.7	0.8	1.3	0.9	0.1	0.0
S. Africa (SABC)	294	52.3	12.9	19.7	6.4	2.0	2.0	3.0	1.7
Spain (TVE-2)	180	47.0	12.7	28.8	5.5	1.6	2.2	0.0	2.2
Catalonia (C. Olímpic)	357	62.7	8.4	16.5	5.3	2.8	0.5	0.8	3.0
UK (BBC)	339	56.6	21.7	12.6	2.9	4.7	0.8	0.5	0.2
USA (NBC)	406	44.6	18.4	24.6	2.4	4.9	2.2	2.9	0.0

Within the primary limits of sport (team attributes and history) and geo-political associations, commentary patterns about others fall, with remarkable ease, into the following six subject areas: (1) Olympic sport participation or performance; (2) national personalities; (3) size, dress and demeanour of the entering athletes; (4) location references; (5) defining national events or characteristics; and (6) nation-specific linkages.

These findings can be explained by three primary influences, noted earlier, on the media presentation of nations in this Olympic context: the Olympics as a sports event, the visual nature of television and the nature of national images.

The Olympics as a sports event

Olympic sport participation or performance. Without surprise, the majority of commentary across most broadcasts relates in some way to the team or nation as part of the sports competition in Barcelona or in some prior Olympic Games or other athletic event. Clearly, a primary narrative structure during the Parade is the Olympics as a sports event.[7]

Five of the broadcasters in this study – those from Cuba (Tele Rebelde), Germany (ARD), Indonesia (TVRI), Romania (RTV) and Slovenia (2nd channel) – concentrate at least 80 per cent of their commentary about entering nations on sports or a nation's (or athlete's) prior Olympic performances. Thirteen more broadcasters devote at least 60 per cent of their commentary to sport and Olympic sport history themes. Broken down further, the most common introductory topics concerning sport were: the country's medal history, strong sports coming to Barcelona, or the naming a specific athlete or the flagbearer. Broadcasters that focused a notable amount of commentary on topics other than sports were CTV (Canada), ERTU2 (Egypt), TF1 (France), Canal 13 (Mexico) and ET1 (Greece). Accordingly, these are same broadcasters noted above who framed their introductions more in terms of entering nations than of teams. The French TF1 commentary stood alone in focusing 10 per cent of its introductions on social or cultural issues related to the entering nations.

Television visuals as commentator cues

National personalities. Nations and teams were commonly associated with well known personalities. Sometimes this was the mention of an infamous athlete such as Ben Johnson with Canada (referencing the 1988 drug scandal), but most often this category of association was prompted by commentators responding to a visual close up inside the stadium. Sitting with every commentator (whether in the stadium or studio) is a television monitor showing what visual images home audiences are experiencing at any given moment. While a few commentators become stadium spectators and lose themselves in the live event, most pay close attention to narrate the specific images being received in their home country. So, while the commentator might be introducing an entering team, a visual image

---

7   As discussed in Chapter 6 and 7, however, this is not the case for other parts of the ceremony, where broadcasters depart from one another in their characterization of and commentary tone associated witih the Opening Ceremony.

of a head of state or sports celebrity might prompt an abrupt shift in commentary. The visual nature of television clearly influenced the associations made with specific nations.

For example nearly all broadcasters coupled Nelson Mandela with South Africa, Fidel Castro and Cuba, and Magic Johnson and the USA. These personalities were all present in the stadium and included in the international signal. In fact, Magic Johnson was the most frequently mentioned personality across all 26 Opening Ceremony broadcasts due to excessive visual attention by the host broadcaster.

Size, dress and demeanour of the entering athletes. Also prompted by visual images were commentator references to the 'look' of the teams. First, the size of each team was readily available to commentators and easy to express to home audiences. Broadcasters noted both the large size of teams such as the United States, as well as questioned the very minimal presence of others as when the Cuban (Tele-Rebelde) commentator said of Brunei, 'What's it doing with only 1 athlete!' or when the Colombian (Canal A) commentator expressed concern that these 'small', non-competitive teams would eventually get pushed out of the Olympics by the IOC.

The second most prominent discussion category in this area was that of athlete dress. The French Canadian broadcaster (TVA) suggested the importance of team uniforms by saying that each uniform 'gives us a vague idea of the country and its traditions'. The Russian Ostankino 1 commentator, however, was more to the point when he introduced the Parade by calling it a 'fashion, or beauty contest'. Several broadcasters paid notable attention to what each team wore to the Opening Ceremony. Among these were broadcasters from France, Russia, the UK, Mexico and Egypt. The TV anchors from Cameroon argued at length about the role of wearing traditional (versus modern) uniforms. Much to their distress, the Cameroon team entered the stadium in athletic wear, while several other African teams arrived in traditional dress.

In another example, French commentators clearly enjoyed noting the 'superb outfits' of Algeria and the 'famous Bermuda shorts' of Bermuda. They pointed out US team member Carl Lewis by saying 'What a nice tie!' (the Catalan, Canal Olímpic commentator said the tie was 'stunning'). At the same time, the French broadcast was also the most critical of team uniforms, noting sarcastically the 'relaxed outfits' of Belgium (the athletes looked as though at a 'country fair') and exclaiming upon the entrance of Denmark, 'look at those jackets with red sleeves ... the tailor didn't finish his work!' One Eurosport commentator suggested the Unified Team uniform looked spray painted.

Finally, team demeanour – also visually prompted – was a popular topic. The Colombian (Canal A) commentator said its own athletes were 'too serious' and that the Italians were 'fun' and 'simpáticos' for their antics peering into RTO cameras. The Greek commentators concurred about the Italians, but with a disapproving and sarcastic tone said, 'Of course the Italians *never* embarrass themselves'. French commentators said of Romania 'they don't look too happy'. They also commented on teams that looked 'friendly' (Benin, Bahrain), 'cheerful' (Belgium) or 'breathing easy' like the Chilean athletes. They described the Bahamas as a 'joy of life team' looking as though they dance as they walk (compared to the US athletes who were 'not very well lined up'.) By contrast, Egyptian (ERTU2) commentators thought the Korean team was 'very disciplined' in its entrance. The Eurosport commentator, apparently lacking any relevant facts to offer, simply said the Puerto Rican team came in a 'variety of shapes and sizes'.[8]

The nature of national images

As noted in the introduction, research into our images of others demonstrates their tendency to be vague (due to a lack of knowledge), subjective and narrowly defined. When broadcast commentators spoke about *nations* (rather than about sport specifics of each team), these same findings emerge across nearly all broadcasts.

Location references. At least half of the broadcasters incorporate location references into their commentary, reflecting a perceived lack of audience knowledge. This explanation is supported by the fact that not one broadcaster felt a need to offer location markers for the USA, China, Russia, or most European nations. Some broadcasters even made direct references to geographic distance or obscurity: TVA (Canada) commentators talked of 'far away Iceland'; Canal 13 (Mexico) spoke of India as a 'distant, mystical land'; Eurosport referred to 'way out there in Korea'; and others admitted no knowledge whatsoever, as when one commentator asked where a country, Myanmar, was in the world and a French TF1 commentator said, 'Belize, a million dollar question, isn't it? Where is Belize?' For part of the Parade duration, the Canal Olímpic (Spain) commentators played what they called 'geography lesson' playfully testing each other on country locations and capital cities. One SABC South African commentator would have flunked the test when he introduced Costa Rica as Southern African nation. This need for location markers mimics a common practice in national news programming when geographic labels or maps are provided to locate infrequent newsmakers for audiences. It is an explicit acknowledgment of how little we often know about our others.

Defining national events or characteristics. Kong notes the distinction between enduring and time-based national images.[9] This essentially refers to the repetitive association of a given nation with some event, action, or attribute consistently over time, or instead, with intensity within a given time frame. As noted, media producers contribute to the persistence of these portrayals through their desire for content that is recognizable to audiences. In the athletes' parade, these brief, familiar characterizations are also encouraged by the short time between team entrances. In this analysis, broadcasters shared several enduring and time-based associations. For example, common time-based associations included: Bosnia-Herzegovina as defined by civil war; Germany by reunification; the Unified Team by dissolution, Iraq by the Gulf War; and South Africa by the abolition of policies of apartheid and its return to the Games. Examples of more enduring shared images were those of Israel as defined by the Munich tragedy; Greece as the Olympic birthplace; China

---

8 All quotes come from the 1992 Opening Ceremony transcripts of these different broadcasters.

9 Kong (1991).

as having a large population; Lebanon as war ravaged; Bermuda by its triangle (and shorts); and Brazil with the samba.

The choice of certain associations, however, were clearly prompted by some specific national relevance. Greek (ET1) commentators, from a country with a long and fractious history, were the most likely to associate other nations with disputes and conflicts. The commentators named several border disputes, civil wars, and referenced many countries involved in the Gulf War. One Greek commentator mentioned that it was acceptable that Taiwan was forced to change its name to Chinese Taipei (for use in the Olympics), most likely prompted by Greece's name dispute concerning Macedonia.

Broadcasts from Canada (CTV) and the USA (NBC), representing capitalist democracies long entrenched in the rhetoric of the Cold War, brought special attention to nations moving from communist or socialist systems to a free market or democratic system. For example, the Canadian CTV commentators made a point of characterizing: Bulgaria as 'former communists'; Albania as 'shedding nearly half a century of communist rule'; and Poland as 'one of the first communist nations to begin to press against threads of communist yoke'. The Cuban and Chinese commentators, not surprisingly, never made such mentions.

Nation-specific linkages. In this same vein, broadcasters select ways in which they explicitly link their own nation with others, thereby defining some aspect of their national identity. Bilateral linkages present themselves primarily as references to geographic neighbours, pointing out sport competitors (as with a medal rival in a particular sport), or noting former colonial relations. These linkages are motivated by direct political, geographic, economic, or sport salience of the broadcasting nation to another nation and represented cooperative, oppositional and stratified types of relationships.

More intriguing are the broader groupings of nations which emerge through the course of the Parade commentary. This might be conceptualized like small clusters or constellations of nations defined by certain types of alliances or dimensions – whether political, cultural, ethnic, religious, geographic, economic, or sport. Prior researchers have investigated this idea of perceived linkages with some fruitful results. For example, Robinson and Hefner found that communism, economic development, ethnicity and geography were common organizational frames within which countries are related to each other.[10] Further, nations differ on the kinds of sentiments they promote to reinforce and reflect nationhood – whether language, ethnicity, birthplace, or more civic orientations such as community values.

This study found the same sort of clustering phenomenon. Figure 8.2 shows a sampling of these clusters with the broadcasting nation positioned in the centre of the cluster in which they specifically identified themselves. Some broadcasters allied their nation by a sense of geography or common 'home'. For example, South African SABC commentators took pains to point out other 'African' nations. Colombian Canal A commentators did the

---

10 Robinson and Hefner (1967).

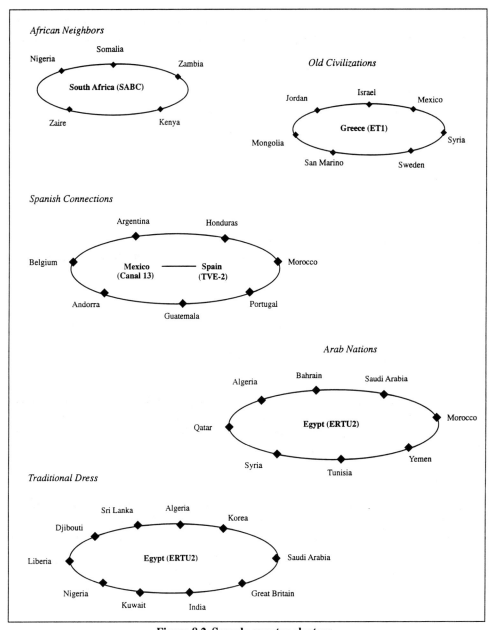

Figure 8.2. Sample country clusters.

same thing with Latin American countries, pointing out 'neighbours' and 'friends' in this manner.

Egyptian ERTU2 commentators clearly expressed an affinity with those teams, like the Egyptian team, that entered the stadium in traditional dress. Egypt also associated itself with the community of Arab nations. The Greek commentators found a camaraderie with countries boasting old civilizations, as well as long Olympic traditions. Some examples from the Greek ET1 commentary included: Mexico as 'centre of one of the oldest civilizations, the Maya'; Mongolia as 'one of the oldest countries in the world'; Israel as 'centre of one of the oldest civilizations on earth'; and Papua New Guinea as having 'human remnants dating 10,000 years ago'.

Most often nations put themselves 'inside' the cluster as when commentators from Cuba and Mexico discussed Spanish connections, the Colombian commentator noted soccer-playing nations, or broadcasters from former Olympic host nations regularly pointed out former Olympic hosts. These examples reveal aspects of a national self-identity as expressed through selected linkages with others.

Evaluating others in a broader world context

Michael Real once said that each Olympics is like a tribal fire where people of the world come together to meet each other in the spirit of cooperation and understanding, regardless of political ideology, economic well being and sport ability.[11] Indeed, the visual intent of the Olympic Opening Ceremony is for each team to march into the stadium on equal footing before the eyes of the world. However, through both the capabilities of the camera and the addition of commentary, disparities in national power and ability, geo-political alliances and cultural preferences all emerge as national broadcasters present images of others in the Opening Ceremony. Nations position themselves and others around the tribal fire.

Within the Parade context this sort of global positioning manifested itself in three primary ways: the broadcaster choice to introduce a national team, the ranking or placement of a team or nation on some evaluative scale, and through the use of commentary techniques that served to trivialize or marginalize others.

Countries not mentioned

To most countries the entrance into the Olympic stadium is a moment of great pride. Yet, contrary to Olympic philosophy, it is the rare case that all teams are introduced by broadcasters.[12] Table 8.4 summarizes how many teams – or not – each broadcaster introduced during the Barcelona ceremony. It also notes the reason teams were not introduced. Although commercial breaks are a significant cause, commentator talking – about topics other than the entering team – is the most common reason for missed introductions.[13]

---

11 Real (1989: 240).

12 Larson and Rivenburgh (1991).

13 It should be noted that countries that speak the Olympic languages can rely on the team introduction made by the stadium announcer (as the sound is often heard via television) or the visual of the country name on a placard preceding the team. Some of the nations not introduced did show up on television screens. But this seems to be the exception. Commentators tended to verbally introduce those teams to which they wish to bring attention. Similarly, as noted by our Cameroon correspondent Wete (1992), not all audiences can read the signs.

Table 8.4. Team introduction totals – athletes' parade

Nation (broadcaster)	Delegations mentioned 172 = total	Delegations not mentioned	Reason for exclusion	
			Breaks from ceremony	Other
Australia (Ch. 7)	159 (92.5%)	13 (7.5%)	4 – ads	8 – while talking about own team
Brazil (TV Globo)	167 (97%)	5 (3%)		5 – talking
France (TF1)	132 (77%)	40 (23%)	33 – ads for France; to studio for Cameroon	7 – talk about French team
Canada (CTV)	117 (68%)	55 (32%)	26 – ads 25 – to studio	4 – talking
Canada (TVA)	129 (75%)	43 (25%)	29 – ads	14 – talking
China (CCTV)	171 (99.5%)	1 (0.5%)		1 – talking about Unified Team
Colombia (Canal A)	62 (36%)	110 (64%)	43 – ads	18 – technical 49 – talking
Cuba (Tele-Rebelde)	171 (99.5%)	1 (0.5%)		1 – talking about prior team
Egypt (ERTU2)	168 (98%)	4 (2%)		4 – talking
Germany (ARD)	88 (51%)	84 (49%)		84 – talking
Greece (ET1)	128 (74%)	44 (26%)	40 – ads	4
Indonesia (TVRI)	72 (42%)	100 (58%)		100 – just stops introductions
Japan (NHK)	172 (100%)			
Korea (MBC)	56 (32%)	116 (68%)		116 – edited out
Mexico (Canal 13)	159 (92.5%)	13 (7.5%)		13 – talking
Romania (RTV)	132 (77%)	40 (23%)		40 – talking
Russia (Ostankino)	111 (65%)	61 (35%)	22 – ads	39 – talking
Singapore (SBC 12)	143 (83%)	29 (17%)	28 – ads	1 – talking
Slovenia (2nd Channel)	169 (99%)	3 (1%)		3 – talking
Spain (TVE 2)	95 (55%)	77 (45%)	15 – ads	62 – talking
Catalonia (Canal Olímpic)	133 (77%)	39 (23%)	21 – ads 7 – video feature	11 – talking
South Africa (SABC)	114 (66%)	58 (34%)	20 – ads	38 – talking or uses announcer
United Kingdom (BBC)	167 (97%)	5 (3%)		5 – talking
United States (NBC)	134 (78%)	38 (22%)	24 – ads	14 – talking
Eurosport	52 (30%)	120 (70%)	23 – ads	101 – talking

Only one broadcaster in this study, Japan's NHK introduced each of the 172 teams that marched in the Parade. In addition, commentators from CCTV (China), Tele-Rebelde (Cuba), BBC (Britain), TV Globo (Brazil), 2nd Channel (Slovenia) and ERTU2 (Egypt) – all broadcasts without commercial interruption – introduced to their audiences over 95 per cent of the teams that marched in the stadium. Although in the case of CCTV of China little else was said beyond the country name.

By contrast, broadcasters that inserted commercial breaks into the Parade segment tended to miss strings of countries – such as all the countries that start with a 'B' – while away from the ceremony. Even when not showing an advertisement, commercial broadcasters such as Canada's CTV or the USA's NBC, feel the competitive pressure to keep an entertaining and fast pace so audiences won't change channels. To this end, they took breaks from the Parade to conduct interviews, show home team close ups, or visit the studio. Another common instance of missed introductions for all broadcasters was to skip teams that entered directly after their own, as they talk in more detail about their own athletes.

The Eurosport channel introduced the least number of teams: 30 per cent or 52 out of 172 countries. While one might expect only broadcasters with commercial breaks to fail to introduce teams. The next group of broadcasters to consistently ignore teams marching in were Korea's MBC and networks in Indonesia (TVRI) and Germany (ARD), who introduced only 32 per cent, 42 per cent and 51 per cent of the nations that marched in, respectively. None of those broadcasts had commercials.

Although some missed introductions are haphazard (as in missing all the 'B' nations), an analysis of introduction choices readily reflect the world of international news and sports activity – with western nations making up a dominant and powerful core. There were only eight national teams introduced by all the broadcasters looked at in this study. They were Greece, South Africa, Germany, Australia, Canada, Cuba, the USA and Spain – with the United States team receiving exceptional attention across all broadcasters by virtue of its basketball 'Dream Team'.

In stark contrast, nations like Burkina Faso, Guinea, Laos and the Maldives are all but ignored. However, the record for the least mentioned countries went to three tiny nations: San Marino, St. Vincent and the Grenadines, and the Solomon Islands. These nations did not exist for over 50 per cent of the broadcasters studied.

If one looks more generally at those countries which were ignored by 40 per cent or more of the commentators, they tended to be small, non-sports powers. They are also the same countries ignored by the major international news organizations. Geographically the most 'ignored' nations were either small island nations or African nations. Even if introduced, however, it was as if some did not even qualify for nationhood as when the French TF1 commentators joked of the Cook Islands, 'I thought it was a travel agency' or called Bahrain a 'charming little emirate'. A Eurosport commentator, after skipping several teams to talk of other topics said, 'So far we've had only a contingent of the smaller teams, the huge nations are still to come' implying he had only missed introducing insignificant countries – nothing important.

One disturbing demonstration of a television broadcaster selectively introducing nations was the case of MBC of Korea. This delayed broadcast edited out 116 or 68 per cent of the entering teams. However, in a stretch of cutting out 80 teams (from Kenya through Zambia), the Korean broadcaster *put back in* only the teams of Italy, Jamaica, Japan, Jordan (all in a row), Mexico (alone), Norway and New Zealand (marching next to each other), North Korea and Romania (also together), Sweden, and Switzerland. MBC only introduced four African countries – and largely by accident because of their position in the parade: Cameroon and Central African Republic which marched in on either side of Canada and before China; the Congo which marched right before Korea; and Zimbabwe which entered right before the host team Spain.

Another factor in attention to nations, noted at the outset of the article, is that the athletes' parade is the longest and most repetitious segment of the Opening Ceremony. Some broadcasters simply become bored with introducing the teams – or at least are afraid that the audience will be bored. At one point, Russia's Ostankino commentator said, 'I think our audiences won't be offended if we pass over the title of some of the countries ...' then proceeded to skip introducing 61 entering teams. The Indonesian TVRI commentator claimed he didn't have information available on the teams, so after the first 71 teams he just stopped introducing altogether – skipping the next 100 teams until Spain appeared at the end of the Parade. While these last examples do not reflect any intent to ignore particular nations, the broadcasts contribute to the invisibility of several teams. On the other hand, some omissions are with motivation as when the Romanian broadcaster, from a country bitter over the Moldova annex, chose not to say anything about the Unified Team. One of the study correspondents from China felt that it was a generous act for the CCTV to show Chinese Taipei's entrance. He said:

> There is only one China in the world, the People's Republic of China. That the image of Chinese Taipei could appear for almost 30 seconds during the Parade of Athletes showed the concern of the lead broadcaster [CCTV] for China.[14]

Positioning in the global arena

Through their commentary, broadcasters 'place' other nations in relation to themselves. In this sense, broadcasters not only describe others, but evaluate and position them in the world system using familiar scales of comparison. This was found to be done in three ways: by sports, politics and economics. This is reflective, of course, of the primary arenas of international relationships. Accordingly, they also represent the type of image content commonly found to comprise people's perceptions of other nations.

Sports status. Ranking nations on sports ability takes two forms. Either the commentator ranked a nation by number of medals in Olympic competition or by national sports ability

---

14 Kong (1992).

more generally. The broadcasts most likely to provide medal rankings were, in order of emphasis relative to other topics, were from Australia (Channel 7), Indonesia (TVRI), Romania (RTV), Slovenia (2nd Channel), Brazil (TV Globo), French Canada (TVA), China (CCTV) and Korea (MBC). This included pointing out nations that had won a lot of medals or, as the Slovenian commentator consistently did, pointing out nations that had never won a medal. By contrast, South African commentators rarely mentioned medal counts, rankings, or records possibly reflecting a lack of confidence in that nation's participation after 32 years.

Commentators also ranked nations in terms of sports ability more generally. For example China and the United States were widely labeled as sports giants or powerhouses. The Slovenian commentator, again, offered some contrary examples when he said of Saudi Arabia, 'a country without big success in the Olympics'; of Aruba, 'more success in tourism than sports'; of the United Arab Emirates, 'known more for financial success than sports success'; of Costa Rica, 'not rich in athletes'; or of Bhutan, 'Here's come Bhutan. In sports they are an undeveloped country.'

Political stability. Hierarchical placement in the political realm was expressed not in terms of power or influence, but by pointing out political instability. For example, Afghanistan, Syria, Sri Lanka, Laos, Lebanon, Myanmar, Chad, El Salvador and others were consistently associated with instability or conflict by broadcast nations who, by implication, would consider themselves both developed and stable at that time. Along these lines the Mexican Canal 13 commentator noted, with obvious approval, that Hungary was able to make the transition to democracy without violence.

Olympic participation. Broadcasters from nations who have long participated in the Olympic Games – like Australia, Japan and Greece – paid close attention to the participation history of other nations. There was an obvious approval of those nations who have long been part of the Olympic Family and, in fact, nations were ranked by the number of Olympic Games they've attended. At the bottom of this scale, according to the Australian Channel 7 commentator, was Algeria which was noted for the most non-attendance to the Games.

Economic status. To a lesser degree, nations were positioned according to economic status. Most frequently, this took the form of pointing out the poorest countries in the world. Mali and Bangladesh seemed to hold this dubious title, in the eyes of several broadcasters, in 1992. On the other hand Mexican Canal 13 commentators were interested in economic growth and health, singling out Malaysia and its healthy economy, admiring Japan as an economic powerhouse, calling Korea and Singapore 'Asian Tigers', and suggesting that Senegal, although in 'traditional dress [is] undergoing modernization'.

Trivializing and marginalizing techniques

Overall, nations are introduced in a neutral or favourable manner reflecting the inherently positive nature of the Olympics as event. Negative characterizations, however, are embedded in the commentary through the use of evaluative labels and scales noted above or through techniques which serve to marginalize or trivialize the other. For example, several broadcasters pointed out that spectators were 'hissing' at Iraq for its invasion of Kuwait. Not being able to locate a team on the map, as happened with Myanmar, serves to marginalize its salience *vis-à-vis* other nations. A more indirect technique, however, was through the use of humor or sarcasm. This narrative technique, discussed in Chapter 6, seemed to manifest itself most often during the athletes' parade. While this is admittedly difficult to pick up through translations, this technique of trivializing others is found almost exclusively in those broadcasts characterized by more informal bantering among commentators. The broadcasts from the United States, French, Canadian, Spanish and Greece are examples of this style. Examples would include NBC's ill-conceived introduction of the Central African Republic, which noted that 'the former emperor of the Central African Republic ... was found guilty of cannibalism'. Or the Colombian Canal A commentator's humorous tone associated with the entrance of exotic or traditional uniforms, such as the 'peculiar dress' of American Samoa and the 'curious dress' of Togo. Or the commentator from Canal Olímpic (Spain) calling Haiti the 'exotic country' of 'voodoo'. Rather than complimentary, the comments carried a 'they are not modern like us' implication. The French TF1 commentators offered this sarcastic exchange about Swaziland.

> Commentator 1: 'Swaziland ... going to have a lot of success'.
>
> Commentator 2: 'The one of the far left looks in good health'
> [referring to a very fat man entering as part of the team]
>
> Commentator 1: 'And the white people came, too ... Amazing'
> [referring to the few white athletes]
> (TF1, France, Opening Ceremony)

They also referred to badminton, a very popular sport in East and Southeast Asia, as a 'charming sport for little old English ladies and robust Chinese proletarians'.

It was Eurosport, however, (British commentators, yet without the burden nationhood given the presence of the BBC) that provided the most evaluative commentary about nations, generalizing nations as 'troubled' (Albania, Algeria, Colombia), labeling the African continent as 'beset with political problems', calling Colombia a 'disgraced country with wild and erratic soccer performance' and Romania a 'blighted country if ever there was one – emerging from the ice age of Ceausescu', and readily discussing controversial issues surrounding the different teams (such as drugs and payoffs). In addition, there was no pretense to being informative or careful when introducing teams (as an example, they called Bosnia Herzegovina 'Herza Bosgovina'.)

By contrast, the British BBC and Japanese NHK commentators presented the most varied, informative and consistently upbeat broadcasts during the athletes' parade. The commentators introduced the nations, for the most part, in an extremely positive manner – with little negative evaluation in keeping with the ideals of Olympism.

The role of television in expressions of national identity

The Olympics as event constructs a framework within which national interpretations take place. During the athletes' parade a sports narrative was dominant, consisting of athlete names, records, statistics and medal rankings and teams hopes for Barcelona. This finding is greatly influenced by the fact that close to 90 per cent of broadcasters in this study used sports commentators to narrate the Opening Ceremony. In addition, the fast pace of the entering teams lends itself to the use of brief statistics, labels and familiar references – or no information at all. For some, it also encouraged highly repetitive introduction patterns. Camera shots of spectators waving national flags, famous personalities and team demeanour also prompt commentators to react to specific visual images as part of characterizing others.

Despite the character of the Olympics as an international event unprecedented in its levels of cooperation and goodwill, televised images of our 'others' in the Olympic Opening Ceremony have everything to do with national self identity. Most broadcasters who come to the Olympics, whether public or private and whether they like it or not, find themselves as national representatives. As such, broadcasters have little motivation to change their cultural and national lens when interpreting the Games to home audiences.

Within the Parade narrative and influenced by the nature of television, the presentation of nations in the Barcelona Opening Ceremony resembled media attention and portrayal patterns found in research on national images of others, which in turn, supports what is known about fundamental aspects of national identity and intergroup relations. When Opening Ceremony television commentators chose to point out emerging democracies, old civilizations, booming economies, or traditional uniforms they revealed sentiments or pointed to symbols derived from a national consciousness. When commentators linked their nation with others – whether by geography, ethnicity, activity, or other means – they further define who they see their nation to be. When commentators locate others on a map or remind audiences of some familiar event that happened elsewhere, they reveal what information is 'common knowledge' to their national audience. When commentators position or evaluate others as poor, unstable, powerhouses, friends, or otherwise they often do so using their own nation as some sort of reference point and by a criterion of some national salience. Despite the abundance of shared experience found in the Olympics, how the international broadcasters who came to Barcelona in 1992 chose to represent others reveals identity aspects of their own imagined community called a nation.

9   The Olympic Host on a World Stage

The athletes never had a chance. No matter how well they jumped and ran and rowed, they could never dominate these Summer Games.

The city won the Games. The people of Catalonia won the Games. Always, there were the fantastic spires of Sagrada Familia shimmering in the background, or the fountains of Montjuïc, or the towers of Tibidabo in the distance.

Day or night, no matter how exercised we got over the Irish boxer or the Canadian rower or the African runners or the American basketball players, we always knew something was happening on the Ramblas. Somebody was cooking calamaris. Somebody was pouring the cava. Somebody was singing. Real people were dancing the sardana, the sweet folk dance of Catalonia, in some haunting plaza. We could feel it. We could hear it.

New York Times, 10 August 1992

Holding the Olympic Games in one's own home is truly exceptional for any world culture, and in particular for cultures largely unknown as was the case for Catalan culture and the Olympic Games. Catalonia is an Autonomous Community (Nation) within the Spanish state of which the 1992 host city of Barcelona is the capital.[1]

---

1   An introductory note about Catalonia.

Catalonia ('Catalunya' in Catalan) is a historic and autonomous community that covers an area of approximately 32,000 square kilometres. The population is more than 6,000,000 which is about 16 per cent of the total population of Spain. The capital is Barcelona whose metropolitan area has a population of approximately 3,000,000. It is a nation which has managed to preserve its social and cultural traditions throughout the centuries, even in the face of the most adverse political situations. Franco's victory in the Spanish Civil War (1936–39) brought about the repeal of the Statute of Autonomy which had been passed by the republican parliament in 1932. Within the legal framework of the 1978 Spanish Constitution, Catalonia now has a new Statute of Autonomy (1979) which recognizes its *own* government and parliament (the Generalitat) with different responsibilities in communication policies and exclusive legal control in education and cultural affairs. In 1992, the parliamentary majority and the government was made up of a nationalistic coalition (CiU) whose principal leader was Mr. Jordi Pujol. The main opposition is provided by the socialist party of Catalonia, associated with the PSOE (PSC-PSOE) in Madrid. The mayor of Barcelona in 1992 and president of COOB'92, Mr. Pascual Maragall is one of the Catalan socialist party leaders.

Catalonia's own official language is Catalan, a Romance language that reaches a population base of about 10.5 million (of which 6 million speak the language), primarily in northeastern Spain (i.e.

Catalonia has its own national language (Catalan) and a Mediterranean culture, history, personality and folk tradition quite distinct from other parts of Spain.

There is a belief by Olympics hosts that holding a Games represents an opportunity to enhance one's image abroad. While this is not necessarily true, or is true to a much less extent than believed, it is nonetheless a compelling motivation for cities and countries to take on such a challenging and expensive feat as hosting an Olympic Games. For Barcelona and Catalonia, hosting the Olympics held the promise of having a global coming out party. A party where residents could carefully plan for six years just what to wear as their best clothes.

Along with this exciting possibility, however, also comes the inherent fear of hosting an unsuccessful or unflattering event. In reality, the amount of attention brought about by hosting the Olympics far exceeds the amount of control the host ultimately has over the outcome of the Games – despite meticulous planning. This tension is fundamental to understanding how an event which lasts only 17 days can hold a city in the suspense for six years.

This chapter outlines the identity goals of the Barcelona Olympic organizers then compares what international broadcasters presented to home audiences about Barcelona, Catalonia and Spain as Olympic host and Europe as Olympic setting. As with prior chapters on broadcasters' presentation of nations and Olympism, the results can be explained to some degree by the preparation of broadcasters, as well as their motivation to educate or entertain audiences. But it is also apparent, as in prior chapters, that the broadcaster portrayals are also conditioned by domestic contexts, influencing, for example, whether to present Catalonia as a national and cultural entity distinct from Spain.

Planning an identity

Chapter 5 related the basic process of planning the Opening and Closing Ceremonies, as well how the present day ceremony structures allow for significant amounts of cultural presentation by the host. In 1986 when Barcelona was put forward as a candidate, well before the ceremonies were designed, the process of developing a host identity had already begun. That process involved a number of important steps:

    1. selecting the geopolitical reference for the host (in this case, 'how much' of the

---

(contd) Catalonia, Valencia and parts of Aragon), Andorra, several counties of southern France, the Balearic Islands, and part of the island of Sardinia. The Catalan language is going through a period of linguistic normalization. Its use in public and in the mass media is slowly increasing, but it is still far from overtaking Spanish, which still enjoys the status of majority language in Catalan territory. Besides the presence of TVE, the Spanish state public television station, and the private stations Antena 3, Tele 5 and Canal Plus (pay channel), Catalonia has two autonomous television channels, TV3 and Canal 33, which broadcast in Catalan.

The Barcelona Organizing Committee of the Olympic Games (COOB'92) was made up of the Barcelona City Council, the Spanish Olympic Committee, the Higher Council for Sports (Spanish Government), and the Catalan autonomous government (the Generalitat).

host should be identified as Barcelona, Catalonia or Spain, and how these relationships should be presented);

2. defining a desired 'character' for the host (or hosts as in this case), grounded in reality yet promoting the host's most positive features;

3. choosing appropriate symbolic representations of that character, using existing urban and geographic features, as well as newly designed elements such as a logo and mascot;

4. developing an approach for the dissemination of the host identity locally (e.g. sign, city and venue design) and internationally (materials for media); and

5. creating Opening and Closing Ceremony performances which present the host culture in an accessible and appealing way to international audiences.

To locate a starting point, the ceremony producers Ovideo Bassat Sport conducted an international survey. The results revealed that there existed remarkably few image associations (outside Europe) with Barcelona – beyond the fact that it would be an Olympic host. Further, there was absolutely no recognition of Catalonia outside of western Europe. Finally, international associations with Spain were largely limited to tourist-oriented stereotypes: southern European location, beautiful women, sun, cheap wine, siestas after lunch, bull fights and flamenco. While many of these stereotypical images have been attractive for tourism over the years they were considered a drawback for the host in terms of presenting an international picture of Spain as an advanced economy and a modern democracy.

Establishing an Olympic peace among planners

In order to devise a workable plan a consensus needed to be reached between the various actors involved in the organizing efforts: the Spanish Government, the Catalan autonomous government (La Generalitat), Barcelona City Council, the European Community and the Olympic Committees. These actors represented the different 'image' stakeholders in the outcome of the 1992 Games.

For these planners it was a relatively easy task to develop a list of identity goals for each of the host entities. The greater challenge was deciding how, which, and to what degree, these chosen attributes of Barcelona, Catalonia and Spain would manifest themselves in the design of the ceremonies and elsewhere. To make the task even more challenging, good advertising principles dictated that a complex reality be consolidated into a relatively few identity attributes that were easy to grasp and well suited to audio-visual portrayals, thus raising the possibility that the groups involved might have to compete for the inclusion of 'their' desired image agenda as part of the identity campaign.

To an amazing degree the identity goals (outlined below) were ultimately realized in the design of the ceremonies and look of the city despite the diverse interests of the organizing factions entering into the process. In large part this was due to the common desire of the organizing committee, and others involved, for everything to run smoothly. Along the way

165

it became clear that if the Games were not successful, then everyone would lose.[2] Also, each of the parties had slightly different priorities, making compromises possible.

This does not mean there was no controversy over those six years of planning. Quite the contrary. In Catalonia, and throughout Spain, there was much discussion, debate and speculation over what the Olympic organizers should and would do in terms of the balance between Catalonia and Spain as hosts.[3] Interestingly, this continuous and at times contentious local dialogue never found the same intensity in international media and as such did not leave Spanish borders in any significant way.

Identity goals for Barcelona, Catalonia and Spain as Olympic host

To get a sense of the success, or not, of the host's identity campaign as interpreted by international broadcasters, it is necessary to briefly review what was intended by the Olympic planners.

A passionate and democratic Spain

For Spain, one of the main cultural objectives of the ceremonies was to eliminate some of the tourist stereotypes (siestas, bullfights, slow moving). However, not all of the existing stereotypes noted above were seen as negative. The organizers decided to promote the widely held image of Spain as a land of 'passion'. In addition, the 'sun' (also a central symbol in Spain's tourist advertising campaign: 'Spain. Everything under the sun') appeared as elemental to several ceremony performances. More broadly, it was desired that Spain be represented as diverse, democratic, modern and cultured. To emphasize Spain as a land of 'culture', it was decided to focus on artistic representatives that already had international recognition. For example, the artists Picasso, Dalí and Miró were chosen as design models for signs, colour and ceremony settings, and world famous entertainers such as Montserrat Caballé and Josep Carreras were chosen to sing in the ceremony. Politically, the image of the King Juan Carlos I and Queen Sofia in the dignitaries' box and at various venues throughout the Games constituted the primary symbol of Spain throughout the Games.

A politically and culturally distinct Catalonia

The producers of the ceremony themselves suggested that their project was to produce a 3-hour television commercial spot whose aim was to 'put Barcelona and Catalonia on the map'.[4] It was a concern within many sectors of Catalan public opinion that Spain, as the familiar international presence, would overshadow any reference whatsoever to Catalonia

---

2   Two years before the Olympics there was a ceremony for the opening of the Montjüic Olympic stadium. It rained. Everyone got soaked. The event was rife with problems and delays, including nationalistic demonstrations and police preventing Catalan flags from entering the stadium. According to sources, that event acted as a turning point of sorts in that it occurred to all groups that the Olympics could fail and everyone would lose if they didn't work closely together to the end.

3   For a discussion of local discourse about host identity issues see Blain, Boyle, and O'Donnell (1993).

4   Bassat (1992) and Bassat (1993).

and its national identity. Therefore the primary identity objectives for Catalonia were first to become known, and second to be understood as having a distinct political, cultural and linguistic identity relative to Spain. Particularly in the ceremonies it was felt that the presentation of Catalonia and Catalan culture should be 'undiluted' and differentiated from that of Spain (but not necessarily in conflict with Spain). This goal was primarily achieved through the use of Catalan language as an official Olympic language (along with Spanish, English and French), the entrance of the Catalan flag along side the flags of Spain and Barcelona, the playing of the Catalan national anthem, and by dedicating specific performance segments to the avant-garde and Mediterranean spirit of Catalan music, art and folk traditions (specifically the segments of the 'Sardana', a traditional Catalan circle dance, and 'Els Castellers' or the human pyramids). Catalan residents joined in the effort by displaying Catalan flags in the stadium, out windows, and over balconies throughout the city.

Modern, yet historic Barcelona

For the host city, Barcelona, the image objectives were more conventional and along the lines of what is termed 'city marketing', a strategy aimed at attracting projects that encourage local economic activity and development. Barcelona wanted to present itself to the world as a modern city which welcomed economic activity and initiatives; it wanted to promote the city as the economic hub for southern Europe. It was desired that Barcelona be perceived as a thriving, cosmopolitan city ready for the next century, but also a city built upon centuries of colourful history. To serve these goals, it was obvious that the city's outstanding architectural character would provide excellent televisual symbols (for example, the Montjuïc Olympic stadium, the Gaudí-designed Sagrada Familia cathedral, the statue of Columbus, etc.). In addition, certain competition venues, such as that for diving, were designed to offer television cameras scenic background images of Barcelona during the competitions. RTO'92, as host broadcaster, set up five 'beauty' cameras around the city to offer colourful and characteristic city scenes for international broadcasters to use.

Another goal was to demonstrate that Barcelona was economically and administratively capable of successfully organizing one of the most complex and popular events of modern times. In this sense, planners wanted the Games to be seen as technologically innovative and well-organized (yet friendly and human), dispensing with any generalized Spanish stereotypes of lateness, laziness, or inefficiency.

As is the case with any marketing or advertising process, the negative elements also present in the city (pollution, discrimination, rubbish, poverty, traffic, noise, transportation, humidity, asphalt, etc.) were left out of the image selection process.

A Mediterranean Olympics

Central to the host identity campaign was the decision to emphasize the 1992 Games' Mediterranean setting. Using the Mediterranean as an overall framework for the Olympic host identity both respected and solved many issues for the Olympic planners. First, because the Olympic Games are a sports and cultural phenomenon whose historic roots are found in the Mediterranean, and more specifically in Greek culture, this identity strategy conveyed an attitude of respect towards the protagonism of Greece in Olympic history. The Barcelona organizers felt this even more important when it became known that Athens would not be host to the Games in the Centenary year in 1996, and that the US city of Atlanta had been chosen for this anniversary event.

Second, the Mediterranean provided the needed rubric within which the respective identities of Barcelona, Catalonia and Spain – and even Europe – could all comfortably fit. This concept facilitated the establishment of consensus among the different political actors involved in the organization.

Finally, the Mediterranean concept is not only an internationally recognized geographic referent, but also a recognizable 'feeling' and cultural concept that links well to aesthetic expression. The Mediterranean concept was integrated in all design aspects of the host identity, including the Barcelona'92 mascot and logo, the design of the torch, signage colours, and ultimately the Opening and Closing ceremonies.

As an example, the Barcelona'92 logo, a vibrant blue, yellow and red symbol, was intended as an expression of Mediterranean aesthetics. Blue represented the sea and the sky, yellow as the sun, and combined with red was intended to evoke the idea of passion, human qualities and friendship. The logo was also a reproduction of the human body in movement, thus expressing the humanist concepts of classicism, as well as the Mediterranean character of joy for life.[5]

Broadcast presentations of Spain, Catalonia and Barcelona

This part of the study used a quantitative (close to 200 content categories) and qualitative analysis of 25 Opening Ceremony broadcasts to better understand how broadcasters chose to characterize the 1992 Olympic host. (Refer to Appendix A for a list of content categories.) It also considers study correspondent observations concerning the perception of the Olympic host in their respective countries. While Closing Ceremony broadcasts were not subjected to the same analysis, it should be said that through correspondent reports and a review of Closing Ceremony broadcasts it was clear that knowledge about Barcelona and Catalonia as hosts increased substantially over the course of the Games (and should be kept in mind when reviewing the Opening Ceremony findings). Add to this the success of the Games and plenty of visual exposure for the host city and it is safe to say that broadcasters finished their Olympics commentary full of positive regard for its

---

5   The representation of this symbol during the Opening Ceremony caused various international television channels to recognize this 'Mediterraneanness', and some others such as Russian television, for example, to make some quite amazing interpretations:
'Perhaps, after the first look it's hard to determine what this emblem means. However, as its creator Josep Trias believes, everything is obvious: a figure of the man in movement is pictured on the white background; and the colors in which the symbolic parts of the body are colored, unmistakably point at his Mediterranean origin ... Blue represents the sea, yellow the sun, red life ... But, to tell you the truth, it (the emblem) also reminds me of a head of a bull; and corrida and Spain -- these are inseparable.' (Ostankino 1, Russia, Opening Ceremony).

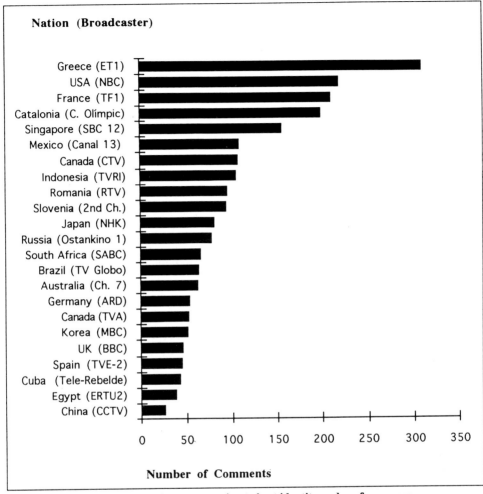

Figure 9.1. Broadcaster attention to host identity and performances.

host. The broad identity objective of creating or enhancing a 'favourable' image was certainly achieved.

But what of more specific identity objectives? Reflective both of differences in the overall quantity of broadcaster commentary (noted in earlier chapters) and interest in presenting cultural aspects of the Opening Ceremony, broadcasters varied in the relative amount of attention spent characterizing the host and narrating the cultural performances in terms which reflected on a host identity. Figure 9.1 compares these levels of attention by comparing the number of distinct comments or associations broadcast commentators made that relate in some way to the portrayal of the host either directly or indirectly (through the characterization of cultural segments). This figure does not reflect purely descriptive commentary about the cultural performances ('There are now 1200 dancers entering the stadium'), but only commentary which educates or presents, in some way, information regarding the host ('they are now dancing the Sardana, a traditional Catalan dance').

Oddly, there is little to explain how broadcasters are distributed along this figure – except at the extremes, where the CCTV (China) commentator not only didn't say much in general, but showed no interest whatsoever in the cultural or political distinctiveness of Barcelona and Catalonia (discussed below), while ET1 (Greece) commentators clearly reveled in the 'return' of the Olympics to a Mediterranean port.

The portrayal of Spain

The Royal Family

Attention to Spain, across nearly all broadcasters, mostly focused on the King and the royal family, most often prompted by visual images of King Juan Carlos I and family in the tribunal. As organizers hoped, a few broadcasters emphasized the success and stability of Spain's democratic transition (in particular NBC, USA; CTV, Canada; Canal 13, Mexico), identifying the King as the protagonist of the new Spanish democracy.

> And so does [King] Juan Carlos deserve this moment, so instrumental in guiding his nation through treacherous waters toward democracy and out of the dark ages of fascism under Generalísimo Francisco Franco (NBC, USA, Opening Ceremony).

Canal 13 (Mexico), Ostankino 1 (Russia) and ARD (Germany) emphasized the popularity of the King in the management of political power. The Russian commentator, in particular, communicated a sense of a country united by love for the King. Several broadcasters emphasized aspects of the King that were significantly less political, such as his sportiness (TVE, Spain; SABC, South Africa; 2nd Channel, Slovenia; and NHK, Japan). Strangely enough, this non-political approach to the royal family is also the case for the BBC which apparently did not want to establish any comparisons between the British monarchy which, at the time of the opening of the Games, was less popular than the Spanish monarchy. CCTV China did not make any political reference to the figure of the King whatsoever.

Passion for life

With one of the performance segments (flamenco dance and opera) titled 'Land of Passion' it was not surprising that 10 of the broadcasts specifically associate this attribute with the Spanish people. All told, 62 per cent of the broadcasts characterized the Spanish people as having a deeply felt passion and love of life expressed through music, festival and colour. Only NHK (Japan) commentators refer to more traditional stereotypes of bullfights and joined NBC (USA) and TF1 (France) in remarking on the beautiful Spanish women. (Also, the BBC UK chose as part of its opening graphic for its daily Olympic broadcast a picture of a bullfighter, flamenco dancer and red carnations). One Chinese press account after the Opening Ceremony was quoted as saying, 'although there was not the symbol of Spain – bullfighting – in the performances at the Opening Ceremony, the performances as a whole were very cultural and colourful.'[6]

---

6 *Wenhui Bao*, 26 July 1992. This is a Shanghai newspaper geared to intellectuals.

A 'cultured' host

The goal of the Olympic planners for Spain to be associated with high culture was met in the sense that most of the broadcasts mentioned well known artists (Picasso, Miró, etc.) and nearly all made general comments about the Spanish love of music and art ('Spain has offered so much to the world in culture, art, architecture, music, sports' – SABC, South Africa, Opening Ceremony). However, any sense of a specific artistic tradition (e.g. modernism) was tied much more to the presentation of Barcelona, than of Spain.

Also, few broadcasts attempted to place various dance or music segments in their Spanish contexts (Anadulsia, Aragón etc.) or show much affinity for the relatively long segments of opera presented by some world famous Spanish artists. As an example, Langer described a central tension in the Australian Channel 7 broadcast as the commentators positioned as 'uncultured' outsiders trying to grasp 'European high culture' (opera, arts, theatre). He said that 'a symptom of this tension was the virtual silence of the commentators while the opening cultural pageant unfolded compared with the verbosity of these commentators once the athletes joined in'.[7] In fact, across several broadcasts the relatively long, performance segments of opera, devoid of action, served more to silence the largely sports-oriented commentators than to provoke commentary about Spain and its high culture. Awatef Abd El-Rahman, reporting perceptions of the ceremony in Egypt, suggested that the opera singing, while consistent with the ceremony, was contrary to 'the Arab mood which is not in favour with that sort of singing'.[8] This attitude was also reflected in the comments of the study correspondents from the United Kingdom:

> Among the less relevant symbolism as perceived through the BBC's coverage was the sight of half a dozen people (including some conspicuous heavyweights) dressed in faintly absurd clothes and singing lollipop fragments of opera. [The BBC commentator] did not indicate what this meant in the context of the ceremony, and it was left hanging uncertainly as a celebration of Spanish or European culture. It also became (through costume, 'classicism' and fat) a celebration of wealth and power ...[9]

Catalonia's coming out party

Much to the delight of the Generalitat of Catalonia there was a much greater recognition of Catalonia in international media than expected. Looking specifically at the broadcasters in this study most found the idea of 'Catalanness' something worth presenting to home audiences. For NHK (Japan), for example, the existence of Catalonia provided a basic introductory framework to the Opening Ceremony as a whole:

> K: Mr. Hirano, for spectators to able to enjoy the ceremony, we need to explain something about Catalonia, right?

---

7   Langer (1992).

8   El-Rahman, Awatef Abd (1992).

9   Izod *et al.* (1992).

171

H: Yes, that's right, because Spain is a country with a strong sense of autonomy. The people of each region insist on his own sense of autonomy and among them the Catalans are strongest. Many centuries ago in this region was a time in which it was independent, very prosperous with its centre in Barcelona. Accordingly, from the point of view of Catalan people and Barcelonians this opportunity is not a Spanish, but Catalan Olympics (NHK, Japan, Opening Ceremony).

Table 9.1 summarizes the percentage of broadcasts that recognize Catalonia, either directly or indirectly, as a distinct political and cultural unit. It should be noted, however, that this particular table represents 'mentions' only and does not mean there was an accompanying explanation of what, just exactly, Catalonia 'is'. For example, every broadcaster mentioned the visual entrance of the Catalan flag into the stadium, but CCTV (China) did not explain its meaning or ever mention Catalonia again in its broadcast.

Table 9.1. Recognition of Catalan political and cultural symbols

Commentary references	% broadcasts*
Refer to Catalonia as a nation or politically autonomous region	32% (8)
Refer to the Catalan anthem	60% (15)
Refer to the Catalan flag	100% (25)
Refer to the Catalan language	68% (17)
Refer to the 'sardana' performance as Catalan folklore	76% (19)
Refer to the 'human pyramids' as Catalan folklore or tradition	80% (20)
Name Jordi Pujol as the President of the Generalitat of Catalonia	64% (16)
Refer to Catalonia as having a distinct history	56% (14)

*$N = 25$.

While the majority of broadcasters recognized the existence of Catalonia as evidenced in the above table, they varied considerably in the clarity and theme of that presentation. Each of the broadcast presentations of Catalonia in this analysis could be described as falling into one of the following four identity orientations:

1. Catalonia is an autonomous political and cultural identity distinct from, and at times in conflict, with Spain. The Opening Ceremony design is seen as representative of both the cooperative and conflictual nature of this relationship.

2. Catalonia has a cultural and political identity distinct from, but fully compatible with, the rest of Spain. The Opening Ceremony is seen as an opportunity for audiences to experience Catalan culture, but the display does not hold any political connotations.

3. Catalonia is mentioned – and thus implied as distinct in some way, but it is not really explained. Catalonia is used interchangeably with Spain as host.

4. Catalonia is not presented in any way as a politically, culturally, or linguistically distinct entity.

The Opening Ceremony as a victory for Catalonia

In contrast to some of the negative pre-event media framing concerning the possibility that North Korea or student activists might disrupt the Seoul Olympics, the international media at Barcelona appeared to reject any central story line involving potential conflict or terrorism. For their part, the call for 'Olympic peace' was well heeded by Catalan nationalist groups who, in line with their general tendency to reject violence as a way of defending their identity, at no time whatsoever decided on mounting a boycott. Instead, they proposed festive ways of demonstrating their identity at all times (encouraging of flags and decorations on balconies, streets festivals, etc.) which, given the inherently positive context of the Olympics, seemed to prove more attractive to international sports media than the staging of nationalist demonstrations. However, there was interest expressed by of several broadcasters in the political dimensions of the Barcelona Olympic Games. In the end, however, this vein of discourse largely ended up as compliments on the ability of all parties to work cooperatively.

Even so, the broadcasts of NBC (USA), ET1 (Greece), CTV (Canada), Channel 7 (Australia), Canal A (Colombia), TF1 (France), Canal 13 (Mexico), NHK (Japan), ARD (Germany), BBC (UK) and TVA (Canada) fall generally within the first identity orientation in that they all recognized the political dimension of the relationship between Catalonia and Spain and saw the Opening Ceremony as somehow emblematic of that relationship.

> Well after the bitter civil war and dictatorship, there was a sensitive question. Should the Games be more or less Catalan or more or less Spanish? It was only settled after semi-formal negotiations between the national government and the Catalonians and tonight we'll see the compromise (BBC, UK, in introductory comments to Opening Ceremony).

These broadcasters readily note the presence of Catalan symbols at the ceremony (flag, anthem, language and folk performance, political representatives) and imply their presence as a victory of sorts for Catalonia. For example, when King Juan Carlos I of Spain made his official declaration of the opening of the Games, he spoke alternately in Catalan and Spanish. Here's how the NBC commentators reacted to the King:

> C: The reaction of the crowd! King Juan Carlos spoke Catalan, and that is significant. The Mayor [of Barcelona] was quoted as saying only a couple of days ago, 'let us make this an occasion of Catalan pride, pride in Barcelona, but not antagonism toward any other region of Spain at large, let's come together for this one'. As apparently they have.

> E: Incredible concession. You heard the appreciative reaction of the Catalans in Olympic stadium ... (NBC, USA, Opening Ceremony).

For NBC, these were definitely Catalan Olympics, and at times the US broadcaster seemed to give the ceremony more political significance than the Olympic planners did. Earlier in the ceremony NBC even went well beyond the boundaries of the ceremony's official script to re-interpret the Mediterranean Sea segment (refer to Chapter 6 for a summary of this segment) as a representation of the Catalans' historic effort to defend their identity.

> E: Many of the great explorers of history were either Spanish or sailed under the Spanish flag: Columbus, Magellan, Ponce de León, Cortez, Pizarro. In a sense, you might think this [the performance] represents their adventures, the peril they encountered, seeking a new world, going off toward uncharted territory. In a sense, that's true, but it's also meant to represent the fierce independence of Barcelona and Catalonia, the vicissitude of their existence, rocked from to and fro by conquerors from other lands, dictators from Spain at large, their fierce determination to fight off those influences and be sovereign, determine their circumstances themselves, again, no matter what evil, what adversity ... (NBC, USA, Opening Ceremony).

And, as if to underscore just who the 'real' host was NBC commentators introduced the 'Land of Passion' flamenco performance segment as 'not a bit Catalan' then cut away to conduct interviews outside the stadium.

As noted, the US broadcast was not the only one to imbue political importance into some of the ritual, folkloric and musical performances of the ceremonies. Here's how two other broadcasters characterized the Catalan folk dance, the 'sardana':

> This sardana was prohibited during the Franco era. It became, like the language, a symbol of Catalan autonomy. (ARD, Germany, Opening Ceremony).

> The interlocked hands represent the solidarity and the collective strength of the Catalan people. (BBC, Great Britain, Opening Ceremony).

The BBC suggested that the tension between Catalan and Spanish nationalism was harmonized in several segments of the ceremony with the inclusion of both the sardana and some 'flamenco steps', too. They also note that a musical 'consensus' was arrived at when both 'El Concierto de Aranjuez' (Spanish) and 'El cant dels ocells' by Pau Casals (Catalan) were played.[10] This idea of consensus was also underscored by other broadcasters at more ritualistic moments of the ceremony, particularly in the choice of the final flame carriers:

> It's [a final torch] relay ... to Juan Antonio San Epitanio, a basketball player, representing the city of Barcelona, whereas Mr. Menéndez [who entered the stadium with the torch] was from Madrid, also a symbol of these two cities sharing the last race, that of the flame to its final destination, at least for 1992. (TVA, Canada, Opening Ceremony)

The French TF1 broadcaster, in particular, focused on the cooperative outcome of the

---

10 *Ibid.*

relationship between Catalonia and Spain throughout its broadcast. Referring to the fact that the Spanish and Catalan flags are both red and yellow, the commentator said:

> ... different tones but ultimately there is that unity of red and yellow which expresses so well the relations between Spain and Catalonia, who are so different but have such close ties. It's something that is not very comprehensible, perhaps not even very logical, but which is profoundly rich and creative. (TF1, France, Opening Ceremony)

Although agreement was not always possible, as when the BBC commentator noted that the use of French to introduce entering teams during the athletes' parade was because 'the Catalans and the Spanish couldn't agree'.

Acknowledgment of the political dimension of Catalonia did not necessarily mean that these broadcasters delved into the same level of historical detail as, for example, the NBC (USA) broadcast did. According to Langer, most of the comments by Australia's Channel 7 about the 'fervently Catalan city' of Barcelona were mostly 'throw away' lines or 'momentary gestures', passing by quickly, without follow up or substance.[11]

The Opening Ceremony as an introduction to Catalan culture

While the two primary 'Catalan' performance segments, the 'sardana' segment and 'Els Castellers' (refer to Chapter 5) were recognized by 75 per cent of the broadcasts as based on Catalan folklore, not all broadcasters chose to bestow any political dimension to their presence in the ceremony. The broadcasts of Ostankino 1 (Russia), 2nd Channel (Slovenia), RTV (Romania) and SBC 12 (Singapore), for example, readily acknowledged the Catalan origins of these performance segments and other ceremony symbols, but did not relate these to any relationship between Catalonia and Spain. For these broadcasters 'Catalanness' is a cultural presence, not a political one. For the Slovenian 2nd Channel commentator, for example, the linguistic attributes of Catalonia found some affinity with the strong linguistic identity associated with Slovenia. Again, while acknowledgments of Catalonia were distinct there was rarely a sense of depth to these comments, as our Russian correspondent noted, 'Catalonia was mentioned, but ignored ... [the image was] positive, but insufficient'.[12]

Catalonia as undefined

For those broadcasters remaining, ERTU2 (Egypt), Tele-Rebelde (Cuba), TVRI (Indonesia), SABC (South Africa) and MBC (Korea), Catalonia 'exists' in that it was mentioned. Any definition, however, not only lacked depth, but was decidedly vague – particularly in relation to Spain. Catalonia and Spain were used interchangeably to describe ceremony features, with Barcelona most frequently cited as host. For example, the Indonesian commentator said, referring to the sardana:

---

11 Langer (1992).

12 Zassoursky *et al.* (1992).

> This dance is often performed in open spaces in the cities around Catalonia ... And if we are seeing on the television screen these dancers do not include only young people but also those who are not young any more. Older people are also participating. Because indeed this dance is owned by all Catalonians. (TVRI, Indonesia, Opening Ceremony).

He then referred to this as a 'Spanish tradition' in the next sentence.

The South African broadcaster (SABC) missed the entire first segment of the ceremony intended to present Catalan culture to the world – and thus missed the opportunity to introduce the ceremony design as reflective of its Catalan host. (In fact, advertisements took up over a third of the cultural performances in SABC's broadcast, affecting any coherent cultural narrative that commentators might have engaged in.)

There is no Catalonia

The fourth identity orientation included only one broadcaster in this study: China's CCTV. Other than one brief, and unexplained reference to the Catalan flag as it entered the stadium (alongside flags of Barcelona and Spain), no aspect of Catalonia – its language, culture or political autonomy – was mentioned at any time in the broadcast. That said, it should also be mentioned that little detail, if any, is offered by the CCTV commentator about the Spanish monarchy, Spain or even Europe. Instead the CCTV commentator's interest concentrated more on aspects such as the unifying tradition of the cultural segments rather than their national origin.

Domestic context influencing broadcaster recognition of Catalonia

Prior chapters readily acknowledge the range of preparation and interest of various broadcasters in interpreting, rather than just describing, the Opening Ceremony. For the most part ceremony planners got their wish that Catalonia would be 'presented' as unique, in some way, to global audiences. The limits to their identity objectives were found in the presentation of Catalonia as an autonomous political community. This outcome, however, was likely beyond the efforts of the ceremony planners to control. Reviewing the findings concerning the presentation of Catalonia it is clear that the broadcasters associated with the three identity orientations that did not underscore the political dimension of Catalonia's character represented specific types of geopolitical and social environments listed below. These domestic contexts may well have affected their presentation of Catalonia as host:

- Broadcasters from countries that have cultural, linguistic or national plurality problems that politically condition the commentators. This is the case, for example, for CCTV (China) and TVRI (Indonesia).

- Broadcasters from countries that have social or development problems which clearly affect the interest their commentators may have in the problem of national and linguistic minorities in Europe. This is the case, for example, for ERTU2 (Egypt) and CRTV (Cameroon).

- Broadcasters from countries that are subject to situations of social conflict that cast a shadow over their interest in these questions of identity. This is the case of the extreme complexity for SABC (South Africa), whose television channel does mention that differences exist between Catalonia and Spain although hardly considers the political dimensions of this difference.

- Broadcasters from countries that are currently experiencing great transformations with dramatic nationalistic implications and which prefer to concentrate their attention on other aspects of the ceremony such as the freedom and creativity of expression (Ostankino 1, Russia), the union of the athletes and the value of Olympism (RTV, Romania and 2nd Channel, Slovenia).

- Broadcasters from countries that are culturally more distant from Europe whose commentators more interested in the global aspects of a Mediterranean culture than in the specific features of the cultural or national identity of Catalonia. Specific descriptions related to Catalan culture are given more global interpretations. This is the case for a broadcaster such as MBC (Korea).

Before leaving this discussion of Catalonia as a host identity, it's worth reflecting on a few special cases.

Surprise and acceptance in Latin America. The image of Catalonia and Spain in Latin America, as a consequence of their important historic, cultural and linguistic relationships, deserves some special attention. Analysis of the commentaries of TV Globo (Brazil), Canal 13 (Mexico), Tele-Rebelde (Cuba) and RCN (Colombia) reveals two interesting reactions to the host identity in the ceremony. First, there is more surprise than in other parts of the world about the presence – and existence – of such cultural and linguistic variety in Spain and, second, there is a special interest that these diversities express themselves in a positive Catalonia-Spain relationship. The Brazilian commentator suggested to his viewers that 'they are becoming immersed in the capital of Catalonia'. With that identification, the duality of Catalonia/Spain or of Spanish/Catalan culture is fully accepted.

> 'Let's see ... this is a symbol of the Olympiad. A smile of all Spaniards, not only Catalans, but from all Spaniards to everyone in the world'. (TV Globo, Brazil, Opening Ceremony).

This surprise and acceptance of the Catalan / Spanish relationship is even more evident when considering the Catalan language, its protagonism as the official language, and its use by some of the most important dignitaries in the ceremonies.

Even more intriguing to several of the Latin American commentators, however, was the modernization of Spain, of which Barcelona seemed an admirable expression.

> J.R.F. Barcelona is proof of a new Spain. A re-urbanized Barcelona, a modern Barcelona with its grand architecture and grand port that's a door to Europe ...

> J.S.: Barcelona has been radically transformed in the last years, a transformation

that cost 7–8 million dollars! But today Barcelona is a beautiful city.(Canal 13, Mexico, Opening Ceremony)

Quebec and Catalonia: birds of a feather? One of the reasons that the French Canadian broadcaster TVA was included in this study was an interest in some of the similarities between Quebec and Catalonia – both nations with a sense of being linguistically and culturally unique within their home state. As it turned out explicit parallels between Catalonia and Quebec were not made by TVA commentators although, without reading too much into their commentary, they did show a special interest in Catalonia, in particular the Catalan language, and suggested at times a sense of camaraderie, as in the following comment:

> [Our] Catalan friends ... a generous people, a warm people ... a people with traditions ... a people which is marked by its culture, but its architects, but its artists and its painters ... by its musicians and by its dynamism during the 1990s (TVA, Canada, Opening Ceremony).

The Spanish broadcasters: self presentation of the most humble kind. One final reference should be made to the truly unique treatment of Catalonia and the Catalonia/Spain issue by the Spanish TVE and Catalan Canal Olímpic television channels. There is a great degree of self-control on the part of the commentators (in contrast to the spontaneity and ease of several other international broadcasters) when dealing with the issue of the Catalonia-Spain relationship. The rhetoric seemed to avoid conflictive questions altogether. In fact, there is not one explicit reference whatsoever throughout both ceremony broadcasts to the national question of Catalonia or to its relationship with Spain. The exception is some emotional references to a Catalan symbol in TVE and making a single unqualified mention of the Catalan language in the Catalan Canal Olímpic broadcast.

The presentation of the official host: Barcelona

Because of the physical presence of Olympic activities within the host city, the image of Barcelona was by nature quite different from presentations of the more imaged entities of Catalonia and Spain. The city was uniformly seen through its unique architectural, artistic and urban planning features. Probably as a consequence of its visual accessibility, the number of items defining its image had more breadth and heterogeneity, but the resulting image was also remarkably consistent across broadcasts.

Most broadly, Barcelona was interpreted as the place where an historic event was occurring which affects the whole of humanity. Barcelona was identified as the capital of Catalonia in nearly half of the broadcasts, but it was a city being transformed – for the duration of the Games – into a 'capital of the world'. This 'special' Olympic capital city status allowed many commentators to present Barcelona as the most fascinating and compelling city, especially regarding the quality of life and the attractions it offers to people visiting it. These references would become more and more persistent and enthusiastic by the time of the Closing Ceremony.

A splendid city. It's a city that gives you a feeling after a few hours of an intensity, a vitality, a creativity, an intense creativity. Life is everywhere, art is everywhere, with a simplicity in community life that is stunning. (TF1, France, Opening Ceremony).

A city of contrasts and creativity

Specifically meeting the goals of the Olympic planners, Barcelona was interpreted at one and the same time as being old and new ('The old and the new mixed in Barcelona', TV Globo, Brazil, Opening Ceremony), as historic and modern, as a city that lives in the streets. Much of this was able to be expressed using the television cameras.

For several broadcasters 'La Rambla', Barcelona's most famous street, offered an excellent visual representation of the 'personality' of Barcelona and its inhabitants. For example, NBC (USA) began its broadcast of the Opening Ceremony with some camera images of this famous promenade, pointing out that the widest part was given over to pedestrians while the narrowest parts on each side were reserved for cars.

> Eight o'clock, Saturday evening in Barcelona, and what you're seeing in this Opening Ceremony, a tribute to the signature boulevard of Barcelona, Las Ramblas. Flower people, bird people, here's a look at Las Ramblas. There's no other boulevard quite like it in the entire world, a pedestrian walkway where those on foot occupy the wide centre cut and automobiles negotiate the narrow sidelines, as if they were consigned to the sidewalks. Newspaper kiosks seemingly almost every ten or fifteen yards. There's the huge food market, you saw just a moment ago, la Boqueria, and just about every twenty or thirty yards you'll see merchants selling caged birds or colourful flowers and that's what the people down on the stadium infield are meant to represent here ... Las Ramblas is a nearly 24 hours a day kaleidoscope of humanity, street performers, mimes, home to vagabond and aristocrat alike, you might say. If you had just one day or night to spend in Barcelona, and you wanted to absorb a good portion of what the city is about, you'd spend it strolling from the centre of the city down to the Columbus statue alongside the Mediterranean, Las Ramblas. (NBC, USA, Opening Ceremony)

Through this type of commentary Barcelona was portrayed as a colourful and creative city, that has been able to offer the world great 'avant-garde' artists such as Gaudí, Miró, Picasso, Dalí, etc. Some broadcasters such as Japan's NHK, used specially designed studio sets which replicated Gaudí architecture or represented other artistic styles of Barcelona as background the television commentators.

A city of renewal

One of the items most emphasized by the international press over the Games' preparatory period was the urban renovation experienced by Barcelona. There were reasons for that, since the urban planning transformations experienced by Barcelona over that period had been really exceptional. During the Opening Ceremony, the television commentators also referred to the urban renewal of Barcelona, especially as related it to the sports facilities (e.g. the renovation of the stadium). References to the modernization process, the wealth of Catalonia and Barcelona, and the efficiency of the organization of the Games were most frequent in the broadcasts of Indonesia (TVRI), Egypt (ERTU2), Cuba (Tele-Rebelde), Romania (RTV), Slovenia (2nd channel) and China (CCTV). Barcelona was definitely not associated with a siesta-style pace.

> The progress achieved by Barcelona, in culture, economics ... gives Barcelona a good chance to become the greatest city in the world. And they have proved this. They are capable of becoming the host of the 25th Olympics. (TVRI, Indonesia, Opening Ceremony).

Broadcasters demonstrated little interest in more strictly economic realms such as trade and industry attributes, although there were generalized references to Barcelona as the 'economic capital' of Spain (e.g. ERTU2, Egypt). Despite a few references in some Opening Ceremony broadcasts to traffic, high hotel prices, unfriendly police, and the like, Barcelona came away looking through the lens of the television camera like a gem of art and architecture with sports-loving and hospitable people, more than capable of hosting a successful Olympic Games.

The cultural context for the games

Europe as part of the host identity

The European Community in 1992 (now European Union) also saw itself as host. To this end, the European Commission established an EC Olympic Programme and contributed money to have a presence in Barcelona (through street flags and banners) and in the Opening Ceremony during a 22-minute performance part entitled 'Music and Europe' which included opera, the human pyramids ('Els Castellers which linked a traditional Catalan folk activity to the symbols of the EC flag and its 12 member nations) and the playing of the European anthem 'Ode to Joy' with accompanying fireworks.[13] Locally, the EC actively promoted itself to visitors and professionals in attendance at the Games. For example, broadcasters in the international media centre were exposed to the EC's promotion of its high-definition television (HDTV) technology. The EC had involved itself in a similar way earlier in the year at the Albertville, France winter Olympics.[14] Did

---

13 In the introduction to the Opening Ceremony Press Guide, a few indirect references to Europe were made: 'Spain is the south-eastern gateway to Europe', 'Barcelona is a great European city'. The guide defined the European Community as: 'Today, twelve countries go to make up the Community Europe, a land where 348 million speak at least nine different languages. United by the blue flag with twelve golden stars, the countries of the European Community share the goals of economic policy and are on their way to political union. Today, the European Community is the world's largest market and the cradle of freedom and democracy that reflects the richness of its cultural diversity. The EC is formed by: Germany, Belgium, Denmark, Spain, France, Greece, Holland, Ireland, Italy, Luxembourg, Portugal and the United Kingdom'. (COOB'92, Opening Ceremony. Press Guide). As noted in chapter 5, the EC also provided a supplementary media guide to broadcasters, which was not noticeably used in the broadcast commentaries.

14 For example, the EC backed a series of advertisements and banners in the streets of Barcelona and Albertville representing the image of an athlete holding a torch decorated with the 12 stars of the European Community flag.

broadcasters notice this publicity campaign? The answer would have to be only marginally and never to the level of centrality that Barcelona, Catalonia and Spain played as host entities. To understand this outcome, it's worth pointing out some of the challenges the EC faced in trying to promote its image through an Olympic Games.

First, the image of Europe that was projected in Barcelona faced the difficulty of confusion over the global idea of Europe and the idea of the European Union as a political and economic entity of 12 European states. The idea of European culture, moreover, extends beyond the present boundaries of the 'Europe of the 12'. Further, any incorrect delimitation could have caused dissatisfaction among the non-Community European countries and posed a problem of matching the European political identity to the cultural identity.

Second, the image of the European Union came up against some special difficulties in the framework of the Olympic Games, dominated by the central role that 'nation-states' play in constructing the mythologies of sports representation and ceremony protocol. The European Union did not act as a nation among nations in the Olympic Games, and did not appear as such in the athletes' parade.

Finally, this was a time of great historic changes, which were presenting difficulties in the consolidation process (Maastricht Treaty), with unresolved expectations of extending the Union (Austria, Sweden, Norwegian, etc.) and the rupture of the historic division between East and West with the subsequent opening up of new European relations.

Under these conditions, the idea of Europe was developed at risk of appearing, in the eyes of other international communities, as a 'competitive community', as a 'market' or even as a yet politically undefined and incomplete entity. Given the challenges noted above, the EC chose the positive aspect of this image, the idea of the cooperative community of the future, as its image focus. However, in the end, even this fairly unthreatening strategy did not find its niche within the geopolitical images of Barcelona'92.

Table 9.2 summarizes references to Europe and the European Community demonstrating the marginal focus put on this aspect of the host identity. The broadcasts that carried no explicit mention of Europe were ARD (Germany), CCTV (China), ERTU2 (Egypt) and Ostankino 1 (Russia). Over 70 per cent of the mentions of Europe came during the human pyramids (Els Castellers) segment as intended. Only six of the broadcasts referred to Europe during the playing of the European anthem 'Ode to Joy', and these broadcasters tended to link their mentions of Europe and its anthem with references to the values of universality, unity, solidarity, and so forth., more in keeping with the Olympic spirit. For the Japanese NHK commentators, the European anthem evoked reference to German unification. For Mexican (Canal 13) commentators, the European anthem was the 'world anthem'. For Russian (Ostankino 1) and Romanian (RTV) commentators, the anthem had more humanitarian and emotional connotations than European ones:

> What's happening in the Olympic stadium now is very symbolic. The Ode to Joy is being performed by a 13-year-old boy (...) Here they are – the Olympic Games! The celebration, that unites all of humanity has finally begun'. (Ostankino 1, Russia, Opening Ceremony).

Only Greek (ET1) television, the broadcaster that emphasized the European context most, described the 'Ode to Joy' in terms of European unity as was the intent of ceremony planners.

> And this is the ode to joy, the European anthem sang by a boy 13 years old ... This year's Olympic Games coincides with a historic event for Europe. Beginning with the first day of 1993 all economic barriers will be removed between the member countries of the European Economic Community. The Olympic Games and the Expo'92 both of which are being held here in Seville, carry a message, important for all Europeans: Unite. (ET1, Greece, Opening Ceremony)

Table 9.2. References to Europe and the EC in the Opening Ceremony

Commentary references	% broadcasts (no. of broadcasts)*
Mention Europe and the European Community	58% (15)
Mention Europe but not the European Community	11% (3)
Do not mention Europe	15% (4)
Mention Barcelona as a European city	7% (2)

While perhaps the image of Europe in the Games was in fact a faithful reflection of the limits and conditions in line with which the image of the European Community at that time,[15] the marginal degree of attention paid to things European also relates to the structure of the narration of the ceremony, which did not situate things European in the centre of its discourse. Inclusion of 'Europe' in the design of the ceremony was as an arbitrary symbolic referent. Thus, for example, in the human pyramid segment, the references to Europe do not arise directly from the narrative of what it represents. Instead, they came from indirect references: twelve human pyramids that represent the twelve countries of the European Community. Thus, two identification symbols are employed: Catalan folklore (cultural referent) and its homage to Europe (arbitrary symbolic referent). In addition, the segment lost some of its intended impact when, ignoring the instructions that they had been given, the spectators began to light up their flares (which were intended to present the EC flag) at the wrong time (earlier when the Olympic torch entered the stadium), effectively ruining the iconic force planned for this segment and, of course, losing the references to Europe that had been foreseen with the participation of the spectators.[16]

---

15 European Parliament (1993).

16 Izod *et al.* (1992) suggest that the design of the segment itself was quite ill conceived. They said, 'It was not a strong moment, not least because only some of the twelve castles were seen [on television] ... Furthermore the major struggle in each tower building exercise was involved in building each castle [symbolically one EC country] – any overarching structure linking them would have been architecturally inconceivable. Thus the symbolism served its ostensible purpose weakly.'

Finally in the segment dedicated to opera lasting 13.5 minutes, performances were given by Spanish singers only, and it did not manage to evoke the idea of Europe in spite of the official indications ('The music the Europe created for the universe', 'A clear example of European culture') offered in the media script and guide. Instead, the opera segment acted more as a sign of prestige for the organizers – Catalan and Spanish – than as a sign of identification of Europe and its culture. The only broadcaster that referred to the European meaning of opera were TVE of Spain and Tele-Rebelde of Cuba.

As NBC (USA) did with the political meaning of Catalonia, only the Greek ET1 commentators take their references to Europe, European culture and Europeanness of the Games far beyond the proposals contained in the official script:

> We have to say to those who are watching what is going on now. People from Catalonia have begun to form 12 human pyramids. This officially marks the third part of the Opening Ceremony of the Olympic Games. What do these pyramids stand for? They represent the 12 member countries of the European Community. I think we mentioned earlier that the people of Spain have put great emphasis on their role in the European Community.

> But so did we. In the ceremony that took place on the hill of Olympia on June 6 and during the festivities in the Panathenaikon Stadium two days later, in both cases we raised the flag of Europe and played the anthem of the European Economic Community (...) it is very obvious that Europe is the future of the world ... These castells, these pyramids that are being formed represent the unity of strength and solidarity of the construction of Europe. (ET1, Greece, Opening Ceremony).

The Mediterranean culture of the Barcelona'92 Olympic Games

Ultimately more attractive to the international broadcasters than the idea of a 'European culture' hosting the Games was the host as Mediterranean culture. In fact, 17 or 68 per cent of the broadcasts studied explicitly identify Catalonia as a Mediterranean country and/or Barcelona as a Mediterranean city, while there were no explicit references to identify either Catalonia or Spain as a 'European countries' (and only two which identify Barcelona as European, Mexico's Canal 13 and Indonesia's TVRI). The Mediterranean, unlike Europe, appears to be a non-political and non-institutional concept, much easier to identify with the Catalan identity than with the concept of Europe. Further it was consistently interpreted as a positive cultural value: historic, representative of renewal, and creative.

 As noted earlier, this interpretation by broadcasters was fully compatible with the desires of the Olympic planners who, from the initial stages of candidature, felt comfortable with the idea of expressing Mediterranean values as a starting point, framework and common denominator in the cultural identity programme.

Chapter 6 discussed various interpretations of the Opening Ceremony performance segment called 'The Mediterranean Sea' which found that many broadcasters related well to the choice of this well known water as context for a performance narrative. It's worth noting that as with the European context, for Greek ET1 commentators the choice of the Mediterranean concept as central to the Games and to the Opening Ceremony held very special meaning. It represented the main link among classical Olympism, the renewal of the Games in Athens in 1896 and the 'new Mediterranean Games' in Barcelona'92.

> We hear the first notes of 'Mediterranea' 360 drums shatter the silence with their loud beat ... And the part that follows ladies and gentlemen has as theme the Mediterranean the Olympic Sea ... , the theme could have also been 'return to the Mediterranean'. After 96 years the Olympic Games returned to the Mediterranean. The first Games were held at the Panathenaikon Stadium of Athens in 1896. Since then all the Olympiads have been hosted by countries close to the Mediterranean but never bordered by this peace offering sea, the sea of civilization. And they have come back to the Mediterranean after 96 years. Understandably therefore, the people of Spain, the Catalans, honor the Mediterranean, our sea, here in Barcelona ... Ryuichi Sakamoto, Japanese, 40 years old has composed this piece dedicated to the Mediterranean and is ironic the fact that someone from Japan has written a music honoring the Mediterranean ... . (ET1, Greece, Opening Ceremony)

The plan succeeds

The strategy to project a favourable host identity succeeded in the ways deemed most important to Olympic planners. They were not only able to balance the presentation the different geopolitical entities involved, but were able to consolidate the discrete needs of these different hosts into simplified visual and cultural themes that truly emphasized the intersection of these identities: Mediterranean, colour, life, modernity, history, passion, art and warmth. Further, the planners seemed to succeed in connecting these local cultural attributes to more universal feelings.

Projecting a local culture as global

In large part the identity goal for Catalonia – to get on the map – was readily met. Catalan culture was presented, by most broadcasters, as elemental to cultural aspects of the ceremony. However, it is doubtful that most international audiences came away with an understanding of Catalonia as a politically autonomous community within Spain. Only a few broadcasts really pursued a story line of a history of political and cultural conflict between Catalonia and the rest of Spain, and even this was primarily used by these broadcasters to promote a more transcendent, universal emotion of the Games as a place for resolution and not to further a political agenda for the Catalan people.

This outcome, however, does not contradict the identity goals of the planners. In fact, it was considered critical to the success of the Opening Ceremony to have the local aspects of the folkloric performances seen within the context of a global event, serving to connect the host to a broader global condition. Thus, for example, the stress the commentators put on the 'Catalan', 'Canarian', 'Madrid', 'Andalusian', etc. origin of the various singers and actors was hoped to seem perfectly compatible with the international nature of these same figures. The opera singer Montserrat Caballé, for example, is on many occasions in broadcast commentaries referenced as both 'Catalan' and 'universal' or 'world famous', and her image upholds this ambiguity perfectly well. Similarly, it was the desire of Olympic planners to give the character of Barcelona, Catalonia and Spain international essence and connection. Rothenbuhler admires the audacity of this attempt: 'Ultimately, it was charming to realize that Barcelona was portraying itself as at the centre of the origin of civilization – and doing it with convincing style'.[17]

The influence of television on host identity

Thinking of television in the Olympics, most broadcaster presentations of the Olympic host discussed in this chapter were prompted by tangible, visual imagery strategically located by Olympic planners within the ceremony and around the city: Catalan flags in the streets of Barcelona prompted Channel 7 (Australian) commentators to characterize the city as 'fervently Catalan', the linked hands of the sardana circle dance provoked an association with the collective spirit of Catalonia, a smiling King Juan Carlos speaking Catalan represented a positive Spanish / Catalonia relationship, and so forth. More abstract identity goals (democratic stability, encouragement of economic initiative, political history, growing industries, a European community) were less noticed by broadcasters and not brought up without some specific connection between a broadcaster's cultural context and the host (e.g. an interest in urban renovation) and in some cases was purposely avoided (China's CCTV not wanting to underscore the political autonomy or nationalism of Catalonia within Spain). In particular, several of the study correspondents wrote of the impact that visual images had on perceptions of Barcelona, by associating local landmarks, people, architecture, cultural performance, Olympic venue settings and design features. Somehow these images encouraged television broadcasters to link the host identity with passion, history, culture, innovation, modernism, Mediterranean, and so forth with great consistency across broadcasts. Thus, it was to credit of the 1992 Olympic organizers that they chose host identity goals not only compatible with the visual character of television, but which held a simplicity of meaning readily understood across many different cultural orientations.

---

17 Rothenbuhler (1992).

10   Advertising and Commercial Messages in Olympic Television

Part of contemporary Olympic discourse surrounds the obvious tension between the idealistic anti-commercial principles which resonate with modern Olympic philosophy and the need to finance the world's largest athletic and media event. More and more, Olympic observers admit that this tension is no longer a conflictual one, but rather a dynamic balance where the identity of the Olympics as embodying a special set of values does a sort of delicate dance with sponsoring commercial entities eager to use that identity to sell products. Chapter 2 on the economics of the Olympics shows the high degree of interdependency – and success in financial terms – which has evolved with this relationship.

This commercial evolution within the Olympic movement has been an 'easy' one in the sense that advertisers are well aware of the positive influence the Olympics can have on commercial messages and, as such, have actively sought to intermingle their products and services with Olympics values. What is less sure, and cause for uneasiness in some, is the question of what results from this mix, or even blur, of commercial concepts with Olympic messages from the perspective of the Olympic movement. This is ultimately a question of 'meaning' rather than of financing and one this chapter seeks to address by offering some data on commercial messages as part of Olympic broadcasts.

This part of the study analysed 28 international broadcasts for the presence and character of advertising and commercial messages during the 1992 Opening Ceremony broadcast and more generally over the course of the Games. Data were collected on: advertising scheduling, frequency, formats and quantity; the products, services and organizations advertised the use of Olympic symbols and values as part of the advertising strategies.

This chapter draws heavily upon the research of Marc Carroggio, whose collaboration the authors gratefully acknowledge.

The study also profiled, in detail, one broadcaster's advertising insertions during a 'representative' Olympic broadcast day (Spain's TVE–2 on 1 August 1992).[1]

A primary goal of this chapter is to assess the degree to which commercial messages visually and thematically 'interact' with Olympic ceremony, thereby contributing to the construction of its meaning. The first section looks at the volume of advertising inserted in the Barcelona Opening Ceremony, raising the question of balance between commercial and Olympic messages within the structure of the ceremony programme. Broadcasters in this study ranged from 0 to over 100 ads placed in the Opening Ceremony alone. The next section addresses the juxtaposition of commercial and Olympic messages by investigating just when and in what form advertising appeared inside the Opening Ceremony. Here the capabilities and innovations of television are shown to be perfectly suited to the pursuit of advertising exposure – and to staying a step ahead of IOC regulations. The final section looks at the amounts and types of Olympic themes and symbols used in the advertisements themselves, considering not only the association of products with the prestige of the Olympics, but the appropriation of Olympic values, spirit and emotions by advertisers for strategic use.

A profile of Olympic advertising

The banning of advertising in the Olympic stadium, facilities and on any athletes' clothing and equipment visible during the Games, as well as strict regulation of the commercial use of the Olympic symbol, flag, flame, motto and anthem makes the Olympics a special case in the context of sports advertising.[2]

Turn on the television to view World Cup Soccer, Tour de France, Wimbledon or any other international sports event and at least one, if not all, of the following sports advertising formats can be seen:

- Static advertising. Advertisements placed in sports installations, especially on hoardings (billboards) around the field of play.[3]

---

1   Obviously, no one day is typical for all broadcasters as sports events with special significance to a nation may occur on different days depending the sport of interest. 1 August 1992 was chosen for analysis because it was halfway through the Games and the day of one of the big athletic finals, the mens' 100 metres.

2   Refer to rule 61, 'Olympic Charter'.

3   Static advertising can be considered sports advertising *par excellence* on contemporary television. This type of advertising is characterized by the presence of a logotype of a brand or a company where the sports event is set. The hoardings (billboards) used continue to improve in design, rotating both physically and through sets of advertisements. This system takes direct advantage of the large number of medium shots used during sports events, allowing commercial messages to be seen continuously without having to interrupt the event. Thus, for example, in a basketball match, the advertising images can be made out on the hoarding at the entrance to the court and on the court itself for nearly 90 per cent of the broadcast time.

- Advertising logos on athletes' dress (shirts, socks, caps, helmets, etc.), easily captured by the television cameras.[4]

- Advertising on sports equipment (sails, skies, motorcycles, etc.)

- Superimpositions. Advertisements graphically superimposed on televised pictures of the sports event.

- Advertising spots. Breaks in programming exclusively devoted to commercial messages.

- Verbal 'plugs'. Sports commentators directly identifying television programme sponsors ('this portion of ... is brought to you by ...').

Because the International Olympic Committee has held tight to the philosophy of commercial-free athletic venues, in theory, only the last three of these advertising formats – those directly contracted by television – are seen by Olympic audiences. (It should be noted, however, that athlete clothing or venue equipment may have the logo of its manufacturer *only*, yet must conform to strict IOC rules concerning discrete logo size.)

Commercial broadcasters sell advertising space to finance broadcasting expenses and the purchase of television rights to broadcast the Olympic Games. While the IOC is involved in the marketing of various Olympic sponsorship programmes described in Chapter 2, it does not regulate the amount and types of broadcaster-contracted advertising placed in Olympic broadcasts around the world. This creates the opportunity for commercial broadcasters to immerse the event in advertising without necessarily contravening 'Olympic Charter' rules.

Advertising as part of Olympic programming

Despite the perception of global popularity of the Olympic Games, an analysis of advertising breaks on 28 different television broadcasts during 1992 Olympic programming reveals that some broadcasters did not manage to sell all the advertising spaces available during 17 days of Olympic broadcasting. The volume and placement of advertising depended on several factors: (1) the level of economic development in each country; (2) the broadcast regulatory and competitive environment (e.g. national or European Union regulations on amounts of advertising allowed within specified time periods; and[5]

---

4   This idea has found its way on to hats and shirts of athlete family members, spouses, and other celebrities in the stands sure to attract frequent television camera attention.

5   For example, the European Union's directive on television without frontiers establishes some maxima concerning the transmission of advertisements: 15 per cent of the total daily broadcast time; 20 per cent of each broadcast hour; the maximum interruption of films every 45 minutes; a minimum period of 20 minutes between two commercial breaks in a single programme. The daily total time limits are only exceeded in the most developed countries, where there is a wide range of advertisements offered, and in the majority of countries these limits are only exceeded during prime time or the athletic events with the largest audiences.

(3) local attributes of Olympics programming, such as the timing of the broadcasts and audience interest in different sports events.

Advertising quantity also fluctuates throughout the duration of the Games depending on the outcome of the Olympic competition. When a national team or athlete makes (or does not make) final rounds of an event this inevitably links to audience size which in turn links to ad prices, ad quantity and broadcaster revenue. For example, in Colombia audience interest in the Games dropped off considerably after the Colombian soccer team lost 4–0 to Spain in a preliminary round right before the Opening Ceremony.

Accordingly, this analysis revealed a large variety in the number and positioning of advertisements across broadcasters who typically carry commercial messages. Cameroon television (CRTV) demonstrated an extreme case where commentators actually asked advertisers to buy space in the Olympics as it was being broadcast.

> JL: Every day on CRTV, three hours a day, we ask for sponsors. Contact CRTV directly, or telephone, or even write, telephoning in better ... For your advertisements on CRTV during the Olympic Games (CRTV, Cameroon, Opening Ceremony).

Wete suggests that the absence of local sponsors in the Cameroon broadcast was reflective of the lack of preparations made by CRTV to cover the Games. Ironically, he says this resulted in little perceived relationship on the part of viewers between the Olympics and commercialism.[6]

That was not the case for broadcasters in more highly developed commercial markets (e.g. United States, NBC; Canada, CTV; Australia, Channel 7; and European Union broadcasters) who faced the opposite dilemma: trying to balance the desire to deliver large numbers of selective audiences to advertisers (by selling a lot of ad space at prime times) with the awareness of audiences' increasing dislike of the super-abundance of advertising in Olympic programming.

TVE – 2 Spain: an example of advertising packaging and placement

To illustrate how broadcasters such as these latter ones approach Olympic advertising, it is instructive to look at the case of Spain's TVE–2. It serves as a reasonable example of a commercial broadcaster that sold a large number of commercials throughout the Olympic telecast.

TVE–2 advertising packages. Before the Olympics began TVE–2 created and sold special advertising packages. Examples of these packages are shown in Table 10.1. They included a variety of spots bundled together at different value levels. Along with these 'variety' packages, the broadcasters also marketed 'sports' packages in much the same way. The sports packages listed in Table 10.1 also give a sense of the relative value assigned to different sports, with athletics, basketball and field hockey as Spanish favourites.

---

6   Wete (1992).

Table 10.1. Sample TVE–2 advertising packages

Name of package	Number and description of advertisements per package	Package price in pesetas*
Olympic Rings	**49-spot package**, distributed as follows: – 2 in the Opening Ceremony – 2 in the Closing Ceremony – 15 in the afternoon summaries – 15 in the night summaries – 15 in the summary of TVE's second channel	140,000,000
Big Finals	**20-spot package**, distributed as follows: – 1 in each ceremony (opening and closing) – 6 in the special summaries (3 each week) – 3 in the afternoon summaries – 3 in the night summary – 1 in the finals of soccer, basketball, handball and waterpolo – 2 in the tennis final	50,000,000
Olympic Games Celebration	**33 spots** shown during the Games, at a variety of time slots guaranteed by TVE, but *not* during ceremonies or the principal finals	16,000,000
Olympic Games Celebration – weekly	**18 spots** shown during one of the two Olympic weeks. TVE only guaranteed the broadcast time slot but not the specific moment	8,500,000
Athletics	**17 spots**	25,000,000
Basketball	**14 spots**	25,000,000
Handball	**14 spots**	11,000,000
Football (Soccer)	**13 spots**	13,000,000
Gymnastics	**14 spots**	14,000,000
Field Hockey	**15 spots**	15,000,000
Swimming	**11 spots**	10,000,000
Waterpolo	**7 spots**	7,000,000

Source: TVE, Circular Informativa, 290-A. XXV Juegos Olímpicos, Barcelona, 1992.
*While most of these packages would have sold at various times in advance of the Games, as a reference, during the Games US$1 = approximately 119 pesetas.

TVE also offered smaller packages and individual insertions, (e.g. 20-second spots ranging between 2 and 17 million pesetas). The basic price for individual advertisements varied according to the time slot and the day of the week. Advertising 'surcharges' were added to the basic price if the insertion was paired with any of the following factors: (1) the participation of Spanish athletes in the event; (2) specified popular sports (e.g. athletics, gymnastics, swimming and basketball); or (3) final rounds of a competition (semi-finals,

finals). To determine the price, if all three factors coincided with the insertion time the basic price was multiplied by 3.3, if two factors coincided it was multiplied by 2.2, and if only one of the factors was applicable it was multiplied by 1.5.

Adhering to IOC recommendations TVE offered companies that were official Olympic sponsors of the Games preferential rights to purchase its advertising packages or individual spots for a month beginning from the publication of the offer. After one month all advertisers, sponsors or not, had the same opportunity to invest in Olympic advertising and to choose spaces for broadcasting their commercials.

TVE–2 advertising placement. Table 10.2 summarizes one complete day of Olympic programming on TVE–2. It shows the time slots designations made by TVE–2, the average interval between commercial breaks during each time slot, and then the number of ad breaks that interval rate translated into. During a 16-hour broadcast day, TVE–2 inserted 64 commercial breaks. While that divides nicely into 8 breaks per two-hour slot, that is not how an advertising day is organized. Instead, it is easy to see that the time slots with the largest audiences (evening and night time) coincided with shorter intervals between commercial breaks. In contrast there was a 2-hour absence of advertising between 10:00 and 12:00. On this particular day, 1 August 1992, the shortest interval between breaks (9 minutes and 3 seconds) coincided with the live broadcast of one of the most awaited of Olympic events, the men's 100 metres final (broadcast in the 20:00 to 22:00 time slot).

Although not shown on this table, the interval length also related to the number of spots within each break. However, it was the *shorter* interval periods between breaks that related to a larger number of commercials per break (again, relating to the largest audiences). For example, the overall average of commercials per break on this day was 2.25, but in the popular 20:00 to 22:00 time slot one could watch up to 9 commercials per break.

Table 10.2. TVE–2 advertising schedule: 1 August 1992

Broadcast times (24 hour clock)	Intervals between breaks (min.' sec.")	Number of ad breaks
From 08:00 to 10:00	26' 00"	2
From 10:00 to 12:00	120' 00"	5
From 12:00 to 14:00	15' 00"	5
From 14:00 to 16:00	32' 05"	3
From 16:00 to 18:00	16' 02"	13
From 18:00 to 20:00	36' 04"	14
From 20:00 to 22:00	09' 03"	14
From 22:00 to 24:00	12' 02"	8
	34' 00" average time interval between breaks	64 total ad breaks

Source: compiled by Núria García, Centre d'Estudis Olímpics i de l'Esport. Universitat Autònoma de Barcelona.

Advertising breaks during the Olympic Opening Ceremony

For advertisers, the Opening Ceremony by virtue of its large audience and social and historical significance is highly desirable for product exposure. Accordingly, the price of advertising spots during the ceremony is at premium levels for all commercial broadcasters. To continue with the TVE–2 example for a moment, the Spanish broadcaster's advertising rates during the Barcelona Games peaked at 22:15 on 25 July, the day of the Opening Ceremony. The price was 17,000,000 pesetas (roughly US$ 150,000) for 20 seconds of advertising. The moment was the entrance of the Olympic flame into the stadium. The buyer was Kodak.

In this study sample of 28 broadcasters, 18 broadcasters presented commercial messages during the Barcelona Opening Ceremony. Of those, 17 broadcasters departed from the ceremony 176 times for commercial breaks totaling 1109 commercials (one broadcaster, Canal 13 of Mexico, only used superimposed advertisements and did not 'leave' the broadcast for ad breaks). This figure would be even higher if it included advertising that was inserted into the pre- and post-ceremony programming that several broadcasters added as part of their Opening Ceremony broadcast. In fact, the advertising spots that were broadcast before and after the ceremonies generally cost the same as the spots broadcast during the ceremony and had the same size viewing audience.

As discussed in Chapter 5, the insertion of advertising into the ceremony alters not only the flow and structure of the ceremony that television viewers experience, but obviously takes away from what they see. Across all 28 broadcasters in the study an average 7.1 per cent of the Opening Ceremony was used for advertising purposes. This figure increases to an average of 11 per cent of the ceremony if calculated only for those 18 broadcasters which used advertising. At the extreme were broadcasters from CTV (Canada) and NBC (United States) who dedicated more than 40 and 60 minutes respectively to advertising during the event, effectively preventing viewers from seeing that much of the official ceremony.

Table 10.3 summarizes the inclusion of paid advertising during the Opening Ceremony – both in the form of advertising spots and superimposed corporate logos. While the table offers a general guide to the most commercially driven broadcasters in this study, it should also be noted that some broadcasts in this sample occurred in middle of the night because of time zone differences with Barcelona, and as such, might not reflect typical levels of advertising for those broadcasters.

As an example of how to read Table 10.3, South Africa's SABC devoted a total of 20 minutes, 14 seconds (column 1) to advertising both in the form of commercial spots and superimposed corporate logos. That is the equivalent of 10.7 per cent of the official 3:09'36' ceremony. Of that 20'14" of advertising 5.7 per cent (or 1 minute 9 seconds) was in the form of superimposed advertising graphics (column A), and the remaining 94.3 per cent (or 19 minutes, 5 seconds) was in the form of advertising spots (column B). Finally, SABC broke away from the ceremony 19 times (column C) during which time they showed a total of 48 distinct advertisements (column D).

Table 10.3. Summary of advertising in the Opening Ceremony

	1	A	B	C	D
	Total advertising volume in minutes and as % of official ceremony	% of total ad time devoted to super-imposed ads	% of total time devoted to ad breaks	Number of advert-ising breaks	Total number of ads within breaks
ET1 (Greece)	57' 49" (30.4%)	82.2	17.8	4	19
NBC (United States)	62' 32" (39.9%)	2.5	97.5	23	97
CTV (Canada)	40' 35" (21.3%)	0	100	15	107
Channel 7 (Australia)	33' 45" (17.7%)	0	100	12	87
CANAL A (Colombia)	26' 21" (13.9%)	19.1	80.9	19	54
TV3 (Malaysia)	20' 25" (10.7%)	0	100	5	32
SABC (South Africa)	20' 14" (10.7%)	5.7	94.3	19	48
TVA (Canada)	30' 55" (16.3%)	0	100	22	67
MBC (Korea)	15' 12" (8.0%)	0	100	3	58
Bandeirantes (Brazil)	14' 00" (7.4%)	10.5	89.5	3	64
Eurosport (UK)	12' 15" (6.4%)	0	100	8	42
SBC 12 (Singapore)	11' 55" (6.1%)	0	100	10	57
TVE (Spain)	10' 55" (5.6%)	0	100	5	25
C. Olìmpic (Catalonia)	10' 25" (5.4%)	0	100	5	23
TF1 (France)	8' 58" (4.5%)	0	100	3	37
Ostankino 1 (Russia)	6' 35" (3.4%)	0	100	19	22
CANAL 13 (Mexico)	3' 50" (1.9%)	100	0	0	9
ERTU2 (Egypt)	1' 35" (0.7%)	0	100	1	3

Source: Compiled by Núria García and Marc Carroggio. Centre d'Estudis Olímpics i de l'Esport. Universitat Autònoma de Barcelona.
Notes: Column 1 figures include the total time devoted to both advertising spots and superimposed advertising graphics and then lists that figure as a percentage of the official broadcast (3:09'36' in length). Percentage figures in columns A and B equal 100 per cent of the figure in column 1. They show the ratio of advertising time devoted to superimposed ads versus advertising spots. Column C shows the number of breaks for advertising spots only. Column D shows the total number of advertising spots composing those breaks. The data in columns C and D do not reflect superimposed advertising graphics.

The broadcasts in this study with no advertising *during* the Opening Ceremony included: CCTV (China); TV Globo (Brazil); CRTV (Cameroon); ARD (Germany), Tele-Rebelde (Cuba); 2nd Channel (Slovenia); NHK (Japan); BBC (UK); RTV (Romania) and TVRI (Indonesia). Please note that for this chapter, the analysis includes two broadcasts from Brazil.

Also, as noted in Chapter 5, despite the revenue potential not all commercial broadcasters chose to interrupt the Opening Ceremony for advertisements. Slovenia's 2nd Channel and

Brazil's TV Globo are examples of broadcasters that considered the ceremony 'special' enough not insert commercials inside of it (instead they clustered ads around it). This, in fact, surprised the study correspondents from Brazil, for as Mader in his discussion of Brazilian television notes: 'Advertising is the *raison d'être* of every channel [in Brazil]. Advertising comes before, during and after every programme without warning or rational regulation.'[7]

Who are the advertisers?

Advertisers during Olympic ceremonies represent a broader range of product and service arenas than for other sports events, correlating to the more heterogeneous demographics of Olympics audiences in general, as well as to the non-sports nature of the ceremonies themselves. The distribution of advertisers in the Barcelona Opening Ceremony by commercial sector, listed in order of importance, is shown in Table 10.4. This table also breaks out the individual sector distributions for four broadcasters (NBC of the US; TV Bandeirantes of Brazil; TVE–2 of Spain; and Ostankino 1 of Russia) for comparison purposes.

Table 10.4. Advertisements by commercial sector

Sector	Average across 28 broadcasters $N = 1109$ %	US $n = 97$ %	Brazil $n = 64$ %	Spain $n = 25$ %	Russia $n = 22$ %
Non-durable goods	27.3	26	39	29	13
Durable goods	16.9	17	17	6	9
Financial	14.9	7	21	17	31
Transportation	13.1	18	14	12	0
Media and publishing	12.6	17	3	25	12
Data processing and electronics	4.4	3	0	0	14
Retailing and consumer services	3.5	4	0	0	0
Energy	1.7	1	1	4	0
Healthcare	1.5	4	1	2	0
Basic industries & related equipment	1.0	2	0	2	0
Construction	1.0	0	0	0	0
Defense and security systems	0	0	0	0	0

Note: For 2.1 per cent of the ads it was not possible to distinguish the sector.

Table 10.5 gives a further breakdown of the sectors, showing the 12 most represented product groups, again listed in order of importance (note: repeats of the same ad were included in frequency counts). Advertising covering these 12 sub-product categories

---

7   Marques de Melo and Loturco Pittelkow (1992). The quote comes from Mader (1993).

accounted for 70.5 per cent of all the advertising contained in this study's Opening Ceremony broadcasts. The remaining 29.5 per cent of that advertising space (not shown on the table) covered an enormous range of other products and services.

Table 10.5. Primary sub-product categories of advertisements broadcast during the Opening Ceremony

Product category	% of all advertisements*
Media self-promotion	11.0
Cars	10.0
Banking	8.0
Food	8.0
Non-alcoholic beverages	7.2
Cosmetics	6.5
Sport	5.8
Electronics (audio/video)	4.0
Clothes (clothing maker)	3.0
Alcoholic beverages	3.0
Financial services	2.0
Insurance	2.0

*$N = 1109$.

Most noticeable in the above tables, besides a high presence of products related to sport (5.8 per cent), is the importance of the mass media (11 per cent) as advertiser. The sport link to the Olympics is obvious. And, while media self promotion is common to audiences in some countries included in this study, there seems to be an extraordinary attempt on the part of nearly all broadcasters – through advertising spots, superimposed graphics, verbal 'plugs', and commentator head shots – to flaunt the momentary prestige of being a rights-holding (i.e. exclusive) broadcaster.[8]

Completing the profile, advertisers were divided up almost equally between national companies (49.4 per cent) and multinational companies (45.29 per cent), with a little room left for local companies (2.2 per cent) and a group of companies that were not identifiable through this analysis (3.11 per cent). Further, 53.8 per cent of the advertisements (N = 1109) were *not* official Olympic sponsors. Table 10.6 shows this distribution, breaking these figures down further to show per cent of ads by type of official sponsor across all broadcasts with advertising (refer to Chapter 2 for a description of Olympic sponsorship categories). This analysis shows a relatively limited presence of official sponsors in television advertising during the Opening Ceremony. This could be proof of an insufficient use of the strategic resources available to these companies or it could also be evidence of a dilemma between directly investing in advertising during the transmission of the Games

---

8   For some broadcasters this is not a case of enjoying the prestige of exclusivity, but rather a head on competition with other broadcasters in that country. In Russia, Korea, Brazil, and Japan, for example, the Olympics was broadcast on more than one channel, although often at different times or divided by sport event.

or indirectly investing in Olympic sponsorship. Using Spain's TVE–2 again as an example, only 7 of the 21 sponsors of the Spanish sponsorship programme (ADO'92) were represented in the Opening Ceremony broadcast. Even fewer of the TOP sponsors appeared.

Table 10.6. Advertising during the Opening Ceremony by category of sponsorship

Advertiser category	% of ads*	
Non-sponsoring companies	**53.84**	**(597)**
Sponsoring companies	**46.16**	**(511)**
Sponsor of Olympic TV programmes	65.0	(332)
NOC sponsorships	26.0	(132)
TOP sponsorships	22.0	(112)
COOB'92 sponsorships	4.0	(20)

*$N = 1109$.
Note: Sponsors of television programmes are companies that sponsor a whole time period of programming and are identified as such by the broadcast commentators and often through superimposed logo graphics. The sum of the sponsor category percentages is greater than 100 because in some cases the sponsors of TV programmes are also sponsors of one of the three following categories.

Commercial messages inside of the games

Despite IOC regulations dictating commercial free venues, commercial messages do mingle with Olympic ceremony and event images in more subtle ways. This section considers the placement of advertisements at key 'Olympic moments', as well as the visual juxtaposition of corporate images with official ceremony activities.

The placement of commercials in the Opening Ceremony

Table 10.7 summarizes where in the ceremony broadcasters placed commercial breaks. The first column shows the actual times for each key part of the ceremony (and breaks this down further into its distinct segments). This particular table also includes the opening and closing RTO sequences just before and after the 'official' ceremony. These 5–7 minutes sections are part of the international signal and allow broadcasters to making introductory and closing remarks. The second column shows, as a percentage, how all advertising spots (the total in all broadcasts) were distributed throughout the ceremony. Thus, for example, 41.2 per cent of all advertisements across broadcasters in this study were placed into the athletes' parade.

Individual broadcasters generally tried to space out advertising throughout the ceremony, although there was a certain tendency to insert advertising breaks into the athletes' parade, a segment which lasted 79 minutes making it the longest segment of the ceremony (Chapter 8 discusses the impact this had on which teams were introduced to audiences, or not, by broadcasters). Over 36 per cent of all advertising occurred during the opening or closing host cultural performances. The moments before and just after the ceremony were also preferred by broadcasters for the insertion of commercials – an approach which conveys the most respect for the cultural and ritual character of the Olympic ceremonies. Finally, as Table 10.7 shows, several broadcasters did not hesitate to insert advertisements into the Olympic ritual segments.

Table 10.7. Distribution of commercial breaks during the Opening Ceremony

Segments of the Opening Ceremony (min.' sec.")	% of Advertising*	
Introductory screen – before the official start (05' 00")	8.2	
Opening cultural performances (51' 53")	**26.6**	
consisting of:		
Hola – Barcelona'92 logo (04' 18")		2.5
Arrival of king and queen of Spain (03' 42")		2.6
Welcome/Land of passion: flamenco opera (16' 56")		11.2
The Mediterranean, Olympic sea (26' 57")		10.3
The athletes' parade (79 '01")	**41.2**	
Olympic rituals (33' 40")	**6.3**	
consisting of:		
Speeches and opening (10' 32")		1.6
Entry of the Olympic flag (07' 16")		0.7
The Games reach their XXV Olympiad (07' 01")		2.0
The Olympic torch (06' 27")		0.3
Positioning of flags and oaths (02' 24")		1.7
Closing cultural performance (25' 23")	**9.6**	
consisting of:		
The great flag of friendship (03' 30")		1.6
The human pyramids (03' 54")		2.3
Opera (14' 27")		2.2
The anthem of Europe and music (03' 32")		3.5
Athletes' exit, after the official end (07' 01")	8.1	

*N = 1109;
Source: Moragas and Carroggio (1994).
Note: This analysis includes the immediate presentation and closing of the Opening Ceremony, but not the various longer programmes before and after the ceremony. These, in some cases, included blocks of commercials lasting over 10 minutes.

As noted earlier, Kodak chose the scene showing the arrival of the Olympic torch as a prime time to insert advertisements on TVE (Spain), NBC (USA) and Canal Olímpic (Spain), among other television channels. The 'proximity' of this advertisement to the ceremony moment deemed most sacred by the IOC and its 'Olympic Charter' raises important questions about the kind of impression left with viewers about the value of Olympic rituals. It also seems an interesting advertising risk, as viewers are less likely to want to 'leave' the ceremony at this time to experience a Kodak moment – and may actually resent having to do so. See Chapter 7 for a discussion of other examples.

Sharing the screen: Olympic and corporate images

Superimposed advertisements

A significant piece of data for consideration is the use of superimposed ads. The majority of the corporate logo graphics appeared over either a transitional camera shot (e.g. a view of Barcelona) before going to a commercial break or other screen image (e.g. the logo on a dark screen) *after* the camera had left the live ceremony activity. However, that was not always the case. There were several examples of corporate images (e.g. logos) sharing the screen directly with ceremony actors and symbols. The most extreme case was Greek television (ET1). During a full 25 per cent of the Opening Ceremony a superimposed corporate logo was maintained on the television screen. This banking and insurance company was a sponsor of the ET1 telecast. Canal A (Colombia) superimposed corporate logos of various companies several times during the ceremony and notably when the Olympic torch entered the stadium and later when the large Olympic flag was spread over the athletes, allowing these corporate symbols to visually link to these powerful Olympic symbols. In another case, Canal 13 of Mexico flashed, in 5 second shots, the logos of various corporations on top of country delegations and cultural performances 40 different times throughout the ceremony.

Television 'side by sides'

In another version of the visual juxtaposition of commercial messages with the Olympic ceremony, South Africa's SABC kept the ceremony in a reduced-size box in the corner of the screen while advertisements were shown (this happened 7 times during the broadcast). In a similar style, Canada's TVA reduced the ceremony image and placed it in the centre of screen while showing a superimposed graphic of the broadcaster logotype next to it.

Not only do these practices visually mix the corporate image with the Olympic one, but the presentation of a commercial message at the same time viewers are watching the official Olympic ceremonial contravenes the spirit of the regulations established by the IOC concerning advertising inside of Games venues.

While only occurring on the television screen, this ability of commercial messages to effectively get 'inside' of Olympic venues is a direct result of the evolving technological capabilities of television. Commercial messages can not only be superimposed on top of ceremony images, but positioned next to and around Olympic events and ceremonies in a variety of creative ways.

Camera capabilities and brand labels

Enhanced television capabilities also allow cameras to magnify the smallest of corporate logos on clothes, equipment, spectators and elsewhere inside Olympic sports venues beyond the sizes allowed for by IOC rules if so desired. This latter type of advertising appears repeatedly in Olympic transmissions. The recognition of the brands (SEIKO, IBM, etc.) on official measuring equipment, for example, at Olympic venues is very noticeable.

(In fact, current television wizardry could place, for television viewers only, the image of corporate logos or signage on walls inside of Olympic venues without their actual physical presence – much like weather maps are positioned in news casts.)

Increasingly faced with this 'gray' area of advertising intervention, the IOC does attempt to address issues such as superimposed advertising in their television rights agreements with international broadcasters. For example, the IOC rights contract with the EBU for the Albertville'92 Games included language to the effect that there was to be no superimposed images without prior approval of the IOC except those of the host broadcaster and event-related data (e.g. results, start lists, etc.).[9]

In a sense, however, it will be hard work for the Olympic movement to stay ahead in this type of race. Mixing the Olympics with a world of technological innovation, advertiser pressures to gain more viewer exposure, and broadcasters desiring lucrative advertising presence, guarantees that these issues will need to be continually addressed as part of Olympic television.

Use of Olympic symbols and themes

An advertising presence during the Olympic Opening Ceremony, and throughout the Games, is not only an opportunity to capitalize on a high profile sports event, but to associate one's product with a unique, and at times emotional, global gathering. Many advertisers – whether official sponsors or not – explicitly tailor or produce advertisements for the Games. According to this study 60 per cent (665, $N = 1109$) of the commercials broadcast during the Barcelona Opening Ceremony were specifically produced and customized for the Olympic Games, containing themes linked explicitly or implicitly to this event. Of the customized commercials 15 per cent (or about 100) were produced by non-sponsors.

Olympic values and commercial strategies

Some sponsors simply add Olympic logos to existing commercials. As a result, it was easy to confuse their ads with non-sponsor advertisements actively employing references to sports, the host city, or indirectly to the Olympics (although not using official symbols).

Further, some Olympic references are more popular than others. The Olympic rings, 'official sponsor' title, and Barcelona'92 logotypes make frequent appearances, while the mascot and motto (*Citius, Altius, Fortius*) are virtually absent in international advertising.[10] Table 10.8 shows how the companies in different sponsorship categories chose to use the Olympic references available to them. This is not an exhaustive list, but rather it shows the most frequently used references.

---

9   IOC (1991).

10   This was not the case for Spanish advertising where companies used the mascot more frequently. In fact, the Barcelona Olympics represented the first time that an official mascot (Cobi) was physically adapted to each sponsor firm by its designer. For example, the Ray Ban Cobi had sunglasses on, the Coca-Cola Cobi held a bottle of Coke, and so forth.

Table 10.8. Olympic/sports references in sponsor advertisements

Olympic or sports references	TOP advertisers *N* = 112 ads %	NOC advertisers *N* = 132 ads %	COOB'92 advertisers *N* = 20 ads %
Olympic rings	72	9	5
The sentence 'Official sponsor ... '	55	33	26
Competing athletes	42	29	10
The adjective 'Olympic'	25	13	0
Uses Olympic athletes as stars	22	16	5
Barcelona'92 Logo	18	11	47
'Sport for all'	9	7	10
The Olympic torch	8	2	5
NOC emblem	0	58	0
The Olympic mascot (Cobi)	0	0	10

Table 10.9. Olympic references by non-sponsoring advertisers

Reference used	% of non-sponsor ads that use an Olympic reference*
Non-professional practice of sport	26
Olympic athletes, start of advertisement	24
Use of the word 'Olympic' (verbal)	24
References to the city of Barcelona	18
Olympic rings**	18
Sport-Olympic facilities	17
Reference to medals	6
Spanish music	5
References to the ceremony	4
Barcelona'92 Logo**	4

*N = 100; **IOC and COOB'92 regulated Olympic symbols. This usage is not permitted.

Non-sponsors

Official sponsors are not the only advertisers to use Olympic meanings in a strategic way. Not having the right to associate their brands with regulated Olympic symbols, non-sponsoring advertisers have to adapt their messages to the legal conditions that regulate the use of the symbols. In order to achieve this they use various rhetorical forms and, sometimes, subterfuge. In the place of regulated Olympic references, non-sponsoring advertisers use symbols which are not exactly regulated such as the torch, medals, stadium, spectators, images of victory, or images of Olympic athletes who are known on a national or international level. That said, there were cases in the Opening Ceremony analysis of the unauthorized use of regulated Olympic symbols (Olympic rings, logo) by non-sponsoring companies. In fact, 22 per cent (22 ads) of non-sponsor advertisements who customized their commercials used legally protected Olympic Games references (i.e. they used

Olympics symbols in violation of IOC rules). For some additional perspective, however, these ads constituted 2 per cent of the universe of 1109 advertisements in our sample of 28 broadcasts. Table 10.9 summarizes the Olympic-related themes used in non-sponsor advertisements. With the exception of those 22 ads which used the Olympic rings (18) and the Barcelona'92 logo (4) shown below, these presentations are not regulated by the IOC.

Capturing that Olympic feeling

At the other extreme from simply adding a logo to the corner of an advertisement were several highly creative campaigns prepared exclusively for presentation during the Games. Companies such as Kodak, Coca-Cola and Visa put a lot of money and time into developing specialized advertisements incorporating Olympic symbols, themes, feelings and visuals.

Barcelona as romantic, exciting host

Among the contents that were adapted to the circumstances of the Olympic broadcast, the use of references to the host city stand out clearly against more generic sports references Advertisers hoping to evoke the Barcelona setting included generalized Spanish images of flamenco and bull fights, as well as more accurately 'Barcelona' images of historical monuments, famous painters and artists. For example, the commercials broadcast by American Express (a non-sponsor company competing with Olympic TOP sponsor VISA), used some of the most representative symbols of Barcelona: Miró, Picasso, images of the streets, Gaudí, etc. Taking more stereotypical approaches in their Opening Ceremony advertising were Volkswagen (shown on TV Bandeirantes of Brazil) in which one of their cars was advertised with the image of a bull (the car) and a bullfighter in a bullring and Malaysia Airlines' commercial in which their logotype danced flamenco (shown on TV3 of Malaysia). Ironically, and as discussed in Chapter 9, some of these stereotypical images (such as bull fighting) were exactly what Olympic planners did not want broadcasters to portray in the coverage of the Games.

Cashing in on Olympic values

Olympic sponsors who produce spots specifically for the Olympics become, in their own way, influential cultural actors in the Games. Although using very different forms and rhetorical resources, advertising always consists of some form of association between the product and a set of positive values which generally produce a feeling of well-being. Those responsible for selling the TOP programme assured advertisers that they would profit by associating their product with Olympic values. In turn, these sponsors organize an advertising strategy around the Games that goes well beyond an association strategy and the linkage of logotypes (e.g. a commercial logotype with the Olympic rings).

While some advertisers placed their ad campaigns in the host context of Barcelona, others tried to make the viewers (consumers) feel involved in the more transcendent story and emotional context of the Olympics. Thus, for example, Kodak's commercial (broadcast by TVE during the transmission of the Barcelona Games) showed images of previous

Olympic Games in which spectators are seen forming colour mosaics in the stands, as well as other images which suggested that taking a photo at an 'Olympic moment' was similar to taking a photo at that right moment during intimate and family events, such as children's parties or family birthdays. This approach was also very noticeable in the case of Coca-Cola, who in its narration evokes 'Olympic' values of friendship, universality or the community of races and peoples. TVE of Spain, for example, broadcast various Coca-Cola spots during the Barcelona Games in 1992 that, while making references to sport, also showed their link to a transcendent Olympic spirit. In one of these spots showing images of children practicing sport a voice-over could be heard saying:

> Coca-Cola sponsors sport for children so as to discover the Olympic spirit that we all carry inside. (TVE–2, Spain).

In advertising rhetoric success, outcomes of victory, triumph, satisfaction, happiness and sports records are the consequence of the effort, will, perfection and passion represented by the athlete but also identified for the viewer as the consequence of consuming the product being advertised. Many of these commercials are based on the dialectic between effort and reward. The multiple drinks commercials are an example of this, in which the relationship between thirst (as a result of physical effort) and satisfaction, the prize (brought about by the consumption of the advertised drink) is expressed.

Another common strategy is advertisers' use of sports stars as an authoritative attraction. This is done to hopefully induce consumers to follow the positive example of sports idols. Thus, for example, a Spanish banking company (Banca Jover) produced a spot for the Barcelona Games in which images of a well known swimmer (Martín López Zubero) appeared in competition, which were followed by images of the swimmer signing a contract in the bank. The script simply went as follows:

> Voice-over: 'Effort, consistency, professionalism, these are the keys to success in order to be a number 1'.

> Athlete's voice: 'I'm Martín López Zubero and I'm a client of Banca Jover'. (Canal Olímpic, Catalonia).

An issue related to this latter strategy of using athletes as product spokespeople is the fact that these famous athletes can also be Olympic athletes. As such, they not only are associated with commercial products outside of the Games, but can carry that association with them into the Olympic Games, whether they wear a logo or not. Langer suggests that, with the admittance of professional athletes into the Games, this is yet another way in which commercial and Olympic messages will increasingly become mixed:

> Select athletes become corporate signs. They stand in for advertising ... or actually become synonymous with the advertising logos of particular products ... Their presence [in the Olympics] intertextually references an already established presence in television ads, magazine ads, etc.[11]

---

11 Langer (1992).

To some observers, all the above strategies – while no secret in their intent for most television viewers – still represent the appropriation of Olympic values and symbols for commercial use and serve to alter or dilute, in some way, their meaning. The following IBM ad spot which was broadcast by TVE–2 (Spain) during the Lillehammer'94 Winter Games is an example of a corporate entity attempting to alter a common Olympic association, the Olympic medals, by adding the IBM 'big blue' to the list. The voice-over said:

> IBM has developed the entire technical infrastructure of the Winter Olympic Games so that they are a success from beginning to end. Gold, silver, bronze and blue. (TVE–2, Spain)

What comes out of the mix?

The Olympic Games offer an undeniable set of positive references and values highly attractive to advertisers. This is confirmed by the large volume of advertising incorporated into television broadcasts and the interest expressed by sponsoring and non-sponsoring companies in identifying themselves with the Games in many countries around the world.

By placing restrictions on advertising in the stadium and Olympic venues, the Olympic regulations actually transfer the tension, the need for advertising exposure by sponsors, from the physical event to the television screen. Olympic sponsors are forced to buy television advertising space not only to gain satisfactory levels of exposure, but to prevent counter-marketing actions by competitor companies who do not hold any sponsorship rights.

At the same time, the sponsors have developed tremendously in their ability to exploit Olympic symbols and phrases and insert themselves into the most ritualistic moments of the Games ceremonies. This is done either by bringing the Olympic messages inside of commercials or by inserting commercial messages – via actual commercial spots, logos, or celebrity athlete associations – inside the Olympic ceremony.

In fact, considering the data presented in Chapter 7 about broadcaster presentation of Olympic values, it is readily apparent that many advertisers, particularly in the dedicated TOP sponsor category, put more energy than broadcast commentators into attempting to communicate Olympic values and sentiments to television viewers. This should raise the difficult question for the IOC about media responsibility as exclusive rights holders to the Olympic broadcasters (and, as such, primary interpreters of the Olympic event for world audiences). While the IOC readily takes steps to prohibit the intrusion of commercial messages into Olympic venues, it does not take similar steps to promote the presentation of Olympism by international broadcasters.

For their part, a few commercial broadcasters still refuse to interrupt the Opening Ceremony with commercials, however most are anxious to recoup their financial invest-ment in rights to broadcast the Games and, as such, offer a variety formats and advertising frequencies within their broadcasts – from 5 second superimpositions to a variety of ad slot lengths. They are aided in this endeavor by technological innovations which allow advertisements – and the Olympic ceremony itself – to literally take many shapes and sizes on the television screen. In commercial television terms, a 3-hour programme is a very long time to broadcast without advertising breaks. And, while the broadcasters in this study avoided missing any Olympic rituals completely due to commercial breaks, there was no hesitation to alter to flow of the ceremony with commercial insertions. As a result, there were plenty of instances where advertisements prevented audiences from seeing cultural presentations, national team entrances, or parts of ritual segments. This raises the question of whether more could be done on the part of ceremony planners to work with broadcasters in order to allow for needed commercial breaks without compromising ceremony design – or perhaps more important – the integrity of Olympic 'moments'.

All of the above issues arise quite naturally within the interdependent context of sponsorship, television and sport in modern society. But they take on special meaning when considered in the Olympic setting, where that 'special set of values' embodied in Olympic symbols and events acts as its most important asset. It is apparent from the evidence in this study that the mixing of commercial and Olympic messages are headed for increasingly murky waters. So, it is with special attention that the patrons of the Olympic movement will need to stay abreast of these relationships and monitor the evolution of Olympic messages associated with Games so that they hold their value or, more critically, their intent.

PART III
The Viewing Experience

Introduction

This part of the book looks at aspects of audience. There was not a reception analysis component to this study. However, from the data received it became apparent that there was much that could be said about the viewing experience around the world. As part of this it seemed necessary to evaluate claims of such extraordinary audience figures as 3.5 billion people simultaneously watching the Barcelona Opening Ceremony. This is the central question addressed in Chapter 11. Are such claims simply media trying to bolster their own importance? In the process of investigating audience figures an interesting variety of factors affecting audience viewing emerged. Maybe an awareness of these could help researchers better devise such audience calculations in the future. Chapter 11 also looks at the capacity of the Olympics Games telecast to alter the routines of daily life around the world, shedding light on its impact as a global television event.

Finally, many of the study correspondents provided perspectives as to the viewing experience in their respective countries, including insights into local political, cultural and economic contexts affecting the 'experience' of the 1992 Olympics. While, to some degree, differences in cultural context was expressed through broadcast presentations, these country by country perspectives allowed for a more sensitive evaluation of Olympic 'meaning' around the world. In our sample, there were countries being touched by war, political crisis, tremendous sport expectations, and more. While narratives on all 25 countries in our sample are not presented, Chapter 12 tries to give a sense of the Olympics on the African continent, in Russia, Slovenia, China and Latin America.

11 The Worldwide Audience for the Olympics

T he Olympic Games are one of the most representative examples of what has been called 'global television', a concept which has been used to identify the world-wide scope of the television broadcast of exceptional events. The landing of man on the moon (1969), the wedding of Charles and Diana (1981), the first night of the Gulf War, and sporting events such as World Cup Soccer championships would be examples of this phenomenon. Attributes commonly associated with global television events are the size of the viewing audience, as well as the ability the broadcast to disrupt the routines of daily life.

This chapter investigates the Olympic Games by considering those two attributes. The first section attempts to shed light on popular estimates of Olympic television audiences. The second section offers a cross cultural picture of television viewing behaviors during the Games. While this section does not represent a systematic analysis of audience, it does offer up some insights into different viewing cultures and factors which provoke interest in the Olympic Games.

The international audience for the Olympics

Newspaper commentaries about the Olympics readily use the size of its world television audience as proof of the Games' significance, and certainly there is reason to believe that the Olympic Games garner among the largest of global television audiences. As a television event the Olympics involves nearly all nations of the world engaged in a universally popular form of entertainment: sport. But international media also place the worldwide viewership figure in the billions even though there are no sufficient statistical bases available on the event itself. While appealing to a sense of awe, such estimates contradict available world audience and television equipment data. Therefore, one aim of this chapter is to estimate the real potential audience for global television phenomena such as the Olympic Games.

The first section of this chapter, on international audience estimates for the Olympics, draws heavily upon the research of Nicolás Lorite and Núria Garcia, whose collaboration the authors gratefully acknowledge.

Methodological problems of measuring world audiences

Before any evaluation of audience data relative to the Olympic Games, it is essential to consider the scientific value and the methodological problems of measuring the audiences on a worldwide scale. The obstacles to any kind of accurate audience figures – particularly when considering the media presentation of isolated events – are numerous.

A barrel of apples, oranges and other fruits

It is well known that in countries such as the United States, Germany, Japan, Canada, France and Spain, television audiences are routinely analysed. This activity is largely driven by the strategic interests of advertisers and broadcasters to attract select audiences. All of these countries have research centres or agencies (e.g. Nielsen in the United States, Sofres in France and Spain, and Eurodata in Europe) dedicated to the observation, daily analysis and detailed description of audiences. In addition, these organizations work continuously to refine their techniques of audience analysis and have employed an interesting array of methods over the years: audimeters, home surveys, weekly panels, immediate memory tracking, telephone surveys, etc. While servicing the needs of national markets, audience research across these countries uses different samples, variables, analysis techniques and measuring criteria which impede or make very difficult comparative or cumulative audience interpretation. The picture becomes even murkier when trying to include even less systematically collected data from other countries.

In fact one can identify four general types of countries as television data sources:

- Countries for which there is reliable television audience information, although with methodological limits when it comes to making cross national comparisons. This is the case of the most developed countries including the United States, Japan, Canada and the European Union.

- Countries for which the data obtained are inconsistent methodologically or incomplete in terms of sample. This is frequently the case in Latin America where data might be available relative to the urban concentrations, but not for scattered villages in rural areas.

- Countries with highly centralized or controlled television systems where official data come from state television corporations. These data should be cautiously interpreted both for their method and motivation. This is the case, for example, of China whose government owned CCTV attributed an audience of 500,000,000 people to the Barcelona'92 Opening Ceremony, which would mean an audience of nearly 45 per cent of the population.

- Countries, representing close to 70 per cent of the world's population, for which there are no direct audience data.

It is obvious then that only some type of deductive approximation, for example by considering the population and the number and distribution of television sets needs to be used in lieu of such insufficient direct viewership data. These other data must then be considered relative to other factors such as access to the television signal, the estimated number of people in front of each television, the degree of national involvement in the televised event, programme schedule, electricity rationing, and so forth. The complexity and subjectivity of worldwide audience analysis quickly becomes apparent.

Estimating potential world television audience

As a starting place from which to analyse Olympic audience potential, one can look at the level of participation of nations in the celebration of the Olympic Games. Athletes belonging to a total of 172 teams, corresponding to 183 countries, paraded at the Barcelona Games. These delegations were 'representing' a total of approximately 5,342,306,000 people – almost 100 per cent of the world's population, calculated at 5,358,344,000 people at the end of 1991. Barely 16,000,000 people were excluded from direct or indirect representation at the Barcelona Games. The breakdown of these data is shown on Table 11.1. These figures represent UNESCO estimates for 1991.

Table 11.1. Population representation at the 1992 Olympic Games

	Olympic delegations	Population represented
Africa	47	658,179,000
Asia	39	3,130,012,000
Europe	39	502,338,000
North America	2	279,845,000
Latin America	37	454,210,000
Oceania	11	26,650,000
USSR (Former)	4	291,072,000
Total participants	**172**	**5,342,306,000**

Non participants	16,038,000
Total world population	**5,358,344,000**

Source: Statistical Yearbook (UNESCO, 1993).

Only a little over 16 million people, mainly from the African (Burundi, Cape Verde, Reunion and Sao Tome and Principe) and Asian (Cambodia, Gaza, Macao, Diego García) continents were not represented in the Opening Ceremony of Barcelona'92.

That such a large population was represented does not mean, of course, that television reception was available to them. Large groups of people in Africa, Asia and also in America, still have no access to electricity. Television sets are expensive in many countries. Further, despite technological advances using satellites, coverage is still far from universal due to interference in the reception of the television signal.

Table 11.2 offers information relative to television sets per 1000 inhabitants by world region. Using primarily UNESCO data, and bearing in mind methodological drawbacks in collecting this kind of data, one sees that the estimated 1991 average individuals per television set was at 6.3 individuals, a lot higher than that of 1.3 television sets per individual corresponding to North America, for example.

Table 11.2. Television sets by regions

Geographic region	Number TV sets	% World TV sets	Total population	TV x 1000 people	People per TV
Africa	24,000,000	2.8	658,179,000	37	27.4
Asia	225,000,000	26.3	3,130,012,000	72	13.9
Europe	202,000,000	23.6	502,338,000	402	2.5
North America	223,000,000	26.1	279,845,000	797	1.3
Latin America	74,000,000	8.7	454,210,000	163	6.2
Oceania	10,000,000	1.2	26,650,000	375	2.7
USSR (former)	96,000,000	11.3	291,072,000	330	3.1
Developed	610,000,000	71.4	1,234,924,000	494	2.1
Developing	244,000,000	28.6	4,107,382,000	59	16.8
World total	854,000,000	100	5,342,306,000	160	6.3

Sources[1]

These averages make clear that the possible audience for the Olympic Games on a continent such as Africa, with an average of 37 television sets per 1000 inhabitants, would be substantially less than that of Europe, for example, where there are 402 television sets per 1000 inhabitants. Sweden, with 468 television sets per 1000 inhabitants, or the United States, with 814, contrast sharply with the 44 television sets per inhabitant in Cameroon or the 31 per inhabitant in Nigeria. Ethiopia's 53 million inhabitants only possess 130,000 television sets. Something more than 30 per cent of the world's television sets are to be found in the United States and Japan, countries which represent only 7 per cent of the world's population.

Countries from the so-called 'Group of 7' representing the most developed economies in the world – the United States, Japan, France, the United Kingdom, Italy, Germany and Canada – possess 49 per cent of the total number of television sets in the world. By contrast, the African continent, with a similar population to that of the G–7 (approximately 12 per cent of the world's population) possesses 2.8 per cent of the total sets in the world. If one adds, by rough calculation, what might be considered the rest of the 'developed' countries (according to UNESCO) to the G–7 countries then 71 per cent of television sets belong to 23 per cent of the world's total population.

---

1   This study used various information sources on world television equipment, including:
    Statisical Yearbook, UNESCO, 1993;
    World Communication Report, UNESCO, 1992;
    World Radio TV Handbook, 1993;
    TV World, EMAP, Business Publications, London 1993;
    The Complete Guide to World Television, TBI, 1993.

One can state that a relatively stable 98 per cent of people in developed countries have at least access to television. However, such calculations are much more difficult for developing countries, especially in areas of dramatic development. For example, more recent Chinese government estimates put the number of TV sets in China alone at 230,000,000 or roughly the same as was considered to exist in all of Asia in 1991 by UNESCO and other sources shown on Table 11.2. Considering the presence of Japan and Korea in this same region, it is clear that either the UNESCO 1991 numbers are very conservative or growth in television set ownership has been nothing less than phenomenal in that country.

Specific event audiences

Trying to estimate potential audience for a television event really asks how many people could be conceivably watching television simultaneously around the world. Organizers first began to attribute to the Games event audiences measured in millions in Mexico'68, and the figure has been rising dramatically ever since. Audience estimates of 600 million viewers (e.g. for the Opening Ceremony) for Mexico'68 was followed by 900 million for Munich'72, 2 billion for Los Angeles'84, 3 billion for Seoul'88 until it reached 3.5 billion which was readily attributed to Barcelona'92. Even allowing for dramatic levels of growth in number of television sets in some areas of the world, the figures still do not allow for such high viewer estimates.

In other words, if it is true that there was an audience of 3.5 billion viewers for any event during the Barcelona Olympics then different combinations must have been produced which, in fact, would be impossible. As an example scenario (using the UNESCO TV set data), the audience for this event would have had to reach 90 per cent in the developed countries, which would amount to a figure of 1,111,431,600 viewers, as well as managed to attract another 2,388,568,400 in developing countries, which would only have been possible if all 244,000,000 television sets were tuned into this event and the amount of viewers per television set was 9.7 people.

These figures are highly unlikely, and adjustments to these numbers result in similarly improbable formulas. Even with significant alterations to the UNESCO data toward the outer limits of probability, such as an adjustment downward of viewers per television set in the less developed countries to 4 and 5 people, the potential television audience in this part of the world would fall between 976,000,000 and 1,220,000,000, respectively allowing a *maximum* potential world television audience of around 2.3 billion people at any one point in time. Further this kind of formula does not consider any of a number of intervening factors that would affect the viewing of a particular Olympic events, whether ceremonies, team sports, individual sports, finals, qualifying rounds, etc. A sample of such factors are mentioned below.

Competitive channel environment. In highly developed, competitive television markets, as one finds in the United States, Canada, Japan, etc., the audience for big television events would rarely exceed 30 – 35 per cent of the television share (the percentage of people who watch a specific programme from among all those watching television) because of competitive programming alternatives.

In media environments of limited channel choice, but with a relatively high number of television sets (e.g. Russia, China, Cuba, Romania, etc.) viewer estimates can be much higher than that in the above example.

Timing. Timing differences also affect the potential for simultaneous worldwide audience. Even peak viewership of middle of the night programming in a select number of countries did not exceed top programme ratings during a 'typical' television week, let alone a week with a 'special' event. In a broader sense, time of the year also affects viewership when one considers school vacations, harvests, competing events of interest, etc. Related to this (see Chapter 4, is number of programming hours available at various times of the day.

Local relevance. National audience varies in terms of event interest with the highest audience ratings corresponding to local-national events of greatest interest, but these events are not always of world-wide interest or on a world-wide scale. However, this does help explain the general popularity of the Opening Ceremony as television event because, in that case, national participation in the Games gains world-wide relevance.

Technical or environmental factors. Availability or rationing of electricity as was experienced in Cuba and Colombia relative to the Barcelona Games affects audience access to programming. In Ghana, technical difficulties affected the quality of the Opening Ceremony to the point where it was visually indecipherable and served to discourage many viewers. In Russia, the loss of sound during the Closing Ceremony, causing the need to use a local commentator, might also have deterred audience interest. Even the weather can affect viewership in a variety of ways.

Promotion of the event. While extensively marketed as a television extravaganza in many countries, broadcasters in places like Ghana and Cameroon – or even Australia for specific events – did not publish television schedules of Olympic events. This could have a few different outcomes – either the encouragement of viewing longer hours (in hopes of 'catching' one's favourite sport) or as a message that the Olympics is not of high importance.

Competing events. In 1992, many countries had other things on their minds. War in Bosnia-Herzegovina; reunification adjustments in Germany; dissolution in Russia; radical political transformations in South Africa – all serving to distract viewers from watching television sports. In Cameroon, the death of Mrs. Jeanne Irene Biya, wife of the President of Cameroon, caused the Olympic broadcast to go off the air for four days (29 July – 1 August). As noted by the study correspondent in Germany:

> The Olympic Games of 1992 were not a big media event in Germany, perhaps because of a lot of other things required greater attention – the war in former Yugoslavia, economic problems in Germany, vacation time in many German regions.[2]

---

2   Rath (1992).

The audience for the Opening and Closing Ceremonies

Even with the above factors causing great country variability in audience levels, various audience studies carried out on Barcelona'92 show that the Opening and Closing ceremonies did in fact achieve the highest average audience of all the Olympic events on a world-wide scale, breaking global audience records. However, these figures were far short of the oft-cited 3.5 billion viewers.

Remember that the potential world television audience calculated above at 2.3 billion viewers was done considering a 90 per cent audience in developed countries. However, the Olympic Games audience in these areas was, at best, between 25 per cent and 32 per cent. Even with limited channel media environments, such as in Cuba, China and Russia, reporting viewership around 30 to 40 per cent (and up to 85 per cent of potential audience for Romania during the Closing Ceremony) the highest possible audience for a single event, such as the Opening Ceremony, must be estimated to be between 700 million and one billion, depending on the factors listed above: alternative programming availability, local interest, timing, the number of viewers per television set, etc.

Sports events with the largest audiences

The Opening and Closing ceremonies achieved exceptionally good audience ratings in most cases analysed in this study and was nearly always in the top four Olympic event ratings for each country in this study. In some countries, the ceremonies achieved the highest rating for Olympic programming (CTV, Canada; FS2, Austria; TF1, France; ARD, Germany). This unanimity of interest makes the ceremonies the Olympic events with the highest cumulative audience on a world-wide level. Otherwise audience was influenced most by national interest or participation in particular sports. And of these events, the programme ratings were highest when there was a chance of victory by a national team or athlete. Even sports that are not very popular in certain countries managed to achieve high rating positions as long as there was a chance of a compatriot winning a medal.

Some brief examples illustrate this point:

- In the United States, the audience for the finals of the women's gymnastics achieved the highest rating figures of the Olympic audience, 22.3, 8.5 points above the 13.8 audience rating achieved by the Opening Ceremony. The indiscriminate interest of female and male audiences in this sport, the clear chance for victory of the American team, along with NBC's placement of gymnastics largely in prime time, combined to create top ratings.

- The participation of Scottish athlete Liz McColgan in the womens' 10,000 metres brought about the highest audience figure for the Games in Central Scotland.

- The football final between Spain and Poland attracted the highest audience in Spain with an audience of some 3.5 million viewers.

- In France the same happened for the womens' 400 metres final which was won by María José Pérez. The event was simultaneously retransmitted by four television channels: TF1, A2, FR3 and Canal Plus, and it achieved the highest audience figure of 13 million viewers.

It is also noticeable even in the above examples that television viewers' favourite events, in contrast to the sports transmissions of each season, tended to be indiscriminate as to whether it was a men's or women's event. In fact, competitions in which women took part occupied the first position in audience ratings in many countries such as, for example, the USA, South Africa, Romania, Korea, England, France, Canada, etc. This is due to the greater importance given to national prospects at winning medals than of watching particular sport or gender events.

That said, popular sports do certainly attract viewer interest even without gold medal potential (but with at least national participation), such as, womens' gymnastics in Romania, badminton in Malaysia, and football in Ghana and Colombia. In fact, Colombian interest in Olympic events altogether fell considerably after the national football team was eliminated. Table 11.3 shows the most popularly watched Olympic sports for the countries in this study as reported by study correspondents and derived from a variety of national sources.

In some cases, social and political expectations generated by the athletes' participation increased the audience figures. In South Africa, for example, political leaders began to make statements from the moment people began to discuss the athlete Elana Mayer's chances in finishing in one of the first three places in the final of the womens' 10,000 metres. The media divulged that the country's president. F. W. de Klerk and the person in charge of sport each sent a fax to wish her the best of luck, building anticipation toward the event.

As might be expected, television in Catalonia paid more attention to the Olympic Games than television in the other nationalities and autonomous regions in Spain.[3] However, even in this case – the case of the host city itself – the rule of greatest interest in sports events of national and local significance remained true. It is significant that in the case of Barcelona the audience for the 1992 European Cup Final between F.C. Barcelona and Sampdoria managed to exceed the audience for the Opening Ceremony. While the ceremony obtained a high audience index of 35.7 per cent – the sum of viewers who tuned into TVE (18.2) and Canal Olímpic (17.5) – it still did not exceed that of the European Cup Final which managed a 37.4 per cent audience index, about a point more than the Opening Ceremony.

---

3   Although the audience for the Olympics in Spain was large, it could not be considered an audience leader in television programming. Very few Olympic episodes managed to be included among the major programs of 1992. Thus, for example, the Opening Ceremony was followed by an average audience of 16.7 per cent, far below the highest rated programme of 1992 – a show called *Que te den concurso* which obtained an average audience of 29.5 per cent.

Table 11.3. The most watched Barcelona'92 Olympic sports

Country	First	Second	Third
Germany	Gymnastics men's final	Athletics Triple jump (m.)	Athletics Hept.800 m.(w.)
Cameroon	Wrestling	Not available	Not available
Canada	Women's synchronized swimming	Not available	Not available
Colombia	Football	Not available	Not available
Cuba	Men's baseball	Boxing	Volleyball
China	Basketball 'Dream team'	100 m. (m. & w.)	Women's basketball
Spain	Football Spain-Poland final	Basketball 'Dream team'	Football
France	Athletics 400m. final. (w.)	Judo	Women's gymnastics
Ghana	Football	Boxing	Athletics in general
Netherlands	Athletics in general	Women's gymnastics	Judo
Indonesia	Football	Badminton	Boxing
England	Athletics Women's 10.000 m.	Athletics Men's 100 m.	Boxing
Italy	Men's football	Basketball 'Dream team'	Athletics Men's 100 m.
Japan	Womens' marathon	Athletics in general	Women's synchronized swimming
Korea	Women's archery	Wrestling Greco-Roman style	Women's handball
Malaysia	Men's badminton	Hockey	Football
Mexico	Basketballl 'Dream team'	Men's 50 km walk	Men's pole vault
Romania	Women's gymnastics	Athletics in general	Basketball 'Dream team'
Russia	Athletics in general	Gymnastics	Boxing
South Africa	Athletics 10.000 m.(w.)	Athletics 100 m. (m.)	Athletics 100 m. (w.)
USA	Women's gymnastics	Men's swimming	Not available

(m.) – Men's event (w.); – Women's event.
Source: Information provided by study correspondents.

After national participation, it was the participation of the most famous athletes or teams in the world, among the international sporting elite, in the Games that drew the largest audiences. The most representative example in this sense was the world audience success achieved by the United States basketball team ('Dream Team') that included the best players from the NBA. The opportunity to see such charismatic players as Magic Johnson, Michael Jordan or Larry Bird, possibly for the last time, drew the interest of audiences from the most varied of countries. The basketball final between the 'Dream Team' and Croatia obtained the highest audience figures in such culturally and politically different countries as China and Mexico as well as high ratings in Spain, Italy, Romania, and more.

The same audience interest was shown for the performances of other famous American athletes whose stardom in the Games was reminiscent of the international fame of the great Hollywood film stars. This is the case of Carl Lewis who was striving to beat the mythical long jump record of Mexico'68.

The degree of interest in following these elite teams and athletes on the television was less than that of the interest provoked by reasons of a popular, local or patriotic character which have been already described. Nevertheless, as happened in the case of the ceremonies, the presence of these famous stars among the highest audience rating positions in almost every country in the world led to higher cumulative audience rating figures on a world-wide level.

The debate that follows the international Olympic movement about the participation in the Games of the great athletes of professional sport – especially relevant in the case of baseball, soccer and cycling – should keep this important audience characteristic in mind.

Cumulative audience figures

Data compiled by the IOC through various sources offer some comparisons of estimates for cumulative audience of the past several summer and winter Olympic Games. These figures are shown in Table 11.4.

The cumulative audience concept is highly relevant in relation to advertising, especially taking into account that Olympic Games, are actually a set of events that take place over 17 days and offer numerous television audience profiles, and therefore numerous possible advertising opportunities.

Table 11.4. Cumulative audiences for recent Olympic Games

Summer	Winter	Summer	Winter
Seoul'88 10.4 billion	Barcelona'92 16.6 billion	Calgary'88 6.5 billion	Albertville'92 8 billion

Source: IOC 1993.

The viewing experience

Rothenbuhler has demonstrated that in the United States the Olympic Games generates a wider and more diverse type of audience network than that for usual sport or even general television programming.[4] From mostly anecdotal evidence provided by study correspondents this finding may also hold generally true cross nationally. In addition, television audiences for the Olympic Games seem to have quite similar sociological characteristics in very different regions of the world. In general the demographics are broader, by age and gender, than for typical programming (and definitely when compared to sports programming). There were a few peculiarities such as an increase in youth viewership because of summer holidays coinciding with the Olympic schedule in many countries. Also in Russia, the 1992 Opening Ceremony was said to hold a special interest for 'intellectuals' to whom it was seen as an interesting political moment given the dissolution of the Soviet Union.

In any case, this broader demographic sweep of viewers associated with the Olympics can be explained by any combination of the following general factors in a given country, including.

- The multidimensional nature of the event: multicultural, multi-political, multi-sport.

- The spectacular and historical nature of the Opening and Closing Ceremonies.

- The presence of sports such as gymnastics, diving and swimming which are of a clearly different aesthetic nature to competition sports.

- The attention devoted by rights holding broadcasters to the promotion of the Games as a special television event.

- The feelings of involvement with some social collective involved in the Games, whether cultural, racial, sexual, national or linguistic.

Such attributes explain how sports such as gymnastics, which attract very small audiences in the sports programming season, saw some of the largest audiences for Barcelona'92 in countries such as the USA, Romania, Germany, Australia, The Netherlands, Russia and France.

Viewer setting and configurations

It seemed the consensus of study correspondents that typical viewing group sizes and settings were increased or are expanded during the Olympic Games. If it is common for television to be watched in family settings, then these patterns continued but maybe with larger family groups or spending more time. Even in the most developed countries such as the United States, Germany, Italy, etc., an increase in the amount of people in front of one television set was detected, with the addition of friends or relations to the family group.

---

4 Rothenbuhler (1988).

If, as in Ghana, television viewing is primarily a medium of the urban middle class with a significant amount of group viewing, this skew of television demographics was accentuated during the Games. In Ghana, for example, the social characteristics of housing – shared courtyards and shared television sets – lent themselves to such increases in group viewing during the Games. While people mostly watched the Olympics at home in urban settings Karikari cited larger than usual group viewing sizes ranging from 5 to 50 people in community centres, dorms, churches, or other open places.[5]

Commercial incentives

There were many reports of commercial settings using the Olympics as a means to attract or keep customers eating or drinking in their establishment by adding television sets, fixing the channel to the Olympics, and actively trying to attract customers to come watch. In Malaysia, for example, the Olympic Games were tied to location promotions for shopping centres, products, restaurants and more. Drinking establishments of several major hotels promoted specialty drinks and slogans such as the 'Olympic bowl', 'drink your way through the Olympics', enjoy 'Happy hour with the Olympics', and so forth.[6] In other countries it was common to see the Olympics on television sets in pubs, restaurants and even in small shops and local markets.

Changing the daily routine

Along these lines, there was an increase in public viewing as well as the creation of additional public viewing spaces. Television sets appeared in hotel lobbies, airport lounges, public square and subway stations to allow people to follow the Games outside their homes. In African villages it was reported that people got together in larger than usual groups in front of public television sets to follow the main events, especially football. Similarly, some correspondents reported an increase in portable televisions brought into the workplace. And some viewers, as reported in Cameroon, covered quite some geographic distance in order to watch the most important events (boxing, weightlifting and wrestling) with friends and family who had television sets.

Some changes were caused by more environmental factors. For example during the Olympic Games it was very hot in China, and with air-conditioners rare in private houses, many people moved their TVs outside to watch, attracting larger than usual family and neighbour groups for 'patio' viewing.

However, it was time zone differences that accounted for the most disruption in the routines of daily life during the Olympics. As noted by the study correspondent from Australia:

> Because the 'live' broadcasts of some of the most important finals events for Australian audiences – for example swimming – took place between 12 and 6 am there was a tendency to watch through the night, to arrange sleeping time so that

---

5 Karikari (1992).

6 Mohamed (1992).

the event could be watched at a certain point. Hence, one might assume that Olympic coverage tends to create unusual patterns of viewing ... Even press commentaries emphasized the 'Olympian' quality of the watching experience itself, which required a certain discipline and dedication.[7]

In Japan the increase in the number of sets in use during the late night hours was 60 per cent higher than for the same time period the year below, correlating directly to Olympic Games viewing. Summed up nicely by the study correspondents from Japan, they said, according to such figures, 'it's possible to say that well over eight million Japanese lost sleep over the Olympics'.[8]

Broadcasters themselves encouraged changes in viewing routines by adding programming hours onto their regular broadcast schedules. This was the case in Indonesia and China, for example where broadcast hours were extended just for the Olympics period later into the night to accommodate more live coverage.

While this analysis could not support the idea that 3.5 billion people simultaneously viewed the Olympics in unusual circumstances around the world. The audience levels that were attracted at various peak moments, combined with notable changes in many daily routines still allow the Olympics to be labeled as a global television event of extraordinary proportions around the world.

---

7   Langer (1992).

8   Kosaka *et al.* (1992).

12   Local Visions of the Global: some perspectives from around the world

Visions of the Olympic Games, in professional and academic circles, have largely come from western, developed countries. These views have shaped, and somewhat confined, modern images of the Olympic Games. Yet, most serious observers of the Games realize this and know, that for many cultures around the world the Olympics creates more a sense of participating in the festival of 'others' than of participating in a universal event.

This chapter offers just a few different perspectives from around the world. It even has the audacity to combine the views of several countries into more regional overviews. The limitations of such ventures are obvious and, while for each area a more in-depth analysis could certainly have been conducted, the idea here is just to offer a sense of how different countries and geographic regions live the Olympics, largely through the eyes of the study correspondents.

Africa

The old adage that from where one sits determines what one sees is particularly pronounced in the interpretations of African nations looking at the Olympic Games. The analysis of some selected African perspectives highlights the diversity in the forms of interpreting and experiencing the Olympic Games. It also underscores the pervasive theme of hierarchy – or have and have nots – that has run through this entire analysis, as well as issues concerning ways in which identity is manifested through televised images.

Limitations in television production and reception

The different technical conditions of television reception and production colour every

The sections of this chapter concerning Africa and Latin America draw upon contributions from Carmen Gómez Mont, whose cooperation the authors gratefully acknowledge. Further, each section draws primarily upon the contributions of the study correspondents from those countries.

aspect of the presentation and understanding of the Olympic Games in Africa. When referring to the African continent one cannot speak of 'universal coverage' let alone viewer 'choice' in selection of television programmes. Although this study did not collect specific audience data across Africa, it is clear that the Olympic Games were mainly of interest to literate sectors of the population who have better access to television and speak the primary languages (English and French) used in broadcasts. Of the countries involved in this study, Cameroon has a literate population above 15 years of age of 46 per cent, Ghana 40 per cent, Egypt 52 per cent and South Africa 24 per cent.[1] As expected however, it was the radio, and not the television, that allowed much of the population to keep in touch with the Games. Within African society the radio has a considerable audience and broadcasts the most popular modern sports on the continent, mainly soccer and long distance running.

Second hand broadcasts

The most significant characteristic of television coverage of the Olympics in Africa was the virtual absence of images of Africans or images produced by Africans on objects of local interest to television viewers.

> From beginning to end nothing was shown or said about the participation of Cameroon on the television, except when the country was identified during the Parade of the Nations in the Opening Ceremony.[2]

Cameroon appeared on camera for only 16 seconds during the opening ceremony.

The broadcasting of the Barcelona'92 Olympic Games reached the majority of African countries by means of European international networks produced for very different 'home' audiences. For example, Cameroon Radio TV (CRTV), via an arrangement through URTNA, used Canal France International as an intermediate broadcaster. As a consequence of this the viewers in Cameroon saw an Opening Ceremony narrated by French commentators for French television viewers. The presence of Cameroon broadcast personnel during the Opening Ceremony was limited to the participation of two commentators situated in their own television studio in Cameroon and not in Barcelona. These commentators, one speaking French and the other speaking English among themselves were only able to intervene in the presentation during the brief advertising breaks destined for the French audience.

> J.L.: We're going to return to Barcelona in a few moments. Perhaps we need to explain the reason for these brief interruptions in this ceremony that has to last three hours. We are receiving the images from TF1 and this channel cuts the ceremony in order to introduce their advertising and we cannot pass on an advert that comes from France (...) (CRTV, Cameroon, Opening Ceremony).

The dependency on foreign television channels also had consequences for programming and quality of reception. Karikari pointed out in his report that:

---

1   UNESCO (1993).

2   Wete (1992).

In Ghana the majority of the broadcasts were carried out by people other than Ghanaians, in English and in French, the broadcast was in black and white (due to the lack of technical link-up), and there were constant interruptions in order to improve the image. The timetables were not published in advance and many of the major events of most interest for Ghana were excluded.[3]

Wete says something similar in relation to the experience of television in Cameroon:

The programming of the Games wasn't announced in advance ... they were simply discovered on the television. Cameroon television coverage was fragmented and irregular ... The commentators were French and spoke of France, the European Union and the West in order of importance.[4]

Local commentaries were added to the end of the programmes or, as mentioned, during advertising breaks of the original broadcasts – spaces in which the local commentators quickly referenced issues of most relevance to the local viewers.

The Olympic host seen from the South

Looking south to north, the African countries saw the Olympic host – Barcelona – as a land of development, wealth and modernity. In this sense, the Olympic Games represented for African countries the chance to contrast their position in relation to the modern world, a world that uses economic development as its primary evaluative standard.

These types of comparisons were not necessarily made in a negative sense. As Awatef Abd El-Rahman from Egypt said, Spain is seen as 'a developed country with a heritage of civilization and modern technology' and that 'the Egyptians see a synthesis of East and West in the Olympic Games'. These observations are interesting in that they project an idea of symbiosis between the ancient and the modern, between tradition and technology, the central idea around which the new African identity is trying to be constructed.

Yet other observers of the Barcelona Games were less accepting of the displays of wealth bundled up into the Opening Ceremony when considering north/south comparisons and even implicate television in this display of world economic disparity:

A ceremony of this kind is designed to depend on extravagant spectacle and thus it also sharply conveys a celebration of conspicuous wealth. This is no doubt a by-product of the fact that television coverage is dominated by requirements of audiences in the world's richest nations. But the gigantism of the whole event has the inadvertent consequence that the arrival of the world's poorer nations in the great parade of athletes with only a handful of people looks almost embarrassing – as if they cannot they cannot [pay to send] a hundred or more lusty youths.[5]

---

3   Karikari (1992).

4   Wete (1992).

5   Izod *et al.* (1992).

Non-national African identity

As discussed in Chapter 8, although an event based in the philosophy of internationalism, the design of the Games ceremonies and competition is such that the concept of the nation state is central to identity differentiation. Yet for African participants in the Games whose identity is linked to different types of membership groups such national symbols are not highly relevant. In other words, the central role of 'nation' found in the Olympic concept of identity is more compatible with western forms of identity representation, where symbols such as national flags, national anthem, presidency or royalty have strongly reinforced historical, legal and cultural representation functions. That is not to say, however, that there wasn't an acute interest and pride on the part of Africans in being at the Olympic Games. There clearly was.

Uniforms instead of flags

This interest is African self identity was most deeply expressed in what for some western countries could be interpreted as a trivial question: the clothes worn by the athletes in the Opening Ceremony parade.

At the time of choosing their attire some African countries were equally divided between those who opted to show off their traditional style of dressing and those who opted to dress in the 'western' style, with a majority of the Arab delegations opting for the traditional style of dressing.

Various reasons can be put forward for this difference in choices. On the one hand those who chose to wear western style clothes seemed to do so just to adopt symbolical forms of the modern world. On the other hand, it is possible that those who opted for the traditional form of dressing did so as a consequence of attributing to the athletes' clothes and uniforms even greater importance than their own flags and national symbols. The choice of athletes uniforms clothes were clearly more than a fashion statement. It was seen as a sign of identity that referred to the most ancient of their traditions, as well as contrasted with western ways.

The analysis of the coverage of the Opening Ceremony on Cameroon television under-scores the importance of this choice. The athletes of Cameroon appeared in the Barcelona stadium wearing elegant western style suits. This circumstance went unnoticed by the French commentators who were broadcasting the ceremony for France – and to Cameroon. However, it was noticed by the commentators situated in the television studio in Cameroon and in their brief appearances during French commercial breaks the main theme com-mented on was, precisely, the merits of the western style attire worn by the Cameroon athletes:

> Yes, it has to be said that large sports events are also great opportunities for cultural and even political propaganda because each country that participates wants to announce a message ... And we thought that Cameroon would wear the national dress ... We paraded wearing typical dress in the African Games, and now we are unfortunately parading wearing [Western] suits ... When the people in charge from

the Ministry of Youth and of Sport return they will be asked why they allowed Cameroon to portray a cultural image that isn't theirs ... The Africans are becoming westernized, the Arabs are becoming westernized, Egypt too ... Traditional dress is culture and isn't that all we have left when we have lost everything. This is what we will be left with ... (CRTV, Cameroon, Opening Ceremony).

Despite the reference in the quote to Egypt, the Egyptian ERTU2 commentator noted literally even team that entered the Olympic stadium, African or not, wearing traditional attire.

The athlete, the hero and personification of the nation

African athletes, as representatives of popular identity and associated with strength and success, are important in the construction of African identity. More than political representatives, flags or national anthems, it was the athlete-hero who took centre stage for the Africans. This has not just been the case of the Olympics. As Baker affirms, when the victorious athletes returned home from any sports events:

> They were received with full honors, they went on national and international tours, their photographs appeared in many public places, troubadours sang of their exploits and public works and streets were named after them. In 1970 African athletes became important symbols of national identity ... and, more than political heroes, it was the athletes who represented for a large number of young Africans a chance of success within their reach.[6]

But these idols are not 'national' ones as is understood in western countries where they are linked to the performance of the nation state and wrap themselves in the national flag upon victory or cry on the medal stand at the playing of national anthem and raising of their national flag. The idol of an African nation is an African idol. 'With Kenya we're also hoping for a handful of gold medals, above all in the long distance races'. (CRTV, Cameroon, Opening Ceremony).

As in the case of Latin America, it is not just the pride of the country (nation state) that is at stake while being represented in a sport, but rather the identity of the whole continent. The idea that a sports person or a team has a chance of winning, strengthens the whole of Africa against everyone else.

> We think that the African countries who went in traditional dress are the pride of Africa in these Olympic Games ... Ghana, Egypt, Morocco, I'm convinced that one of these countries will bring back gold from the Games.

> As for the football which began yesterday with the Republic of Qatar and Egypt, one-nil, it was a poor beginning for Africa on this occasion ... I hope that all will be put right in the name of Africa. (CRTV, Opening Ceremony).

This idea of collectivity and importance of strength of identity is even stronger in the case of the Arab countries, as evidenced by Egyptian television's keen attention to every

---

6   Baker (1987: 272–273).

entering Arab delegation, as well as explicit praise for any team dressed in a traditional costume. In fact it was the commentators from these countries who expressed the biggest reservations about and criticisms of the cultural forms of the ceremonies' spectacles (e.g. opera) and even the costumes of the spectators caught by the television cameras (such as bikini tops). A special attitude of rejection was perceived towards western cultural forms, attitudes and life styles that contrasted with religious and, above all, moral principles.

South Africa: an identity crisis

The South African media faced an enormously difficult task when it set about dealing with the Barcelona Olympic phenomenon. On the one hand, South Africa's return to the Olympics after 32 years was generally seen as a cause for celebration. But on the other hand, South Africa's participation became yet another site of politico-cultural conflict in an already tense society.[7]

Re-admittance in the Games was, for many South Africans, an important symbol of having re-joined the world community and 'being normal again' as a nation.[8] Yet at the same time South Africa in 1992, had no national identity to bring to this significant event – an event that demands teams come with a suitcase of national symbols (anthem, flag, uniform).

The South African team performed under a specially designed National Olympic Committee of South Africa (NOCSA) flag explicitly to avoid conflicts which would most likely arise using the blue, white and orange flag identified with the apartheid era. Ironically, RTO'92 as host broadcaster unwittingly served to spoil the positive intent of this by showing South African spectators at the Olympics wildly waving the flag of 'white South Africa'. South African athletic officials at the Games even tried to stop, to no avail, the spectators from waving the flags.

Other apartheid era national symbols, the official anthem and the springbok logo (long associated with South African sport), were also dropped leaving the team and country with little to speak of in terms of meaningful identity, yet much to argue about between groups as a consequence of those moves. In addition there were several other areas of turmoil related to athlete's selection, de Klerk not receiving an invitation to the Games (although Nelson Mandela sat with other heads of state), and other events which served to disillusion some audiences only days into the Games.

The result was that, rather than being a unifying experience, the Games provided one after another reminder of the painful transition the country had been going through. As such, the Olympics became part of the domestic crisis – the struggle among groups to, in fact, define just what South Africa should be. In this sense, South Africa's return to the Games in 1992 was ultimately bittersweet. This was accentuated by the fact that the team performance was disappointing, causing 'much soul-searching' in the press during and

---

7   Louw (1992).

8   de Beer *et al.* (1992).

after the Games as to the reasons. While the Olympics did not serve, in any way, to construct a sense of national unity in South Africa during this period it is suggested that the Olympic broadcast, which occurred during one of the most politically violent periods of South Africa's history, at least offered an escape.[9]

Ironically, the international media offered a chorus of celebration for the return of South Africa and demise of apartheid in their commentaries without any reference, whatsoever, to the continuing domestic crisis in that country. Rather, the presence of South Africa was presented – and symbolized by commentators through the stadium presence of Mandela – as a victory already won. The SBC 12 commentator from Singapore exemplified this sentiment when he said, upon entrance of the South African team, 'What a moment for those athletes. [visual of Mandela] Nelson Mandela, I'm sure with a tear in his eye'. Or the Australian Channel 7 commentator who noted the dove symbol on their track suits 'to demonstrate their commitment to peace and democracy'.

The South African experience, as with other African nations, was another reminder of the skewed nature of the international Olympic audience – and of television reception in general on the African continent. As Louw noted, not all South Africans could participate in the Olympics as a television event because only about 25 per cent of South Africans own, or have access to, a television set effectively skewing Olympic audiences to the favour of middle class whites, coloureds (people of mixed blood) and Indians (people who ancestors came from India). Black TV viewing, according to Louw, is mostly concentrated in the 'formal' black townships. This viewership profile was also reflected in the television coverage. Of the five SABC presenters, all were middle class, four were white, two of those spoke Afrikaans. In this sense, the Barcelona Olympics was for a 'westernized' South Africa. Only 36 per cent of South Africans use the three languages of the broadcast presentations as a primary language (English, Afrikaans, Xhosa).[10]

Not to be daunted by some of the problems accompanying this first foray back into the Games, the cities of Cape Town, Durban and Johannesburg began to work on applications to host a 2004 Olympics shortly after the Barcelona Games. If successful South Africa would be the first Africa nation to host an Olympics Games.

Russia

The Barcelona 1992 Olympics represented a special case in the history of Russian participation in the Olympics due to the disintegration of the Soviet Union. Nearly every aspect of the television coverage of the Games – the production quality, the commentary, the audience, the broadcast scheduling, and even the criticisms of the coverage – reflected

---

9   *Ibid.*

10 Only 6 per cent of the South African population is English speaking. The Afrikaans-speaking population constitutes 9 per cent of the total population. About 20 per cent of the population are Xhosa speaking, although 46 per cent of the population can understand Xhosa (Zulus, Swazis and Ndebeles). None of the SABC presenters catered to the Sotho-speakers (about 23 per cent of the population), and the black presenter used mostly English in his commentaries. Louw (1992).

in some way the changes and problems going on in Russia and the former Soviet republics at that time.

In the Barcelona Games, Russian athletes, as well as those from other former Soviet republics, participated as part of the 'Unified Team'. Although they marched into the Olympic stadium together, each republic had its own identity and if a medal was won – of which there were many – it was the anthem of the newly independent republic or Russia that was played.

For audiences, the Barcelona Games represented a transition time from the old to the uncertain new. As the study correspondents from Russia put it, 'In a certain way the attitude of the Russian public towards the Barcelona Olympics was unique in its mixture of nostalgic images of the victories of the powerful Soviet team in the past and ... of the appreciation of the achievements of Russian athletes still in the framework of the Unified Team.'[11]

A difficult time for media in Russia

For broadcasters, Barcelona also represented a new way of doing things, reflecting both structural changes and financial hardships of the media inside the former Soviet Union. The two main Russian channels 1 and 2, although still owned by the Russian state now sported new identities. Channel 1 'Ostankino' broadcast to Russia and practically all other former Republics. Channel 2 had become the Russian Television and Radio Broadcasting company (RTR) broadcasting almost exclusively to Russia. However, the two broadcasters competed for audiences within Russia.

For the coverage of the Barcelona Olympics both channels were hampered by a lack of resources that seriously affected their abilities to provide quality commentary from Barcelona. The two channels were able to send only 34 people to Barcelona for television and radio operations (contrast this to 1300 broadcast personnel brought by NBC of US). They occupied a small, two-room office without a television studio. This was a significantly smaller operation than had attended the Seoul'88 Games. Russian print media, although now flourishing within a new post-censorship atmosphere, was suffering from similar financial hardships as broadcasters, resulting in very few journalists traveling to Barcelona. This put the main burden for covering the Games on television.

The two Russian broadcasters had come to Barcelona having agreed to share coverage of the Games by alternating the days on which each channel would broadcast the most 'popular' sports. However, given a new atmosphere of competition within Russia, it was not long before one accused the other of 'breaking' the agreement and soon they both ignored any prior complementary programming agreement. By the Closing Ceremony, Russian viewers could watch two versions of the ceremony, each with its own commentator, on two different channels. In a related sign of the times, for the first time ever in Russian coverage of the Olympics the Games were also interrupted by commercial breaks.

---

11 Zassoursky *et al.* (1992).

The Games as a distraction from domestic problems

At first the Olympics seemed neglected in relation to domestic media coverage of the difficult political situation within Russian and tensions with the former republics. However, ultimately there were significant amounts of daily television attention devoted to Olympic coverage with RTR broadcasting close to 9 hours a day (including summaries) for much of the Games. One RTR commentator in Barcelona confessed that he thought the amount of Olympic television coverage was excessive given all that was going on in Russia. He quipped that the government actually wanted it that way, suggesting that the long hours of Olympic broadcasting kept people from going outside to protest the domestic situation. He said, 'the government is happy the Olympics are in August ... it keeps everyone inside watching TV'.[12]

Post-Cold War commentary

The television coverage itself was criticized by Russian press and viewers for its poor quality of both sports and cultural commentary. That aside, the commentary did exhibit several important features also reflective of the changes going on. There was a distinct absence of confrontational, Cold War style rhetoric that had characterized prior Olympic broadcasts. If there was any rhetoric apparent it related more to the beauty of sport and notions of international friendship and peace – both concepts were brought up repeatedly during the ceremonies. At one point in the Opening Ceremony, commentators reminded audiences that in ancient Greece war had always stopped during the Olympic Games. For the war-torn [then] Commonwealth of Independent States (CIS) this value seemed of special importance.

Further, the commentary reflected a transition period in the national identity of Russia. For example, when the Unified Team entered the stadium during the Opening Ceremony very little was said by the commentators and what was, seemed routine, matter of fact, and made up of disjointed comments.

> Here is the team of CIS. You know, of course, (name of co-commentator) that all former republics of the Soviet Union, with the exception of the Baltic states, are suppose to perform as one team. And in case of victories, the flag of their country will be flown and the corresponding anthem will be played in their honor. So, the team of the Commonwealth of the Independent States: representatives from Azerbaijan, Armenia, Belarus, Georgia, Russia, Tadjikistan, Turkmenistan, Uzbekistan and Ukraine. The largest delegation is from Russia. The Olympic flag is carried by by Alexsandr Kerelin, the champion of the Olympics in Seoul, our famous wrestler. (Ostankino 1, Russia, Opening Ceremony).

As Zassoursky noted, 'In some respect we watched a disunited team of a disunited nation ... [in that sense] "national identity" was adequately portrayed'.[13] Interestingly, twice as

---

12 Interview with Vladimir Gomelsky, commentator for Russian Television and Radio Broadcasting, 3 August 1992, Barcelona.

13 Zassoursky *et al.* (1992).

much was said about the next team which entered: the United States. It seemed easier for commentators to talk about the US athletes.

> EV: Just at this moment you see the delegation as a whole. The delegation of the USA – one of the most numerous – has just entered the field.

> AS: To be precise, they are the largest.

> EV: Yes, 591 athletes will go to the starting line in the competitions that are part of the compulsory programme. But overall the American delegation here in Barcelona includes 365 people who are coaches, doctors, managers, participants of the demonstration sports and, of course, the most numerous team – track and field – numbering 141 athletes. They have the most realistic chances for Olympic medals. In swimming 52 people will go to the starting line and Americans suggest that in this Olympics they expect to achieve the highest results in all of history and win the most medals.

> AS: We'll note that Americans ... have brought fantastic basketball led by Magic Johnson, a legend of American basketball, the strongest ... in the world today. And that's exactly why, perhaps, the tickets to the final game cost enormous amounts of money, and are, of course, all already sold out. Everybody will watch the performance of the wonderful sprinter Carl Lewis, the swimmer Michael [name] and many, many other athletes from the United States of America.
> (Ostankino 1, Russia, Opening Ceremony).

At the same time, the sports coverage of the Russian broadcasters was also generous in its recognition and applause of the achievements of athletes from the newly independent Baltic states, Lithuania, Latvia and Estonia and former Soviet athletes now on the Israeli team, throughout the Games. It is also interesting to note that the Russian commentators offered an extremely favourable portrayal of the Spanish Royal Family. During the Closing Ceremony, the Spanish horse-riding skills were compared to those of the old Russia's guard. As Zassoursky suggested, 'This description of Russian traditions may set a future model of a nation's portrayal'.[14]

More generally, the Russian perspective was one that has been consistently stalwart in its support of the Olympic movement. As one of many examples throughout the broadcast commentary, toward the end of the Opening Ceremony, the Ostankino 1 commentator said, in a very impromptu outburst:

> And now we say good luck to all the participants of the Games and to the Olympic Games as a whole. We want this unique festival, that has lasted on our planet for almost 100 years not to end, ever, but become more wonderful and bring joy to all of us. (Ostankino 1, Russia, Opening Ceremony).

---

14 *Ibid.*

Slovenia

The Barcelona Olympics were the first time Slovenia participated in the Olympic Games as an independent state. Thus, the playing of the Slovene national anthem, *Zdravlijica*, upon the entrance of the Slovene athletes held a very special meaning for the Slovenian people. For the media, it also provided a natural interpretive framework within which to view the Games: as a promotion of nationhood. For the commentators of Slovenia's 2nd channel the Slovene athletes marching behind the national flag represented a 'historic' moment: a moment of national and international recognition of Slovenia as a legitimate nation-state. Through the course of the Games Slovene athletes were repeatedly presented as national symbols and, as such, incorporated into a dialogue of national promotion. When Slovenian rowers won two bronze medals, they were portrayed as 'heroes'.

The Olympics and war

However, only 200 km south of Slovenia, in another newly independent state of Bosnia and Herzegovina, civil war raged. Each day the media were flooded with horrific pictures of refugees, concentration camps and war. The proximity of this tragedy was to dominate the media agenda and overshadow the pure joy of seeing Slovene athletes compete for the first time under the national flag in an Olympic Games. Unfortunately, 'for the Slovene audience the reality of war was closer than the reality of the Olympic Games'.[15] In a telling cartoon published in *Delo*, a Bosnian athlete is waiting to start a race, listening to the starter saying, 'it is important to participate', while the starter points his pistol at his head.

These two realities would meet briefly in the commentary of the Games. For example, the Slovene 2nd channel stressed repeatedly that both Serbia and Montenegro were absent from the Games' roster of countries. While Slovenia news and sport commentary isn't known for rhetoric or hyperbole, the dual interpretive frameworks of proximity of war and the relishing of new nationhood also seemed reflected in the distinct lack of broadcast discourse about Olympic and universalistic values of peace and internationalism common to other broadcasts. Here was one isolated reference:

> Peace and friendship through the world is symbolized with 15,000 doves released from the stadium. In ancient Greece, during the Opening Ceremony all the wars came to a stop. Unfortunately, today's reality does not follow the old Greek habit. (2nd Channel, Slovenia, Opening Ceremony).

And, later in the Opening Ceremony, at the sight of the Olympic flag, the commentator added:

> Unfortunately, the world is not at peace today. While we have the Olympic Games in one part of the world ... in other parts we have wars and destruction ... Let this unfolding of the Olympic flag be a symbol of the Olympics, peace, friendship, love ... (2nd Channel, Slovenia, Opening Ceremony).

---

15 Splichal *et al.* (1992).

China

Late July was extraordinarily hot along the coastal areas of China. This did not dampen the enthusiasm of an estimated 500 million Chinese for watching the Opening Ceremony of the Olympic Games.[16] If not at home, they watched in courtyards, restaurants, night markets and stores, or in the village centres. Li Liangrong states that according to a newspaper report there were 'thousands of people ... watching outside on the street July 26' the Opening Ceremony in the cities of Nanjing, Shanghai and Wuhan. Further, he said that the Barcelona Games was a significant topic of daily conversation as viewers commented and argued about various events and outcomes.[17] The roots of this interest can be found in the broad, government supported integration of sport in society, the tremendous growth and reach of television, and the very social nature of Chinese TV viewing as a form of entertainment.

Setting television broadcast records

As noted in Chapter 11, the broadcasting of the 1992 Olympics did disrupt the routines of daily life across China. Because of an awkward time delay between Barcelona and Beijing, live Olympics programming aired during the middle of the night, well after CCTV's normal broadcast hours. Although an extreme rarity in Chinese broadcasting history, CCTV extended its hours past its normal sign off time of 23:00 to broadcast an unprecedented 276 hours of Olympic broadcasting replacing much regular programming (setting CCTV records for both hours of programming and reach for a televised event).

And people readily stayed up to watch. Both sport and television viewing in China are very important parts of public life. In a 1986 study of 367 urban Chinese, sports programmes were found to be second only to drama as a favourite programme type with men favouring sports over women.[18] In a 1987 *China Daily* poll of TV viewers, 50 per cent said that sports programmes are 'an indispensable part of their lives'.[19] For the Barcelona Games, men and women's basketball, table tennis and track events – all popular school sports – were the most watched sports events for Chinese audiences. For students, the Olympics was held during summer vacation, so viewing the Games was popular.

Given this favourable public attitude toward both sports and the integral nature of television viewing as entertainment in China, it is not surprising that television and print coverage of the Barcelona Games was both comprehensive and positive in China. Spurring this high level of attention has been a steady increase in Chinese worldwide sports accomplishments since the early 1980s. And Chinese audiences in 1992 were, once again, rewarded by a stellar performance of the Chinese team at the Olympics.

---

16 CCTV estimates cited in Li Liangrong (1992). By calculations in Chapter 11, this figure seems somewhat high.

17 Li Liangrong (1992).

18 Lull (1991).

19 Brownell (1993).

International sport as linked with stature

Media coverage of the Games portrayed China's very successful participation in the Games as proof of Chinese prominence and cooperative stance in the Olympic Family – and by extension in world affairs (a philosophy made clear by the Chinese government's avid promotion of China as an international sports competitor). The Chinese team, as noted in Chapter 8, clearly carried the full burden of national identity with them to Barcelona. In this sense, international sports are inextricably linked with national prestige in China. So it would come as little surprise when Olympic gold medial Chinese diving champion Gao Min announced shortly after the Barcelona Olympics that she wanted to sell another gold medal she won at the world swimming and diving championships (earlier in the year) so that the proceeds could go to Beijing's campaign to host the 2000 Olympics.

Brownell explains this attitude by suggesting that types of 'face' work with much more moral force than western or Olympic ideals of fair play and friendly competition. As an example, she says that the Chinese keep a point system concerning Olympic performance (not simply medal counts as many countries do). She notes that, 'The general public is not aware that these are unofficial' and they talk about one country 'beating' another in the very specific sense of point tallies. According to Brownell, China's performance in the world of international sports is not just participation in a game, but for China are as 'real as military defeat, economic accomplishments, or political reversals'.[20]

Possibly as a result, the broadcast of the Olympic Opening Ceremony tended to be solemn and grand presented with an attitude of the team on a serious mission, rather than endowed with any character of Olympic festival. This is reflected in Kong Xiang'an's (1992) observation that the Chinese athletes entering the stadium in Barcelona were 'lined up neatly and their spirit inspiring' and that the visual attention given to China by the international signal (much longer than the 30-second average) 'was correct given China's due place in the Olympic Family'. The commentary was formal, poetic, inexact, and full of common sports slogans ('The torch symbolizes the bright future; it lights up all corners of the globe' CCTV, China, Opening Ceremony). It also atypical for this kind of event in that it was very sparse. This was largely due to a combination of language barriers and the late-arriving media script for the ceremonies not allowing the Chinese commentators to follow their usual pattern for this type of event and prepare, and rehearse, an elaborate script. As such, the commentary offered little flavor of the host city culture.

The Beijing Olympic bid

It was also of no small consequence that Beijing was in 1992 still in the running to host the 2000 Games. China's bid was discussed frequently in the media along with a campaign of sorts for convincing the Chinese people of the importance of this effort. For example, media gave accounts of the positive impacts of hosting for Barcelona's urban development. Newspapers praised the 'miracle' of Barcelona's supposed transformation from an

---

20 From 'Face and Fair Play': Sports and Morality in the Economic Reforms. Chapter 11 in Brownell (1995).

old city to a modern city in just a few years. Newspapers also wrote admiringly of the wide participation of Barcelona's citizens in the Games, suggesting that China could learn from the 1992 in terms of both development and volunteerism.

More generally, the Games were defined in terms of not just peace and friendship, but progress. Olympic spirit was explicitly linked with economic modernization. One article in *Liberation Daily* headlined, 'Let the Olympic Spirit Spread in China', advocated that China's economic reform and modernization would benefit from some Olympic spirit.[21] Conversely there was virtually no attention to any of the usual problems identified with the Olympics, such as drugs, professionalism and encroaching commercialism.

As such the 1992 Olympics from the Chinese perspective was very serious business. In fact, one Chinese study correspondent even lamented this fact. When discussing the obvious joy, frivolity and friendship among the Olympic athletes dancing together at the end of the Closing Ceremony, he wrote:

> Regrottably, since at the time of the Closing Ceremony most of the Chinese athletes had already returned home ... one could not see any Chinese athlete. This was not due to the bias of the [television] director, but was the inevitable result of the traditional Confucian teachings learned by Easterners ... In the free activities of the Closing Ceremony, the defects in the personalities of Eastern youth were easy to see. If Beijing's bid for the 2000 Olympic Games is successful, simply having the smiles of the city residents is not enough; the national character still ought to change towards openness.[22]

Latin America

In order to analyse the significance the Barcelona Olympic Games had for Latin America it must be remembered that 1992 was the year of the 500th anniversary of Columbus' voyage, the year that Latin America met Spain once again, in a new tone dominated by the region's democratization and economic modernization processes.

It is not difficult to imagine this self image of transformation would link to heightened, and even unrealistic, expectations of sporting triumph. It is in this context – a continent looking for some acknowledgment and reward as players in a changing global environment – that Latin America approached the Barcelona Games.

> More than a parade of sport teams this could be an example of the new world map, the new geopolitic distribution (TV Globo, Brazil, Opening Ceremony).

But instead of playing as equals with the imaginary west, through sport, as it had hoped, Latin Americans experienced the emotional highs and lows of a local television drama.

21 Li Liangrong (1992).

22 Kong Xiang'an (1992).

Sport, television and soap opera

Across many parts of Latin America, sport provides the 'ordinary' people with a space in the open air which they do not have at their disposal in their homes. There are abundant football clubs in the neighbourhoods where playing and organizing matches becomes a question of identity and territory. Football is played anywhere, even in the middle of the street, but within the neighbourhood. Sundays, and in certain cases, the end of the working day, are organized around this activity. Big sports stars such as Pele, Maradona and Romario have emerged from the common people, from the street.

In another aspect of life, the majority of homes have video cassette recorders, cable television or else satellite dishes. Audiovisual technology is now part of the urban and rural landscape. For a Latin American, the television is a terminal from which he or she establishes contact with the outside world for simple curiosity, entertainment or a desire for news. However, it is also the medium through which is created fantasies as a form of escape. The creation of fantasies finds its perfect television format in the 'telenovela', an extremely popular Latin American form of soap opera. The telenovela is a story that allows viewer to come in contact with lifestyles in which success is one of the key values.

The Olympic Games, in the Latin American context, adapts perfectly to the telenovela structure. It embodies festivity, drama, spectacularity, suspense, reward, punishment, hero, anti-hero, tears, laughter, embraces and more. Its sports competitions are like episodes condensed into sixteen days during which the viewer is passionately involved. The characters suffer, cry, laugh, cherish victory and are turned into heroes and anti-heroes. If they take shape as winners parts of their lives appear surrounded in glory. The element of surprise comes into play, hope for the victory of one of 'ours' keeps the people glued to the television screen. Identification is sought with the hero of the telenovela: the athlete. Such was the case of Ximena Restrepo, the first woman to win an Olympic medal in the history of Colombia.

In the Barcelona Olympics all the above elements converged. The hope and need of Latin America for international recognition, the channeling of these hopes through sport expectations, and the playing out of these expectations through the Olympic broadcast as dramatic story. And, in true telenovela style, the story had some peak experiences, but ultimately ended with dashed expectations and self examination.

A proud start

Latin America has been falsely understood as a quasi-homogeneous region. In fact, it is a complex mosaic of historical and cultural diversity, in which races, languages and various historical levels coexist. Strong nationalist feelings exist, but they do not exclude the idea of belonging to the same region. Latin American first introduced itself during the Barcelona'92 Opening Ceremony through the athletes' parade with its broadcasters noting the appearance of each Latin American nation and by drawing attention to the large presence of Latin American political figures in the tribunal (due to the celebration in Madrid of the Summit of Latin American States in the days before the Games). Commentators emphasized national pride by evoking their neighbours as both fellow countries and rival countries, but always as belonging to a common 'group'.

> The first representative that appears from South America is Argentina. There is President Menem. (TV Bandeirantes, Brazil, Opening Ceremony).

> And here is ... president of Brazil, also with problems ... Brazil, a big power, without doubt, on the American continent. (Canal 13, Mexico, Opening Ceremony).

> Argentina, not many possibilities to win ... Brazil, a South American giant ... Chile, the first Latin American country to win a gold medal in 1896 and first to participate in the Olympic Games ... Mexico, a brother country. (Tele-Rebelde, Cuba, Opening Ceremony).

> After 12 years, Cuba returns to an Olympic Games ... Here is President Fidel Castro applauding the entrance of Cuba. (RCN, Colombia, Opening Ceremony).

> Get Belho who is the shot-putter of South America ... And don't forget that we made the Australian basketball girls cry when Brazil won the pre-Olympic match' ... In Seoul, when Cuba was not there, only two medals went to South America ... Our eternal sports rival, thank God, Argentina. (TV Bandeirantes, Brazil, Opening Ceremony).

> Without taking into account the US, Cuba has won 14 gold medals and the rest of the continent 8; Cuba has won 6 silver and the rest of continent 11, Cuba has won 11 bronze and all America 13. That is what gives superiority to Cuba. (Tele-Rebelde, Cuba, Opening Ceremony).

But soon to be disappointed

Realistically, Latin America knows that its sports potential, in contrast to other countries, is particularly poor. The United States and the Unified Team won large amounts of medals, Cuba, the exception, was in fifth place in the medal table, Brazil was in 25th place, Jamaica 35th and the rest of the countries were positioned between 50th and 60th place. For these countries winning a medal seemed to be more the result of a 'miracle' than the consequence of sports planning.

> Large countries, powerful ... with good teams ... sports powers ... high levels of literacy ... favourable economic conditions, the United States, a team that will fight for all. (Canal 13, Mexico, Opening Ceremony).

> But the truth is that the people know that victory is taken by the richest countries. (TV Globo, Brazil, Opening Ceremony).

> But there are no countries that can equal what the United States is ready to do, that is to sweep all the metal in the Olympic Games. (Canal A, Colombia, Opening Ceremony).

Moments of festival

In Latin America a victory immediately led to a popular celebration – for the Games are, above all, 'a fiesta'.

> All is joy in this moment ... nice, colourful spectacle ... the tears, the emotion, happy faces ... (RCN, Colombia, Opening Ceremony).

> And finally, it is evident that the Olympics is the true fiesta of humankind. (Canal 13, Mexico, Opening Ceremony).

When Brazil won the volleyball 'the fiesta became Brazilian'. Television images would show how the people threw themselves onto the court forming piles of people with some on top of others, embraces, tears of joy, praying on their knees and the coach asking the television not to ask him anything else about the victory so as to allow him to get back to the festivities. The rest of the Olympic Games were forgotten, as if there were no other medals nor other countries nor other competitions.

Attempts at 'Luck'

These moments, however, were few. In fact, most Latin American countries had little hope of widespread victory at the Games, since to achieve it a sustained sports policy over a long period of time, ten or fifteen years is required. Such an effort was not possible for Latin American children and youth who trained in the 1980s, the crisis years, and precisely those who participated in Barcelona'92. For this reason in the television commentaries there was insistent talk of luck, luck or faith in God being the things that could bring about success, other factors not being considered by the media.

> China ... it's good to remember that they can give us a headache in women's basketball ... but Brazil, here, was lucky to win the game. Because of that we hope to win a medal for Brazil (TV Bandeirantes, Brazil, Opening Ceremony).

But ultimately the face of disappointment

In the context of Latin America, success and failure tread a fine line and when hope disappears, the festivities can turn into mourning and the expression of disillusionment can be great. Marijosé Alcalá, the Mexican jumper who reached the ten metre finals, raised hopes too soon – two days after the beginning of the Games. Hopes were kept alive during nearly all the competition. In Mexico the morning news bulletins were canceled, there was a reduction in traffic in the city and the people held their breath. In the end the press were saying that 'the medal slipped through our hands'. The athlete stated: 'My tears are not of sadness, but of courage, sport is one of the most beautiful activities, but sometimes is really very cruel'.[23]

This lack of winning athletes ultimately seemed a painful thorn in the side of a region that saw itself gaining prominence on a world stage. A few days before the Closing Ceremony

---

23 Xicotencatl (1992).

the press was once again complaining that 'the Olympic Games go and the Olympic Games come and we always write the same story of frustration. Oh, it's a horrible feeling to specialize in the chronicle of defeat.'[24]

Playing with the imaginary West

Not to be put off by athletic defeats, Latin American broadcasters still found ways to join with the imaginary West in other ventures and show the extent of the changes Latin America had undergone.

> Barcelona and the Olympic Games is associated with modernity, here will stay the Colombians (RCN, Colombia, Opening Ceremony).

> Through sport, Latin American television shows reach to high levels of organization. Projecting efficiency, precision, coordination, professional and sports spirit. (RCN, Colombia, Opening Ceremony).

In 1992 the Olympic Games seemed an opportunity for Latin America to construct a new self image in the presence of the world using television and the Olympic Games. The Latin American countries approached the Olympic Games with realism recognizing their limits in contrast to the world sports powers. However, television's commercial and dramatic interests led them to build up their hopes by creating stories inviting success.

Unlike soap opera, where the outcome can remain in the fantasy realm, the results of the Games are written into history. The medals table has direct implications for the image that a country offers in the face of international and national scrutiny. For all these reasons sport is seen as an element of identity for the peoples of Latin America. It is for this reason that the Olympics acquire such dramatism and are celebrated – and felt – so much within Latin American culture.

---

24 Gutiérrez Pérez (1993).

13 Television in the Olympics: some final thoughts

The Olympics holds great allure for communications researchers. It is a philosophy that attempts to express itself through a mega-media event. It is an event that transforms a city into a technological laboratory and showcase for the key actors in the communications industry. It is a gathering of unprecedented intercultural co-operation and exchange. Every four years, its Opening Ceremony breaks records in attracting the largest media audiences in history. In many places Olympic programming changes the routines of daily life. And, while Olympic symbols are among the most recognized on earth, the Games themselves mean different things to everyone involved.

This study focused on television in the Olympics; it is only one perspective on the Games. However, it is a perspective that allowed a look inside and behind-the-scenes at its organization, economics and production processes. It also offered a glimpse of various phenomena outside of the Games – at cultures, world events, communication industries, the Olympic movement. Finally, a television perspective revealed something about the processes of meaning construction. It provided clues as to how diverse world audiences might come to define the Olympic Games relative to their own cultural contexts and using television as their primary source of Olympic imagery.

The shape of Olympic television

Part I of this book investigated the context of television in the Olympics: the astounding human and technological convergence which makes it possible for the Olympics to be an international broadcast experience. Its most obvious finding is that communications-related revenue such as television rights, advertising, sponsorship and sales of Olympic symbols constitutes the fundamental capital for the organization of the modern Games and, as such, greatly influences its global presentation.

Further, Part I offered a glimpse at the communications industry by looking inside the Games at media organizations, technological infrastructures and current production processes which literally link and wrap around all Olympic activities. The experience of visiting the Main Press Centre and International Broadcast Centre of the Barcelona Olympics revealed an international community with a remarkable degree of shared knowledge, language, professionalism and purpose. Even within this group one can see the emergence of multicultural broadcast specialists: an international cadre of broadcast technicians, producers and artists who are able to make a career out Olympic and international sports broadcasting.

Olympic broadcast 'haves' and 'have nots'

At the same time, the collection of broadcast organizations responsible for Olympic programming in their respective countries reflect a worldwide television industry coloured by vast economic disparities. In our study sample, two broadcasters, both from the African continent, did not have the resources to send broadcast personnel to the Barcelona Games. They both received French broadcasts via the African broadcast union URTNA. Others in the study had some personnel at the Games, but did not have the resources available to customize the broadcast much beyond adding commentary. The study sample moved along this spectrum of resource capability to a final group of predominantly European, North America, East Asian broadcasters who arrived in full force with both the technological means and hundreds of broadcast personnel to offer well-researched, highly 'produced,' and customized versions of the Games to home markets.

These disparities influence the presentation and interpretation of the Olympic Games and its actors by broadcasters around the world. Financial resources directly relate to the ability of broadcasters to prepare in-depth commentaries, to use unilateral cameras to show one's own athletes, and be live at the stadium to convey the experience of Olympic ceremonies and sport – all of which enhance a sense of connection to and understanding of the Olympics. Without a doubt, 'being there' expresses itself qualitatively in the broadcast experience.

A technology showroom

As an artifact of the communications industry, this study found the Olympics to be more a site for the promotion of proven technologies – for example, digitalization, high definition television, fibre optic networks, mobile and underwater camera – than a site for experimental technology. That said, the technological infrastructure of the Games does highlight important industry trends that are certain to affect the broadcast industry worldwide. For example, the Barcelona Olympics underscored the importance of communications mobility – in particular the role of cellular telephony and mobile camera set-ups – in allowing not just live, but more intimate and multiple perspectives on unfolding events. These link to the emergence of more personalized technology where these sorts of capabilities will be increasingly available at the end user stage with implications for how audiences might some day choose the 'version' of the Olympics they wish to see.

In addition, the information systems central to the Barcelona Games demonstrated how technology convergence continues to reconfigure the toolbox of the broadcast industry – as computer electronics, audiovisual equipment and telecommunications networks merge in extraordinarily complex ways to produce, control and deliver information and entertainment programming.

Such transformations in technology are reminders that the Games are an event of affluence from the perspective of organization and production. A host city such as Barcelona required extensive communications infrastructures and power needs – certainly not now available in many parts of the world. Along these lines, broadcasters need to get to able to 'keep up' with technologies used by the host broadcaster – technologies that are necessarily geared to high end broadcast quality levels in order to satisfy the highest paying right holders.

Changing broadcast strategies

Despite such concerns, Olympic television, once the domain of a few broadcasters from the most developed countries, has seen spectacular growth in international broadcaster attendance, reflecting the continued growth in the availability and use of television worldwide. The media organizations involved with the Barcelona Olympics also reflected an industry adapting more and more to commercial formats. While this study did not analyse a strictly representative sample of broadcasters or countries, its purposive sample based on geographic distribution and inclusion of a variety of media environments showed close to two-thirds of the broadcasters in this study use commercial messages in their programming.

Perhaps more interesting from the perspective of industry configuration was the range of cooperative strategies used to gain rights to broadcast the Games. This is also indicative of industry maturation and change. Broadcast pools, broadcast unions, re-selling rights deals, exclusive rights, pay-per-view, formal and informal sharing arrangements of unilateral signals and other cooperative (and competitive) ventures were in abundance at the Barcelona Games – several crossing national borders. As in the industry as a whole, the impetus for these arrangements are rising costs, converging goals and the growing number of personnel necessary to broadcast such a large international event. Now, for the first time, there has been a multi- Games rights agreement deal signed with NBC of the US for the Sydney 2000 summer Games and Salt Lake winter Olympics, introducing yet another broadcaster strategy with implications yet to be seen.

Many of these strategic arrangements also speak to changing industry demographics. World political and economic change has been transforming centralized television systems with one or two channels into multi-channel environments, often with a mix of public and private ownership formats. Already mature television societies are seeing a proliferation of new channels resulting from the increased transmission capacity offered by cable, fibre optics and signal compression technologies. Satellites circling the globe have introduced pan-regional television. Further, many of these new channels use programming formats that are localized or thematic (sports, religion, language, movies, etc.). In a surprising number of countries for the 1992 Games, viewers were not limited to the Olympic programming offered by the 'exclusive' national rights holder, but could refer to alternative Olympic programming provided by cable or regional satellite sports channels. This is a trend sure to continue.

Olympic programming fragmentation

All of the above points raise questions about whether Olympic broadcasts might become increasingly fragmented across multiple channels within a geographic region. While such arrangements may help broadcasters share costs, and indeed facilitate IOC goals of maximizing exposure (by allowing for more total hours of coverage), they do run counter to the IOC strategy of exclusivity in television rights and sponsorship. Further, as with NBC's pay-per-view experiment, there do seem to be limits to audience size, time and willingness to inconvenience themselves to view the Olympics. So, broadcast strategies that fragment programming by sport, level, national participation, or other means, may instead limit exposure and allow viewers to easily avoid the sport and cultural diversity that makes the Games so unique.

Television and Olympic meaning

Part II looked at the Olympic Games as multiple television presentations. It compared 28 broadcasts of the Barcelona Opening Ceremonies seeking both similarities and differences in terms of their structure, verbal and visual narratives, and interpretations of Olympism, other nations, and the host culture. Here it was possible to see not only how the efforts of COOB'92 and television production processes influenced these presentations, but how different broadcasting norms and cultural and political mindsets came to influence how the ceremony was interpreted, by broadcasters, to home audiences. The results were analysed in a variety of ways, but the overall finding is best summarized by considering the example of fireworks.

A simple fireworks display

Both the Opening and, in particular, the Closing Ceremony of the Barcelona Opening included a fireworks display. In the view of Barcelona ceremony planners this was very appropriate. They felt that fireworks were a universal celebratory experience. And sure enough, as a denotative symbol, all broadcasters described the fireworks as a spectacle to behold. Further, the presence of fire has a long history in Mediterranean folk festivals. As described in the organizing committee's media script for the Closing Ceremony:

> Pyrotechnics are characteristic of the Mediterranean, expressive of joy and its fleeting nature ... Fire appears in all the Mediterranean festivals. It is a spectacular show of visuals and sound of great force. The languages of the sense and the universal language of life.[1]

However, the fireworks display, although deemed spectacular, held different connotations across broadcasts. To the German (ZDF) and Slovenian (2nd Channel) commentators the fireworks display was likened to the bombs dropping on Sarajevo – a harsh reality not so

---

1   COOB'92 (1992d).

very far away in 1992. The study correspondent from Australia echoed those sentiments more generally:

> Ironically, despite the extended references to peace and friendship through the [Closing] ceremony the detonation of the fireworks finale, with its intensity and prolongation, also had unsettling echoes of wars and battle zones.[2]

Through the Singapore (SBC 12) broadcast, the viewers saw fireworks presented as a questionable extravagance. In Cameroon, fireworks symbolized a display of wealth on behalf of the host city. As Wete suggested, this perspective was not necessary a negative one – but rather a way of reading fireworks from a different economic perspective. He said:

> The splendour of the fireworks, the cultural fares and the organizational genius of Barcelona '92 [was] perceived as a legitimate sight of the host city, nation and continent to present itself to the world. It is seen as another aspect of the 'competition' between the cities that hosted the last and the present Olympic Games and extending to the city that will host the next. To this effect, Barcelona confirmed current local impression of the enormous material, financial, human resources and organizational ability required to host the Olympic Games.[3]

In Latin America the fireworks display represented a fiesta, the beginning of a night long festival. In Canada and US the display symbolized a typical, yet entertaining close to two very long weeks.

In a similar way, the comparative analysis revealed different perceptions of cultural performances (e.g. opera, the Mediterranean segment, the Catalan sardana), team uniforms (e.g. as connoting wealth, tradition, or informality), the King of Spain (as a sportsman, a hero for democracy, or a 'regular' guy), and more.

The differences in the above interpretations, and others, brought to light the fact that the broadcasts are significantly influenced by societal and cultural conditions, whether politics, economics, sport or folklore. In that sense they also revealed aspects of self identity. Narratives in the Slovenian (2nd channel) broadcasts made it clear that this first Olympics for Slovenia meant international legitimacy. For South Africa (SABC) commentators the broadcast seemed to reveal a bittersweet sensation: a return to Games, yet clothed in national self doubt as to South African identity. The Japanese (NHK) experience of the Games was that of evoking the 'Japanese spirit' through its athletes, implicitly recalling the surprise triumphs of Japanese athletes in 1964 Tokyo Olympics – an experience still firmly rooted in Japan's collective consciousness.[4] China's CCTV commentator never mentioned the Olympic host Catalonia or its meaning. Yet other broad-

---

2   Langer (1992).

3   Wete (1992).

4   Kosaka *et al.* (1992).

casters, from countries less concerned with restless nationalities within their borders, showed plenty of interest in Catalonia's political and cultural identity.

Broadcasters also approached the narration of the Opening Ceremony in different ways, thereby framing the activities, for example, more as entertainment, as history, or as cultural festival. Here, the backgrounds and experience of the broadcast commentators – who were mostly from the world of sports – also came into play. In addition, the pace and flow of the broadcasts reflected the professional norms of various media environments – from competitive, commercial environments with commentators as polished insiders always with a secret to reveal (after the commercial break), to more heavily scripted and formal commentator tones, without concern over losing audience to other channels.

That said, there was much that was shared across broadcasts. Foremost was the presentation of the Olympics as a unique and positive event. Even the most staid of commentators styles could not suppress the thrill at the sight of the athletes gathered together in the stadium or the moment the flaming arrow set ablaze the Olympic cauldron. Broadcasters also displayed a common global news agenda for 1992, with war in Bosnia Herzegovina, a reunited Germany, a dissolved Soviet Union, a post-apartheid South Africa and the presence of Magic Johnson and the Dream Team appearing in all broadcast commentaries.

Understanding the Olympic movement

Important to the patrons of Olympism should be the finding that an alarming number of broadcast presentations of Olympic values were both narrow and sparse – and in a few broadcasts absent altogether. (Although a few broadcasts spoke of Olympism and its values at great length and with considerable emotion.) Of those values articulated by broadcasters those of participation and peace were most prevalent with international friendship following third. Beyond that, however, there was no sense of obligation displayed on the part of broadcast commentators to educate audiences about Olympic history, family, values, and so forth. That said, there was indirect evidence of an imagined sense of Olympic community, in that shared personages, past events, symbols and accepted standards of behaviour for athletes, teams and nations were both expressed and implied across most broadcasts.

The mix of commercial and Olympic messages

Actually, it was the advertisers who seem most concerned about expressing Olympic values and emotion. Here raises the question of what meanings might emerge from the mix of commercial messages surrounding and appearing inside Olympic sport and ceremony (at least on the television screen). The sophisticated strategies used by advertisers to access audiences, assisted by television wizardry, allow commercial messages to circumvent existing restrictions placed on advertising in Olympic venues. There are no obvious answers here, but this is an area that should spur active IOC concern.

The encroachment of commercialism into the Olympic Games was easily the most common and emerging topic of discourse across both print and broadcast observers of the Barcelona Olympics. On the part of broadcasters, there is a certain double standard to questioning the impact of sponsorship and professionalism on the Games, then lauding the US Dream Team in the next breath. However, this topic was clearly one of concern and should serve as a warning that the 'definition' of the Olympics is changing. As noted by our study correspondents from Russia, then Malaysia:

> We cannot remember a case when Olympism in general was ever criticized by any Russian (or Soviet) publication in modern history. Olympic ideas and ideals have been widely propagated here. Still, a new approach to the Olympics is being taken by some of the Russian press: the noble Olympic ideas, say those publications, are leaving the actual Games under the pressure of commercialization and professional sport.[5]

> For the past two Olympics, and yet another in Atlanta, endorsements and financial gains have become central themes of the Games, rather than putting the quality of athletic performance and endurance as the soul of this world event.[6]

Maintaining the Olympics as a 'special' event

Perhaps as a testament to its popularity and prestige, the world of sports has appropriated attributes common to the Games: opening ceremonies, torch lighting, medal giving rituals, etc. At the same time, the Olympic movement has embraced, with certain limits, many of the formats of high level international sport. Professional athletes now participate. Sponsorship programmes are an integral part of the financing package. Olympic symbols are sold for advertising use. This leads to the question of who is responsible for the Olympic message. Given the central role of television, advertisers and even other sports events in bringing Olympic images to world audiences, more evaluation is necessary. What is necessary to maintain that 'special' character of the Olympics?

The fact remains that Games organizers lack any control over how television broadcasters adapt the international television signal or what role they play as primary intermediary between audiences and Olympics. In this study, television broadcasters were found to play a variety of roles relative to the Olympics, the host city and their home audiences during the Opening Ceremony. At any given time, commentators in this study acted as interpreters, observers, participants, experts, obstructions, patriots, self-promoters (of television), and more. Whatever the role, broadcaster commentators saw themselves as sole arbiters of the event, and as such, did not fear about the quality or veracity of their commentary. This allowed much to pass unexplained about the host culture, the Olympic movement, about other nations, and more.

So, with seeming irony, one suggestion is for the Olympics to further adapt to the needs of television. Much has already been done. In sport, rules have changed. The ceremonies have become more visually spectacular and technically controlled to maximize television impact. But there is more that could be explored in terms of providing timely information

---

5   Zassoursky *et al.* (1992).

6   Mohamed (1992).

about the Olympics (beyond sports statistics) to broadcasters in formats and languages conducive to their use. The structure of the ceremonies and rituals might be altered to better guide when advertising insertions take place leading to less interruption of the intended narrative structure. Cultural informants might be made available to broadcast organizations well in advance of the Games. More feature materials could be made available – especially for those broadcasters without unilateral camera capabilities – and more.

The viewing experience

The study design did not request country correspondents to gather, in any systematic way, audience data related to perceptions of the Olympics. It was too enormous of an undertaking given all that was to be collected and analysed concerning the broadcasts alone. However, from the data received for Part III it was possible to extract a sense of both interest in the Olympics as a television event and the viewing experience from a few places around the world. While this study found that access to viewing the Games is hardly universal, that the global audience is not as big as often estimated, and that attention and interest varies considerably country by country, the Olympic Games are, without question, as close to a truly global event as mankind has experienced.

Local dimensions of the global

But probably the most interesting finding regarding the viewing experience is that while certainly the global character (so many nationalities gathered together for elite level sport) of the Games contribute to their attraction, it was the local dimensions of the Olympic telecast that were critical to sustaining broadcaster and audience interest. The 'liveness' and excitement of the Olympics as event seemed sustained mostly by attention to specific performers and mostly to a nation's own athletes. Without question, those broadcast countries whose athletes did not appear on the international signal (because they were not participants or contenders in various sports events) saw viewer interest in the Games drop off considerably after the Opening Ceremony and first several days of competition. Viewership, while influenced by programme timing, was most influenced by the participation of – and ability to view – one's own national athletes.

Perhaps symbolic of this desire to see the local (self) as part of the global (Olympics) was the fact that in many of the Opening Ceremony broadcasts, commentators mentioned the large applause 'the world' (as represented by the spectators in the stadium) was giving their national athletes. As an example, when the Australian team entered, the Channel 7 commentator said:

> They are getting a terrific hand. Australians are very popular in this city. (Ch 7, Australia, Opening Ceremony).

Such findings provide further support for the idea that opportunities should exist for all broadcasters to be able to customize the international signal for participating national and cultural groups so they may 'see themselves' at the Olympics. In the spirit of universal access and the goals of programs like Olympic Solidarity, it does not seem unreasonable to consider offering broadcasters from countries without abundant resources or medal contender athletes a better chance not only to come to the host city, but to personalize their programming, to talk to their athletes while in the host city, and thereby increase local interest in and spirit surrounding the Olympic Games.

A final word

There are many possible directions to go from a study like this. There is much to explore about many of the relationships embedded within the complexity of the Olympic Games. To mention only a few, in the future Olympics study would benefit greatly from more systematic and cross cultural reception analysis. This study certainly found evidence not just of different perceptions of the Olympics through broadcast presentations, but of evolving meanings associated with Olympism. These should be also investigated further. In addition, there is much more to understand about how increasing channel fragmentation and new configurations of the television industry will affect the Olympic Games in the future. Certainly, the issues surrounding advertising in Olympic television need more research attention. This list could go on.

This project was a challenging undertaking. It involved many people, cultures, languages and logistical challenges. It took a long time to translate, transcribe, analyse and attempt to understand all the documents, broadcast video, interview notes and other materials gathered at the Barcelona Games and received from around the world. As such, the project missed nearly every deadline originally set. However, in the end, as in the beginning, it is still abundantly clear that this kind of multicultural, multidisciplinary, multimethod comparative work is not only rewarding, but essential to understanding any kind of globally placed phenomenon. Further, it is clear that this type of international project can only be taken on through international collaborative efforts which encourage the kinds of important contributions that were received here from research correspondents around the world. Their work – and patience – was invaluable to the success of this project.

Also of critical importance was the institutional support both at the university level, through places like the Centre for Olympic and Sport Studies at the Autonomous University of Barcelona, and the cooperation of the International Olympic Committee and other organizations in facilitating access to the Games themselves. Without that kind of support, the central researchers would also have missed the sensation of 'being there' and not been able to gain the perspectives they did on the Olympic television experience.

Appendix A
Content Analysis Categories for the Barcelona Opening Ceremony Broadcasts

Section I: Commentary about Olympic and Sport Values

Olympic Values, Meanings
friendship, fraternity (among individuals)
international cooperation, community
peace or harmony (free from conflict)
number of nations or athletes participating
meeting place for peoples, athletes
equal participation
modern Olympics
balance, development of body and mind
culture and education
joy found in effort, will
ethical or moral principles
human dignity

Sport values embodied in Olympics
excellence, 'Citius, Altius, Fortius'
fair play
friendly competition
hard work or training
sport as universal or common language

Olympic Symbols, Rituals
Olympic Rings
Olympic Flag
Olympic Music: Hymn or Fanfare
Torch, Cauldron, Lighting
Olympic village or sport venues.
Olympic mascots
Official speeches or oaths or proclamations

Olympic languages
Olympic Family

Collective Memory: History, Heroes, Events
ancient Olympics
past Olympic named
past Olympic records
past Olympic athlete(s)
past event positive or neutral
past event negative
Munich tragedy
Mexico City
boycott
history of an Olympic sport
fun 'facts' or statistics or human interest
number of spectators

Olympic festival or feelings
historical event or moment
excitement, importance of participation
happiness, goodwill
celebration of the world, unity
celebration of youth
celebration of sport
emotional, sentimental
solemn, serious moments
anticipation
spectacle

Olympic personalities or institutions
Pierre de Coubertin
former IOC president Avery Brundage

IOC President Juan Antonio Samaranch
Pasqual Maragall (Head of COOB'92)
COOB'92 or other OCOGs
NOCs (National Olympic Committees)
sports federations

International Olympic Committee
games organizer, chooses Olympic sites
regulate activities involved in the Games
political organization
above or independent of politics
criticisms of IOC or members
secret or secrecy of votes

IOC conflicts with other institutions
Olympic Discourse
professionalism (vs. amateurism)
politics in the Games.
nationalism
judging conflicts or bias
fierce competition, revenge, rivalry
merits of commercialism, sponsorship
media financing of the Games
drugs, doping related issues
apartheid or race discrimination or issues
gender discrimination
world change, flux
conflict in Bosnia-Herzegovina
conflict (elsewhere or general)
terrorism, security threats
athletes or teams 'breaking the rules'
discussion of merits of an Olympic sport
costs of sending athletes, preparing

Media
number of of media personnel
name of media (other than own)
media facilities (IBC, MPC)
services for media
media from all over the world
size of TV audience

Section II: Presentation of Nations and National Teams

Olympics History
number of medals won, medals rank
no medals
new or first time participant
recent or infrequent participant

long time participant
once boycotted or banned
mention prior athlete, event or record
prior Olympic host or future host
attempts at Olympic host

Sport / Team 1992
identify flagbearer
size of team
specific athlete name
sports participating in
favoured medal or strong sport(s)
national attitude toward sport
team character or impression
team actions in stadium
team uniform
gender mix
non-Olympic sport event
Dream team or Magic Johnson
provisional recognition by IOC
not favoured to win medal
order of team in parade
Magic Johnson with AIDS

Feelings, sentiments of nation/team
happy, pride at participating
sad or conflict because of situation
crowd applaud, approval of team
change, impression of Barcelona
team wants medals
crowd disapproval

Natural Geography

Political / Geopolitical
population
size
capital city
location reference
type of government
change in government
historical event, era former name
current event reference
famous / official personage
military, war
ethnicity, racial mix
national symbols (flag, icons, colours)

Economic
economic statistic
economic status

economic type
economic change
specific industry or product
media general

Social / Cultural
family
gender
education-literacy, school, student
religion or religious place
cuisine
language or communication
folk custom, art, leisure activity

National / Cultural / Team Distinctions, Traits, Character

Section III: Commentary about Barcelona, Catalonia, Spain, Europe

General Barcelona'92 Olympic / 25th Olympiad
proud to host
pior attempts to host
goals of Hosting Games
improvements, changes due to Olympics
'sport' city or area
Olympic village
Olympic stadium
Olympic venues
Montjuïc stadium or venues
cost of hosting; Games profits; ticket costs

Barcelona'92 Symbols
Cobi as mascot
Cobi present everywhere
Cobi's popularity
Cobi designed by Mariscal
description of Cobi
specific association of Cobi with a dog
Cobi as Catalan culture or art
Barcelona 92 logo
description of Barcelona 92 logo
logo as Mediterranean or Catalan
'92 motto 'Friends for Life'
colours of ceremony (yellow, red, blue)

General reference Barcelona
Barcelona: capital or city of Catalonia
Barcelona: Spanish city

Barcelona: European city
Barcelona: Mediterranean city
Government Barcelona (P. Maragall)
Barcelona flag

General reference Catalonia
a region, territory, or area
a nation or country
European city or country
nationalist sentiments, nationalism
cultural pride, distinctive, unique
reference Catalan history

Symbols of Catalonia
Catalan anthem
flag of Catalonia
Catalan flags on display
Catalan Olympic Committee
Generalitat de Catalonia or Jordi Pujol

Catalonia/Barcelona within Spain
cooperation between Catalonia/Barcelona and Spain
conflict between Catalonia/Barcelona and Spain
separatist sentiments from Spain
cooperation Catalonia/Barcelona and other region(s)
conflict Catalonia/Barcelona and other region(s)

General reference Spain
Democratic
Socialist
Stable or secure (government)
Unstable or changing
Multi-party or conflicting parties
Parlimentary monarchy
Government representatives of Spain and family
Spanish historical references
Spanish Civil War
Franco
Spanish Inquisition
1992 events
Expo 92
500th Anniversary of Columbus
Spanish flag or anthem
Name of location / region in Spain, outside of Catalonia

General reference Europe
European Community
European Hymn or Anthem
European Community flag
reference to 12 towers representing 12
stars on EC flag
Maastricht Treaty, European unification
changes going on in Europe

Make up of population
Catalan people
Spanish people
mixed races
immigrants
gypsies

Population number or geographic size
large
medium
small
specify population #
specify size (e.g. square km or miles)

Language and Communication
Catalan speaking
Spanish speaking
Characterization of Catalan language
association with French, Italian
Specific references to Catalan language
　　　　in learning and education
　　　　in media
　　　　as a political symbol
language was suppressed at one time
use in Games as official language

**Economic references Barcelona,
Catalonia**
rich, prosperous, wealth, well off, modern
growing, booming
poor, undeveloped, less developed
declining, recession, unstable
important economic centre
in Spain
in southern Europe or Europe

Economic references Spain
rich, prosperous, wealth, well off, modern
growing, booming
poor, undeveloped, less developed
declining, recession, unstable
important (economic centre) in Europe

EC member

**Specific references: trade arts, industry,
technology**
technology
furniture making
graphic arts or design
fashion or jewelry
textile
chemical
manufacturing
tourism, tourists
banking

Urban Character and Environment
modern 'look'
traditional and modern, old and new
architecture
historical, full of history, old, traditional,
ancient
beautiful (city or buildings)
enlightening, rich, educational
cultural, cultured, strong culture
city of art, full of art
foreign, exotic, different
inviting, open, hospitable
cosmopolitan, fashionable, chic
crowded, close together, congested, traffic
resort like, vacation
churches, cathedrals
Sagrada Familia
museums, castles
statues, outdoor art
street markets, peddlars, fruit stands
bullrings
plazas or open cafes
parks or promenades
Las Ramblas
Park Güell
restaurants, small shops
port, docks, harbor
highways, traffic
construction
adobe, clay, stucco, stone
colour associations (e.g. red)

**Specific architectural influences styles or
locations**
'Spanish'
Mediterranean (as an architectural style)
European

Gothic
Modernism
Gaudi
Roman
Moorish
Arab or Muslim

People Associations
beautiful women
dark skinned, tan, dark hair, eyes
relaxed, tranquillo
romantic, sensuous, passionate
friendly, warm, smiling
colourful, lively, festive, spirited,
beautiful, handsome, pretty
seny or rauxa, common sense, eccentric
unfriendly, cold, arrogant, closed
intelligent, smart
from the hear, deeply felt

Work and Play Habits
bustling, busy, hard working, efficient, organized
lazy, siestas, disorganized, inefficient
fiestas or parties, night clubs
groups of people
walking, strolling

Natural Geography
General reference: nice, good climate, beautiful
weather
hot, warm
sunny
dry
blue sky, clear
hazy
humid, tropical
landscape features
hills or mountains
sea or ocean
blue water
beach
flowers
green or greenery
specific locations
      Costa Brava
      Montserrat
      Pyrenees
birds

Social Institutions
religion
education
family
holidays, festival
Gegants (Catalan folk tradition)

Food/drink
good food and/or drink
different food and/or drink
bad food and/or drink
seafood, fish
tapas
paella
cava (champagne)
wine
bread and tomatoes

Sport
Non Olympic – competitive
tennis
Tour de France
World Cup Soccer
bull fights

Performing and Fine Arts
General references
music
dance
painting
writing, poetry
Picasso
Miro
Tapies
Goya
Dalí
Pau Casals
Velázquez
Miralda

Identification of some performers, performances
Opera
Flamenco
Sardana
Top Models
Els castellers
Montserrat Caballé
Josep Carreras
Plácido Domingo:
Alfredo Kraus

Cristina Hoyos
Antonio Rebollo
Other

About the Ceremony in General
the best in Olympics so far
a big success, everyone likes it
a grand spectacle, exciting, big
well organized, efficient, no problems
different from other ceremonies
artistic, cultural, creative
hard to understand

technological, special effects, modern
typically, representative of Spain
typically, representative of Catalonia /
Barcelona
numbers of participants or volunteers
made for TV
creative, innovative
surprises
spectators participation
reflective of world changes

Appendix B
International Radio and Television Rights Holders in Barcelona'92

Country	Television stations		Radio stations	
BROADCAST UNIONS				
ABU (Asian Pacific Broadcasting Union)				
Hong Kong	TVB	Television Broadcast Ltd.		
China	CCTV	China Central Television	CPBS*	
Iran	IRIB	Islamic Republic Iran Broadcasting		
Pakistan	PTV	Pakistan Televisions Corporation	PBC*	
Malaysia	TV3M	TV3 Malaysia	RTM*	Radio and Television Malaysia
Singapore	SBC	Singapore Broadcasting Corporation		
Thailand	TPT	Thailand Television		Radio Thailand*
Indonesia	TVRI	Television of the Republic of Indonesia	RRI*	Radio of Republic of Indonesia
India	DDI	Doordarshan India*		
EBU (European Broadcasting Union)				
France	A2F	Antenne2	SRF	Radio France
	FR3	France Régions	EU–1	Europe 1
	TF1	Télévision Française 1	RFI	Radio France Internationale
	CPF	Canal Plus France		
Spain	TVE	Televisión Española	A3R	Antena 3
			COPE	Cadena Cope
			RNE	Radio Nacional de España
			ONDA	Onda Cero Radio
			SER	Sociedad Española de Radiodifusión

Country	Television stations		Radio stations	
Catalonia	RTVE CCRTV	Canal Olímpic		Catalunya Ràdio
Germany	ARD	Arbeitsgemeinschaft der Offentlichrechtlicher Rundfunksanstalten der Bundesrepublik Deutschland	ARD	Arbeitsgemeinschaft der Offentlichrechtlicher Rundfunksanstalten der Bundesrepublik Deutschland
	ZDF	Zweites Deutsches Fernsehen		
United Kingdom	BBC	British Broadcasting Corporation Eurosport	BBC	British Broadcasting Corporation Capital Radio*** Southern Sound
Belgium	BRTN RTBF	Belgische Radio en Televisie Radio-Télévision Belge de la Communauté Francaise	BRT RTBF	Belgische Radio en Televisie Radio-Télévision Belge de la Communauté Francaise
Cyprus	CYBC	Cyprus Broadcasting Corporation*		
Denmark	DRTV2	Danmarks Television	DR	Danmarks Radio
Algeria	ENTV	Entreprise Nationale de Télévision		
Egypt	ERTU	Egyptian Radio & Television Union	ERTU	Egyptian Radio & Television Union
Greece	ERT	Elliniki Radiophonia Teleorasis	ERT	Elliniki Radiophonia Teleorasis
Tunisia	ERTT	Radiodifusion Télévision Tunisienne*		
Israel	IBA	Israel Broadcasting Authority	IBA	Israel Broadcasting Authority
Slovenia and Croatia	JRT	Jugoslovenska Radio Televizija	JRT	Jugoslovenska Radio Televizija
Jordan	JTV	Jordan Television*		
Libya	LJB	Libyan Jamahirya Broadcasting*		
Malta	MBA	Broadcasting Authority Malta*		
Netherlands	NOS	Nederlandse Omroep Stichting	NOS	Nederlandse Omroep Stichting
Norway	NRK	Norsk Rikskringkasting	NRK	Norsk Rikskringkasting
Austria	ORF	Österreichischer Rundfunk Fernsehen	ORF	Österreichischer Rundfunk Fernsehen
Italy	RAI	Radiotelevisione Italiana	RAI	Radiotelevisione Italiana
Portugal	RTP	Radiotelevisao Portuguesa	RDP	Radiodifusao Portuguesa
Monaco	RMC	Tele Monte Carlo	RMC	Radioo Monte Carlo
Ireland	RTE	Radio Telefis Eireann	RTE	Radio Telefis Eireann
Luxembourg	RTL	Radio Tele Luxemburg	RTL	Radio Tele Luxemburg
Morocco	RTM	Radio Television Marocaine*	RTM	Radio Television Marocaine*
Iceland	RUV	Rikisutvarpid Sjonvarp	RUV	Rikisutvarpid Sjonvarp
Sweden	SVT	Sveriges Television	SR	Sveriges Radio
Switzerland	SRG	Schweizerische Radio uns Fernseh Gesellschaft	SRG	Schweizerische Radio uns Fernseh Gesellschaft
	SSR	Societé Suisse de Radiodiffusion et Télévision***		
	TSI	Televisione Svizzera Italiana***		
Lebanon	TL	Tele-Liban S.A.L.***		

Country	Television stations		Radio stations	
Turkey	TRT	Turkish Radio and Television Co.	TRT	Turkish Radio and Television Co.
Finland	YLE	OY. Yleisradio Ab.	YLE	OY. Yleisradio Ab.
OIRT (Organisation Internationale de Radio et Télévision)				
Bulgaria	BT	Bulgarian Television	BGR	
Byelorussian	BTV	Byelorussian Television***		
Czechoslovakia	CST	Czechoslovak Television	CSR	Czechoslovak Radio
Estonia	ETV	Estonian Television*	ER	Estonian Radio
Cuba	ICRT	Instituto Cubano de radio y Televisión	ICRT	Instituto Cubano de radio y Televisión
Lithuania	LITV	Lithuanian Television*		
Mongolia	MOTV	Mongolian Television		
Hungary	MTV	Magyar Television	MR	Magyar Radio
Poland	TVP	Polish Television	PLR	Polsky Radio
Romania	TVR	Romanian Television	ROR	Rumanian Radio
CIS (former USSR)	RTO RTR	Radiotelevidenle Ostankino Russian Television		
CIS			SUR	Soviet Union Radio
CIS	TVMO	Moldavian Television***		
CIS	UTV	Ukrainian Television***		
OTI (Organización de Televisiones Iberoamericanas)				
Brazil	SBT	Televisao Bandeirantes Ltd. Rede Globo Ltda. Canal 4 Sao Paulo TV Manchete		Radio Bandeirantes Radio Italiala* Radio Record
Argentina				Radio Gaucha*
Chile		Canal 7 TV Nacional de Chile		
Venezuela	CRCAS	Radio Caracas Televisión		
Mexico		IMEVISION Instituto Mexicano de Television Televisa		
Colombia			RCN	Radio Cadena Nacional* Radio Caracol* Datos y Mensajes*
ASBU (Arab States Broadcasting Union)**				
CBU (Caribbean Broadcasting Union)**				
URTNA (Union Radio Télévision National d'Afrique)** Secured rights through French broadcasters.				

BROADCAST POOLS

BOJP (Barcelona Olympic Japan Pool)				
Japan	ANB	Asahi National Broadcasting	JOFU	FM Hokkaido

Country	Television stations		Radio stations	
Japan	CX	Fuji Television	JOQR	Bunka Hoso
Japan	NHK	Nippon Hoso Kyokai	JOLF	Nippon Hoso
Japan	NTV	Nippon Television Network Corporation		
Japan	TBS	Tokyo Broadcasting System Inc.		
Japan	TX	Television Tokyo		
BOKP (Barcelona Olympic Korean Pool)				
Korea	KBS	Korean Broadcasting System		
Korea	MBC	Mun-Hwa Broadcasting Corporation		
Korea	SBS	Seoul Broadcasting System		
NZTV Pool (Television New Zealand)				
New Zealand	TVNZ	Television New Zealand	RNZ	Radio New Zealand
New Zealand	ATV	Asian Television		
TAIWAN Pool (Taiwan)				

BROADCAST NETWORKS

WIPR (Puerto Rico Public Broadcasting Corporation, Canal 6, Puerto Rico)

AuBC (Australian Radio)

CH 7 (The Seven Network, Australia)

CTV/TVA (Canadian Television Network Ltd., Canada)

NBC (National Broadcasting Company Inc., United States)

SABC (South African Broadcasting Corporation, South Africa)

HIGH DEFINITION TELEVISION:

VISION 1250 (European HDTV)

NHK/HDTV (Nippon Hoso Kyokai / Hi-Vision, Japan)

*= Personnel from this broadcaster attended the Games, but did not have facilities at the IBC in Barcelona.
**= There were no members of this broadcast union accredited to attend the Barcelona Games – only broadcast union personnel.
*** = This radio or television station was accredited to attend, but it is unknown for certain if it did.

Appendix C
'The Arrival of the King and Queen of Spain'

A Comparision of RTO'92 International Signal and the NBC (USA) Broadcast

RTO'92 Opening Ceremony International Signal (visuals and stadium sound only)	NBC Opening Ceremony Broadcast	
	Visual images	Commentary
Flags of Barcelona, Catalonia and Spain enter into the stadium	*NBC uses RTO'92 image*	BC: Colorguard, on the left, flag of the region of Catalonia. The Catalan flag, the Spanish national flag, and then the flag of the city of Barcelona. It'll be interesting to see what sort of reception King Juan Carlos receives. When he re-opened the stadium for a soccer tournament in 1989, he was boo'd by Catalan nationalists, Dick. DE: Bob, that's because of his link to Franco and Madrid, and the county of Spain itself, more than against the man whose inspiration in reviving this country has been quite profound. C: It's a story almost out of a 'B' movie, something you'd expect long ago, rather than in a modern great nation. And I'll tell you that story. King Juan Carlos is now entering, and generally speaking, the reception is cordial.
Musicians playing and director directing (MCU)	Shot of field, three flags at far end (LS)	
Section of Catalan politicians in the stands (MS)		
The three flags (Barcelona, Catalan and Spanish) in the hands of the guard of honor of the city of Barcelona (FS to MCU)	Zoom in to Catalan flag (CU) then over to Spanish flag (CU) then over to Barcelona flag (CU)	
fade to Three flags (MCU) Zoom in to Spanish flag		
fade to Three flags (MCU) Public applauding in stands (MS) Three flags (MCU)	fade to Flag bearers turning toward audience (MS) then pull back to audience (LS); Zoom in to MS of VIP tribunal in stands.	

Boxed areas of the RTO'92 international signal description denote which images were substituted by NBC with images from its own unilateral camera. The substitutions are in the middle column.

FS = fullshot; MS = medium shot; CU = close-up; BC = Bob Costas; LS = long shot; MCU = medium close-up; ECU = extreme close-up; DE = Dick Enberg

RTO'92 Opening Ceremony International Signal (visuals and stadium sound only)	NBC Opening Ceremony Broadcast	
	Visual images	Commentary
The King and Queen of Spain arrive in the grandstand and salute to the crowd, while the rest of the VIPs remain standing and applaud the King and Queen (MCU then zoom out to MS)	*NBC uses RTO'92 image*	Following the Spanish Civil War, when Franco's fascist dictatorship went into place, King Juan Carlos' father, Don Juan de Bourbon, lived in exile in Portugal. He was fiercely democratic, critical of Franco. Eventually, the dictator and the exiled monarch drew up a deal in international waters in 1948.
fade to Catalan flag (ECU) fade to crowd applauding in stands fade to Catalan flag (ECU) fade to the King and Queen saluting the crowd while VIPs applaud King listening, with serious expression to the Spanish anthem. (CU)	fade to King Juan Carlos waving (CU) fade to King Juan Carlos (ECU) add superimposed graphic of King's name fade to King and Queen (CU) fade to King (ECU)	Juan Carlos, the prince then just ten years old, would come live in Spain. He would live in the palace in Madrid, and Franco would annoint him as his successor, and the full powers would transfer to Juan Carlos. Young Juan Carlos gave every indication that he supported
Three flags (MCU) Zoom in to Spanish flag fade to King Juan Carlos looking serious (ECU) Airplanes fly over the stadium leaving colour trails behind (MS) fade to The King turns toward Juan Antonio Samaranch and nods his satisfaction with the spectacle, indicating to the stand that they can sit down.	fade to CU of Spanish flag waving against a blue sky fade to audience applauding, Catalan flag shows in the middle of the crowd (MS) fade to King Juan Carlos smiling and then sitting down (MCU)	'El Caudillo' and his 'movimiento national', that he himself was a fascist. But upon Franco's death in 1975, instead of taking all that power for himself, what the king did was to ease the way toward the creation of a democratic system, the constitutional monarchy which is now in place. The pivotal moment for the infant democracy came in 1981. – and the 'fly-by' outside the stadium E: that's going to come right over our heads, Bob ...

Segment time: 5 min. 40 sec.

Appendix D
Description of the
Barcelona Opening Ceremony

As designed, the Barcelona Opening Ceremony was divided into general performance segments listed below.

Time min' sec"	Segment title	General description
Part One	**Welcome to the Mediterranean**	
4' 18"	**Opening Hola!**	
	The gaiety of birds invades the arena and the word symbolizing friendship, Hola!, is formed in the centre of the stadium.	Dancers representing flowers, birds, musicians enter the stadium. The crowd cries 'hola'. The performers form the symbol for the Barcelona Olympics
	Arrival of the King of Spain	
0' 46"	Entrance of the flags of Barcelona, Catalonia and Spain	Flagbearers march in with flags and stop in front of King's box. The King is announced
0' 41"	Entrance of the King and the Hymn of Catalonia, 'El Cant dels Segadors'	King Juan Carlos enters and the anthem of Catalonia plays
0' 35"	The King Listens to the Spanish anthem.	The Spanish anthem plays
0' 40"	Planes fly overhead.	Sound of planes. Visuals of VIPs

Time min' sec"	Segment title	General description
	Welcome	
2' 25"	Give us your Hands	*Dancers in white perform the Catalan dance the sardana.* *M. Caballé and J. Carreras sing.* *The orchestra performs.*
0' 53"	The Olympic rings are formed.	*The dancers form the Olympic rings.*
1' 37"	A Heart is formed.	*The dancers move into the form of a heart.*
	Land of passion	
3' 44"	Entrance of musicians	*Musicians walk down the stadium steps into the main stadium field.*
1' 06"	Entrance of the Flamenco dancers	
2' 24"	Plácido Domingo sings a passionate love song	
6' 19"	The fires of Flamenco	*Cristina Hoyos rides in on a horse and does a dance performance on the stage.*
4' 23"	Sighs of Emotion	*Tenor Alfredo Kraus enters and sings.* *There are images showing the orchestra playing.*
	The Mediterranean, Olympic Sea	
2' 31"	The sun, the force of life	*Performers dressed like sun enter the stadium.*
3' 43"	Hercules, hero of heroes	*A robot-looking hercules enters the stadium and moves across the field and up onto the stage.*
10' 34"	The Mediterranean Sea Journey	*Performers, dressed in blue swirls to represent the sea enter the stadium. A metallic looking ship enters the stadium and makes its way across fighting evils on the way. This segment is long and ends with the blowing of conch shells and the ships arrival at the stage.*
4' 15"	Civilization Triumphs	*On the stage there is an altar and flame. The men disembark onto the stage in victory.*
2' 59"	The Joy of Civilization	*An orchestra segment as flags file into the stadium.*
Part Two	**The Games Begin**	
79' 01"	The parade of Athletes	
	The teams begin to enter.	*Young rhythmic gymnasts enter the track. The Greek team enters the stadium, followed by the rest of the Olympic delegations and ending with the Spanish team.*
	Speeches and opening	
1' 08"	Samaranch ascends the platform	
3' 54"	Speech by Pasqual Maragall	
4' 31"	Speech by Samaranch	
0' 59"	The King declares the opening of the Games	

Time min' sec"	Segment title	*General description*
	Entry of the Olympic Flag	
4' 35"	The Olympic flag comes into the stadium	*The flag is carried around the track.*
2' 41"	The raising of the flag	*The flag is hoisted up the flagpole.*
	The Games reach their XXV Olympiad	
3' 14"	Top models	*Music begins and fashion models parade across stage.*
3' 47"	Past Olympiads	*Men enter stadium with flags of past Olympiads.*
	The Olympic flame lights up the Stadium	
0' 59"	The torch arrives	*H. Menéndez enters stadium and comes down stairs.*
1' 06"	The torch makes its way around the track	
2' 12"	The torch is passed	*The athlete stops and makes a circle, then passes to a second runner who runs through the athletes down the centre of the stadium.*
1' 10"	The archer takes the torch	*The runner passes off the torch to the archer who lights the cauldron by shooting the flame by arrow.*
	The oaths	
2' 21"	The athletes oath	*Two athletes take an oath.*
1' 03"	The judges oath	*A representative official takes an oath.*
	The great flag of Friendship	
3' 30"	A flag is unfurled over the athletes	*The flag covers all the athletes gathered in the centre of the stadium.*
Part Three	**Music and Europe**	
	The human pyramids	
3' 54"	Perfomers build human pyramids	*In the Catalan tradition of castells, or human pyramids, 12 pyramids of men and women are constructed 7 to 8 levels high. A small child waves from the highest point. The 12 castells are intended to represent the 12 countries of the European Community.*
	Opera, music for the universe	
14' 27"	Opera segment	*Six of the world's finest opera singers put on a recital of 17 arias.*
	The anthem of Europe, the Ode to Joy	
0' 57"	The Ode to Joy	*Barcelona Orchestra plays.*
0' 52"	The Stars of Europe	*Fireworks light the sky*
1' 47"	Opera Singers on stage join the anthem	*Opera singers join the choir.*
0' 45"	Finish of Ceremony	*Officials applaud.*

Bibliography

Abad, Josep Miquel (1993). 'Balanç de les realitzacions del COOB'92', *Working Paper n.22*, Barcelona: Centre d'Estudis Olímpics i de l'Esport, Universitat Autònoma de Barcelona.

Alaszkiewizc, R. and Thomas McPhail (1986). 'Television Rights', *International Review of Sociology of Sport*.

Alkemeyer, T. and A. Richartz (1993). 'The Olympic Games: From Ceremony to Show', *Olympika*, vol II, 79–89.

Anderson, Benedict (1991 revised, 1983). *Imagined Communities*. New York: Verso.

Andreff, Wladimir and J. F. Nys (1987). *Le Sport et la télévision. Relations économiques pluralité d'intérêts et sources d'ambiguités*. Paris: Dalloz.

Arbeláez Ramos, Ramiro (1992). 'Correspondent Report for Colombia', *Television in the Olympics Project Archive*. Barcelona: Centre d'Estudis Olimpics i de l'Esport, Universitat Autònoma de Barcelona.

Aris, Stephen (1988). 'The Great Olympic Soap Sell', *Financial Times*, June 11.

Atlanta Committee for the Olympic Games (1995). *Press Guide*. Atlanta: ACOG'96.

Baker, William (1987). 'Political Games: the meaning of International Sport for Independent Africa', in William Baker and James A. Mangan (eds), *Sport in Africa*. Essays in Social History, Africana Publishing Co.

Barcelona Press Service (1992). Barcelona: BPS.

Barnett, S. (1990). *Games and Sets: the Changing Face as Sport on Television*. London: British Film Institute.

Bassat, Lluís (1992). 'The Olympics and History's Longest Commercial', *Viewpoint*. Chicago: Ogilvy and Mather.

Bassat, Lluís (1993). *El libro rojo de la publicidad*. Barcelona: Folio.

Benkoski, H. (1993). 'Droit du sport et de ses images télévisuelles'. *STAPS*, n. 30.

Berger, A.A., ed. (1987), *Television in Society*. New Brunswick: Transaction Books.

Blain, N., R. Boyle and H. O'Donnell (1993). 'Centrality and Peripherality at the Barcelona Olympics: Spain, Catalonia, Scotland, Portugal', *Sport and National Identity in the European Media*. London: Leicester University Press, 156–199.

Botella, Joan (1995). 'The Political Games: Agents and Strategies of the 1992 Barcelona

Olympic Games', *The Keys to the Success*. Barcelona: Centre d'Estudis Olímpics i de l'Esport, Universitat Autònoma de Barcelona.

Bourgh, Jean François (1990). 'L'information sportive sur un marché monopoliste', *Médiaspouvoirs*, n. 18.

Bourgh, Jean François (1991a). 'Le sport et la television: economie des relations', *Revue Juridique et économique du sport*, n. 19.

Bourgh, Jean François (1991b). 'Aspects économiques des relations entre le sport et la télévision', *Médiaspouvoirs*, n. 23.

Bourgh, Jean François (1993). 'Ordre télévisuel et éthique sportive', *Médiaspouvoirs*, n. 29.

Brownell, Susan (1993). 'The Olympics and Television: The Chinese Perspective.' A paper presented at the International Symposium on Television and the Olympic Games, Olympia, Greece, July 2–6.

Brownell, Susan (1995). *Training the Body for China: Sports in the Moral Order of the People's Republic*. Chicago: University of Chicago Press.

Brunet, Ferran (1993), *The Economics of the 1992 Barcelona Olympic Games*. Lausanne: The Olympic Museum.

Brunet, Ferran (1995). 'Economy of the 1992 Barcelona Olympic Games', *The Keys to the Success*. Barcelona: Centre d'Estudis Olímpics i de l'Esport, Universitat Autònoma de Barcelona.

Busquets, Jordi (1992). *El Cobi al descobert*. Barcelona: Parsifal.

Carey, James W. (1989). *Communication as Culture*. Boston: Unwin Hyman.

Carroggio, Marc (1994). *El Patrocinio: fuente de ingresos para el deporte y modo comunicativo para la empresa*. Barcelona: Centre d'Estudis Olímpics i de l'Esport, Universitat Autònoma de Barcelona.

Carroggio, Marc (1995). *Patrocinio, deporte y olimpismo: estrategias de comunicación*, doctoral thesis, Universidad de Navarra. Also available at the Centre d'Estudis Olimpics i de l'Esport, Universitat Autònoma de Barcelona.

Cashman, R. and McKernan (1981). *Sport: money, morality and the media*. Kensington: New South Wales University Press.

CCE (1992). *Balance de la participación de la Comunidad Europea en los Juegos Olímpicos de 1992*. Brussels: CCE.

Centre d'Estudis Olímpics i de l'Esport (1992). *Olympic Games, media and cultural exchanges. The experience of the last four summer Olympic Games*. Barcelona: Centre d'Estudis Olímpics i de l'Esport, Universitat Autònoma de Barcelona.

Chandler, J.M. (1988). *Television and national sport: the United States and Britain*: Urbana: University of Illinois Press.

Commission of the European Communities (1992). *Olympic Programme 1992*. Barcelona: Commission of the European Communities.

Congreso Paralímpico Barcelona'92 (1993). *I Paralympic Congress Barcelona'92*. Barcelona: Fundación ONCE.

COOB'92 (1990a). *Cobi Animation Guide*. Barcelona: COOB'92.

COOB'92 (1990b). *Master Plan* . Barcelona: COOB'92.

COOB'92 (1991a). *Barcelona'92 Guide*. Barcelona: COOB'92.

COOB'92 (1991b). *Finanzas, in 500 días para los Juegos Olímpicos. Dossier de prensa*, March, Barcelona: COOB'92.

COOB'92 (1991c). *Criteria for commercial sponsorship and collaboration in the Games of the XXVth Olympiad Barcelona'92*. Barcelona: COOB'92.

COOB'92 (1992a). *The Opening Ceremony of the Barcelona 1992 Olympic Games: Press book. Guide to coverage by the press*. Barcelona: COOB'92.

COOB'92 (1992b). *Barcelona'92, The pictogrammes*. Barcelona: COOB'92.

COOB'92 (1992c). *Barcelona92, Llibre Oficial dels Jocs de la XXVa Olimpíada* . Barcelona: Plaza & Janés.

COOB'92 (1992d). *The Closing Ceremony of the Barcelona 1992 Olympic Games: Press book. Guide to coverage by the press*. Barcelona: COOB'92.

COOB'92 (1993a). *Barcelona 1992 IX Paralympic Games Official Report* . Barcelona: COOB'92, Enciclopèdia Catalana.

COOB'92 (1993b). *Official History of the Games of the 25th Olympiad Barcelona'92*. Barcelona: Enciclopèdia Catalana.

Crexell, Joan (1994). *Nacionalisme i Jocs Olímpics del 1992* . Barcelona: Columna.

Dayan, Daniel and Elihu Katz (1992). *Media Events: The Live Broadcasting of History*. Cambridge: Harvard University Press.

De Beer, Arnold S., Daan P. van Vuuren and Elanie Steyn (1992). 'Correspondent Report for South Africa', *Television in the Olympics Project Archive*. Barcelona: Centre d'Estudis Olimpics i de l'Esport, Universitat Autònoma de Barcelona.

Dimitras, Panayote (1992). 'Correspondent Report for Greece', *Television in the Olympics Project Archive*. Barcelona: Centre d'Estudis Olimpics i de l'Esport, Universitat Autònoma de Barcelona.

Dirección General de Electrónica e Informática (1986). *BIT'92 Planificación de las necesidades informáticas y de telecomunicaciones de los Juegos Olímpicos de 1992*. Madrid: Dirección General de Electrónica e Informática.

Edelman, Murray (1988). *Constructing the Political Spectacle*. Chicago: The University of Chicago Press.

El-Rahman, Awatef Abd, with Ashraf Abd El Mogeith, Fahima Ahmed Gouda, Hani Mohamed, Khalid Salah El Din and Mohamed Houssam El Din (1992). 'Correspondent Report for Egypt', *Television in the Olympics Project Archive*. Barcelona: Centre d'Estudis Olimpics i de l'Esport, Universitat Autònoma de Barcelona.

EMAP (1993). *TV World*. London: Business Publications.

Eriksen, Thomas H. (1993). *Ethnicity & Nationalism: Anthropological Perspectives*. London: Pluto Press.

Espy, Richard (1981). *The Politics of the Olympic Games*. Berkeley: University of California Press.

European Parliament (1993). *Reflections on Informations and Communication Policy of the European Community*. Brussels: R.P. 1051/93.

Faure, Roland (1991). *Le sport et la télévision: analyse, avis et propositions.*. Paris: Conseil Supérieur de l'Audiovisuel.

Geertz, Clifford (1973). *The Interpretation of Cultures*. New York: Basic Books.

Gómez Mont, Carmen, assisted by Lorena Martín del Campo, Vincente Arancon, Francisco Briseño and Pablo Herranz (1992). 'Correspondent Report for Mexico', *Television in the Olympics Project Archive*. Barcelona: Centre d'Estudis Olimpics i de l'Esport, Universitat Autònoma de Barcelona.

Gonzalez Manet, Enrique (1992). 'Correspondent Report for Cuba', *Television in the Olympics Project Archive*. Barcelona: Centre d'Estudis Olimpics i de l'Esport, Universitat Autònoma de Barcelona.

Gordon, G. (1993). 'TV and radio: two powerful tools for sport for all', *XIV Congreso Panamericano de Educación Física*.

Gould, D. (1992). *Superbook of television sports*. New York: Barry Gould.

Greenberg, Stan (1992). *Guiness book of Olympic record: the complete 1992 winter and summer Olympic schedule*. New York: Bantam Books.

Gross, Peter, assisted by Radu Cosarca and Cristian David (1992). 'Correspondent Report for Rumania', *Television in the Olympics Project Archive*. Barcelona: Centre d'Estudis Olimpics i de l'Esport, Universitat Autònoma de Barcelona.

Gusfield, Joseph R (1987). 'Sports as Story: Content and Form in Agonistic Games'. A paper presented at the First International Conference on the Olympics and East/West and South/North Cultural Exchange in the World System. Seoul, Korea.

Gutiérrez Pérez, Fernando (1993). 'Hay que decirlo ...', *Exelsior*, August 4.

Hargreaves, John E. (1986). *Sport, power and culture: a social and historical analysis of popular sports in Britain*. London: Polity Press.

Hitchcock, J.R. (1991). *Sportcasting*. Boston: Focal Press.

Hitchen, Adrian L. (1992). 'Sponsorship Gold at the '92 Olympics?',*Sponsorship Europe*, Conference Proceedings. Expoconsult: Marssen.

Hoberman, John M. (1986). *Sport and political ideology*. Austin: University of Texas Press.

Holaday, Duncan and Eugenia Peck (1992). 'Correspondent Report for Singapore', *Television in the Olympics Project Archive*. Barcelona: Centre d'Estudis Olimpics i de l'Esport, Universitat Autònoma de Barcelona.

Huerga, Manuel and Josep Sol (1992). The Olympic Ceremonies. M. Ladrón (Ed.) *Olympic Games, Media and Cultural Exchanges: the experience of the last four Summer Olympic Games*. Centre d'Estudis Olimpics i de l'Esport, Universitat Autònoma de Barcelona.

Idris, Naswil (1992). 'Correspondent Report for Indonesia', *Television in the Olympics*

Project Archive. Barcelona: Centre d'Estudis Olimpics i de l'Esport, Universitat Autònoma de Barcelona.

Institut Nationale de l'Audiovisuel (INA) (1988). 'Sport & Television', *Dossier de l'audiovisuel*, n. 18.

Institut Nationale de l'Audiovisuel (INA) (1993). 'Sport et Television: vendre ses images sans perdre son image', *Dossier de l'audiovisuel*, n. 50.

International Olympic Committee (IOC) (1984). *Symposium International on Sport, Media and Olympism:: Official Report*. Lausanne: IOC.

International Olympic Committee (IOC) (1990). *Media Guide*. Lausanne: IOC.

International Olympic Committee (IOC) (1991). *Sponsorship and Advertising Guidelines for EBU members, XVI Olympic Winter Games, Albertville 1994*. Lausanne: IOC.

International Olympic Committee (IOC) (1992a). *IOC Olympic Marketing Press Dossier*. Lausanne: IOC.

International Olympic Committee (IOC) (1992b). *Marketing Manual. Olympic Solidarity*. Lausanne: IOC.

International Olympic Committee (IOC) (1992c). *Olympic Charter*. Lausanne: IOC.

International Olympic Committee (IOC) (1993). *Marketing Matters*. Lausanne: IOC. (1994a). *1992 Olympic Broadcast Analysis Report. The World is Watching*. Lausanne: IOC.

International Olympic Committee (IOC) (1994b). *Centennial Olympic Congress Report*. Lausanne: IOC.

International Olympic Committee (IOC) (1994c). *The Centennial Olympic Congress Texts, Summaris or Plans of papers*. Lausanne: IOC.

International Sport, Culture and Leisure Marketing (1985). *TOP: The Consumer View. An International Research Survey into Sponsorship of the Olympic Games*. London: ISL Marketing.

Izod, John, Peter Meech and Tim Thornicroft, with the collaboration of Richard Kilborn (1992). 'Correspondent Report for United Kingdom', *Television in the Olympics Project Archive*. Barcelona: Centre d'Estudis Olimpics i de l'Esport, Universitat Autònoma de Barcelona.

Jackson, Roger C and Thomas L. McPhail, eds. (1989). *The Olympic Movement and the Mass Media: Past, Present and Future Issues*. Calgary: Hurford Enterprises.

Kang, Shin-Pyo, John MacAloon and Roberto Da Matta, eds. (year), *First International Conference on the Olympic and East/West and South/North Cultural Exchanges in the World System*, Seoul.

Karikari, Kwame (1992). 'Correspondent Report for Ghana', *Television in the Olympics Project Archive*. Barcelona: Centre d'Estudis Olimpics i de l'Esport, Universitat Autònoma de Barcelona.

Kim, Jong-gie, Sang-woo Rhee, Jae-cheon Yu, Kwang-mo Ku and Jong-duck Hong (1989). 'Impact of the Seoul Olympic Games', *National Development*.

Kong, Lily (1991). 'Mental Images of Foreign Places: The View from Singapore'. *Singapore Journal of Tropical Geography* 12, 1: 44–51.

Kong, Xiang-an (1992). 'Correspondent Report for China', *Television in the Olympics Project Archive*. Barcelona: Centre d'Estudis Olimpics i de l'Esport, Universitat Autònoma de Barcelona.

Kosaka, Nobuko, Hiroshi Matsuyama and Andrew Painter (1992). 'Correspondent Report for Japan', *Television in the Olympics Project Archive*. Barcelona: Centre d'Estudis Olimpics i de l'Esport, Universitat Autònoma de Barcelona.

Kürten, Dieter (1992). *Olympische sommerspiele Barcelona'92*. Munich: Mosaik verlag.

Landry, Fernand, Marc Landry and Magdeleine Yerlès (1991). *Sport ... The Third Millenium*. Quebec: Les Presses de l'Université Laval.

Langer, John (1992). 'Correspondent Report for Australia', *Television in the Olympics Project Archive*. Barcelona: Centre d'Estudis Olimpics i de l'Esport, Universitat Autònoma de Barcelona.

Larrègola, Gemma (1994). *La alta definición en Barcelona'92*. Doctoral thesis, Universitat Autònoma de Barcelona.

Larson, James F and Nancy K. Rivenburgh (1991). 'A Comparative Analysis of Australian, US and British Telecasts of the Seoul Olympic Opening Ceremony', *Journal of Broadcasting and Electronic Media*, 35, 1, 75–94.

Larson, James F. and Park Heung Soo (1993). *Global Television and the Politics of the Seoul Olympics*. Boulder, Colorado: Westview Press.

Lever, Janet and Stanton Wheeler (1993), 'Mass media and the Experience of Sport', *Communication Research*, vol. 20, n. 1. [check author names]

Li, Liangrong (1992). 'Correspondent Report for China', *Television in the Olympics Project Archive*. Barcelona: Centre d'Estudis Olimpics i de l'Esport, Universitat Autònoma de Barcelona.

Louw, Eric, with Nhlanhla Nkosi (1992). 'Correspondent Report for South Africa', *Television in the Olympics Project Archive*. Barcelona: Centre d'Estudis Olimpics i de l'Esport, Universitat Autònoma de Barcelona.

Lull, James (1991). *China Turned On: television, reform and resistance*. London: Routledge.

MacAloon, John (1984). Olympic Games and the Theory of Spectacle in Modern Societies. In J. MacAloon (Ed.). *Rite, Drama, Festival, Spectacle: Rehearsals Toward a Theory of Cultural Performance*. Philadelphia: Institute for the Study of Human Issues Press.

MacAloon, John (1987). 'Encountering Our Others: Social Science and Olympic Sport', *The papers presented at the First International Conference on the Olympics and East/West and North/South Cultural Exchange in the World System*. Seoul, Korea: The Institute for Ethnological Studies, Hanyang University Monograph No. 1.

MacAloon, John (1991). 'Comparative Analysis of the Olympic Ceremonies, with special reference to Los Angeles, 1984', *Olympic Games, Media and Cultural Exchange*. Barcelona: Centre d'Estudis Olimpics i de l'Esport, Universitat Autònoma de Barcelona, 35–54.

MacAloon, John (1995). 'Barcelona'92: The Perspective of Cultural Anthropology', *The Keys to the Success*. Barcelona: Centre d'Estudis Olímpics i de l'Esport, Universitat Autònoma de Barcelona.

MacAloon, John and Kang Shin-Pyo, (1991). 'Uri Nara : Korean Nationalism, the Seoul Olympics and Contemporary Anthropology', *Toward One World Beyond All Barriers. The Seoul Olympic Anniversary Conference*. Seoul: Poon Nam Publishing.

Mader, Roberto (1993). 'Dominance and democratisation in the Globo village', *Intermedia*, 2 4, 15–17.

Marques de Melo, José, assisted by Nanci Laura Loturco Pittelkow (1992). 'Correspondent Report for Brazil', *Television in the Olympics Project Archive*. Barcelona: Centre d'Estudis Olimpics i de l'Esport, Universitat Autònoma de Barcelona.

Melucci, Alberto (1982). *L'Invenzione del Presente: Movimenti, Identità, Bisogni Individuali*. Bologna: Il Mulino.

Millet, Lluís (1991). 'Urban Impacts of the Olympic Games', *The Keys to the Success*. Barcelona: Centre d'Estudis Olímpics i de l'Esport, Universitat Autònoma de Barcelona.

Minquet, John Paul (1992). 'Le Marketing dy sport', *Revue Française du Marketing*, n.138.

Mohamed, Ramli (1992). 'Correspondent Report for Malaysia', *Television in the Olympics Project Archive*. Barcelona: Centre d'Estudis Olimpics i de l'Esport, Universitat Autònoma de Barcelona.

Moragas Spà, Miquel de (1988). 'Local culture and international audience facing Barcelona '92'. In John MacAloon, Kang-Shin Pyo, Roberto DaMatta (eds.) *The Olympics and East / West, South / North Cultural Exchange*. Seoul: Hanyang University.

Moragas Spà, Miquel de (1989). 'The Mass Media, Olympic Values and the Opening Ceremony', *Toward One World Beyond All Barriers. The Seoul Olympic Anniversary Conference*. Seoul: Poon Nam Publishing.

Moragas Spà, Miquel de (1992a). 'Los pictogramas en la historia de los Juegos Olímpicos de Tokio'64 a Barcelona'92', *Mensaje olímpico*, n. 34.

Moragas Spà, Miquel de (1992b). *Cultura, símbols i Jocs Olímpics: la mediació de la comunicació*. Barcelona: Centre d'Investigació de la Comunicació.

Moragas Spà, Miquel de (1992c). *Los Juegos de la Comunicación: las múltiples dimensiones comunicativas de los Juegos Olímpicos*. Madrid: Fundesco.

Moragas Spà, Miquel de and Miquel Botella, eds., (1995), *The Keys to the Success*. Barcelona: Centre d'Estudis Olímpics i de l'Esport, Universitat Autònoma de Barcelona.

Moragas Spà, Miquel de and Marc Carroggio (1994). *Models de patrocini esportiu*. Barcelona: Centre d'Estudis Olímpics i de l'Esport, Universitat Autònoma de Barcelona.

Moragas Spà, Miquel de, et al. (1992). 'Correspondent Report for Spain and Catalonia', *Television in the Olympics Project Archive*. Barcelona: Centre d'Estudis Olimpics i de l'Esport, Universitat Autònoma de Barcelona.

Melucci, Alberto (1982). *L'Invenzione del Presente: Movimenti, Identità, Bisogni Individuali*. Bologna: Il Mulino.

Müller, Karl (1992). *Barcelona Olympia 1992: die Höhepunkte der XXV. Olympischen spiele* . Erlangen: Karl Müller verlag.

Papa, Françoise (1992). 'Correspondent Report for France', *Television in the Olympics Project*

Archive. Barcelona: Centre d'Estudis Olimpics i de l'Esport, Universitat Autònoma de Barcelona.

Pappas, N., (1981), *Development and symbolism of the ceremonies of the Modern Olympic Games*, Bloomington, Indiana University.

Park, Heung Soo and Kang, Tae-Young (1992). 'Correspondent Report for Korea', *Television in the Olympics Project Archive*. Barcelona: Centre d'Estudis Olimpics i de l'Esport, Universitat Autònoma de Barcelona.

Pastor, Ferran and Jordi López (1995). 'Barcelona'92: Strategies of Technology', *The Keys to the Success*. Barcelona: Centre d'Estudis Olímpics i de l'Esport, Universitat Autònoma de Barcelona.

PC Week (1992). *Especial Juegos Olímpicos*.

Perelman, Richard B. (1984). *Report: press radio-television operations at the games of the XXIIIrd Olympiad*. Los Angeles: Los Angeles Olympic Organizing Committee.

Plimpton, G. (1992). *The Official Olympics Triplecast viewer's guide*. New York: Pindar Press.

Pujadas, Xavier and Carlos Santacana (1990). *L'altra Olimpíada. Barcelona'36: esport, societat i política a Catalunya (1936–1990)*. Barcelona: Llibres de l'Index.

Rader, Benjamin, (1984). *In its own image: how television has transformed sports*. New York: The Free Press.

Rath, Claus-Dieter (1992). 'Correspondent Report for Germany', *Television in the Olympics Project Archive*. Barcelona: Centre d'Estudis Olímpics i de l'Esport, Universitat Autònoma de Barcelona.

Real, Michael (1986). *Global Ritual: Olympic Media Coverage and International Understanding*. Paris: UNESCO.

Real, Michael (1989). *Super Media: A Cultural Studies Approach*. Newbury Park: Sage.

Retevisión and Telefónica, (1990). *Servicios de telecomunicaciones para entidades de televisión*. Barcelona.

Ribas, Susanna (1993). 'El CIO y la negociación de derechos de Televisión', Working paper. Barcelona: Centre d'Estudis Olimpics i de l'Esport, Universitat Autònoma de Barcelona.

Rivenburgh, Nancy K. (1992). 'National Image Richness in US-Televised Coverage of South Korea during the Seoul Olympics', *Asian Journal of Communication* , 2, 2.

Rivenburgh, Nancy K. (1993). 'Images of Nations During the 1992 Barcelona Olympic Opening Ceremony', *Olympic Congress*. Lausanne: Media Ad Hoc Committee for the IOC.

Robinson, John P. and Robert Hefner (1967). 'Multidimensional Differences in Public and Academic Perceptions of Nations', *Journal of Personality and Social Psychology*, n. 7.

Rome Olympic Organizing Committee (1960). *Official Report* available in Lausanne: The Olympic Museum.

Rothenbuhler, Eric W. (1988). 'The Living Room Celebration of the Olympic Games', *Journal of Communications*, vol. 38, n. 4, 61–81.

Rothenbuhler, Eric W. (1992). 'Correspondent Report for the United States', *Television in the Olympics Project Archive*. Barcelona: Centre d'Estudis Olimpics i de l'Esport, Universitat Autònoma de Barcelona.

RTO'92 (1992a). *Report to the IOC Radio and TV Commission on the Summer Olympic Games*. Barcelona: RTO'92.

RTO'92 (1992b). *Broadcasters Handbook*. Barcelona: RTO'92.

Russett, Bruce and Harvey Starr (1992). *World Politics: A Menu for Choice*. New York: W.H. Freeman and Co.

Schlesinger, Philip (1991). Media, the Political Order and National Identity. *Media Culture & Society*, vol. 13.

Serra, Joan (1993). 'The Production of the Olympic Games'. A presentation given at the International Symposium on Television and the Olympic Games, Olympia, Greece, July 2–6, 1993.

Shaikin, Bill (1988). *Sport and Politics: The Olympics and the Los Angeles Games*. New York: Praeger Publishers.

SLOOC (1988). *Beyond all barriers : scenario for the Opening and Closing Ceremonies*. Seoul: Seoul Olympic Organizing Committee.

Smith, Anthony (1992). Is There a Global Culture? *Intermedia* Aug/Sept.

Splichal, Slavko, with Sandra Basic and Breda Luthar (1992). 'Correspondent Report for Slovenia', *Television in the Olympics Project Archive*. Barcelona: Centre d'Estudis Olimpics i de l'Esport, Universitat Autònoma de Barcelona.

Stolze, Raymund, (1992), *XXV. Olympische sommerspiele Barcelona 1992*, Berlin, Sportverlag.

Telefónica (1992). *Telecommunications at the Olympic Games*, Press Dossier. Barcelona: Telefónica.

Thomas, Raymond (1993). *Le sport et les medias*. Paris: Vigot.

Tokyo Olympic Organizing Committee (1964). *Official Report* available in Lausanne: The Olympic Museum.

Tomlinson, A. (1990). *Sport in society: Policy, Politics and Culture*. Brighton: Leisure Studies Association.

Tremblay, Gaëtan, with M. St. Laurent (1992). 'Correspondent Report for Canada', *Television in the Olympics Project Archive*. Barcelona: Centre d'Estudis Olimpics i de l'Esport, Universitat Autònoma de Barcelona.

Ueberroth, Peter (1985). *Made in America*. New York: William Morrow.

UNESCO (1992). *World Communication Report*. Paris: UNESCO.

UNESCO (1993). *Statisical Yearbook*. Paris: UNESCO.

United Nations (1993). *Assembly Proclaims 1994 Internationsal Year of Sport, Urges Member States to Observe 'Olympic Truce'*, Department of Public Information Press Release. New York: United Nations.

Wallechinsky, Davis (1992). *The Complete Book of the Olympics*. Boston: Little Brown & Co.

Wenner, L.A. (1989). *Media, Sport and Society*. London: Sage.

Wete, Francis Nguepmenye (1992). 'Correspondent Report for Cameroon', *Television in the Olympics Project Archive*. Barcelona: Centre d'Estudis Olimpics i de l'Esport, Universitat Autònoma de Barcelona.

Whannel, Gary (1992). *Fields in vision: television sport and cultural transformation*. London: Routledge.

Xicotencatl, Arturo (1992). 'Mis lágrimas no son de tristeza , sino de coraje', *Exelsior*, July 28.

Zassoursky, Yassen, with Svetlana Kolesnik and Andrei Richter (1992). 'Correspondent Report for Russia', *Television in the Olympics Project Archive*. Barcelona: Centre d'Estudis Olimpics i de l'Esport, Universitat Autònoma de Barcelona.